KNOWING THE TIMES

KNOWING THE TIMES

*Addresses Delivered on
Various Occasions
1942–1977*

D. M. Lloyd-Jones

THE BANNER OF TRUTH TRUST

THE BANNER OF TRUTH TRUST
3 Murrayfield Road, Edinburgh EH12 6EL
PO Box 621, Carlisle, Pennsylvania 17013, USA

*

© Mrs D M Lloyd-Jones 1989
First published 1989
ISBN 0 85151 556 8

*

Set in Linotron Sabon 10 on 12pt at The Spartan Press Ltd,
Lymington, Hants
and printed and bound at The Camelot Press Ltd, Southampton

Contents

Introduction

Martyn Lloyd-Jones was a man who, in terms of his influence, lived in several worlds at once. From 1938 he ministered to one congregation in the centre of London. Simultaneously he commonly itinerated mid-week as an evangelist, preaching at churches to which he had been invited or sometimes sharing in student missions. Yet another (and no less significant) part of his life had to do with conferences, ministers' fraternals, and public gatherings on special occasions. These were times when he had the opportunity to speak on subjects of a more general nature than he would normally deal with in public worship and many of those who heard him received inspiration and a sense of direction which was never to leave them. Hundreds who knew Dr Lloyd-Jones chiefly in this context could say with Dr James I. Packer, 'I know that much of my vision today is what it is because he was what he was, and his influence has no doubt gone deeper than I can trace.'[1]

If Dr Lloyd-Jones' addresses at such gatherings had all been recorded their number would easily run into hundreds. Many can never be published for records of them exist only in the brief notes of hearers or in newspaper reports. He never spoke from a full manuscript, always from nothing more than an outline of his thoughts. This volume, however, can be said to provide for the first time a representative collection of the most valuable of these addresses. Eleven of the seventeen items included have not previously been in print in English. Items 2 and 3 were published in Welsh in 1947[2] and we are indebted to Mr Dafydd Ifans of the National Library of Wales in Aberystwyth for his generous work in their translation. For material here reprinted from earlier booklets grateful acknowledgements are due to the Universities and Colleges Christian Fellowship (formerly the Inter-Varsity Fellowship) for

[1] *Chosen Vessels: Portraits of Ten Outstanding Christian Men*, ed. Charles Turner, Vine Books: Servant Pubns, 1985, p. 110.
[2] *Crefydd Heddiw ac Yfory* [Radio talks], Llandybie: Llyfrau'r Dryw, 1947.

'The Presentation of the Gospel' (first published by the Crusaders' Union), 'Maintaining the Evangelical Faith Today', 'Conversions: Psychological and Spiritual', and 'The Basis of Christian Unity'. These addresses all had a powerful impact on students across Britain. 'The Weapons of Our Warfare' and 'Westminster Chapel (1865–1965)' were first published by the Westminster Chapel Bookroom. All the remaining material, previously unpublished, which is included in this volume has been produced from transcriptions of tape recordings. The one exception to this is 'A Policy Appropriate to Biblical Faith' which was taken down by the speaker's friend, Dr Douglas Johnson, the General Secretary of the IVF. It is full but not necessarily exact.

Dr Lloyd-Jones' addresses can be classified into several types and for good reasons some of these types are not to be found in these pages. The historical addresses which he gave at the Puritan and Westminster Conferences are already in print.[3] The same is true of most of his speeches at Christian medical gatherings.[4] None of the nine addresses given by him for the British Evangelical Council from 1967 onwards is to be found here as there are plans that these should be printed together in due course. One further group of addresses consists of the informal talks which Lloyd-Jones gave annually for a number of years to the friends and supporters of the Evangelical Library, London. It is not yet determined whether they will be published in book form but if, as we hope, they can be, then it is again better that they should all appear together.

By the time the first item in this book was originally published Dr Lloyd-Jones was already a leader in the Christian world. Dr Donald Maclean, Principal of the Free Church of Scotland College, Edinburgh, could write of him in April, 1941, 'In the religious world of today Dr Lloyd-Jones occupies quite a unique place.' 'He is increasingly becoming a channel of blessing to the Christian world through his fine biblical testimony', said Clarence Bouma in the columns of *The Calvin Forum* (February, 1943) which he edited. The Glasgow press spoke of him that same year as a preacher 'who has become one of the most powerful Evangelical forces of our time'.[5]

---

[3] *The Puritans: Their Origins and Successors*, Banner of Truth Trust, 1987.
[4] *Healing and Medicine*, Kingsway, 1987.
[5] See *David Martyn Lloyd-Jones, Volume Two of the Authorized Biography*, Iain H. Murray, Banner of Truth Trust, 1989. This work provides background to the addresses contained in the present volume.

Introduction

Many changes were to occur in the churches in the thirty years covered by the later addresses. While the basic message remains the same, it will be noted how Dr Lloyd-Jones' interpretation of the times, their dangers and the corrective emphases which he judged to be needed, was never static. He sought to bring everything freshly to Scripture and the wisdom and insight given to him in so doing has been regarded as one of his most outstanding characteristics. If, in later years, his counsel placed him further away from current trends in evangelical thought and practice he committed his case to the final adjudication of the Word of God. He differed also from many of his contemporaries in his convictions respecting the plain language which ought to be used when dealing with truth and error. In this respect, as in others, he agreed with Robert Haldane who wrote: 'Many religious persons have a dread of controversy and wish truth to be stated without any reference to those who hold the opposite errors. Controversy and a bad spirit are in their estimation synonymous terms; and strenuously to oppose what is wrong is considered as contrary to Christian meekness. Those who hold this opinion seem to overlook what every page of the New Testament lays before us. In all the history of the Lord Jesus Christ we never find him out of controversy.' Nonetheless, it should be added that Dr Lloyd-Jones generally maintained the respect of those with whom he differed. His life and spirit confirmed his testimony that he took no pleasure in controversy.

Dr Lloyd-Jones' thought needs to be taken as a whole. It would not be difficult, for instance, to interpret his comments on new translations of the Bible in his address 'How Can We See a Return to the Bible?' as the words of an inveterate traditionalist. But his general emphasis in the 'sixties and 'seventies would disprove any such thesis. He was not against modern translations in principle and indeed gave one of them to his grandchildren. What he was strongly against was the policy that was encouraging evangelicals to think that effective 'communication' with the contemporary world was *the* main problem to be addressed. He saw that as a deceptively superficial diagnosis.

Dr Lloyd-Jones' addresses also show that he was never merely reactionary. If a certain influence or teaching was wrong at some points that did not mean that the whole was to be treated as totally unhelpful. While he believed that controversy may be unavoidable he also stressed the constant necessity for moderation and balance.

Thus, in the considerable upheaval in church life and worship that occurred in England in the 'seventies, which was often heralded in terms of 'liberty' and 'freedom of the Spirit', he refused to condemn the whole thing, and, on the contrary, is on record as saying, 'There is something right in the ferment today . . . We must reject the idea that everything new is wrong.'[6]

Along with other leaders of the Christian church the influence of Martyn Lloyd-Jones will live in the future as well as in the past. Many of the issues raised in these pages continue to affect the lives of the churches and are by no means settled. It could be wished that several of these addresses had been in print much earlier. They remain in a real sense 'tracts for the times'. It is to be fervently hoped that they will be owned of God in this present form and used to prepare another generation like 'the children of Issachar, which were men that had understanding of the times, to know what Israel ought to do' (1 Chron. 12:32).

THE PUBLISHERS
May 1989

[6] Quoted by Robert Horn in *Martyn Lloyd-Jones: Chosen by God*, ed. Christopher Catherwood, Highland Books, 1986, p. 29.

One

*

The Presentation of the Gospel[1]

*

The presentation of the gospel is a subject which is always important. It is always important because of the eternal consequences that depend upon our attitude towards the gospel. There is no need for me to argue that it is especially important at the present time, and for two reasons: because of the general apostasy, of the failure on the part of the churches to present the gospel of our Lord and Saviour Jesus Christ in the way in which it should be presented; and because of the consequent godlessness and the sheer materialism which, increasingly, characterize the life of the people. It is a subject of urgent importance also because of the nature of the times through which we are passing. Life is always uncertain, but it is exceptionally uncertain today. We who are Christians should always weigh our words and be careful how we present the gospel; surely, that ought to be impressed upon us more definitely than ever before as we come into contact with men and women in the Services, who may lose their lives at any moment, and as we live daily in a world where bombs are dropped, and where death comes suddenly to people. So we are met to consider what I venture to affirm is the most important question that men can ever consider. And as we do so, we must be struck afresh by the remarkable way in which God has committed this all-important task of the presentation of the gospel to us. What a marvellous privilege it is, what a striking honour, that the Lord God Almighty should have entrusted this work of propagating and preaching the gospel to men like ourselves! It is a wonderful privilege, but, at the same time, it is a terrifying responsibility; it is a responsibility that devolves upon us all, and it devolves upon the

[1]The report of an address given at a Conference of Leaders of the Crusaders' Union, Sion College, London, on 7 February, 1942.

leaders of the Crusaders' Union in a very special manner. You are in contact with boys; your position as leaders of these young lives makes your work one of great seriousness.

This subject is so large and important that it is obviously impossible to deal with it adequately in one address. All I can do is select what I regard as some of the most important principles in connection with it; and I shall try to be as practical as I can. There are two main things I wish to emphasize: first, the positive principles which govern this work; and second, some of the dangers which are ever ready to threaten us as we engage in this ministry. We shall not only deal with this subject in general, but also in terms of work among boys. That is an important distinction, and one also, unless we are very careful, which we can turn into a very dangerous distinction. There has been a marked tendency in the last years or so to divide up Christian work according to age groups. I have never been very enthusiastic about these divisions into age groups – old age, middle age, youth, children, and so on. By that I mean that we must be careful that we do not modify the gospel to suit various age groups. There is no such thing as a special gospel for the young, a special gospel for the middle-aged, and a special gospel for the aged. There is only one gospel, and we must always be careful not to tamper and tinker with the gospel as a result of recognizing these age distinctions. At the same time, there is a difference in applying this one and only gospel to the different age groups; but it is a difference which has reference only to method and procedure.

The Nature of the Gospel

Now were I asked to speak on this subject in certain circles, my first business would be to attempt to define the nature of the gospel, and I would go on to ask, What is the gospel? In many circles people have gone astray; they have fallen into heresies; they preach a gospel that, to us, is no gospel at all. To such I would need to define the content of the gospel, but with you here that is unnecessary. I take it for granted that we are all agreed about the great fundamentals, the foundation principles of the Christian faith. What we are especially concerned about is the presentation of that gospel to the boys with whom we come into contact. There may be some of you who may ask, 'Is it necessary that we should thus spend time in considering the presentation of the gospel? Is that not something that we can take for granted?

The Presentation of the Gospel

If a man believes the gospel he is bound to present it in the right way. If a man is orthodox and believes the right things, his application of what he believes is something which will take care of itself.' That, to me, is a very grave error; and anyone who is tempted to speak in that way ignores not only his own weakness, but, still more, the adversary of our souls, who is always attempting to frustrate the work of God.

This is a contention which I think I can prove in two ways. I am concerned to show you how you cannot take it for granted that a man who believes the right thing is of necessity one who can present that right thing in the right way. There are, for instance, men who are sound evangelicals in their belief and doctrine; they are perfectly orthodox in their faith, yet their work is utterly barren. They never get any results; they never hear of a convert as a result of their work and ministry. They are as sound as you are, yet their ministry leads to nothing. On the other hand – and this is my second proof – there are those who seem to get phenomenal results to their work and efforts. They take a campaign, or preach a sermon, and as a result, there are numbers of decisions for Christ, or what are called 'conversions'. But many of these results do not last; they are not permanent; they are merely of a temporary or passing nature. What is the explanation of these two cases? It seems to me that the only explanation is that, somehow or other, there is a gap between what the man believes and what he actually presents in his teaching or preaching. The danger in regard to the first type is the danger of just talking *about* the gospel. This man believes the truth, he exults in it; but instead of preaching the gospel, he praises it, he says wonderful things about it. The whole time he is simply talking about the gospel instead of presenting the gospel. The result is, that though the man is highly orthodox and sound, his ministry shows no results whatsoever.

The danger in regard to the second man is the danger of being so interested in, and so concerned about the application of the gospel and with getting results, that he allows a gap to come in between what he is presenting (and what he believes) and the actual obtaining of the results themselves. As I have said, it is not enough that you believe the truth; you must be careful to apply what you believe in the right way.

Methods of Study

There are two main ways in which we can study this subject of the presentation of the gospel. The first is to study the Bible itself, with special reference to the Acts of the Apostles and the Epistles of the New Testament. That must always be put first if we would know how this work is to be done. We must go back to our textbook, which is the Bible. We must go back to the primitive pattern, to the norm, to the standard. In the Acts and in the Epistles we are told, once and for all, what the Christian church is, what she is like, and how she is to do her work. We must always make certain that our methods conform to the teaching of the New Testament.

The second method is a supplementary one; it is to make a study of the history of the Christian church subsequent to the New Testament times. We can concentrate especially on the history of revivals and the great spiritual awakenings; and we can read also the biographies of men who have been greatly honoured by God in the past in their presentation of the gospel. But here we must notice a principle of the greatest importance. When I say that it is a good thing to go back and read the history of the past and the biographies of great men whom God has used in the past, I hope that we are all clear in our minds that we need to go back beyond the last seventy years. I find so many good evangelicals who seem to be of the opinion that there was no real evangelistic work until about 1870. There are those who seem to think that evangelistic work in Great Britain was unknown until Moody came to this country. While we thank God for the glorious work of the last seventy years, I do plead with you to make a thorough study of the history of the church in the past. Go back to the eighteenth century. Go back to the time of the Puritans and even further back still, to the Protestant Reformation. And go back even beyond that, and study the history of those groups of evangelical people who lived on the Continent at the time when Roman Catholicism held supreme sway. Go right back to the time of the Early Fathers who held evangelical ideas. It is a history which can be traced back unbroken even to the primitive church itself. Such a study is of vital importance, lest we tend to assume, through taking a false view of history, that evangelistic work can only be done in a certain way, and by the application and the use of certain methods.

I would commend to you a very thorough study of that great American divine, Jonathan Edwards. It was a great revelation to me to discover that a man who preached in the way he did could be honoured of God as he was, and could have such great results to his ministry. Jonathan Edwards was a great scholar and philosopher who wrote out every word of his sermons. He was very shortsighted, and he used to stand in his pulpit with his manuscript in one hand, and a candle in the other hand, and as he read his sermon men were not only converted, but some of them literally fell to the ground under conviction of sin and the power of the Spirit. When we think of evangelistic work in terms of the popular evangelism of the last seventy years, I think we might be tempted to say that a man who preached like that could not possibly get conversions. Yet he was a man who was used of God in the Great Awakening on the American continent in the eighteenth century. So I would plead with you to be thorough in your study of church history and of the great things which God has done in various eras and periods. Those, therefore, are the two main lines along which we approach this subject – the study of the Bible and a study of the Christian church.

Having done that, we shall find that the following great foundation principles stand out very clearly as governing this whole subject.

1. The supreme object of this work is to glorify God. That is the central thing. That is the object that must control and override every other object. The first object of preaching the gospel is not to save souls; it is to glorify God. Nothing else, however good in itself, or however noble, must be allowed to usurp that first place.

2. The only power that can really do this work is the Holy Spirit. Whatever natural gifts a man may possess, whatever a man may be able to do as a result of his own natural propensities, the work of presenting the gospel and of leading to that supreme object of glorifying God in the salvation of men, is a work that can be done only by the Holy Spirit. You see that in the New Testament itself. Apart from the Spirit, we are told, we can do nothing. You read in the Bible of men attempting to do things in their own strength, but they fail completely. In the subsequent history of the Christian church you find men who cease to be the instruments of the Holy Spirit, and their ministry at once becomes barren. There was no change in their natural powers, proving, therefore, that the work is a work which ultimately can only be achieved by the Holy Spirit Himself.

3. The one and only medium through which the Holy Spirit works is the Word of God. That is something which I can prove quite easily. Take the sermon which was preached by Peter at Jerusalem on the day of Pentecost. What he did really was to expound the Scriptures. He did not get up and give an account of his own personal experiences. He unfolded the Scriptures; that was always his method. And that is also the characteristic method of Paul, that 'he

reasoned out of the Scriptures' (Acts 17:2). When he dealt with the Philippian jailer you find that he preached unto him Jesus Christ and the Word of the Lord. You will remember his words in the First Letter to Timothy, where he says that it is the will of God that all men should be saved, and brought to a knowledge of the truth (I Tim. 2:4). The medium which is used by the Holy Spirit is the truth.

4. The fourth principle, therefore, is that the true urge to evangelization must come from apprehending these principles, and, therefore, from a zeal for the honour and glory of God and a love for the souls of men.

5. There is a constant danger of error and of heresy, even among the most sincere, and also the danger of a false zeal and the employment of unscriptural methods. There is nothing to which we are exhorted more frequently in the New Testament than the need for a constant self-examination and a return to the Scriptures themselves.

There, I think, you have five foundation principles which are taught very clearly in the Word of God, and which are confirmed abundantly in the subsequent history of the Christian church.

The Application of the Principles

This brings me to the second main division of our subject, which is the application of these principles to the actual work of the presentation of the gospel. This is a subject which divides itself up quite naturally into two main sections. There is first the work of evangelism, and then the work of edification and instruction in righteousness.

EVANGELISM AND ITS DANGERS

As we engage in evangelistic work, it is of vital importance that we ask ourselves before we begin: What am I out to do? What am I going to attempt? What do I want to achieve? What is my real objective? I suggest that there is only one true answer to these questions, and it is this: I am anxious that souls should be reconciled to God, because, being what they are, they are dishonouring God, and because, being in a state in which they dishonour God, they are in danger of perdition. That is the purpose of all evangelistic work – to bring those souls into a state of reconciliation with God. That is the object. It is not merely to get boys to make a decision; it is not simply to get them to live another way of life; it is not simply to get them to join a class or a church. Your object in presenting the gospel to them is to put them right with God.

Now there are very grave dangers that have arisen, and will arise, in connection with this work of evangelism. There is, first of all, the danger of exalting the decision as such, and this is a danger especially when you are working among the young. I have not time to enlarge upon it, though I must use the term – the *psychological* difference between children and adults. I think we all know enough about psychology to realize that children are very much more impressionable than older people. There is a sense in which it is true to say you can influence children to do almost anything you like. You know the claim of the Roman Catholics, who say, 'Give us a child until he is seven, and we have got him for life.' The danger of exalting decision as such expresses itself in a number of ways. It shows itself sometimes in the use of music. There are people who talk about singing, and the use of music – and especially of choruses – as something which they use to 'work up a meeting'. They rely upon music and the singing of choruses to produce the desired effect of bringing about decision. Others, perhaps, tend to make use of stories, rather than music, in much the same way. There are those who have the gift of telling stories in a moving and effective manner. Others seem to put their reliance upon the personal charm of the speaker. For instance, a man was telling me about a friend of his who was doing some work among the troops, and he described him in this way: 'He is doing a grand work. He is just the right type of man; he is so cheery and breezy.' There is none of that kind of thing in the New Testament. Would Paul, for instance, be described as being a particularly cheery and breezy kind of man?

Perhaps I may be allowed to digress at this point. Have you ever observed that some of the most honoured servants of God in evangelism have been extremely ugly men? Let me commend that to you as a study. There is a danger of the evangelist relying upon the attractiveness of his own personality to produce results. Then there are some who try to develop what I can describe most accurately as the cricket-team spirit. They seem to produce an atmosphere which is comparable to that of a football or cricket team. They stand for the idea of being all in it together, of playing the game. That is something which, of course, appeals very much to boys, and something which of itself is quite harmless, and can be very useful. My point is that there is a danger at times of stressing it to such an extent that decisions are produced by that team spirit rather than by an understanding of the truth. But the most serious of all dangers is that of seeking to produce decisions as a result of pressure brought to bear upon the wills of those who are listening. There is the danger of a man so using his personality, his will power, and his capacity to domineer over others as to force those who are listening to respond to his appeal.

These are some of the results which follow this undue exaltation of the decision as such. I could illustrate what I have been saying at very great length. For instance, I have heard repeatedly of a certain popular evangelist, who has an amazing gift for telling stories; he is quite a genius in this respect. His word-pictures are such that you can see exactly what he is describing. This man tells his stories and he seems almost to mesmerize his congregation. At the close of the meeting he invites people to go to the decision room, and they go there in flocks. But those who work in the decision room are agreed in saying that when they ask them why they have come, their reply is that they do not know, but that the speaker told them to come. It is not that the truth has convinced or convicted them. They are influenced by the stories to which they have listened, and then they seem to act in an automatic manner. Music can produce the same effect. You can so sing a chorus that eventually you become intoxicated. The power of music is such that that is the effect it has upon some people; and, in reality, they do not know what they are doing; they just respond mechanically to any command or invitation given to them.

The second danger is that people may arrive at a decision from a false motive. Sometimes people decide for Christ simply because they are anxious for someone else's experience. Here again is a danger to which boys and young people are particularly exposed. In other words, I am trying to warn you against the danger of basing your message upon the effect of your own experience, or that of someone else. The boy who is listening to you may be anxious to be like you, to have what you have, or to be like someone of whom you have spoken, and to have what that someone else has got. While we think he is deciding for Christ he is simply coveting another's experience. Or it may be a desire to have this wonderful type of life of which he has been told. The gospel of Jesus Christ does give us a very wonderful life, and we praise God for it, but the true reason for becoming a Christian is not that we may have a wonderful life; it is, rather, that we may be in a right relationship with God. Again, Christ is sometimes presented as a hero. The heroic instinct is prominent in all of us, and especially in boys. If we over-emphasize that aspect of the gospel, it may be that the boys, or even older people, may join our Bible class or church simply because the message has appealed to their heroic instinct.

There is also a danger of people coming to a decision, and this again is very true of boys, as a result of what is called accepting the challenge of the Christian life. They regard it as a great adventure, as something to which they must aspire, as setting out upon a great crusade.

And then the last danger which I want to emphasize under this heading is the terrible fallacy of presenting the gospel in terms of 'Christ needs you' and giving the impression that if a boy does not decide for Christ he is a cad. These are not artificial points that I have made. I am drawing not only on my own experience, but on those things which I have discovered in my reading, and from the problems one meets in the Christian ministry as a result of the use of false methods. There is a measure of truth and value in many of the things I have mentioned, but the point I want to emphasize is that none of these things, good as they may be in themselves, must ever be allowed to take the supreme position. I do not mean by this that you must not sing at all in your meetings. Of course we may sing, but let us not rely too much upon our singing. Let us use these things so far as they are legitimate, but let us always regard them as aids and helps, rather than the actual thing which produces the results.

Well, says someone, all that is negative. How do you suggest the work should be done? I reply again, we simply go back to those five principles to which I have referred, and they can all be summarized in this: we must present the truth; it must be a positive exposition of the teaching of the Word of God. First and foremost we must show men their condition by nature in the sight of God. We must bring them (and I include boys here) to see that apart from what we do, and apart from what we may have done, we are all born the 'children of wrath'; we are born in a state of condemnation, guilty in the sight of God; we are 'conceived in sin, and shapen in iniquity' (Ps. 51:5). That is the first thing.

Having done that we must go on to show the enormity of sin. That does not just mean that we show the wrongfulness of certain sins. There is nothing so vital as the distinction between sin and sins. Far too often we spend our time in calling attention to particular sins, whereas our real business is to convict of sin, the thing itself which destroys us, and which shows itself in the form of particular sins. Then we must call upon our hearers to confess and acknowledge their sin in the sight of God and of men. After that we must go on to present the glorious and the wondrous offer of free salvation which is to be found only in Jesus Christ and in Him crucified. We must show that only He can remove the guilt and power of sin; that Jesus of Nazareth, the Son of God, bore 'our sins in his own body on the tree' (1 Pet. 2:24), and that it is only as we yield and surrender ourselves entirely to Him that, at one and the same time, we are made right with God, and are enabled to live a life that is well-pleasing in His sight. The only decision which is of the slightest value is that which is based upon the realization of that truth. We may get men to decide as a result of our singing, as a result of the charm of our own personality, but our business is not to get personal followers. Our business is not simply to increase the size of Bible classes or organizations or churches. Our business is to reconcile souls unto God. I repeat that there is no value in a decision unless it is based on an acceptance of the truth.

EDIFICATION

My second subdivision in regard to the presentation of the gospel is the work of edification. This is a big subject and all I can do is simply to throw out certain principles. Nowhere is the danger of a false method more real than in this particular matter of edification, by which I mean teaching concerning sanctification and holiness. The danger is shown very clearly in the New Testament itself. You cannot read the New Testament without realizing at once that the early church bristled with problems and dangers and with incipient heresies. There were people, for instance, who said, 'Let us continue in sin that grace may abound.' There were those who said that as long as you were a Christian it did not matter what you did, that as long as you were right in your beliefs, your body did not matter and you could sin as much as you liked. That is known as antinomianism. There were those who claimed that they were sinless. There were those who went in for 'knowledge', who claimed some special esoteric experience of which other, inferior Christians were ignorant. There were those who, the First Epistle to the Corinthians tells us, described themselves as the followers of Christ – some of Paul, others of Apollos, and *others of Christ* (1 Cor. 1:12) – the select few at the top. And there were those, clearly dealt with in the Epistle to the Colossians and 1 Timothy, who went in for some kind of asceticism forbidding people to marry or to eat meat. If you read the subsequent history of the Christian church you will find the same thing emphasized constantly. Take the monks, for instance, and the hermits, the people who said you could not really be a Christian while you were engaged in any ordinary vocation. And then various movements arose in the Christian church. The people who went in for those things were very earnest and quite honest; they all started by believing true doctrines, but they were subject to the danger of heresy and error, and wandered from the true path.

If I might summarize all these dangers, it is the danger of isolating a text or an idea and building up a system round it, instead of comparing Scripture with Scripture. It is the seeking of a short cut in the spiritual world. People attempt to arrive at sanctification in one move, and thus to forego the process described in the New Testament. The way to avoid that danger is to study the New Testament itself, and especially the Epistles. We must reject anything which is not based soundly upon the teaching of the Epistles. We must be very careful that we do not take an incident out of the Gospels, and weave a theory around it, when the incident which is described has not even the remotest connection with the subject of holiness or sanctification. We must realize that our standard in this particular matter is to be found in the Epistles. If you go to the Epistles I think you will find very clearly set out the principle that our life is not to be based upon some sudden experience, but rather upon certain deductions that we are to draw from the truth which we have believed. May I commend to your special study the word 'therefore' in the Epistles? It is a very important word. First of all the.writer lays down the doctrine, and then he says, Therefore – in view of that, go on to do this. Our living of the Christian life must be a deduction from our doctrine.

What is the doctrine? Well, it is constantly repeated. The reason why we should live a holy and sanctified life is because of what we claim to believe concerning Christ, because God is holy, and because of the hope that is set before us. In other words, the New Testament does not invite us to live a holy and sanctified life in order that we might enjoy happiness; but it tells us to do so because Christ has offered Himself for us, and because He has shed His blood on Calvary. The New Testament tells us that we have been redeemed from our sins by the precious blood of Christ, and therefore we have no right to live a sinful life. It does not leave a gap between our believing on Christ as our Saviour and our receiving Him as our Lord: the two things are one. Sanctification of life arises directly out of the doctrine of the death of Christ on the cross. It teaches us that we are to grow in grace, and in the knowledge of the Lord. That is what we get in every single New Testament Epistle. There is constant exhortation to those early believers to apply, and to put into practice in their lives, the truth which they claim to have believed and accepted.

Let me summarize all that I have been trying to say to you thus. If you want to be able ministers of the gospel, if you want to present the truth in the right and only true way, you must be constant students of the Word of God, you must read it without ceasing. You must read all good books that will assist you to understand it, and the best commentaries you can find on the Bible. You must read what I would call biblical theology, the explanation of the great doctrines of the New Testament, so that you may come to understand them more and more clearly, and may therefore be able to present them with ever increasing clarity to those who come to listen to you. The work of the ministry does not consist merely in giving our own personal experience, or talking about our own lives or the lives of others, but in presenting the truth of God in as simple and clear a manner as possible. And the way to do that is to study the Word and anything and everything which aids us in that supreme task.

You may say to me: Who is sufficient for these things? We have other things to do; we are busy men. How can we do this which you have asked us to do? My reply is that none of us is sufficient for these things, but God can enable us to do them if we are really anxious thus to serve Him. I am not much impressed by these arguments that you are busy men, that you have much to do in the world and therefore have no time to read these books on the Bible and to study theology – and for this good reason: that some of the best theologians I have met, some of the most saintly, some of the most learned men, have had to work very much harder than any of you, and at the same time have been denied the advantages that you have enjoyed. 'Where there's a will there's a way.' If you and I are concerned about lost souls, we must never plead that we have no time to equip ourselves for this great ministry; we must make the time. We must equip ourselves for the task, realizing the serious and terrible responsibility of the work. We must learn, and labour, and sweat, and pray in order that we may know the truth ever more and more perfectly. We must put into practice in our own lives the words to be found in 1 Timothy 4:12–16. God grant us the grace and the power to do so, to the honour and glory of His holy name.

Two

*

Religion Today and Tomorrow[1]

*

I

One of the first questions if not *the* first, which our fathers used to ask each other when they met was, 'How are things with your "cause"?' The state and condition of religion was the most important thing with them, not because they had retreated from the world, but because they believed that religion determined and regulated the state of society. And to the Christian this is still the case, and the most important question still remains, 'How are things with your "cause"?' I do not refrain from posing this most important question even in these days because that which sets the Christian apart and makes him different from everyone else is the fact that he views everything from the standpoint of religion, and he looks in that direction for an explanation for everything. We can see this, for example, in the context of this war. The things which perturb most people are the horrible consequences of the war itself, but what vexes the Christian is that such events are at all possible in a world created by God. And in an attempt to explain the cause of war, the same difference is seen. Most people look for political, economic, or psychological reasons, and so forth, but to the Christian there is but one satisfactory explanation, and that is sin, and the backsliding of people from God and His ways.

The same holds with regard to the future. It is not how much food and clothing and money and education and many other possessions we shall have, it is not the type of houses we shall be living in which will be in the forefront of a Christian's mind, although he knows and allows that these things are all legitimate; rather, the important

[1]Three radio addresses for the BBC in Wales given in 1945.

factor is what sort of men we shall be and what we will make of our lives.

This is not an academic question, but a completely practical question for the following reasons.

Firstly, this is God's world and not man's world. There are rules and laws in life. God made a declaration of His way of living to the Israelites through the law, and chiefly through Jesus Christ in the New Testament. If we are to be blessed and to enjoy a happy life, we must obey God's ordinances. On the other hand, the Bible makes it very clear that 'the way of transgressors is hard' (Prov. 13:15).

The second reason is that man's religion is not something private; it is not merely what a man does with his loneliness, as Whitehead puts it. It starts there, but it affects the whole of life. There is a religious reason for everything; and consequently there is no one question which is more important or more relevant than the old question which today is the subject of jokes and sarcasm, 'How are things with your "cause"?' But the factor which lends urgency to this question today is the state of the world. On many fronts it could be said that there has not been a better chance to preach the gospel for centuries, and that for the simple reason that the world has not been in such a dilemma. But in order to see the true light of the present situation, it is imperative for us to look at it in the face of the accusations and claims which were made during the last century. We were taught that man was quickly advancing towards a state of perfection through the strength of his innate powers, and that we have only to educate him and give him a chance to use his faculties in order to create a perfect world. The self-confidence of man was never stronger. Man had only one thing to do, and that was to believe in himself. Religion was something which belonged to the past and to the childhood of mankind. In fact, nothing was more opposed to true life than belief in God. Everyone is familiar with these ideas; I do not need to enlarge on them.

But now we have had two world wars in a quarter of a century, and events happening on the European continent between the two wars which were unheard of for many centuries. There is little mention today of evolution and progress; the hopes have been dashed, the dreams have faded and disappeared. Fear and uncertainty lie in the hearts of men, and according to those who are in a position to judge, the chief features in the minds of the servicemen and women are the doubts, the uncertainty, and the unwillingness to believe that which is said by the politicians. The big word today is *frustration*, and the spirit of despair is abroad. While this does not mean that people are more prepared to listen to the message of the gospel, it does suggest that there is a great chance to preach the message. But the question remains: Is the church aware of this opportunity and ready to take advantage of it? What is the state of religion among us? What is the state of the church?

If we look at the church in general, unfortunately, there is very little difficulty in answering that question. There has not been such a dry and hard period for two centuries. Statistics alone prove this. The number of church members decreases from year to year, and the number of those who used to be called 'listeners' has virtually disappeared altogether. Small gatherings are the norm almost everywhere, and we are surprised when we see the words on some chapels 'Built in the year such and such, *enlarged* in the year . . .'!

The same decline is to be noticed in the Sunday School, which was once so popular. Everyone looked forward to it and prepared for it, but now with few exceptions it is in a poor state. And as far as prayer meetings, society meetings and fellowship meetings[2] are concerned, everyone knows that they are weak and feeble almost everywhere and that many a church today fails to hold such meetings.

In one sense, these facts prove nothing, except that the number of religious people is very small in these days. We must ask another question if we are to find out exactly what the state of religion is today. I do not like asking this other question because it sounds unkind to those who are still religious, but we must face it. What about those of us who still hold with religion? We tend to console ourselves that we are better than the irreligious, and we measure ourselves by a standard which is below us. But that will not suffice. Our standard is that of the saints, and the New Testament, and the church of the past when religion counted in the land. Have we life in us? Do we give people the impression that the main element in our lives is our religion? Do we stand out in society as God's people, and do we shine in our life and our behaviour? Are zeal and enthusiasm apparent in our religion? Or do we give the impression that religion is a matter of duty for us? I wonder how many of us can say that 'the joy of the Lord is our strength' (Neh. 8:10). How many of us can be 'more than conquerors' (Rom. 8:37) face to face with the trials of life

[2]These meetings were set up during the eighteenth-century revival in Wales for the care and encouragement of the converts.

in days such as these? Why is it that the numbers of those who are able to pray and those who have a spiritual experience to declare and share with others are getting smaller from year to year? These are the tests to set on our religious life, and if we set them we must admit that we are dead and lifeless and very like the world around us.

Who can claim that he feels a burden for the lost souls in this country and in foreign countries as our fathers did? How many of us truly mourn and cry out when we look at the state of the world? Do we think at all about the work of rescuing the world, or do we just satisfy ourselves by 'carrying on the cause' and keeping things going? Are we as keen about the cause of religion and the eternal gospel as are the millions over the cause of their country in the face of an enemy? Is our faith in our message as much as the faith of millions of Germans in Nazism and Hitlerism? Do we portray the same adventurous spirit and the same willingness to sacrifice everything for the sake of God's cause?

It is obvious that we do not fully realize what the state of the world around us is when we speak of religion tomorrow, because our ideas and our aims for the future depend to a great extent on the way we interpret our present situation. Moreover, there is nothing which shows our spiritual condition more clearly than our ability to comprehend the signs of the times. Do we realize that the problem of religion today is very different from what it was, say, forty years ago, and even twenty years ago? Today, we are producing men who are almost totally ignorant of the Bible, and from the point of view of morality, the problem is not so much immorality but the total absence of morality – amorality, a tendency to doubt all types of moral standards. Indeed, some would go so far as to say that all those who acknowledge moral standards live an incomplete life and do an injustice to their personalities. These people claim that what was once called sin is nothing but self-expression. The old foundations are being shaken, and the old boundaries and hedges are being swept away. From the point of view of the claims of religion, the problem is not that men are anti-religious, as they used to be, but that they ignore religion completely, and do not think about it at all. A leading public figure has said, 'We don't need an anti-God movement in Britain as they have in Russia, because the majority have forgotten God completely.' Are we aware of this new situation?

Time does not allow us, as we would wish, to trace the pitiful state of religion today. And yet, it is impossible to understand the present situation properly, not to mention to face the future, if we do not do this. The kindest thing we are able to say about ourselves is that we are the inheritors of the sins and shortcomings of our forefathers. Why has religion lost its hold on us as a country? There are some reasons which are common to us and to every country, the main one being, of course, the question of authority, and especially the authority of the Bible. While men accepted the Bible as the Word of God, and accepted the category of revelation, religion flourished, but around the middle of the nineteenth century a tendency to replace revelation with philosophy arose. The ideas of men were the important elements from then on, and the ability of man to understand was the standard. It was said that the miraculous and the supernatural were impossible, and that the Lord Jesus Christ was no more than a man. The gospel was seen as a way of persuading man to save himself rather than as God's way of saving man. The stress was laid on works and life-style rather than on faith in Christ; the term 'a good man' became synonymous with 'a Christian', and morality became synonymous with religion. The important thing was to improve the world rather than to make peace between men and God. The idea that the church was a place where God met with people through the Holy Spirit was lost, and people began to look upon the church as what Karl Barth termed an 'inspirational conventicle'. The ultimate in this way of thinking, of course, is that there is no need for a church at all.

Another reason for the decline is that the zeal and fervour once shown in the world of religion have been transferred into the field of politics. This was a natural progression from the first change. Man, rather than God, was placed on the middle of the stage. After they had lost their belief in another world and had stopped thinking of man as a pilgrim travelling towards 'a city which hath foundations, whose builder and maker is God' (Heb. 11:10), it is easy to understand how men began to concentrate their ideas whole-heartedly on this world and to replace the prophet with the politician.

As well as this, the standard of church membership was devalued, not so much in terms of behaviour as in the matter of belief and experience. Adults and children were encouraged and persuaded to become members, and it was made easy for them to be members. The idea that to become a member in the church of God is the greatest honour that can come to us while on earth was lost. It was believed that rich men and those who had been educated and had achieved a position of importance in the world were honouring the church by their presence.

I wonder, also, if we should not say, that as far as Wales is concerned, preaching has, to a great extent become something which can be enjoyed from the point of view of performance only? The message disappeared more and more from the forefront, the 'powers of the eternal Spirit' were forgotten apart from singing about them to a popular tune, and the important thing was to hold meetings and singing festivals. The forms and ways of the fathers were followed, but their liveliness and the living element which they possessed were lost.

That is how I, at any rate, see religion today. The picture is a bleak one, but it is not hopeless. Even so, we have to face it because the first step towards revival and salvation is an honest mind and true repentance.

II

In the previous talk we glanced over the state of religion today and tried to discover what is responsible for this present terrible situation. But our review was not completed for lack of time, and I did very little more than outline the situation in general, and, to a great extent, outwardly only. And so, it is not possible for us to discuss 'religion tomorrow' without looking once again at the religion of today. Everyone would agree that this is necessary because the future is determined and regulated by the present. More than that, the preparations and arrangements for the future are being made, and we are forced to study them and give our opinion on them. It is necessary not because we are trying to prophesy what the future holds but rather that we might prepare for the future by trying to remind one another of the standards which we should keep in mind at all times when we think of religion.

Before we suggest anything ourselves, we must survey that which has been done already and the ideas which are popular among us. Although we stressed the element of apathy, indifference, and sloth which is typical of religion in general today, it is fair to say that there are signs of dissatisfaction, and indeed unrest, on the part of many.

This is the most hopeful sign in the present situation. I do not suggest that discontent is enough in itself. Indeed, that which we say quite often betrays our motives, and these are often totally foreign to the true religion which stimulates us. For example, some people's anxiety is for the future of the cause, and how they are to keep the doors open. Others are vexed not because of the present disgraceful situation of the church, which is sinful before God, but only because this means that there will be no comfortable hearth in the churches to which the boys and girls may return at the end of the war. It is easy for us to get mixed up in our aims and to forget what religion is in truth.

However that may be, there is a sort of moving in the church, and men are beginning to ask themselves what is wrong and what can be done about it. It is not only the war which is responsible for this, because trends in this direction were obvious in the life of the church even in the barren and disgraceful days before the war. Let us look at them. Perhaps the best way will be for me to divide them under two headings: that which is being done and is already visible, and the intentions and arrangements for the future.

As we look at that which is already happening, perhaps we should again divide the matter into two parts. The first point includes the theological and philosophical trends which make themselves plain to us, and I use these terms to draw attention to three elements which stand out clearly today.

We must begin, of course, with the awakening in the world of theology as such. This is the most striking feature in the field of religion during the last twenty years. We can only touch upon the matter here, but the fact is that a new interest has arisen in theology, and there is more mention of, and debate about, theological matters than there has been for fifty years or more. We must attribute this mainly to the work of Karl Barth and others on the Continent, and through them to Reinhold Niebuhr in America. In this country the movement influenced Sir Edwyn Hoskyns, C. H. Dodd, Nathaniel Micklem, J. S. Whale, and others. It is interesting to note that Professor Vernon Lewis was the first to draw attention to Barth in Britain, and that another Welshman, D. R. Davies, was very prominent among the pillars of the movement. This movement's greatest stress is that we must return to God's Word in the Bible. These people feel that we have lost sight of the idea of revelation, and that, under the influence of other philosophical ideas, we have turned religion into nothing more than elevated humanism. They tend to say that reason and philosophy are the chief enemies of true religion, and they call upon us to re-read and reconsider what God's Word tells us. A new attitude towards a study of the Bible can be seen to emanate from this, and the new commentaries tend to concentrate on the message of the Word, rather than on criticism and language and all that is contained in the term Higher Criticism. The questions of who wrote the book, or when it was written, or where that was, are not important to this school's teaching, the important factor being the content of the book. The important factor is the teaching of the Bible and our realization that God speaks to us here.

The result of all this is that old terms which were ignored for years have come back into vogue, terms such as God's sovereignty, sin, man's inability, and atonement. The same trend is also to be noticed in Mr C. S. Lewis's popularity, both in his lectures and his books. He does not belong to the school of Barth, but he lays the same stress on the importance of the need to submit and confess our inability and to accept the revelation. He is chiefly an apologist who likes to contrast the all-sufficiency of the Christian faith with other philosophies. At the same time, the popularity of books by Jacques Maritain and Christopher Dawson shows that Thomism is gaining ground rapidly.

Side by side with this new interest in theology as such, we find another trend towards High Church ideas, even among Nonconformists. This movement lays its stress on the idea of the church, on worship and the forms of worship, and on the necessity of having an order and a dignity in our public worship, in a word, the devotional side of religion. To these people there is great value in a liturgy, and they all tend to read prayers and have the congregation taking more of a part in the service. They tend to think that most free churches have lowered the standards of worship and have laid too much stress on preaching and preachers. More than that, they tend to believe that we are lacking in a fitting and reverent spirit, and that the flesh and an unsightly spirit are all too prevalent in our gatherings.

These friends are not content with just criticizing. They put their ideas into practice. The result is that more and more ministers wear Geneva gowns in the pulpit; they read their prayers and often their sermons also; they persuade their congregations to read or to sing psalms, and to develop orders of service. In other words, there is a High Church movement among Nonconformists, and it is interesting for us to notice that one of the chief leaders of this movement is a young Welshman, Daniel D. Jenkins, author of the book *The Nature of Catholicity*, who is joint-editor of the *Presbyter*. Another result of these ideas is that many have withdrawn from their fathers' and grandfathers' church and joined the Episcopal Church. It is interesting to note the stress these people put on the word 'dignity'! It would be even more interesting to make a study of the psychological standpoint of some of them, and to try to establish to what extent the idea that Puritanism is alien to the Welsh nature and spirit, is responsible for their point of view.

I must name one other factor under this heading, and that is the movement towards church unity. Many people feel that this is the most important development in the religious world. They argue that the senseless divisions which split the church constitute the main reason for keeping people away from religion, that these divisions today are to a great extent meaningless to the majority of those who belong to different denominations. The vital thing which is needed, according to these brethren, is for us to come together to form one large world-wide church which will be proof of our unity in Christ, and proof, therefore, of the power of the gospel. This idea has resulted in ministers of all churches, even the Episcopal Church, meeting together regularly and forming committees to work together and to worship together. There has never been so much mention of church unity, and some go on to say that nothing will save the church from extinction except this.

We must now turn to the second heading, namely, the practical side, or that which is being done in order to deal with the religious situation. The main factor in this sphere is that which is called the Movement of Religion and Life. This movement covers all parts of the Christian church, apart from the Roman Catholics, though in some places, even they join in. Under the auspices of this movement, ministers of religion come together not only to meet and pray together, but also to arrange public meetings, which are called Religion and Life Weeks. Meetings are arranged for a week at a time and famous speakers come to address them, the first usually being the bishop of the province. The same programme is almost always followed and the content is arranged as follows: religion and the home; religion and education; religion and social life; religion and morality; religion and the individual. Their purpose is to show what religion has to say on these matters, and they try to persuade people to adapt their religion to these various spheres. Those who are involved in the movement feel that what keeps many from religion is that they feel it has nothing to do with practical everyday life, and that the way to win these people is to state the gospel's relevance to all aspects of life. It can be said, therefore, that this is a way of evangelizing in an indirect manner.

At the same time, others who follow the old paths hold evangelistic campaigns for eight to ten days under the leadership of a popular evangelist or a number of evangelists, some speaking, others singing. Many such campaigns have been held in England during the past year under the auspices of the Faith for the Times Campaign.

To turn for a moment to that which has been suggested with regard to the future, it is a fact that committees and commissions are meeting, as they did during and after the last war, to try to re-organize the work of the churches. No-one yet knows exactly what these will have to offer. I shall refer, therefore, to that which is often heard and believed by many. Some things stand out clearly. It is difficult to ignore the idea that a prejudice is developing against preaching and in favour of debates and free discussions on religious topics. For years many have tried to lay stress on personal work, not as something which follows on from, and which adds to, preaching, but on personal work rather than preaching. Many therefore feel that there is a need for less preaching. Others lay stress on the week-night church meeting. According to these people, these society meetings and fellowship meetings must be turned into meetings to cultivate body as well as mind and spirit. The church's business and work, according to them, is to be a social centre in the district in every respect. This is the way to win over and to keep the young people especially. Others feel that the days of chapels and large congregations are numbered, and that the future trend will be preaching here and there in the open air, and the appointment of chaplains in the factories and shops and wherever men work, as is done in the Armed Forces. In a word, many tend to believe that there is no future at all for religion in the manner to which we are accustomed today.

It is obvious that we have no time here to deal with these many and varied ideas. I hope, in the last address, to look at them from the New Testament standpoint and to stress what its teaching has to say about religion in every age. But some things may be said here, or at least we may answer a few questions. Has the time come, I wonder, to ask,

[23]

What is the true value of the new theological movement? Although it dismisses the value of the mind and the reason, does it really impinge upon anything apart from the minds of men? And while it pays little respect to philosophy, is it any better than a new emphasis in philosophy? Is not this also the reason why it is so difficult to comprehend it? While we are thankful for the new emphasis on the Word and on theology, we must remember that there is a radical, basic difference between preaching the Word and preaching *about* the Word. It is only the preaching of the Word which saves men, and that is the purpose of the gospel – not just to give man an intellectual change and to persuade him to alter his philosophical viewpoint but to have him re-born and changed completely.

With regard to the movement which stresses the devotional side, we are ready to agree with many, if not all, of the things that are said about the unworthy elements which so often typify our meetings – the casual responses ('amen-ing'), the self-centredness, the noise and the turmoil; we agree that there is a need for nurturing a worshipping and reverent spirit. But after all, although order and dignity are splendid, the one element which is needed above everything else is life. The forms are important, but the essence is much more important. Paganism thrives in the outward things and the forms; simplicity and freedom are the feature of true religion always.

Every true Christian hates the small, narrow spirit of denominationalism and sectarianism, but the biggest catastrophe in the world today is not the disunity of the church, but the fact that every part of the church and every denomination is so dead and so devoid of the power and ability of the Holy Spirit. Spiritual power is not something which belongs to the world of mathematics; if we united all the denominations and added all the powers of each together, even that would not create spiritual life. The burial of many bodies in the same cemetery does not lead to resurrection. Life is more important than unity.

For the same reason, the great call today is not to teach men how they should apply religion to life, but first and foremost to make them religious. Before there can be any learning there must first be disciples. It is imperative to see that conviction and salvation come first. I wonder if I am in error when I say that the Religion and Life Movement is typical of the Anglican – not English – idea of religion, the philosophical idea which stems from Oxford? As for the proposals which are made for the future, suffice it to say that there is nothing new in them. What surprises us is that everybody does not see that the chief need of the world is to be reminded of the spiritual side of life. Everyone is interested in food and clothes, houses and lands, work and education, pleasure and entertainment, and there is a multitude of societies to call for that sort of thing and to make arrangements on their behalf; but there is nobody to talk about God and about the soul, about life everlasting and eternal destiny, not to mention the only strength which helps a man to live decently in this world, nobody apart from the church of God. There has never been such a need for spiritual specialists. How can we find them and produce more of them? We shall try to answer that question in the next talk.

III

In the previous talks we attempted to describe the religious scene today, and we also looked hurriedly at the trends and movements which are becoming evident in the life of the church at this time. We came to the conclusion that some of those things which are done or suggested for the future are not only insufficient, but also heretical from the point of view of true religion.

Perhaps some may feel that we have spent too much time on this investigation, and with that which they consider to be negative only, but we did this for a number of reasons. For one thing, we had to make a diagnosis, and be certain of it, before we began to think of a cure. The sick man always wants relief and something to ease his pain, but the doctor's first task is to discover the cause of the illness. It is a very unworthy physician who tries to cure before he knows exactly what the trouble is. But the same principle is seen in action in the work of the prophets of Israel. They spend the greater part of their time convicting the nation of sin and condemning her actions before there is a turning back to God. The nation was willing to try anything and to take hold of any invention, but it was always necessary to do the same thing first. It was not enough for the prophet to tell Israel what to do – he had first to show that everything else was worthless and, indeed, that it was a hindrance. We must also stress the element of hindrance. The great danger in a crisis is to rush to do things, and then just to be satisfied with our actions. Being busy subdues the mind, the heart, and the conscience, and gives us a feeling of relief. We feel, therefore, that just because we are doing something, we are dealing with the problem. The result is that we avoid the problem. Lessening the tension in a crisis is not of itself a good thing. Indeed, it can be altogether a bad thing. Morphia lessens the pain and the tension, but it does nothing to cure the illness. In short, the big danger today is to rush into dealing with the signs, the symptoms of our religious illness, rather than discovering and treating the true cause of all these signs. We had to stress all these things for the reason that treating these symptoms is, necessarily, a hindrance to finding out the true nature of the illness. The purpose of symptoms in the pattern of nature is that they lead us to the illness itself. The symptom is not the illness itself; the symptom is merely a signpost which points in the direction of the illness.

The way to avoid this danger of staying with the symptoms is to go back to the New Testament and to look again at the picture of true religion which is seen there. That is the ultimate authority which we have.

Perhaps the best way for us to reconsider this matter would be to ask a number of questions which would force us not only to face the basic facets of the problem, but also to do that in a practical way.

The first question is: What is the intention and the aim behind our religious strivings and efforts? What is the target which we have in mind? What is the true purpose of religion? We need to face this question because of strange and heretical ideas which are abroad. The important factor in the mind of one group is to have people attend meetings and to have large gatherings. These people are worried that our places of worship are becoming empty and that the number of church members is decreasing. If they could only succeed in persuading people to come to the services, they would be perfectly happy. The reason for their sorrow is the terrible difference between what they saw fifty years ago and the state of things today. Flourishing religion to them means big gatherings and successful meetings from the numerical point of view. To others the function and business of religion is to uphold morality and to influence the life-style of the community. These worry about the moral tone of our country – the drunkenness and dancing and the corruption which are so blatant in the life of the world. They speak of statistics concerning young offenders, of divorce, and many other things, and they worry as they consider the future. We need to deal with these problems, they say, and it is the function and business of religion to do so. Undoubtedly, this is the idea which is behind the intention of giving religious education in the day schools.

Another group of people sees the issue in terms of the point of view of the country generally. They say that religion has been the foundation of the life of this country, that it has accounted for the success and the importance it has among the countries of the world. Therefore if we lose our religion, we will have lost our backbone, and that will be the end of us as a world power. For the sake of our country, for the sake of Britain, we must have a religious awakening, they say.

For still others the purpose of religion is to be a general influence on politics, and on important issues such as education and culture, war and peace, business and trade, and on the life of man in all its spheres.

There is no need to say that all these matters issue from religion, but there is a need to pronounce, clearly and definitely, that this is not the main aim of the Christian religion. This religion's main aim is to re-unite men with God, to convict them of sin, and to lead them to the Lord Jesus Christ as their only Saviour. The aim is not to create a church of great numbers, but people who know God and who are 'in Christ'. The aim is not to produce good men, but to create new men, not to improve society as such, but to deal with individual men. Nothing stands out more clearly in the New Testament than the perpetual contrast between morality and spiritual life. Without the life which is in Christ Jesus, everything else is filth and loss; and to know Him properly is the only target which we should have before us.

This leads us to the second question, an all-important question, What is the church? No-one can answer such a question fully in a few minutes, but we can look at the picture which the New Testament affords us, and find there the central important truth. The name given to the place of worship very often by our forefathers was *Tŷ Cwrdd* [Meeting House]. It was a good name. But the question which arises today is, For what reason are we meeting? We have already seen that many think of the church as a social centre or a cultural centre. To them the church is a place where people meet together on a Sunday, in a public religious service, but they also insist that they should meet one another there during the week to speak together, to debate, to listen to lectures on all sorts of topics, to play together, to perform plays, to dance, and so on.

[27]

The church, they say, should do all these things, more especially in order to entice the young people and to keep hold of them. Now, the important question is not what we think about these things in and of themselves, but does the church have anything to do with such matters? What is the church in the New Testament? There is only one answer to that question – a fellowship of saints. What we see there is a number of people coming together for a special purpose. Who are those people? What brings them together? What is the common interest which is so strong in their hearts, that they often endanger their lives in order to be present at such meetings? They are people who are very different from others, people, according to the apostle Paul, who have been pulled out from the world and divorced from society; people who have proved things which the world knows nothing about; people who have had an experience of God's grace in the Lord Jesus Christ, people who have come to see that the most important thing in life is a knowledge of God, in a relationship in accord with His commandments. They have seen their pitiful, desperate state before God, but they have also seen God forgiving all of their sins in Jesus Christ. They are aware of a new life and an uplifting power which makes them more than conquerors – even when face to face with the temptations and trials of life. Everything is new to them, and they see life in this world as a pilgrimage towards God and heaven. They do not scorn the world, but they do not live for it, or because of it, either. 'For here have we no continuing city,' they say, 'but we seek one to come' (Heb. 13:14). They meet together – for what reason? To worship God, to praise His blessed Name, to thank Him for the grace which has led to the forgiveness of sins, and for new life in Christ. They meet together also so that they may know Him better and come to understand His providence more perfectly. They hunger and thirst after righteousness. They also thirst for the sincere milk of the Word, and there is nothing they enjoy more than to study the Word, and to listen to it being proclaimed. They feel a strong urge to meet with one another, in order that they may exchange experiences, that they might help one another to unravel many a problem, and that they should stimulate one another to go forward. They all have the same basic experience, they are all travelling in the same direction. They feel, therefore, that 'the company of brothers who have their faces set towards that country is sweet'. A church is a place where they recite 'His faithfulness to them in the burning desert' and where they love to speak about 'journey's end'. This is the picture which we have in the New Testament, the portrayal which has been seen a hundredfold since then in the life of the church. The church portrays a collection of people, of whom it can be said: 'But ye are a chosen generation, a royal priesthood, an holy nation, a peculiar people; that ye should show forth the praises of him who hath called you out of darkness into his marvellous light' (1 Pet. 2:9). No-one else has the right to be a member of the society.

I can imagine someone asking the question: If the church is this type of society, what hope do you have of getting people to come in? These criteria do not appeal to men today; this is not their field of study; they do not take any interest in this sort of thing. Would it not be better to reach out to them along common lines of interest, and in terms of the things which appeal naturally to them? The question contains nothing new. It is simply the age-old question concerning the authority of the church.

Some seek for authority, as we saw, in ceremonies and religious rites; others look for it in tradition and yet others in priesthood and special church government. Some feel that the authority of the Bible lies in our response to it. We have no time to weigh these ideas here, but we must pronounce fearlessly and fervently that the church will not find, in these ways, the authority it needs to speak to the world and to make it listen. The Word is all important, but the only power which provides authority is the Holy Spirit. This is the secret of the strange sermon which the apostle Peter preached on Pentecost day in Jerusalem, and of the unbelievable results which followed. Paul speaks in similar terms: 'And my speech and my preaching was not with enticing words of man's wisdom, but in demonstration of the Spirit and of power. That your faith should not stand in the wisdom of men, but in the power of God' (1 Cor. 2:4–5). That is the story down through the ages and in every period of revival and awakening. The world was not better or more anxious to listen to the message of the gospel at the beginning of the eighteenth century than it is today. We cannot explain the big events which happened in the history of religion in Wales in terms of men only. They all have one explanation – Daniel Rowland, Howel Harris, and William Williams of Panty-celyn were men who spoke 'as those with authority'. The same feature is present with the Puritans, in the Protestant fathers, in Savonarola, and everyone who has been used of God to revive religion in their generation. When 'the live element' comes to the church, the world begins to listen, and they flock in. The problem then is not how to get people to come and listen, but how to find enough room for them all. The world is keen to recognize the difference between man's voice and the voice of God, and in the end it is not prepared to listen to anything apart from His voice.

It is not difficult for us, therefore, to answer the next question: What is the call for us today? It is obvious that we must concentrate our energies on the church, and that the chief need is the revival and the awakening of the church itself. It is in the church, and often through individuals who belong to the church, that the big spiritual movements have always started. When the church operates in the power and strength of the Holy Spirit, it does more in one day than it would otherwise do through all its activities without the Spirit in years. In the end all our fears for the future of the church and religion, our feeling of hopelessness as we see the world falling deeper into sin and vanity, our inclination towards multiplying arrangements, committees, and movements, stem from the same blindness, namely our lack of faith in the workings of the Holy Spirit.

What can we do then? The first thing is to realize that we can never create a revival; but after reaching that point, we have a lot to do.

If I had to express this all in one sentence, I would say that what is needed today is for us to forget the nineteenth century completely and make a detailed study of the beginning of the eighteenth century. If we were to do that, we should learn special lessons. Above all else we would see that the first step is not to bring down the standard of church membership, but to raise it. We must grasp once again the idea of church membership as being the membership of the body of Christ and as the biggest honour which can come a man's way in this world. Through discipline, we must lay great acclaim on membership of the society and we must re-emphasize the truth that God gives the Holy Spirit only 'to them that obey him' (Acts 5:32). The need is not for widening the appeal, but to proclaim that 'strait is the gate, and narrow is the way, which leadeth unto life' (Matt. 7:14). This means possibly that many will shy away from the churches and will leave them; and from the point of view of statistics and accounts and collections everything looks hopeless, and those who try to keep the churches alive are afraid. But as sure as that, the Lord's word will be verified: 'whosoever will save his life shall lose it; but whosoever will lose his life for my sake, the same shall save it' (Luke 9:24). Like Paul in Athens long ago, we must realize that our work is not to argue about the truth but to declare it and proclaim it with authority. We are not just to get people to take an interest in the truth, and to appeal to their minds only; that is not our business, but rather to awaken their consciences by proclaiming God's judgment on sin, and God's wrath against 'all ungodliness and unrighteousness of men' (Rom. 1:18), and to warn them to flee from the wrath that is to come. We must convict men of the truth of the extreme importance of the spiritual side to life, of an everlasting world and everlasting destiny. No-one will see the need of the Lord Jesus Christ as a Saviour but the person who has seen himself as lost before God; and the only true motive to live a moral and worthy life is thankfulness to God and the realization that one day we shall stand before Him.

This is the call which goes out to religious people today: we must realize our unworthiness before God, our distance from the saints of the ages, our terrible dissimilarity from the Christians of the New Testament; then we must repent and re-consecrate ourselves to God in Christ, and we must make sure that our religion regulates our lives. But more than anything, we must realize that the state of the world is such that nothing but the power of the Holy Spirit can cure it, and we must feel this to such an extent that we are brought down upon our knees to pray to God in His mercy to look down upon us in pity, and for His great name, that He should send a mighty revival among us. That is the only way, that is the only hope, because with men it is impossible, but not with God, for 'with God, all things are possible' (Matt. 19:26).

Three

*

John Calvin[1]

*

Nothing is more significant of the great change which has happened in the field of theology during the past twenty years than the place now afforded, and the attention given, to the great man of Geneva who is the subject of this address.

Up to almost twenty years ago there was very little attention paid to John Calvin, and when someone spoke of him it was in order to heap insults on him scornfully. He was looked upon as a cruel, masterly, hard person. As for his work, it was said that he was the author of the most oppressive and iron-like theological system that had ever been seen. The main effects of his work in the field of religion, according to this belief, were to place and keep people in a state of spiritual bondage, and in a wider sphere, to open the way for capitalism. It was believed, therefore, that his influence was totally harmful and that he was of no apparent interest to the world apart from being a specimen, if not a monster, in the museum of theology and religion.

But that is not the situation today. In fact, there is more mention of him than there has been for almost a century, and Calvin and Calvinism are the subjects of many an argument and debate in theological circles. Perhaps it is the theological revival that is connected with the name of Karl Barth, which chiefly accounts for this, if one looks at things outwardly. But one has to explain Barth and his standpoint also. What sent him back to Calvin? His own answer is that he could not find a satisfactory explanation of life, and especially of the problems of the twentieth century, anywhere else, nor an anchor for his soul and faith in the bitterness of the storm. Whatever the explanation, the fact is that Calvinist societies have

[1] A radio address for the BBC in Wales, 25 June, 1944.

been formed in this country, in the United States and Canada, in Australia, New Zealand, and South Africa, apart from those that were formed in other countries in Europe before the war. Indeed, an International Calvinistic Congress was held in Edinburgh in 1938, and two similar conferences have been held in America during the war. As well as this, periodicals are published regularly to discuss topics and problems from the standpoint of Calvin's teaching; and this year the textbook being studied in the theological classes at New College, Edinburgh is *Institutes of the Christian Religion* by John Calvin. It would please me a great deal if I were able to add that there was a similar movement in Wales.

The time is ripe, therefore, for us to cast another glance at this man who has influenced the life of the world to such an extent.

What of the man himself? He was born at Noyon in Picardy in 1509. We know very little of his father and mother, except that his mother was renowned for her godliness. Calvin showed from the beginning that he had exceptional mental capacities. His parents were Roman Catholics, of course, and their natural intention was to prepare their clever son for an eminent career in the Church. His fields of study, therefore, were philosophy, theology, law, and literature. Although he excelled in every field, his favourite sphere was literature, and we see him at twenty-two in Paris as a humanist scholar, his main ambition in life being to earn a name for himself as a writer. He was such an exceptional student that he would often lecture to his fellow students in place of their teachers, and as for his life-style and conduct in those days, he was renowned for his sobriety. Indeed, he was so keen to emphasize the moral note that he won for himself the nickname 'The Accusative Case'. But as with Luther before him, and John Wesley and many others after him, morality was not enough to quench his thirsty soul. When he was twenty-three years old he experienced an evangelical conversion and the course of his life was altogether changed. Having seen the evangelical truth, and having experienced its power in his soul, he turned his back on the Church of Rome and became a Protestant. We have no time to follow his life story, but we know that he spent almost the whole of the rest of his life in Geneva as a minister of the gospel. He worked there from 1536 until his death in 1564 with the exception of the period from 1538 to 1541 when the Genevan authorities drove him out, and he went into 'exile' in Strasburg.

Calvin was a thin man, of average height, with a high forehead and piercing eyes. His health was very fragile throughout his life because he suffered from asthma. It was extremely difficult to persuade him to eat or to sleep. Although he had a masterly spirit, the evidence of those who knew him best suggests that there has never been such a humble and holy man. His chief aim in life was to glorify God, and he devoted himself to doing that completely, without any mercy on his body or on his resources. He liked to think of himself as a Christian writer, and if he had followed his own inclination, he would have confined his work solely to this field; but a friend threatened him with God's judgment if he did not undertake to preach, and the result was, according to the chief authority on his life, that he preached on average every day, and often twice a day, in Geneva for twenty-five years. Because of the asthma he spoke slowly, and one could not describe him as an eloquent speaker. We must not think of him, either, as a preacher who appealed only to the mind and the intellect. A certain godly tenderness would often break upon the meetings, so that the congregation would be quite overpowered.

The world remembers him not so much as a preacher, but as the author of fifty-nine thick volumes. He wrote thirty commentaries on the books of the Bible, including the whole New Testament except for the Second and Third Epistles of John and the book of Revelation.

On top of this Calvin was a constant letter-writer and 4,000 of his letters have been published. He had endless opportunity also in an age so fond of debates to use his incomparable ability as a debater. There was no-one ever like him in the use of the 'rapier' and when one adds to this his special gift in logic, we find possibly the greatest 'controversialist' which the world has ever seen.

When we remember that he was perpetually involved in contentions or consultations with the authorities in Geneva concerning the moral and social state of the city, we are not surprised that he died when he was only fifty-five years old. The mystery is how he managed to accomplish so much in so little time. No-one knows where he is buried, but his main contribution to theological literature, the *Institutes of the Christian Religion*, stands as a memorial to him. He wrote this when he was about twenty-five years old, and it was first published in Basle in 1536, but Calvin worked on it, adding to it and republishing it all through his life.

This is undoubtedly his masterpiece. Indeed, one could say that no book has had such an influence on man and on the history of civilization. It is not too much to say either that it was the *Institutes* which saved the Protestant Reformation for this was the *summa theologica* of Protestantism and the clearest declaration which the evangelical faith has ever had.

In the *Institutes* we see Calvin's place in the Protestant Reformation. He belongs to the second wave of reformers. Luther had virtually finished his work before Calvin began. Luther was the 'Morning Star'; in God's hand, he began the movement. Luther is the great hero of Protestants; he is characterized especially by his originality and his audacity, and the dynamic element in his life. Luther was a volcano, spewing out fiery ideas in all directions without much pattern or system. But ideas cannot live and last without a body, and the great need of the Protestant movement in the last days of Luther was for a theologian with the ability to arrange and to express the new faith within a system. That person was Calvin. It can be said, therefore, that it was he who saved Protestantism by giving it a body of theology within his *Institutes*; and it is from this that the faith and theology of most of the Protestant churches has sprung. This was the backbone of the Thirty-Nine Articles of the Church of England and of the Westminster Confession, which regulates the belief of the Presbyterian churches in Scotland, the United States, and every other country. On the *Institutes* was based the faith of the Puritans, and the history of Switzerland and Holland cannot be explained except in this context.

Just a word about his doctrine. Calvin's main feature is that he bases everything on the Bible. He does not have a mixture of Aristotle's philosophy and the Scripture, with the first practically as important as the second, as in the *Summa* of Thomas Aquinas. The Bible for Calvin is the only authority, and he does not wish for any philosophy apart from that which emanates from the Scripture. It is in the *Institutes* that one gets biblical theology for the first time, rather than dogmatic theology. Calvin does not reason in an inductive way like the Roman Catholics, but rather he draws conclusions and works out in a deductive way that which is taught in the Bible. Revelation is not an addition to reason and one cannot reason properly outside of revelation. For him the great central and all-important truth was the sovereignty of God and God's glory. We must start here and everything else issues from here. It was God, of His own free will and according to His infinite wisdom, who created the world. But sin entered and if it were not for God's grace, there would be no hope for the world. Man is a fallen creature, with his

[35]

mind in a state of enmity towards God. He is totally unable to save himself and to reunite himself with God. Everyone would be lost if God had not elected some for salvation, and that unconditionally. It is only through Christ's death that it is possible for these people to be saved, and they would not see or accept that salvation if God through His irresistible grace in the Holy Spirit had not opened their eyes and persuaded them (not forced them) to accept the offer. Even after that, it is God who sustains them and keeps them from falling. Their salvation, therefore, is sure, because it depends, not on them and their ability, but on God's grace. The church is a collection of the elect. It is, therefore, free and there is no king over it except the Lord Jesus Christ, and, because of that, it claims complete and perfect spiritual freedom.

As for the world outside the church, it would quickly be destroyed by sin if God through common grace did not keep it and set bounds on the effects of sin. The world is still God's world, and even sin and Satan are, ultimately, under the control of God. Before the foundation of the world, God had His infinite purpose, and this purpose can be seen being worked out gradually, but surely, through the Old Testament, and especially in the life of Israel; but chiefly it is seen in Jesus Christ, what He did while on earth, and what He continues to do through the centuries. Nothing can hinder His purpose, and in the fullness of time the kingdoms of the world will become the property of our Lord and His Christ; and He will reign evermore. In the meantime we must teach men that this world is God's world, that every gift which man possesses is a gift from God, that men are all one as sinners before God, and that no king, nor any other, has a right to tyrannize his fellow men. We must have order, we must have discipline. Man has a right to freedom, but not to free licence. That is the essence of Calvin's teaching. He worked it out minutely to cover every aspect of life.

During his ministry in Geneva he persuaded the authorities to put these ideas into action, and there was never a town like it. Mark Pattison does not exaggerate when he says: 'He was the means of concentrating in that narrow corner a moral force which saved the Reformation and indeed Europe. It may be doubted if all history can furnish another instance of such a victory of moral force.' It is no wonder that far-seeing men today, in a world such as this, turn back to the prophet of Geneva. What apart from the gospel he taught can save the world? And this is the teaching: 'The Lord reigneth; let the people tremble' (Ps. 99:1). 'The Lord reigneth; let the earth rejoice' (Ps. 97:1). *Soli Deo Gloria.*[1]

---

[1]The republication by James Clarke in 1949 of Calvin's foremost work carried the following cover blurb by Dr Lloyd-Jones:

> The announcement that Messrs James Clarke & Co. are about to issue a new edition of Calvin's *Institutes of the Christian Religion* is the best news I have heard for some time. That they are able to do so at the remarkably low price of thirty shillings, in these days, is astonishing.
>
> Someone may ask why a work like this, which was first issued over four hundred years ago should be reprinted and why anyone should read it.
>
> I would suggest the following answers as a minimum.
>
> The *Institutes* are in and of themselves a theological classic. No work has had a greater or a more formative influence on Protestant theology. It is not always realized, however, that in addition to its massive and sublime thought it is written in a style which is most moving, and at times thrilling. Unlike most modern theology, which claims to derive from it, it is deeply devotional. No book repays reading more than this, and especially so in the case of preachers of the Word.
>
> It is particularly appropriate that the new edition is appearing now. There has been a new interest in reformed theology during the past thirty years, and the name of Calvin is more frequently quoted than it has been for over half a century. It is in the *Institutes* that one finds the systematic and formulated statement of his essential position. It is imperative, therefore, that one should read the *Institutes* in order to understand much of the present-day theological discussion.
>
> The most urgent reason why all should read the *Institutes*, however, is to be found in the times in which we live. In a world which is shaking in its very foundations and which lacks any ultimate authority, nothing is so calculated to strengthen and to stabilize one's soul as this magnificent exposition and outworking of the glorious doctrine of the sovereignty of God. It was the 'iron ration of the soul' of the Reformation martyrs, of the Pilgrim Fathers, the Covenanters, and many others who have had to face persecution and death for Christ's sake.
>
> Never was it more needed than today. Messrs James Clarke & Co. have placed us all greatly in their debt.

Four

*

Maintaining the Evangelical Faith Today[1]

*

For the last thirty years, although I would not for a moment have chosen such a course for myself, a great deal of my time has been taken up with the task of maintaining and defending the evangelical faith. This fact calls, perhaps, for a personal reference and explanation, necessary because in these days Christian people are less accustomed to the earnest discussion and debating of their theological differences.

Though some may not think it, I am by nature a pacific person, who does not like controversy and all that often has to go with a whole-hearted contention for a matter of theological principle. I envy those who have placid temperaments and easy-going, good-natured personalities, who never seem to be worried by all the wrongs, both small wrongs and big wrongs, which impede the progress and lower the standards of our churches. It must be very much easier to be one of those who can be considered good 'denominational leaders' and good 'party men', those who happily pursue 'the even tenor of their ways' no matter what is happening around them. In some moods there is nothing I would more like to be than a mountain shepherd – above and away from it all, upon the silent slopes of the hills I love. But time and again I have been thrust back into, and driven constantly to engage in, this difficult, searching, and strenuous task, the maintenance of the evangelical witness.

Many evangelical Christians could speak similarly of their own

[1]The Presidential Address given at the Inter-Varsity Fellowship Conference at Swanwick in 1952.

experience. It is therefore important that we should together take stock of the position, that we should examine our aims and motives. We must ask ourselves the question, How do we justify ourselves in making strenuous efforts to maintain, and even, if necessary, to fight for the evangelical faith? We are not challenged from one side only. The challenge now comes from several directions. I propose therefore to consider some of the opposing forces and what they would urge upon us. I also want to show why I believe, as I do, that we must more vigorously than ever stand to our job and refuse to surrender any single part of what is vital to the full evangelical faith as recorded in the Holy Scriptures.

First, let us consider the general challenge. It comes to us in numerous forms, but mainly at the present time in what is called the 'ecumenical' outlook and way of life. Almost all of us meet it in the churches to which we belong and in the many young people's and other organizations which supplement the work of our churches. We meet it most in the form of an all-pervasive climate of opinion which dislikes anything that is really distinctive in doctrine or in life, which demands, indeed, ever less emphasis on doctrine, on definition, or on ethical principle. Never was a time when polemics in any form was at such a discount. There have been periods in history when the preservation of the very life of the church depended upon the capacity and readiness of certain great leaders to differentiate truth from error and boldly to hold fast to the good and to reject the false; but our generation does not like anything of the kind. It is against any clear and precise demarcation of truth and error.

There is one common argument, a stock argument, which is widely used to justify all this intellectual torpor and moral enervation. The enemy, they say, is outside the church. It is not for a brother in the church to be worried about what his brother believes, however wide it may apparently be of all that has hitherto been characterized as orthodoxy. The real enemy, they continue, is Communism. This is something which threatens the whole of the Christian church throughout the world. It persists in attacking the whole of Christian life and threatens us all equally. There is no time for debating and arguing when the whole edifice is threatened. Will you be like those who linger, arguing which is the best room or the best furniture, when the whole house is about to burn down over their heads? We must stand as one man. The enemy is at our gates and threatens the whole. That is the argument.

This challenge confronts any church or society which seeks to maintain a distinctive evangelical witness. This is no time to accentuate differences, they are told. Ought we not all to join together in face of the alarming situation? It is encountered, too, surprisingly enough in view of what has already been said, in a new 'denominationalism'. One effect of ecumenicity has been that some denominations and denominational societies have increased in self-consciousness and have begun to emphasize their own particular identity and outlook. Here we have a single denominational 'consciousness' offering itself as, at least, a social refuge.

Why do we not agree with these arguments? Why do we not all take the far less difficult road of simply becoming members in this developing mammoth society of Ecumenicalism?

First, let us look at some negative considerations. We certainly must not adhere to our policy and course of action merely out of loyalty to a tradition, that is, any other than the 'tradition' of the gospel. A tradition, though it may often be a good one, is not in itself to be considered sacrosanct. Even in the case of a good tradition, and one which ought to be preserved, the whole motive for its preservation must not be just 'traditionalism'. A Christian man is not called upon to be a mere antiquary, or one who is simply concerned with maintaining the *status quo*. We must not preserve our evangelical principles simply because they have a venerable pedigree, valuable as the example of our predecessors may be. That which the New Testament calls upon us to perpetuate is something which is living and dynamic, and which carries its own authentication.

Nor must we be animated by a mere party spirit. We must not simply contend, as in history men have often done, for family or for locality or for political party for its own sake. Some of our friends and allies tend to give the impression that they are not fighting for truth itself so much as for their own particular theological party.

Nor must we be actuated by anything in the nature of a spirit of fear. 'For God hath not given us the spirit of fear; but of power, and of love, and of a sound mind' (2 Timothy 1:7). Some people seem to be conservative evangelicals simply because they will not examine anything other than the contentions of their own school of thought. The type of person who says that he believes the whole Bible in the

Authorized Version 'from cover to cover, including all the commas as well', is almost certainly one who is unaware of the problems of a translator and is probably equally oblivious of the nature of the writing in the earliest manuscripts and their lack of punctuation marks. Such a man is often one who fears to look into such matters lest he should be confronted by tests of his faith.

Further, we must disown any such negative attitudes as those which we associate with bellicose personalities. We must not hold tenaciously to our evangelicalism simply because we have a contentious spirit. It is all too easy for most of us to confuse mere prejudice with vital principle.

Our attention was recently called to an instructive example. In a certain British dominion, several leading figures, who were prominent in their denomination, had been considering what their attitude should be concerning their joining in support of their denomination's intention to affiliate with the World Council of Churches. They believed that they had good reason and sound principle for declining to support this course of action and were prepared to act according to their convictions. A little later, two visitors from another country came to their city. These visitors addressed a representative gathering of Christian leaders in order to give their views on this very matter. The two local Christian leaders were appalled at the venom and acrimony with which these visitors attacked the WCC, and were repelled by their whole manner of speech. Later, when his turn to speak came, one of these two anxious and saddened local leaders intervened as follows: 'I rise to say that I am in agreement with what the visiting speakers have said concerning the momentous character of this issue. I am also in agreement with most of the reasons adduced why Christian people may have to refuse to be drawn into courses of action which appear dangerously to compromise, and even to betray, the treasures and liberties which were won for us by reformers and evangelical fathers at such great cost. But I have one very serious disagreement. The speakers seem to be glad that the leaders of the ecumenical movement have revealed themselves to be such blind and unreliable guides. To me it is a matter of the deepest and most profound regret. I wish, with all my heart, that we could forget the past and secure a deep and lasting outward union of all God's true servants. It is in deep sorrow and with a heavy heart (and at real personal cost) that I agree with the conclusion that those who wish to remain loyal to New Testament

Christianity are compelled to refuse the superficial and dangerous scheme of comprehension which has virtually no safeguards against repeating the evils which have wrought such havoc in church history.'

This surely is the right attitude. We must not be animated by a contentious spirit. If it is necessary to take a stand about any matter, then we should do it with real regret and sorrow.

Now we must look at some positive reasons why we should maintain our evangelical witness. In answer to any questioner who enquires as to why we adhere to our particular outlook and methods, we have the duty to give such answers as these.

First, we believe and do these things because our understanding of the biblical principles of doctrine and ethics leads us to the conviction that this is the only right course. We have been led to it by the Holy Spirit speaking in and through Holy Scripture. We may even go further and, indeed, if we really believe what we often say we do, we must not hesitate to affirm that we hold our position because we believe that it is essential to salvation for us to do so. Each one of us must be quite clear about this matter. If God has spoken in His Word in such a way that His will and thoughts toward men are clearly revealed, then to follow this way is essential to receiving the life of God in my soul. In other words, the Bible urges us to take a certain view which it clearly defines and which it expects us to adopt. We have no authority for departing from it.

What have we to say to those who argue that in view of the urgency of the times and the dangers threatening the church, we must all get together and minimize our differences, no matter what they may be? Our answer is that the Bible warns us against this very thing. In Acts 20:17–35 we have a clear outline of the duty of the overseers in the church of Christ. St Paul warns the elders of the church in Ephesus that 'grievous wolves' would come, and men would arise from among the number of their own church 'speaking perverse things, to draw away disciples after them'. Such warnings run right through the New Testament, from the words of our Lord in the Gospels to the last pages of the Revelation, where almost the last words of the book warn the reader not to add to, or to subtract from its words. The Christian has been told to expect false prophets within the church and he is clearly told to contend for the true faith, to fight for it. He is to beware of all that leads the church astray.

The New Testament also warns us not to be too ready to take people, even within the church, at their face value. The 'false prophets' could be expected to come in 'sheep's clothing'. They would look like true members of the flock of God. They would be affable men, 'nice' men; but none the less they would be 'false prophets' and 'wolves'. We are not to accept everything which even those who call themselves Christian may say. The church is warned to look for the true 'fruit of the Spirit'. In particular, those who claim to be God's spokesmen must be quite clear concerning the true nature of the person of Christ; the fact of His resurrection, the substitutionary character of His death, the way of salvation, and how the Christian life is to be lived. Anyone who is equivocal or misleading on such matters is to be avoided. The true Christian must not be misled by them.

There are not wanting today men in teaching and preaching positions who are advising us to walk in 'the broad way'; but our Lord and His apostles constantly affirmed that this is the opposite of God's will for us. We must not mind being thought 'narrow'. We must not be afraid of the charge that 'You think that you *alone* are right!' Yes, we *do* think that we are right; but we are not alone. The great stream of evangelical witness runs down through the centuries of church history. The gates of hell have not prevailed and will not finally prevail against it. We believe as our evangelical forefathers did, and we must be prepared for the reproaches of 'intolerance' and 'bigotry' which they also bore. St Paul is in no doubt about the matter. He says: 'Though we, or an angel from heaven, preach any other gospel unto you than that which we have preached unto you, let him be accursed' (Gal. 1:8).

This charge of intolerance is a compliment. For, surely, if our position is that in which God has ordained His elect should stand, we must necessarily be intolerant of all that would divert us from it. We believe and hold to it. We must be prepared to sacrifice everything for it. We must be like Martin Luther when he stood alone against the authority of the Roman Church, which had arrogated to itself such dictatorial power for so many long centuries. We must be like the Puritans, who were prepared to forsake their emoluments rather than to compromise on such principles. We must be humbly aggressive in propagating the true faith, and patiently adamant in the true gospel's defence, if need be, to the utmost degrees of sacrifice.

Secondly, it would be dishonouring to God if we were to act in any other way. To believe that God gave His Son up for us all and that through Him He has clearly revealed His goodwill and grace towards us forbids us to treat such matters lightly. It would be unthinkable that we could really believe the gospel and not contend for it against its enemies and detractors. If it is true, then it is dishonest and dishonouring to God if we do not clearly stand for the truth.

Thirdly, I believe that this position of fidelity to the Word of God is the only one which God Himself will honour and fully bless. If the church lapses from her reverence for, and obedience to, her clearly given instructions, how can she expect the Holy Spirit to bless? In fact, our critics time and time again acknowledge this fact. They say, after bringing forward their usual arguments and excuses, 'We must, however, grant you one thing. You do seem to be more successful in matters of evangelism and bringing new people into Christ's kingdom.' But this, surely, is only what we should expect if the Holy Spirit works through the truth of the Word of God. The whole Bible insists that God honours and uses His Word as the medium of His grace to men. One has only to read the history of any genuine revival in the history of the church to see that what the Holy Spirit normally honours and uses is the Word and nothing else.

Fourthly, those who do not agree with us and want us to join with them in a great, broad, and comprehensive ecclesiasticism, use the argument that even external unity makes for strength. The disunited church, they say, is a scandal before the nations who look on; but if mankind were to be confronted by a great church which united in one all who use the name of Christ, then the Christian forces would recover their morale in the face of the anti-Christian hordes which menace them, and the impact on the non-Christian world would be colossal. But this is a thoroughly unscriptural line of thought. The story of Gideon, at least, teaches us so. He was taught not to be impressed by numbers. What God required was quality and purity. So Gideon deliberately had to reduce his army and take with him to the fight only those who showed adequate signs of their commando qualities. The kind of reasoning which is constantly evinced by the Bible is the doctrine of 'the remnant', which persisted in loyally seeking to do God's will when all others had defaulted. Indeed, God frequently uses just one man. Jonathan, we are told, took on his mission just one man, his armour-bearer, saying as he did so: 'For there is no restraint to the Lord to save by many or by few' (1 Sam. 14:6). As Lloyd Garrison once said, 'One with God is a majority.' The Bible is interested in quality, with that which is 'sanctified, and meet for the master's use' (2 Tim. 2:21).

To concentrate upon external expansion to the neglect of the biblical requirements of doctrinal and ethical purity is to risk internal disloyalty, disunity, and confusion. Such a policy invites judgment which begins 'at the house of God' (1 Pet. 4:17). Our heavenly Father's primary demands are for faith in Himself and obedience. For these there are no substitutes.

It is also necessary for us to examine some of the other arguments which are put forward by those who would earnestly persuade us to consider the policies of a wider comprehension and compromise in order to gain the dubious advantages of an external appearance of unity.

One of the Scriptures most commonly cited is John chapter 17, in which our Lord, in what is usually termed His high-priestly prayer, especially prays for the unity of His own people. We are told, on this basis, that the greatest good for which we should all strive is fellowship. We must, they say, all start to practise this principle of fellowship and subordinate everything to it. If we ignore our differences in order to achieve this fellowship, all other things will look after themselves. But such a way of thinking is thoroughly unscriptural. For example, in Acts 2:42, the earliest activity of the churches is described in the following way: 'They continued stedfastly in the apostles' doctrine and fellowship, and in breaking of bread, and in prayers.' The apostles' *doctrine* comes before fellowship. There must be real agreement concerning the doctrines by which a group of people are bound together and for the extension of which they are working. If there is uncertainty in such matters there cannot be real fellowship. It is our being clear about what we all stand for which gives unity and confidence. In any case, it is important to notice precisely that for which our Lord actually prayed. He asks, 'That they all may be one; as thou, Father, art in me, and I in thee, that they also may be one in us' (John 17:21). The persons of the Trinity exist in a mystical unity. It is, therefore, a *spiritual* unity for which our Lord is praying. Whatever else may be used from Scripture to support an argument for an external joining of denominations of the churches it ought not to be this particular verse. The point of it is that as our Lord is in His Father, so also He is in us, and we therefore, who have union with the Godhead, have union with all others who are in the same relationship. It is the *unio mystica* of the theologians which is more relevant at this point.

Another argument which is sometimes brought up is one which is thought to be based upon the teaching of the parable of the wheat and the tares. Because the parable postpones the destruction of the tares until the time of harvest – 'Let both grow together until the harvest' (Matt. 13:30) – it is suggested that such steps as should be taken to ensure the purity of the church should not be taken now. Such people say to us: 'You set yourselves up as better than other people, and you urge a strictness of doctrinal and ethical principles which divides the church, and so you violate the teaching of the parable.'

The logical conclusion of this particular argument, and one that is patently unscriptural, is that no discipline should be exercised in the church at all. If such reasoning comes to be applied to church history, it virtually condemns those periods in which the church recovered from extreme unfaithfulness and even perversions of her life and doctrine. We must ask our friends whether, after every effort to reform the medieval church from within had failed, the Protestant Reformation was a mistake? Such a reading of the parable would be a condemnation also of the Puritans. Our friends who desire to use this argument must be content to follow through consistently the logic of their own argument. Some, of course, perhaps more honest than the rest, do so even to the extent of being willing to barter away their birthright by capitulating to the unreformed Roman Church.

The New Testament, however, is quite clear about the duty of refusing to tolerate heresy: 'If there come any unto you, and bring not this doctrine, receive him not into your house, neither bid him God speed: for he that biddeth him God speed is partaker of his evil deeds' (2 John 10–11). How idle it is to laud the reformers and to emphasize their teaching as to the marks of the true church if we forget that, in addition to the preaching of the Word and the administration of the sacraments, they emphasized the vital importance also of the exercise of discipline. And what object had they in view in drawing up their confessions and catechisms save the exercise of discipline?

Then there are those who always speak in a way which suggests that to obey the New Testament's commands concerning our attitude to serious disloyalty and error makes us, of necessity, guilty of the sin of schism. It is most important that all due care should be taken to see that none of us ever causes schism in the body of Christ. God forbid that any of us should be guilty of this terrible sin; but it is important for us to note exactly what constitutes schism. From 1 Corinthians 11:18–19 and the whole of chapter 12 we learn that it consists in a separation where vital truths concerning the way of salvation and the life of the church are not involved. At Corinth there had been needless division simply over the personalities of certain preachers and concerning the relative importance of the various spiritual gifts. St Paul ruthlessly condemns any such state of affairs. Elsewhere, however, he has no hesitation in condemning those who 'preach another gospel' or in commanding separation from those who do not follow the apostolic teaching. (See, for example 2 Thess. 3:6; 2 Cor. 6:14–18; 2 John 10–11; and, indeed, the whole of John's First Epistle.)

The important consideration is that we must be quite sure that we are contesting about and contending for a matter which is absolutely essential to the preservation of the gospel. We must not withdraw ourselves from other Christians for anything less. For example, there are among equally devoted Christians at least three possible views with regard to the interpretation of the 'millennium' (that is, one thousand years), which is mentioned in the book of Revelation. It is not possible actually to prove from Scripture any one of the three views to the exclusion of the others, though we may feel convinced that one of them seems more in harmony with the rest of the Scripture than the others. We must agree to differ. In a similar way, it would be wrong, although there have been those who have done it, to separate simply on the mode of administration of Christian baptism.

It is not that we wish to be separate from others, far from it. Nothing would be easier and nothing more comfortable than to drift in the ecumenical stream. But if words mean anything at all in the New Testament, then we must stake everything on the gospel and be content with nothing less than the greatest possible fidelity to the great essentials of the apostolic teaching. We cannot give our full support to anything else. We accept the gospel because we believe it to be the gift of God to us and eternal truth. Because it is the truth, we must take our stand upon it and, with Luther, we can do no other.

Let us turn to the positive side of all this. How are we to maintain the faith? In the first place, we can maintain the apostolic witness only if we really know what it is. In view of its importance, nothing is more astounding than the pitiable ignorance of divinely revealed truth in which some Christians are content to live. The first call to us is to secure a new grasp of the faith which we have to propagate to the world. We are not here merely to contend for our own frills and fancies. It is not some whim or the peculiarity of a few which calls us. We are concerned about the great fundamentals and essentials of the Christian faith and not merely with the theories and fancies of certain people with respect to matters about which there never has been (and probably never will be) general agreement among Christians. We must never lose sight of those things which our Lord and the apostles have declared to be essential and obligatory.

At this point there is a practical difficulty which merits attention. Many youthful leaders of good causes find it especially difficult, in the confused conditions which today are prevalent in various branches of the church and Christian societies, to know how to select those spokesmen who are fully loyal to the New Testament standards, and who embody in their own lives an honest attempt to fulfil them. Certain negative tests are comparatively easy to apply. If a man who ventures to speak in God's name is not adhering strictly to the biblical presentation of the great doctrines and is substituting philosophical speculation, it is generally soon apparent. The sheep fail to recognize the Good Shepherd's voice speaking through the stranger. More clearly still, if a speaker does not teach the uniqueness of the divine-human person of Christ, and fails to accord Him the fullest divine honours, we are instructed to avoid such (1 John 4:1-3, etc.).

Today, however, when so many boundary lines have been blurred, the negative test is not enough. We must go on to ask about any man, What then does he say? This includes noting what he does *not* say, that is, we must take note of his consistent omissions. At first sight, such an attitude might seem too hard upon our spokesman, and asking for more than may seem reasonable. But a moment's reflection will surely show us that it will be impossible for anyone to speak for long upon the great cardinal doctrines of the Bible without showing where he stands in relation to the essentials. If he is a true evangelical he must, sooner rather than later, say certain specific and characteristic things. A pseudo-evangelical betrays himself by his silence or equivocation at just those points where the Bible calls for fearless precision.

What, then, are the characteristic notes of the evangelical? What are the particular truths that he is concerned at all times to emphasize? I cannot do better than to read from a summary embodied in a recent

Memorandum by the International Fellowship of Evangelical Students:

> The evangelical is one who believes that the Bible itself calls for a particular understanding of its nature and message. It declares itself to be a God-given revelation. It does not merely contain the Word of God, but it *is* the Word of God. This means that he takes the Bible as his source-book for understanding all other doctrines. Those to which evangelicals at all times have adhered with tenacity are:
>
> (a) The biblical doctrine of man (based upon the historicity of the record in the opening chapters of Genesis) – including his special creation, the Fall, and his consequent state of sin (which is not merely a deficiency, but is active rebellion in heart and mind against God, and a state of pollution in his nature).
>
> (b) The understanding of the death of Christ as being His own voluntary act whereby He offered Himself as our Substitute to bear the penalty of our sins and to deliver us from the condemnation of the law and from the wrath of God.
>
> (c) The absolute necessity of the work of the Holy Spirit to bring a man to conviction of sin, to repentance, to faith and to rebirth. Man can stand righteous in the sight of God only as he is 'in Christ' and justified through faith alone.
>
> (d) The Church of Christ consists of those who in all ages have been, or are, in vital relationship with our Lord Jesus Christ as a result of the 'new birth'. The New Testament itself recognizes only two aspects of the Church:
>
> > (i) the whole company of all true believers in heaven and on earth; and
> >
> > (ii) the local manifestation, which is the gathering in fellowship of those who are 'in Christ' and in the midst of whom, according to His promise, Christ is present, who is the only Lord and Head of the Church, the 'fulness of him that filleth all in all'.

Because the evangelical believes such things as these, it is impossible for him to be neutral or accommodating in his efforts to secure for them full sway in our Christian churches and particular organizations. He must base his whole outlook and stake his future upon them. He must refuse to compromise upon any matter which is *clearly* revealed in Scripture to be the mind and will of God. He must not venture to modify such things at any point at all. Even though he may not fully understand all that is set forth in Scripture, and must be careful to allow for due charity and divergence of opinion in minutiae, yet he must not water down the message.

[49]

Then, those who would propagate this faith should study the history and biography of those who have been foremost in asserting and defending it. Some people seem to imagine that what we desire to maintain has had no past and is something which is upstart. The fact is that we are simply repeating in our times what has had a glorious and magnificent history. There have been times when evil men have tried to exterminate the truth and the men of God. They have done their worst; but the evangelical witnesses have stood their ground until God, time and time again, has intervened and overruled. It is a story of which the heirs of the evangelical tradition have reason to be proud. The more any Christian acquaints himself with the story, the stronger he will be in spiritual vigour.

Finally, if we desire to witness in the sense in which the apostles meant the word, then our lives must fully reflect our convictions. When the earliest Christians were scattered from Jerusalem they astounded everyone by their holy joy and victorious faith. They even rejoiced that they were accounted worthy to suffer. They did not falter or whimper in the face of impending martyrdom. They triumphed. But not only in the face of death were they victorious. They had learned also the importance of maintaining good works, which our Lord Himself had prophesied would lead men to glorify their Father. Men who had refused to listen to the proclamations of the message were overcome by true Christian charity and living. 'See how these Christians love one another!' was not first exclaimed in irony. It was a tribute to an undoubted fact. The fact is that we Christians should be outliving everybody as we follow closely our divine exemplar and obey our Lord. An evangelical Christian should be outstanding in his sheer personal goodness and capacity for social and public righteousness.

It is your privilege and mine to have entered into this heritage. We believe God in Christ has laid His hand on us and given His life into our souls. Our supreme honour, as well as our duty, now is so to live that in our lives He may continue to will and to do His good pleasure. It is in such a faith and obedience that some of the noblest men and women who ever walked the face of this earth have smiled on tyrants and welcomed a martyrdom on lonely moors, or maintained the faith in crowded cities. Their supreme joy was to add to the number of those who have joined the ransomed throng in which our glorious Lord will see of the travail of His soul and be satisfied. May He give us all grace to be faithful in our turn, and to follow in their train.

Five

＊

A Policy Appropriate to Biblical Faith[1]

＊

At the present time it is obviously a duty for us to face the question of changes which are taking place in the churches as a result of ecumenical discussions. There are some who would ask us, Has the Inter-Varsity Fellowship a right to be doing its special work at all? Has it a right to a separate existence as an organization? These questions and views have been forced upon us more and more by certain things which have been happening during the past few years. There are some who, in effect, demand that there should be only one church organization throughout the world and, consequently, one organization for all Christian work among students. Whether we like it or not we must face the facts. Our movement has received more general attention during the past two or three years than during its entire history. It is only the simple truth to say that the IVF has met with increasing criticism along such lines. There are three main reasons for this.

In the first place, there have been some marked successes in the IVF. It has been making considerable progress. Articles recently have even drawn attention to what is called the 'menace' of this organization. We may well ask, Why call attention to it? The answer seems to be that it is because this movement is successful. Its appeal to the students is of increasing importance. It is growing in numbers. It is permeating the life of college and university. Its

[1]Notes taken by Dr Douglas Johnson of an address given at the Annual Meeting of the Inter-Varsity Fellowship of Students in London on 1 October, 1954.

[51]

success has been one of the chief causes of criticism among those who do not like its essential message.

Secondly, there is the general attitude of the Fellowship towards co-operation with other religious bodies which claim to be doing a similar work among students. This has been the subject of a good deal of comment, not only in university circles, but also in the wider circles of the church. The Fellowship has a definite policy on this whole subject of co-operation. All leading students and graduates, who were formerly office-bearers in the organization, will know that this has always been an exceedingly difficult question. It has been raised again acutely during the past two or three years.

Then, finally, there is what the critics are pleased to call the 'intolerance' of our movement. It has been variously called 'intellectual dishonesty', 'spiritual intolerance', and even *'the* arrogance'! Such expressions of criticism have been levelled not only against the Fellowship as a whole, but against certain of the better-known people among those senior friends who have from time to time supported it.

Such, then, are the three main causes of the unusual amount of attention which the Fellowship has been receiving. Such are the reasons advanced by those who would question its very right to exist. It is time, therefore, that the Fellowship should examine the truth about itself and be prepared to justify its position. For example, what are we to reply to those who assert that, in principle, there ought not to be two movements among students? Has the time come when such a division should be abandoned and all student Christian organizations be one body? An institution or organization which is being attacked should certainly have something whereby to justify its existence, but should we not, rather, examine the situation not simply for the sake of the organization, but in the interests of truth itself?

Here, we would assert that there can be no real question in the minds of most sympathetic observers, but that the essential problem is the *third* of those which have been named above. The ultimate issue is that of our attitude towards *the truth*; for, in essence, that is the basic question which has been raised by the critics, no matter what pretext may be used for the purpose. Here is the focal point upon which the attack is concentrated.

A number of questions immediately arise. Is there such a thing as *truth*? If there is such a thing, can it really be known? Can it be defined? Can it be stated in the form of a proposition? In spiritual affairs, does theology really matter at all? Does it, in the last analysis, matter what a man ultimately believes? These are some of the questions which are not only raised by implication, but which are once more confronting us. It surely behoves us, therefore, to know where we stand in relation to such important questions.

Briefly, some of our critics would not hesitate to say that belief as such really does not matter at all! In effect, they say, nothing matters but *experience*. Surely, they ask, if men and women have found something which gives them happiness, joy, and peace what does it matter what agent has brought them into this experience? The great purpose of Christ, they assert, is to give the answer to, and deliverance from, our many problems. If people find answers, why should anyone question the way it is taking place? Anything that does people good is surely good in and of itself? This is the way some, at least, among our friends would argue.

Another of their common assertions is often stated in the following form: While in other religious spheres adherence to the truth and doctrinal accuracy does matter, it does not matter, or matters far less, when it is a question of *evangelism*. Such an outlook has been very prominent during the past ten years. Such great campaigns as those being conducted by Dr Billy Graham have caused many people to examine themselves and to see their need of religion. Therefore, many who are sincerely desirous of reaching the masses will affirm, while we are evangelizing, theology and doctrine do not count. Let us call, they say, a theological truce while this mission or that campaign is on. The great thing is to bring people to Christ and then, when they have been won and they are in the churches, they can be taught what to believe and how to understand the Christian faith. But while they are engaged in evangelistic activities, such people urge, we should leave doctrine and similar considerations in abeyance.

We are also criticized on the grounds that we persist in propagating an antiquated or perverse view of truth. One speaker, years back, went so far as to declare, 'The great challenge facing us at the present time is the issue of truth versus fundamentalism'! We must reply to such a critic that we, on the contrary, are not interested in fundamentalism, but we *are* interested in truth. We are not concerned to contend for an 'ism', whatever the label may be. We are concerned with the truth as stated by our Lord and His apostles. Yet we are even called 'sub-Christian' because of our insistence upon

[53]

ing to the cardinal doctrines plainly stated in the New Testa-

It is amazing that such criticisms could ever be asserted by a theologically trained person; but they are made. The question confronting us, therefore, is, what are we to say by way of reply? What are we to do in the face of such deliberate distortion of the facts and such flagrant ignoring of the very commands of the New Testament and all in the supposed interests of the church itself? There is one form of reply given us in Scripture. What we should say at a time like this should be rather like the reaction of Nehemiah when he was sent for in the midst of his building operations to come down into the plain to talk with Sanballat: 'I am doing a great work, so that I cannot come down' (Neh. 6:3). It is on this principle that the Fellowship has been acting for years with restraint and with Christian humility and patience. The IVF, has maintained a commendable silence in spite of provocation and in spite of much else.

Within the family circle, however, we cannot leave it at that. What has been said represents our attitude to outside critics. On the other hand, it is very important that among ourselves we should be quite clear where we stand and why we stand there. We must not become insensitive to criticism, nor must we fail to benefit by all constructive criticism. It may be salutary and, even of God-given value. We must continually be reforming ourselves by the Word of God. So, for our own interest and edification, let us look more closely at our position.

Obviously – at least, we trust that it is obvious – it is not our contention that we understand *everything*! We are not so foolish as to imagine that we know the whole truth and can define it down to the smallest detail. There is nobody in our circles who claims, or has ever claimed, any such monstrous thing. We do not even claim to understand all that we believe. Not only that, we must emphasize that there are many smaller and unimportant points of difference among us. There are some doctrines, or applications of Christian doctrine, about which we agree to differ among ourselves. Those who attack the movement seem to think that its officers are like parrots repeating the same thing phrase by phrase and appalled by any suggestion of deviation from some formally prescribed doctrinal decree. This is a travesty of the truth. Such critics would need only to attend some of the conference or committee discussions to be made aware! Let us take one or two samples of divergent views on matters which are of secondary importance. In matters of interpretation concerning the prophecies of the Bible, there are several quite widely divergent views. There are, for example, evangelical Christians who interpret the book of Revelation from a pre-millennialist, others from a post-millennialist, and still others from an a-millennialist point of view. Yet, while holding to their own convictions on such subjects and pointing out to the others why they should adhere to them, there is a true consensus of opinion and a real unity on what may be called the 'hard core' of biblical doctrine. In the same way there is liberty and diversity on such matters as the application to the individual Christian of the Holy Spirit's work of sanctification and also concerning many points of church government. But, while we recognize that there are certain subjects about which there will never be unanimity among us on earth, we do, on the other hand, contend that there are certain basic things about which there must be no disunity. It is at this point that we are asserting what the genius of the IVF as a movement really is. It came into being because of these fundamental matters and has a right to exist only so long as these things are vital to it and central in it. With equal definiteness and firmness, we must affirm that they are fundamental not merely for the health, but for the very existence of the church itself.

Let us look at several practical issues where these things increase in importance. Let us examine those points where the radical cleavage becomes important between us and those critics who cannot understand us, and regard it as 'bigoted' or 'schismatic' to refuse to co-operate in movements and activities which belittle or ignore Paul's constant reiteration of the need to give heed to the doctrine. Let us take, for example, the urgent question as to why things are as they are in the Christian church and in the world generally today. We have been told repeatedly that the state of the church today is the result of two world wars and their consequent aftermath of political, economic, and social changes. Obviously, people say, increasing social pressures of various kinds, greater movements of the population, and a hundred and one other factors have all combined to take people away from places of worship. Such an explanation is constantly given and this superficial diagnosis all too easily accepted, but is it true?

There is only one adequate explanation for the state of the Christian church today: it is *the apostasy of the church herself.* The crucial damage was done by the destructive Higher Criticism movement that came into being during the nineteenth century. The one essential question in the mind of anyone who investigates such a matter must be, What robbed the church of her authority? The certainty of her message was undermined. This is why the church lost her hold upon the masses. God's revelation has been put out of the pulpits and philosophy has been put into them. The authority of the Bible has been virtually denied and in its place have come the plausible suggestions of those who offer a subjectivity derived from religious genius or modern psychology. That is the real explanation of the present position. Until church leaders come to see this and awake to its implications, there is no hope whatever for any large-scale return to the position that once obtained.

But it may be urged that things are becoming brighter. If one were talking of thirty years ago, then what has been said might be true. There has been a gradual change, it is urged, in the climate of theological thinking, and many of those who once differed have now come so near to the evangelical position that they are almost identical. Surely, people argue, there is now no excuse for a separate existence of the two movements? But we must ask, has there been such a change? Is there a new similarity? As one reads the weekly or monthly Christian press, one fails to find any such evidence. If there is a change, then it is in the matter of window-dressing. Phrases are certainly used, which if they were spoken or written by an evangelical would indicate biblical doctrine, but often, alas, the speaker or writer does not mean the same thing. The thought-modes and general underlying principles are still far from being truly evangelical. That is the actual position today.

Surely, then, our own line of action is clear and straightforward. We must continue to take our stand upon the literal written Word. We do not grant and we cannot grant that the advance of modern knowledge has made the slightest difference to spiritual truth as revealed to mankind in the Bible. We cannot, and we refuse to, regard the one whom so many patronize simply as 'the Jesus of history', (and who we claim should be called 'the Lord Jesus Christ') as little more than the greatest of the prophets. We refuse to subscribe to the theory that His mind, His thought, and His speech were so influenced by the tradition and thinking of His own day, that there are errors of attitude or of fact in His words. We would contend that there is no authority whatsoever for such a view. Our duty is to ensure that our whole faith is based on 'the foundation of the apostles and prophets, Jesus Christ himself being the chief cornerstone' (Eph. 2:20). We regard as monstrous the suggestion that in so doing we are propagating what more than one church leader or editor has described as 'the new heresy'! On the contrary, we claim that on the evidence of Holy Scripture and on the plain statements and example of our Lord and His apostles the deviations from orthodoxy lie elsewhere. It is at such points that other people, and not we, are dividing the church.

These are the facts and this is the position. Our answer must be perfectly plain and quite unequivocal. It is being said that the chief need of the church is to repent because of her 'lack of unity'. That is being asserted widely today. It was, in effect, the message of Evanston: 'The church needs to repent for her disunity.' We would suggest that before she repents of her disunity, she must repent of her apostasy. She must repent of her perversion of, and of her substitutes for, 'the faith which was once delivered unto the saints' (Jude 3). She must repent of setting up her own thinking and methods over against the divine revelation given in Holy Scripture. Here lies the reason for her lack of spiritual power and inability to deliver a living message in the power of the Holy Ghost to a world ready to perish.

Then, as for the question of evangelism, a great deal of confusion of thought is widespread concerning it. If the statements and practice of the apostles were to be carefully examined, one thing would clearly stand out in almost all they say: we must never claim that doctrine does not matter in evangelism.

Let us look at certain Scriptures which specifically refer to the matter. Observe what Paul says in 1 Corinthians 15:1–6 and Acts 17. In the Corinthian passage he enumerates certain great cardinal doctrines. On Mars Hill, to a pagan audience, he spoke of the command to repent, of judgment, and of the resurrection. When preaching in Thessalonica, the apostle argues and reasons out of the Scriptures, showing and proving how Christ must needs have suffered. 1 Thessalonians 1:9–10 is particularly clear in illustrating the clarity with which Paul, from the start, affirmed the great doctrines of the faith. We could go so far as to claim that no-one has taken a more uncompromising stand on the facts of the gospel than the apostle Paul. Did he ever appeal to people to come to church? Did he even appeal to people to come to Christ? Did he once say, Come to Christ and you will get this, that, and the other? He himself has outlined for us the message which he brought in the clearest terms. In the Epistle to the Galatians and in 1 Corinthians 15, we are provided with summaries. He asserted these doctrines. He preached the person of Christ and he insisted on the historic facts concerning Him. He declared the facts of the virgin birth, His vicarious death, and His resurrection. He did not leave his hearers or readers in any uncertainty. He insisted that Christ had been 'declared to be the Son of God with power by the resurrection from the dead' (Rom. 1:4). He preached the substitutionary atonement. Similarly, the apostle Peter did not hesitate to say that 'Christ suffered for us, the just for the unjust' (1 Pet. 3:18). He was not loath to declare the coming judgment of God and to.warn his hearers to flee from the wrath to come.

True evangelism, I would maintain, is highly doctrinal. It demands that, in its challenge and its instruction, the cardinal doctrines of the Christian faith shall be made evident. We must beyond any doubt preach Christ who is the Son of God and who came to give Himself for sinners. We must preach the blood of Christ. We must preach the person of the Holy Spirit. There are other clear doctrines taught by the apostles, which are also part of the gospel. Such considerations must influence our response to the question of co-operation with others who view things differently. If we really believe these truths of our faith, we must realize that co-operation with the man who tells us that doctrine does not really matter, is virtually to acknowledge that we agree that doctrine does not matter. Yet, in view of the plain statements of the New Testament, how can we agree with any man who says that doctrine, even when we are intent on evangelizing the outsider, does not matter? How can we work with those who make light of essential parts of our message? We have no choice in this matter if we really believe what we claim to believe.

There is something else to be noticed. Is there any more polemical document than the New Testament? Have you observed the major emphasis in the various apostolic Epistles? They appeal to doctrine and they appeal to argument. Paul's argument in 1 Corinthians 15 is closely reasoned. He is eloquent about the importance of the bodily resurrection of Christ. If this be not true, 'we are of all men most miserable' (verse 19). In the same way in his Epistle to the Galatians, he declares: 'But though we, or an angel from heaven, preach any other gospel unto you than that which we have preached unto you, let him be accursed' (Gal. 1:8). Why did Paul withstand Peter? Because of an important doctrinal matter. In Philippians 3, we read of those who are 'the enemies of the cross of Christ' (verse 18). In such Scriptures as the two Epistles to Timothy and in John's First Epistle we have scorching statements about those who tamper with the facts about Christ and their relevance to the gospel.

We are warned in the New Testament of the antichrist, and how to recognize the spirit of antichrist. We are told of those who 'went out from us because they were not of us' (1 John 2:19). The New Testament recognizes no neutral ground in these matters. There is too much at stake. God's glory is involved, not simply the eternal destinies of mankind. In our churches we have lost this sense of the importance of the glory of God, even those claiming to be evangelical, but the Bible is concerned for the glory of God and then, after that, for the good of man. Both demand that we should leave no possible doubt in our work where the truth is made to give way to error. The Colossians were being ruined by philosophy, so St Paul faithfully warns them: 'Beware lest any man spoil you through philosophy and vain deceit, after the tradition of men, after the rudiments of the world, and not after Christ' (Col. 2:8).

There is another important Scripture which we must notice at this point. In Jude 3 we read: 'Beloved, when I gave all diligence to write unto you of the common salvation, it was needful for me to write unto you, and exhort you that ye should earnestly contend for the faith which was once delivered unto the saints.' Here we are given a stirring call to the defence of the faith. Such a call is not popular today. It is not popular today even in some evangelical circles. People will tell you that it is all 'too negative'. They continually urge that we must keep on giving positive truth. They will tell us that we must not argue and we must never condemn. But we must ask, How can you fight if you are ever afraid of wounding an enemy? How can you rouse sleeping fellow warriors with smooth words? God forbid that we find ourselves at the bar of judgment and face the charge that we contracted out from love of ease or for fear of man, or that we failed to do our duty in the great fight of the faith. We *must* – we *must* fight for the faith in these momentous times.

One final word. Paul in 1 Corinthians 15:2 says of the gospel that it is that 'by which ye are saved'. The only way to be saved is by believing these gospel doctrines, which bring us to the true Christ. We do not believe in some Christ 'in general'. We must ask of the one presented to us: Who is He? Why did He come? What has He done? It is because of who He is and what He has done that we have any gospel at all by which we are saved. Few words of exhortation will be necessary to those who in this Fellowship are aware of these things. Let us thank God for the witness, for the courage and the tenacity of the IVF. May God bless it and defend it. May He use it in these confused and difficult times through which we are passing. May He enable us together to stand as a rock in the raging seas all around us. We must, of course, never pride ourselves on our stand, or become self-righteous or small-minded persons. But in humility and obedience, let us follow the apostolic exhortations, always coming to know more deeply our glorious God, remembering that He has redeemed us, and aware of what a glorious faith it is to which He has called us to bear witness. Here let us take our stand.

Six

*

Conversions: Psychological and Spiritual[1]

*

Much interest in scientific and theological circles has been aroused of late by the publication of the book *Battle for the Mind*. The author is Dr William Sargant, a well-known practising psychiatrist. The subtitle reads, 'A Physiology of Conversion and Brain-Washing' and shows that the author's chief interest is in the use which can be made, for good or ill, of the mechanisms of the human mind. He is concerned with the ways in which political, social, or religious conversion can be induced by psychological techniques.

I must explain at once why I have felt it a duty to review this book with critical care. I do so because I think that in many ways it is an extremely dangerous book. Such a view is not just a personal impression or opinion. Reports have come to me that a number of Christian men and women, some of them undergraduates, have been profoundly disturbed by it and have been asking, Is this, after all, what has happened to us? Have we been deluded the whole time? One does not necessarily take any notice of an occasional remark of that kind, but when it is repeatedly heard in a number of places, there is reason to feel that this book is capable of doing much harm. I am not alone in my impression in this respect. Observe, for instance, what Professor John G. McKenzie wrote in his weekly article for the *British Weekly*: 'The interest in the volume can be judged by the fact

[1]This critique of Dr William Sargant's book *Battle for the Mind* (William Heinemann Ltd, 1957) reproduces the substance of an address to Christian ministers given under the auspices of the Evangelical Alliance at High Leigh, Hoddesdon, Herts. It was first published by the Inter-Varsity Press in January, 1959.

that it has already called for two reprintings.' He goes on to say, 'No single book has brought me so many letters.' I think that is extremely significant, coming, as it does, from a psychologist to whom large numbers of ministers write.

Professor McKenzie goes on to comment: 'I want my readers to recall my first correspondent's letter on the volume. He was really anxious to know where the Holy Spirit came in, if conversion was simply a physiological process, which is at least one of the implications of *Battle for the Mind*. Dr Sargant has himself repudiated the idea that his description of the physiology of conversion based upon Pavlov's almost inhuman experiments upon dogs need disturb any of our religious ideas; but there can be no doubt that his treatment of Wesley's methods and that of some American sects is along behaviouristic lines. That is to say, the conversions were simply the outcome of "conditioned reflexes", analogous to the confessions wrested by brain-washing, Communistic countries from their victims. Whether the author realized it or not, the linking of Wesley's preaching and the practices of beating on drums, chanting, dancing, shaking, and handling poisonous snakes, pursued by some religious cults in order to induce "religious" experience or conversion, with Pavlov's conclusions from his experiments, gave the impression that the whole thing was just a rape of the mind.'

In spite of Dr Sargant's own disclaimers, I am in entire agreement with Professor McKenzie's statement. It is quite clear that the opinion formed by the average reader is precisely as Dr McKenzie says, and the final impression left by the book is that Dr Sargant has, in this way, more or less explained away what we regard as a spiritual conversion.

Dr Sargant's Main Thesis

What is the author of this book really saying? As we have been reminded, his case is based to a large extent upon the well-known experiments by the great Russian physiologist Pavlov, who was undoubtedly one of the greatest physiologists of the last hundred years. Pavlov has long been widely discussed in medical and physiological circles because of certain of his experiments which led to the introduction of the term 'conditioned reflex'. Let me remind you very simply of what that means and of the data on which the idea is based. Pavlov experimented on dogs. He placed small tubes in the salivary glands in dogs' mouths, and also into their stomachs, with the object of measuring the amount of fluids aiding digestion which was produced by both the salivary glands and those in the lining of the stomach. His method was as follows. He would bring into the dog's presence a meal, and at the same time, while producing the meal, would arrange for an assistant to ring a bell. He continued to repeat this sequence of events for some time. The sight of the food, of course, made the dog anticipate the meal, and the digestive juices were poured out from its salivary glands and also from its stomach. We ourselves all do that when we see an appetizing meal. But the point in Pavlov's experiment was that he rang the bell at the same time. Having repeated the experiment over a sufficient period of time, he found that the mere ringing of the bell alone, without the food, would produce the same result. That phenomenon is what he called 'a conditioned reflex'. By thus training and making an impression upon the mind of the dog, the ringing of the bell alone leads to the same state of anticipation, though the food is not actually produced. The inference is that by such training, or by influencing the mind in other ways, you can produce desired reactions.

Pavlov, having done that early in the century, took his experiments on conditioned reflex a stage further, but his later work did not become very well known until almost the beginning of the Second World War. He had gone on to make further and more advanced experiments upon the minds and the brains of dogs. His work in this field may be summarized as follows. He would stimulate the dogs with an electrical current of varying strength and he found that this again produced a variation in the response. He then found that if he increased the current until it became really painful the response was still more variable, and eventually he reached a stage at which the dog was so upset by this stimulus that it got even beyond the state of excitement and finally fell into a state of collapse. Pavlov also found that, at a further point in the continuation of the stimulus, the various conditioned reflexes which he had earlier produced had been seriously interfered with. He finally found that, following this state of collapse, it was much easier than it was before to put fresh suggestions and fresh conditioned reflexes into the minds of these dogs. The numerous experiments along these lines were very varied in their character. The important point, however, was that Pavlov felt that he was able to demonstrate quite clearly that, by applying appropriate stimuli and by continuing to do so, he could more or less, speaking generally, produce many different kinds of conditioned responses. This was even more marked if, in addition, he produced diseased conditions in the dogs by withholding food or by operating on them. He noticed, in addition, that dogs varied in their temperaments very much, even as men do, and that there were four main types of temperament in dogs, as in men. The presence of these types had to be allowed for in these experiments.

What was the ultimate result of all this? Pavlov suggests that here, perhaps, we have a key to the understanding of man and his reactions and, also, of his responses to various ideas which may be put to him. This, at least, is the scientific background in terms of physiology.

The point of interest for Dr William Sargant is the effect on the mechanism of the mind when certain stimuli are brought to bear upon it. In the early days of the last war he, as a practising psychiatrist, had to deal with numbers of patients who had got into difficulties mentally and psychologically as a result of the Dunkirk evacuation, the bombing in London, or, in some cases, acutely distressing experiences on the field of battle. He and others had found that some of the men who had collapsed from such experiences could be helped, and indeed could be cured, in the following extraordinary way. Certain drugs were injected into the veins of these patients, which produced a form of hypnosis. Then, while the patient was under the influence of the given drug, they would recall to him (and, even more important, help him to recall) the incident which had precipitated the collapse. For instance, they would recall to the man's mind the memory of the air-raid, or the experience while being evacuated from Dunkirk, or the experience a man may have had in a tank, or whatever had been the situation at the time of the damage to his mind. They would bring it all back very vividly to him until he had an experience of the same terror, alarm, and excitement as had originally occurred. They would go on until he became extremely agitated. At that point they would stop the process. They found that, when they could reproduce the experience in this experimental manner, the procedure very often led to a cure.

Dr Sargant and others had been doing a good deal of such work. They had found that sometimes, by putting the patient under the influence of the drug, they could even suggest to him an imaginary trying experience. He gives an example of a man in the Tank Corps who had not actually had a very terrifying experience, but who had been rather fearful that he might have, and had become so worried about this that it led to a breakdown. They found that sometimes they could cure such a condition in the following way. First they would put him under the influence of the drug; then they would very vividly suggest to him that he was in a tank which had caught fire and that unless he very quickly scrambled out he would be burned to death. The man would go through a horrible experience and it would so grip him that he might even collapse. On recovering, however, they found that he had often got a release and that he came out a balanced, normal, healed, and whole man.

Dr Sargant states that, having completed a good deal of such work with his colleagues, he happened to meet an American medical officer who quite casually asked him if he had read a report of the work of Pavlov. (The Russian volume had in 1941 at last been translated into English.) He had not. As soon as he did so, he was forced to conclude that this was almost exactly what he and others had been discovering about the production of this phenomenon of 'abreaction'[2] by means of drugs.

There was yet one further link in the chain which led to the writing of his book. Dr Sargant, who is a Methodist, was one day visiting his father and chanced to look at the bookshelves. He noticed a copy of Wesley's *Journal*. He picked it up quite casually and happened to open it at a page which immediately interested him. 'My eye', he writes, 'was caught by Wesley's detailed reports of the occurrence, two hundred years before, of almost identical states of emotional excitement,' – that is, identical with the ones that he had discovered in his medical work and those reported by Pavlov – 'often leading to temporary emotional collapse, which he induced by a particular sort of preaching. These phenomena usually appeared when he had persuaded his hearers that they must make an immediate choice between certain damnation and the acceptance of his own soul-saving religious views. The fear of burning in hell induced by his graphic preaching could be compared to the suggestion we might force on a returned soldier, during treatment, that he was in danger of being burned alive in his tank and must fight his way out. The two

[2]Abreaction is the psychiatrist's term for the removal of an emotional repression by facing it in a vivid form in imagination and reliving the original experience.

techniques seemed startlingly similar.'[3] These reports of seemingly comparable phenomena all came together in Dr Sargant's mind and it seemed to him that they were all of a piece. So he began to evolve the ideas which he has now set before us in this book.

What, therefore, he is concerned to show is this, in his own words: 'It now seemed possible, in fact, that many of the results which were being achieved by abreaction under drugs were essentially the same as those obtained, not only by Wesley and other religious leaders, but by modern "brain-washers," though different explanations would doubtless be given in every case' (p. xxii). A further quotation serves to show what Dr Sargant˙really is suggesting. He writes: 'In succeeding chapters evidence will be provided for the general observations made above. It must be emphasized that this book is not primarily concerned with any ethical or political system; its object is only to show how beliefs, whether good or bad, false or true, can be forcibly implanted in the human brain; and how people can be switched to arbitrary beliefs altogether opposed to those previously held.' That is his concern. 'The conclusion reached', he says, 'is that simple physiological mechanisms of conversion do exist, and that we therefore have much still to learn from a study of brain function about matters that have hitherto been claimed as the province of psychology or metaphysics. The politico-religious struggle for the mind of man may well be won by whoever becomes most conversant with the normal and abnormal functions of the brain, and is readiest to make use of the knowledge gained' (p. xxiv).

Here we have the main thesis of the book. The suggestion is (in spite of Dr Sargant's disclaimers as a professed Christian) that all conversions are really essentially the same; that is, he implies that political conversions and social conversions are really the same as religious conversions. You will have noticed that he says that whether beliefs are good or bad, false or true, the mechanism by which they are produced is almost exactly the same. He goes on to adduce cases such as that of the wife of Professor J. B. S. Haldane, who first of all was converted to Communism and found herself thinking, in spite of herself, along Communistic lines, and then was converted back again from Communism to Western ideas. She says she is perplexed to know how to explain these changes which happened to her. Then there are the writings of Koestler who has

[3] *Battle for the Mind*, p. xxii. Hereafter references to the book are given in the text.

given very graphic accounts of how he first became a Communist and then ceased to be a Communist. The suggestion which the author conveys is that all these are really psychological processes which happen irrespective of the nature of the particular thing which is being taught.

Now the book does seem quite definitely to imply that Wesley's work falls into this category. For instance, on page 235 Dr Sargant quotes Boswell's *London Journal* in which he says: '"We [Dr Johnson and Boswell] talked of preaching and of the great success that the Methodists have. He (Johnson) said that was owing to their preaching in a plain, vulgar manner, which was the only way to do good to common people. . . . He said that talking of drunkenness as a crime, because it debases reason, the noblest faculty of man, would do no service to the vulgar. But to tell them they might have died in their drunkenness and show how dreadful that would be, would affect them very much."' At this point Dr Sargant comments: 'Dr. Johnson was right: to secure such converts one has to try to overwhelm them emotionally. But this is no longer the eighteenth century. Then it did not seem to matter what the common people believed because they exercised no political power and were supposed only to work, not to think; and because they read no book or papers.' Dr Sargant goes on further to contrast those eighteenth-century people with the modern, educated man who is full of reason and understanding. Thereby, of course, he contradicts himself somewhat, because at the same time he is showing that this modern man, who is so different from the eighteenth-century man, can still be influenced in exactly the same way and by precisely the same techniques.

The result of all this is that Dr Sargant talks constantly about 'the technique of religious conversion'. He is interested in 'Wesley's methods' and so on, clearly conveying the impression that all that happened two hundred years ago, particularly under the preaching of Wesley, was really nothing but the employment of this particular psychological technique which he now feels is explained adequately by Pavlov's experiments.

At this point, it is important for us to notice that Dr Sargant makes one very important admission. He admits that he is not discussing what he would call a 'purely intellectual conversion, but only those physical or psychological stimuli, rather than intellectual arguments, which seem to help to produce conversion by causing alterations in the subject's brain function' (p. xii). In other words, he really does confine himself to certain particular evangelistic techniques. All will agree that that is an important admission on his part.

The Thesis Examined

In commenting on Dr Sargant's thesis I propose, first of all, to make a number of general criticisms and then to examine in greater detail some of the arguments which he puts forward. Let me begin by saying that, within his own sphere, and speaking purely medically, it seems to me that we must grant what Dr Sargant is saying. The findings from his own cases and those of other similar workers in this field are substantiated facts and we do not dispute them. In the same way we do know, unfortunately, from what we have read in newspaper reports and in books devoted to the subject, and also from what we may have heard from individuals who have recorded their experiences, that this procedure known as brain-washing is being practised. It has been successfully used both by Fascists and by Communists. There is no question at all that such results can be produced by this continual 'rape of the mind' (as some call it, that is, as the result of a continual bombardment of the mind with suggestions). We have read of the most unlikely people who have been produced as prisoners or witnesses in court and who have testified that they have flagrantly lied and that they have worked against the state. Some, at least, have been men of ability, intelligence, and integrity. As a result of the application of such processes as we described above, in favourable circumstances the continual bombardment of their minds has reduced them to a condition which is reminiscent of that described by Pavlov in the case of his dogs. In other words, it is idle to pretend that the human brain cannot be influenced in the way that Dr Sargant is suggesting. But the basic question that arises is this: Are these phenomena, which most certainly can be produced under these exceptional circumstances, the true explanation, therefore, of what happens in the ordinary or normal circumstances of conversion?

SOME GENERAL CRITICISMS

It is at this point that we must make certain observations and criticisms. My first general criticism is the question: Is this comparison of animals and men a strictly legitimate one? It seems to me that Dr Sargant does not allow for the essential difference between an animal and a man. For instance, he does not seem to allow at all for the presence of reason and the critical faculty that man possesses. Must we not take into account man's power of self-analysis, self-contemplation, and self-criticism? Though he grants in general that, after all, men are not dogs, yet his suggestion is nevertheless that their brains function in the same way, and that when you are dealing with a man you are virtually in the same position as if you were dealing with an animal. In other words, my reply at this point would be just this, that our condition only becomes comparable to that of a dog in very extreme cases, or in most exceptional circumstances such as war, where there is aerial bombardment or continuous heavy gunfire, or some horrifying experience such as many civilians had with the 'V' bombs. In other words, the comparison is only valid at times when what differentiates man essentially from the dog has been knocked out of action, and a man, because of this terrible stress, has been reduced for the time being to the level of an animal.

Here I would like to express my agreement with a quotation which Dr Sargant takes from Aldous Huxley, who writes: 'Meanwhile, all we can safely predict is that, if exposed long enough to the tom-toms and the singing, every one of our philosophers would end by capering and howling with the savages' (p. 149). I am in entire agreement with that. The power of the Holy Spirit alone could prevent it. But the real point is that, as the result of this conditioning (that is, the bombardment of the mind by these various abnormal stimuli), what really made the philosopher, the university lecturer, or the able man of affairs the man that he was, has already been knocked right out of action. He has been put into an abnormal state. Such a consideration seems to me to vitiate much of Dr Sargant's argument.

My second general criticism is this. It seems to me Dr Sargant really answers his own case by proving too much. His book seems to explain away everything, not only religious conversion or political conversion. His thesis can also be used, if we accept it as it is, to explain away heroism and great acts of self-sacrifice. They are, according to this hypothesis, merely conditioned reflexes, so that all the noblest deeds in which mankind has always gloried are nothing but reactions to given stimuli at a given point. Indeed, it seems to me that Dr Sargant goes so far as to say that, in the last analysis, there is no such thing as a real mental conviction about anything; that always in coming to believe one thing or in rejecting something else, we are simply manifesting a physiological process.

Let Dr Sargant himself be quoted again, to show what we mean. He writes: 'For instance, the conversion of John and Charles Wesley was facilitated by a preliminary "softening up" of both by Peter Böhler, the Moravian missionary; yet it was only after Peter Böhler had left the country that John's heart was finally and suddenly "warmed" in a small religious group-meeting in Aldersgate Street' (pp. 221–22). You notice the expression 'softening up'. In other words, while Peter Böhler was quietly expounding the Scriptures to John and Charles Wesley separately, what was really taking place was this 'softening up' process, comparable to the electrical stimuli that Pavlov put into the legs of the dogs. And so, I argue that he is proving too much – that any instruction is just a 'softening up' process; everything is psychological. In other words, it seems to me that we come to this: by this thesis Dr Sargant is really taking away the grounds for our believing in any kind of intellectual conviction or apprehension whatsoever.

But, to be fair to him, we could argue that all he is really doing is to demonstrate up to a point how our brain works, and that the working of the human brain is always the same, whether it is applied to religion or to philosophy or to politics or to anything else. So that, in the last analysis, we are left with this result, that evidence has been produced up to a point to show the working of the brain under certain conditions, and that, therefore, we must emphasize the all-importance of the truth or falsity of the thing which is presented to the brain. In other words, Dr Sargant's book can be entirely dismissed, from the Christian's standpoint in general, by claiming that this book has no religious application at all; the author is simply showing how the brain always works. That being so, therefore, we are left with this question: How do we decide whether Christianity is true or false? This book is no more a criticism of Christianity than it is of any philosophy, any political teaching, or anything else.

THE SIGNIFICANCE OF PENTECOST

We must now come to a more particular criticism of Dr Sargant's thesis and an answer to it from the point of view of the particular case of religion. As I have reminded you, he deals with religion, paying special attention to Wesley and Methodism (largely, I take it, because he himself is a Methodist). He admits, as I have reminded you, that he is not dealing with what he calls 'the intellectual type of conversion', but, in particular, with the kind of thing that happened in the ministry of John Wesley years ago. He also describes some of the curious cults and religious movements in America – those people who embrace snakes, and so on – and some of the various freak and ecstatic religious movements which he has been studying. He does not confine himself to such matters as these, but deals also with what he regards as similar phenomena described in the Bible.

Dr Sargant refers to what happened on the day of Pentecost on pages 102–4. At this point, significantly, he is interested solely in the conversion of the three thousand. I must quote part of the passage in order that we may notice the kind of things he says. It commences: 'The account given in the *Acts of the Apostles* (Chapter 2) of Peter's sermon at Pentecost also emphasizes the effectiveness of the religious methods discussed in this chapter. No less than three thousand converts are said to have been added that day to the very small group of apostles and other believers who remained faithful after Jesus's farewell on the Mount of Olives.' After this he quotes the opening verses of the chapter to show how people had heard that these apostles were able to speak in different tongues and how the crowd came together, and then continues: 'Peter then rises and begins to preach. He adds further tension to an audience already half-stupefied [*sic*] by the news of that strange Gift of Tongues.[4] In a very powerful speech he announces that they are now watching what has long been foretold by the prophets. He quotes the Prophet Joel.'

After this is recorded Peter's quotation from the Old Testament and then Dr Sargant goes on: 'Then he flings an emotional thunderbolt at his scared and excited listeners.[5] He tells them that Jesus of Nazareth was "a man approved of God among you by miracles and wonders and signs . . ." whom the chief priests had handed over to the Romans to be "crucified and slain by wicked hands." He makes them understand just who the man was whom they had allowed the chief priests to hand over for crucifixion to their Roman patrons, but whom God had now raised up from the dead.

[4]It would be interesting to be informed where in the Bible the suggestion of 'half-stupefied' is found!
[5]Such comment on the text, we presume, is supposed to be calm, scientific comment and reasoning!

By not making a mass protest, however busy they may have been on preparing for the Passover, they have become, he insists, murderers in the second degree.' Here the writer quotes the words of Peter and adds: 'Peter's audience had now come to believe that the "Gift of Tongues" was a sign from God, God who, in accordance with eschatological prophecy, had darkened the sun at the Crucifixion and turned the moon to the colour of blood, with a fearful dust-storm from Elam. Now they are assured that the victim was God's representative on the earth and they cannot escape the guilt of his death. It is therefore easy to understand how "when they heard this, they were pricked in their heart, and said unto Peter and to the rest of the apostles, Men and brethren, what shall we do?"' Dr Sargant then goes on to quote what Peter said to them and how three thousand souls were converted. He adds, 'New beliefs and habits now seemed readily imposed on the converts.' In other words, this tremendous stimulus had produced a kind of emotional collapse, and the crowd was in that very condition in which Pavlov finds the dogs are most ready to receive new suggestions and new ideas. So Peter's 'shock tactics' in preaching on the day of Pentecost were so successful that he was now able to indoctrinate the people with comparative ease.

That is the case that Dr Sargant makes from his example taken from the Acts of the Apostles. But the point which is of most interest to us is that (apart from what I have already said about the obvious special pleading and the subtle importing into the narrative of things which are not there at all) Dr Sargant does not take into consideration what had happened to the apostles themselves before this, that is the complete change which had already taken place in them. He does not deal with that; he does not even mention it! Especially he does not consider what it was that enabled Peter to preach in this manner. It is no use his *starting* with the report concerning the apostles' possession of the gift of tongues; the question is, from what source did the gift of tongues come? He does not attempt to deal with that. He simply starts with Peter's preaching and leaves out what is the most significant feature in the whole narrative. We must ask, however, how had the apostles received this power to speak in tongues? How does Dr Sargant account for the change in them? In their case, there does not appear to have been the kind of stimulus which he postulates in the case of the mass. No-one had come to preach to them so graphically; nothing of this sort is recorded. If we are going to take our data from the Bible, the only explanation must be found in the historical details, the facts which are given in the Gospels themselves. Now that, it seems to me, is the real question, and Dr Sargant, in the interests of his theory, evades it altogether.

THE CONVERSION OF ST PAUL

Further, let us consider the way in which Dr Sargant deals with the apostle Paul's conversion on pages 104–6. He describes it in the following words: 'The case of Saul on the road to Damascus confirms our other finding: that anger may be no less powerful an emotion than fear in bringing about sudden conversion to beliefs which exactly contradict beliefs previously held.' After quoting the actual record as it is given in Acts 9, his first comment is: 'A state of transmarginal inhibition seems to have followed his acute state of nervous excitement.' The author means this: Pavlov found in his experience that when you stimulated the dogs with electrical stimuli, they first of all became agitated, then got very excited, and if you went on increasing the dose which you gave, the dog reached a stage at which it more or less collapsed. That is what he means by 'transmarginal inhibition'. The dog seemed at that point to become apathetic. A total collapse took place and, as a result of it, the dog was, as it were, protecting itself against this too great stimulus. And it is just in that stage, again, that the dog becomes so suggestible. Therefore, Dr Sargant, true to his theory, goes on to say that, in the case of Paul, 'Total collapse, hallucinations and an increased state of suggestibility appear to have supervened. Other inhibitory hysterical manifestations are also reported.' He then quotes: 'And Saul arose from the earth; and when his eyes were opened, he saw no man: but they led him by the hand, and brought him into Damascus; And he was three days without sight, and neither did eat nor drink.' Dr Sargant comments: 'This period of physical debilitation by fasting, added to Saul's other stresses, may well have increased his anxiety and suggestibility [That is true in the case of the dogs, you see! M. L-J.] Only after three days did Brother Ananias come to relieve his nervous symptoms and his mental distress, at the same time implanting [Notice the word 'implanting'! M. L-J.] new beliefs.' Then follows a further quotation from Acts 9, after which Dr Sargant goes on: 'Then followed the necessary period of indoctrination imposed on Saul by the brethren at Damascus, and of his full acceptance of all the new beliefs that they required of him.'

[73]

What have we to say about all this? The first comment must be that Dr Sargant himself is here guilty of a most extraordinary contradiction. In chapter 10 of his book we read: 'A safeguard against conversion is, indeed, a burning and obsessive belief in some other creed or way of life' (p. 229). But if there ever was a man who had a 'burning and obsessive belief' it was surely Saul of Tarsus! That, Dr Sargant tells us 'is a safeguard against conversion'. Yet, on pages 105 and 106, these very things are the conditions which seem to be essential to conversion. That is mentioned in passing!

More seriously, what seems to me to be so important is that, on his own thesis, the writer does not show us what was the tremendous stimulus leading to increased suggestibility, in the case of the apostle Paul. There is no reference made to the nature of the stimulus or assault on the mind at all. Paul was not in a mass evangelistic meeting, indeed he was not listening to any preaching, but he was on a journey to arrest Christians. He was also burning with the zeal of an obsessive belief. The reader will remember the facts as recorded in the New Testament. It seems to me that Dr Sargant does not provide us in any sense with a clue concerning the stimulus which his own theory makes an essential desideratum in such a case. Not only that. He does not tell us why it was that Ananias ever went to Paul in the first instance, which is surely a most material point. Why was it? Ananias himself tells us that it was the Lord who sent him. Dr Sargant's suggestion is, of course, that it was just a part of the indoctrination process. Indeed, you will notice that the author goes on to assert quite specifically: 'Then followed the necessary period of indoctrination imposed on Saul by the brethren at Damascus.' He has already stated that Ananias found Paul in the state which was most conducive to the 'implanting [of] new beliefs'. The further suggestion is that the apostle Paul came to believe and to teach what he did as a result of the instruction which he was given, not only by Ananias but, subsequently, by the disciples at Damascus.

Now this is really serious. It is a flat contradiction of what the apostle Paul himself tells us in Galatians 1:11–12: 'I certify you, brethren, that the gospel which was preached of me is not after man. For I neither received it of man, neither was I taught it, but by the revelation of Jesus Christ.' In other words, in the interests of his theory, Dr Sargant has to overlook the details in the documents he is quoting. These, however, are most important in relation both to Paul's call and to his work as an apostle. He became the man he was, and the outstanding apostle, as the result of seeing the risen Lord with his naked eyes on the road to Damascus. Dr Sargant ignores that completely, in the same way as he seems everywhere to discount the miraculous and the supernatural in the Bible. Whereas, if you take the New Testament narrative as it is, it explains everything that happened to the apostle Paul quite straightforwardly. The resurrection of the Lord Jesus Christ and His subsequent appearances are absolutely vital to the Christian faith and gospel. You cannot explain or understand Christianity apart from this. If Christ did not literally rise from the grave in the body, how did Christianity ever come into being? That is the consideration which is at the very heart of our faith. Christianity is not a philosophy or merely an ethical teaching. It is a faith based upon certain great historical events and facts, and unless our religious experience is based upon these, then it is not truly Christian.

These facts Dr Sargant by implication completely denies. Yet, taken as recorded in the New Testament, they provide an adequate explanation of what happened not only in the case of the apostle Paul but also in that of the other apostles. We are told that they went round preaching and teaching 'Jesus and the resurrection'. They did not merely preach an experience, or simply exhort people to live a certain type of life. They preached *facts*. They were heralds of good news, and the whole basis of their preaching was to tell people of certain momentous and crucial events which had just taken place. All this is stated quite clearly by the apostle Paul in I Corinthians 15:1–8: 'Moreover, brethren, I declare unto you the gospel which I preached unto you, which also ye have received, and wherein ye stand; by which also ye are saved, if ye keep in memory what I preached unto you, unless ye have believed in vain. For I delivered unto you first of all that which I also received, how that Christ died for our sins according to the scriptures; and that he was buried, and that he rose again the third day according to the scriptures; and that he was seen of Cephas, then of the twelve: after that, he was seen of above five hundred brethren at once; of whom the greater part remain unto this present, but some are fallen asleep. After that, he was seen of James; then of all the apostles. And last of all he was seen of me also, as of one born out of due time.' Paul goes on to make it quite plain that if this fact of the resurrection is not true, then there is no Christian gospel at all, and any experiences that people may have had are spurious and of no final value. All that, however, is completely ignored by Dr Sargant.

[75]

THE CONVERSION OF JOHN WESLEY

We come now to our third detailed criticism. It refers to Dr Sargant's understanding of the spiritual experience of John Wesley. Here, again, he would explain everything on the lines of his theory. The question is, however, can this be done? Let us look at the conversion of John Wesley. This event would seem to have happened in circumstances that are almost the exact opposite of those postulated by Dr Sargant. John Wesley was not converted in a crowded and excited gathering; it happened, rather, in a small meeting place and in a quiet service. No-one was even preaching. A man was reading out of the preface of Luther's *Commentary on the Epistle to the Romans* when this vital experience came to him. One cannot imagine a set of circumstances further removed from those postulated by Dr Sargant, and especially when we think in terms of Pavlov's experiments with the dogs and the electrical stimuli which he applied to them. Furthermore, Dr Sargant does not explain why, as the result of this experience, Wesley's ministry at once became so different. I am not concerned at the moment with the message as such, but I am indicating that he does not explain why Wesley's ministry suddenly became so effective. Yet this, surely, is a very vital part of the data.

I must also call attention to certain other inaccuracies in Dr Sargant's treatment of the case of Wesley. On page 127 we read: 'Wesley may, in fact, have read Edwards' account before starting his own campaign four years later.' This is a reference to Jonathan Edwards' famous account of the revival in New England. But this suggestion by Dr Sargant is pure hypothesis, and there is no evidence to confirm it. In the same way we must indicate that John Wesley did not start a 'campaign', and it is a travesty of the facts to picture him as a man planning and starting a campaign. John Wesley continued working more or less exactly on the same lines as he had done before, but what had happened to him in the meeting in Aldersgate Street made all the difference. This is no case of a man suddenly deciding to adopt new methods or a new technique which led to results; but it is clearly the case of a man who has been filled with the Holy Spirit and whose ministry, as a result, is made effective.

There is likewise a similar inaccuracy on page 130 of *Battle for the Mind*: 'John Wesley, though attributing to the hand of God the thousands of conversions he induced all over England, in the most unlikely people, nevertheless speculated about possible additional physiological factors: "How easy it is to suppose that strong, lively, and sudden apprehension of the hideousness of sin and the wrath of God, and the bitter pains of eternal death, should affect the body as well as the soul, suspending the present laws of vital union and interrupting or disturbing the ordinary circulation and putting nature out of its course." It was by thus observing scientifically the results achieved by different types of preaching that Wesley was helped to make even Great Britain, which is so notoriously resistant to change, transform some of its traditional religious and political behaviour patterns.'

This seems to me to be quite extraordinary! While I am a great admirer of John Wesley I do not think he was quite as scientific as that, or quite as able to think in twentieth-century terms! Dr Sargant surely misunderstands what Wesley is saying. Wesley was simply trying to account for what took place during his preaching. Indeed, we know from his *Journals* that he was disturbed by these phenomena. He was truly concerned about them and troubled by them. He is here attempting an explanation and suggesting that the influence and the power of the Holy Spirit can be so great sometimes that it is not surprising that one's physical constitution should break under the power and the glory. It is surely quite unfair to suggest that Wesley in a kind of calm, scientific manner observed certain effects as following certain causes and then deliberately evolved a technique to produce such effects.

It seems to me also that Dr Sargant is misleading in his comments upon the results of the work of Wesley and the Methodists. This is how he puts his view on pages 219 and 220 of his book: 'The Methodist revival also helped to condition the English of the early nineteenth century to accept social conditions which would have caused revolutions in most other European countries. Wesley had taught the masses to be less concerned with their miserable life on earth, as victims of the Industrial Revolution, than with the life to come; they could now put up with almost anything.' While we are ready to agree with the historians who believe that the Evangelical Awakening of the eighteenth century may well have saved this country from something similar to the French Revolution, we must point out that Dr Sargant fails at this point to give adequate emphasis to what he has in fact mentioned in passing on page 76.

Students of sociology agree that one of the most potent factors, if not the most important of all, in the rise and development of the Trade Union Movement and the dominance of Liberal ideas in politics in the

nineteenth century (and indeed the whole of the democratic movement in this country in the nineteenth and twentieth centuries), was
the great Evangelical Awakening of the eighteenth century. This
awakening was perhaps the greatest single stimulus to the intellect of
individuals and to the intellectual outlook of the mass of the people
that has ever been known in this country. It created in the common
people a desire to read and to learn. It awakened them to the dignity
of man and of human life. It opened their eyes to various forms of
oppression under which they had been suffering. Indeed it has
generally been regarded as the source of what later came to be known
as the 'Nonconformist conscience', a fact which Dr Sargant himself
admits in the earlier of the two passages referred to above.

John Wesley was a man who applied no kind of technique in his
ministry; and this is equally true of George Whitefield and the other
great men whom God raised up to carry through such a mighty work
in the eighteenth century. To suggest the contrary is to import
something that is quite alien to the whole atmosphere and spirit of
that great movement in the history of the church.

THE NEED FOR A THEOLOGICAL APPROACH

We come now to some further general points of criticism. Dr
Sargant's central trouble, as I have already suggested, is that he
leaves out entirely the fundamental facts on which our faith is based.
He forgets that Christianity is essentially a historical religion and
that the truths which we believe are solidly based upon facts. His
view of Christianity seems to be that it is but a form of moral and
ethical teaching which has to be applied and lived. It may be unfair to
make such a criticism, but it is very difficult to discover Dr Sargant's
view of our Lord Himself. He may argue that he was not concerned
in this book to deal with theology, and yet no man can say as much as
he does say without of necessity raising questions of theology. In any
case, this whole matter must be dealt with *theologically*. The answer
to the suggestion which pervades this book is that the explanation of
the events and experiences such as Pentecost, the conversion of the
apostle Paul, John Wesley, and others, is not psychological but,
always and essentially, *theological*.

Let me illustrate what I mean. Dr Sargant says nothing about the
fact of the resurrection, but it is surely central in the New Testament
records. What he has to explain (on his hypothesis) is the source from

which came the 'suggestion' of the resurrection to the apostles. We know from the records that at the time they were all crestfallen, disappointed, and unhappy, and had throughout failed to grasp our Lord's teaching with regard to His resurrection. There is only one adequate explanation for the marked change in them: it is the fact that our Lord literally rose in the body from the grave and appeared to these disciples on more than one occasion. If we accept that, then there are no difficulties; but if we do not accept that, or if we fail to see its crucial importance, then we are left in a maze of difficulties and without any real understanding of what followed.

It is exactly the same when we come to the question of the doctrine of the Holy Spirit. This, again, is not dealt with at all by Dr Sargant. It is entirely ignored. It is just here, however, it seems to me, that we have the final answer to the case of this book. What happened on the day of Pentecost had already been predicted in the Old Testament. The apostle Peter in his sermon on the day of Pentecost makes this clear in his quotation from the prophet Joel. But there are other similar prophecies in the books of Isaiah and Ezekiel. John the Baptist had also made the same prophecy, saying, 'I indeed baptize you with water; but one mightier than I cometh, the latchet of whose shoes I am not worthy to unloose: he shall baptize you with the Holy Ghost and with fire' (Luke 3:16). Our Lord Himself had similarly taught the disciples of this great gift that was to come. It is the whole burden of the teaching in chapters 14, 15, and 16 of St John's Gospel, as also in chapter 7, verses 37–39. Again, we find Him repeating the same message after the resurrection and especially in Acts 1:4–8. (See also Luke 24:49.)

Now all this is of crucial importance; it is a question of fact. The exact time when this was going to take place had been stated clearly in the Old Testament. (It is the event foreshadowed by the feast of Pentecost.) This is not just a matter of a number of psychological conditions being fulfilled. How could that have been prophesied centuries before the time? If it were but some psychological event, we are left with the problem of explaining how the prophets were ever able to foretell this event in such detail. If, however, we believe that Pentecost was one of the great events in connection with salvation, and that it was literally the occasion when the Lord Jesus Christ sent and poured forth the Holy Spirit who had been promised by God throughout the centuries (and therefore called 'the promise of the Father'), then there are no difficulties. What Dr Sargant unfortunately does not realize is that the power of Peter's preaching on the day of Pentecost was not so much in what Peter said, still less in any kind of technique that he employed, but was rather the demonstration of the power of the Holy Spirit. His analysis of Peter's sermon on the day of Pentecost is a pathetic travesty of the facts as recorded in the Acts of the Apostles. It is the result of a failure to understand the New Testament doctrine of the Holy Spirit and especially of the results of 'the fullness of the Spirit' in the ministry of a man such as Peter, Paul, or any one of the great preachers who were raised up and used by God in subsequent ages. The idea of Peter deliberately applying stimuli, manipulating his congregation, and deciding when to 'hurl in' certain statements is indeed, quite laughable.

In the case of political brain-washing, whether by Fascists or Communists, it is the case, as it is in Pavlov's experiments, that the stimulus must be applied repeatedly for some time in order to produce the conditioning and to get the result. Now what happened on the day of Pentecost does not illustrate that at all. The effect was immediate and, therefore, the actual facts of the case seem to me to vitiate the main argument of this book.

THE NATURE OF RELIGIOUS REVIVALS

I now refer to a quotation on pages 99 and 100 in which Dr Sargant writes: 'The Quakers later settled down to become rich and respectable, abandoning the means by which they had built up their early spiritual strength. It is the fate of new religious sects to lose the dynamism of their "enthusiastic" founders; later leaders may improve the organization, but the original conversion techniques are often tacitly repudiated. The wild militancy of General Booth's early Salvation Army is gone. The frantic scenes of the Welsh Revival are forgotten in new and respectable chapels where the *hwyl* (a Welsh preaching device for exciting the congregation to religious frenzy by breaking into a wild chant) is now rarely heard. The surprise that Dr Billy Graham's success has caused in Great Britain, where all he has to compete with is religious addresses aimed at the congregation's intelligence rather than its emotions, shows how widespread is the general ignorance of matters discussed in this book.'

Again, the same fallacy appears and we are asked to assume that the originators deliberately introduced and employed a technique, which their successors have discarded. The simple answer is that in not one of these instances (with the possible exception of the Salvation Army, a movement which still employs some of its early methods) did any man, or group of men, introduce or employ any such technique whatsoever. In each case we have a movement of the Spirit of God leading to a definite experience, and in each case it began suddenly. Incidentally 'the frantic scenes of the Welsh Revival' most certainly cannot be explained by the *hwyl* of the preachers, for it is a simple fact of history (and, in the opinion of many, a regrettable fact) that there was practically no preaching at all during the last Welsh revival! A *theory* sometimes seems to exert a very profound influence on its author. Furthermore, the explanation of the changes to which Dr Sargant refers, and which have most certainly taken place, is quite different from what he suggests. What has happened is not that certain 'techniques' formerly employed have now been dropped, but that there has been a widespread departure from the faith of the early leaders, and the church's work is therefore not being honoured by the Holy Spirit as it was formerly. Dr Sargant does not seem to be aware of this factor.

In precisely the same way, Dr Sargant does not seem to have grasped the truth concerning revivals as a whole. He does not deal with religious revival as such at all and, indeed, does not seem to be interested in this remarkable phenomenon which takes place from time to time in the history of the church. Take, for instance, the question of the origin of any revival. How does the whole movement start? From whence, according to Dr Sargant does the stimulus come? The actual facts are that, generally speaking, the church, before a revival, has been in a low and lethargic state. Then suddenly, without any apparent explanation, one man, or a small group of men, suddenly begin to be disturbed and become concerned about the state of the church. They become dissatisfied with their own lives and go to God in prayer, confessing their sinfulness and that of the whole church and pleading for a visitation of God's Spirit. God in His grace and in His own time hears and answers the prayer and pours out His Spirit, and so the revival begins and spreads. Sometimes this happens in several places, and even in different countries, at the same time. But on the hypothesis of Dr Sargant's book, the question is, where does the original stimulus come from? The book does not help us at all with regard to that crucial question.

In the same way, we have to try to understand and explain how revivals end. For it has generally been the case that the ending of a revival has been as sudden as the beginning. Dr Sargant quotes Finney,[6] and, indeed, Finney is certainly very important with respect to this whole subject. He was a man who taught quite definitely that, if one applied a given technique, one could have a revival at any time. That is the essence of Finney's teaching in his book on revivals. But history has surely proved that Finney was quite wrong. Many have tried to plan revivals by using his technique and have done so honestly, sincerely, and thoroughly, but the desired revival has not come. One of Finney's cardinal errors was to confuse an evangelistic campaign and a revival, and to forget that the latter is something that is always given in the sovereignty of God. It never results from the adoption of certain techniques, methods, and organization. It seems clear from the historical facts that Finney himself for a number of years was in the midst of a true revival and greatly used by God. During the course of this revival certain things, such as the confession of particular sins, and certain other accompaniments appeared. These results Finney seems to have misinterpreted and as a result, propounded his theory that, if people can be persuaded to confess their sins, revival will take place. It is the fallacy of believing that if we produce the *results* and *consequences* of revival, we shall have the revival itself! Indeed, in copies of the *Oberlin Evangelist* containing articles by Finney (after his period as an evangelist and when he had become a professor of theology), there are indications that the writer himself had become somewhat suspicious of his own technique. There are statements written by Finney such as the following: 'If I had my time over again I would preach nothing but holiness. The converts of my revivals are a disgrace to Christianity, and if I had my time over again I would preach nothing but holiness.' The suggestion is that the tremendous pressure which this evangelist's methods brought to bear upon the will and emotions, produced only temporary results.

To sum up, then, the fallacy which seems to run right through the book *Battle for the Mind* is that the person and work of the Holy Spirit are entirely overlooked. It is assumed throughout that the history of the church can be explained solely in terms of human activity. As we have seen, the very facts of church history utterly

[6]Charles G. Finney, the leader in a revival movement in the USA in the second quarter of the nineteenth century.

disprove the assertion. Nothing is so clear as the fact that, if the church were but a human institution, she would long since have ceased to be. The persistence of the church is due solely to the mighty and exceptional outpouring of the Holy Spirit which God grants from time to time. He does this in such a manner as to indicate clearly that the power is always of God and not of man.

The Positive Value of this Study

We come now to what might be termed a call to Christians to self-examination in the light of the teaching of this book. We must start by agreeing with Dr Sargant that it is possible, by various means and methods and mechanisms, to influence the human mind. That is indisputable. We grant that this can be done by religious movements as well as by political and other movements. We are not for a moment going to attempt to defend some of the freak religious movements to which Dr Sargant refers, such as the snake-handling sects in America, because we hold the view that such practices in any form cannot be justified in terms of the teaching of the Scriptures. So we can grant him, in general, that it is possible, as he says, to influence the minds of many, religiously, politically, and socially. We obviously also have to accept the existence of what is known as brain-washing as carried out by the Fascists and the Communists. This modern tragedy is simply a fact, and it would be idle for us to attempt to reject it as a phenomenon. In the same way we are well aware that all primitive religions employ techniques, such as dancing, drumming, tom-toms, singing of a certain type, and similar things. It is a characteristic feature of all primitive religions that they employ such means in various forms to produce the desired results. We can freely agree that Dr Sargant has called attention to all this in a very striking manner. Up to a point, therefore, his book should be of considerable value in warning people against the serious danger, in the modern world, of political indoctrination. We have been made aware by post-war documents that such practices could become widespread even in a cultured, educated country such as Germany, and obviously, therefore, it is something that can happen in any society. It behoves us therefore to take due note in this general way that clever men by the use of skilful techniques can so influence the minds of men and women as to produce the results they desire.

But now a further question arises: Has all this anything to say to us Christian people, and especially to evangelical Christians? As I see the situation, we have to admit that wrong tendencies *can* develop and spread even among those who are sincerely desirous to spread the true gospel. I think that in all honesty we must take note that some of these tendencies have crept into evangelical circles in the past. Let us examine some examples.

I am second to no-one in my admiration of the great Jonathan Edwards and his preaching; yet it does seem to me that Edwards in his preaching concerning hell went at times well beyond what he was warranted to do and to say by Holy Scripture. He allowed his imagination to run riot. Thereby he began to do something closely akin, to put it mildly, to that which is described by Dr Sargant in his book. Again, we have the facts concerning George Whitefield, who probably was one of the greatest preachers the church has ever known since the apostles. Yet I would have to admit that even Whitefield occasionally exceeded his warrant. I mean that he allowed his own eloquence and his own imagination to run away with him. He reached a point at which he was not so much presenting the message of the gospel as producing an oratorical, not to say a psychological, effect upon his congregation.

I could illustrate this also in the case of a number of other preachers. The graphic use of a story, or of an illustration, can sometimes become an end in itself, so that the congregation is really not being influenced by the truth of God at that point but by the graphic or dramatic character of the story or the illustration which is being employed. For instance, I remember hearing a story concerning a preacher who was endeavouring to convince his congregation of the danger of delaying decision and action. As an illustration, he pictured a number of people staying at the seaside, who had walked one afternoon on to a promontory of rock stretching from the beach. They had walked right out on to this rocky point and the sea lay all round them. They were enjoying the view and looking out to sea. They failed to realize that gradually the tide was coming in on both sides of them and that it was about to cut them off at the point where the promontory joined the mainland. There they were, so enjoying the sunshine and the fishing that they were unaware of their peril. Then, suddenly, someone noticed it and the urgent question arose as to whether their retreat was already cut off. Were they already surrounded? Would the sea soon cover the whole promontory, and were they all to be drowned? The preacher had taken much time in presenting the story, and had done it with such dramatic effect that he brought the congregation to a point when it seemed doubtful whether anybody in the party could escape at all. At that point he suddenly shouted: 'If you do not run at once, it will be too late.' It is said that the whole congregation literally rose to its feet and the chapel was speedily emptied!

What do we say about an occurrence such as that? I would unhesitatingly condemn *that* kind of preaching. None can deny, surely, that at that point the influence was almost purely *psychological*, that the congregation had ceased to be aware of the truth, and that their minds had been so gripped by this graphic picture that they were acting almost automatically. At that point it is the flesh that is operating rather than the Spirit.

We must therefore start with this admission that though our doctrine may be right and true, we may very well transgress and expose ourselves to the kind of criticism offered by Dr Sargant by adopting, even with good intentions, wrong and false methods. I suggest, then, that this book should come to all Christians, evangelicals included, as a challenge. We must not be content simply with replying to it along the lines that we have already indicated, but we must honestly ask ourselves, Is there here a valid criticism of what any of us are doing? Are there any facts which might indicate that we are at all guilty, albeit unconsciously, of what Dr Sargant says? For instance, is there not a tendency in our work always to reproduce the same type? Do not our people always tend to be drawn from one particular type or class? If they are, there is something seriously wrong. Psychological methods and movements always tend to reproduce the same type, whereas it has always been the glory of the Christian faith that it has won its converts from all classes and all kinds of people. Our suspicions should be aroused at once if we find that we are tending to produce a people that are like peas in a pod, or like rows of postage stamps. That savours of the psychological, rather than of the spiritual.

Let me again quote from Dr Sargant at this point. He says, 'The higher incidence of hysterical phenomena among ordinary people under the acute stresses of war, compared with that among the same sort of people under the minor stresses of peacetime, or among chronically anxious and neurotic people either in peace or war, is further evidence (if any were needed) for the point we have been making, namely, that among the readiest victims of brain-washing or religious conversion may be the simple, healthy extrovert' (p. 61). I have a most uncomfortable feeling that 'the simple, healthy extrovert' is very much in evidence in some circles which place great emphasis on evangelism these days.

Another question, I think, which forces us to examine ourselves in the light of Dr Sargant's thesis, is the so-called 'temporary results' of evangelistic campaigns. We must note the discrepancy between the large numbers that go forward at the appeal and the comparatively small numbers that really join and remain in the church. Now that, again, is a fact, a phenomenon, which we must investigate. It is not enough simply to say, Ah, but look at those who do stick. That is all right; but what has happened to the others? What at the outset *did* happen to them? It is something which we must explain. Or, to put it in another form, certain religious organizations, Christian organizations among students and other young people, often bemoan the fact that a terrible leakage takes place when their members go out into the world from the rarefied atmosphere of their college life, their Christian Unions, and their organizations. So many of them 'fall away'. I do not know the exact figures, but there is at any rate a serious leakage. This again, I think, should cause us to seek for the explanation. So I will ask this question: Is it not the case that some of our methods and approach to evangelism are not beyond suspicion?

I feel that we must be concerned about this for three main reasons. The first is that, if our methods are wrong at these points, we open the door wide to the very kind of criticism that is being offered by Dr Sargant. That in itself would be a serious thing. But that is not my only reason. To me it is not even the most pressing reason. Much more important is that such wrong methods are unscriptural, that they bring the gospel into disrepute, and that they allow the man who is outside the church to scoff: 'This is all psychology; you can see it happening at the time, and look at what happens afterwards!' In such a manner the gospel is discredited. The most serious reason, however, which should impel us to examine ourselves is that such tendencies and use of techniques imply a lack of faith. Over-attention to techniques and methods, I would say, is indicative always of a lack of faith in the work of the Holy Spirit.

What then are the more detailed lessons for evangelistically-minded Christians? Clearly in the light of all these modern phenomena (in the political sphere especially) there are certain dangers which we must avoid. The first consideration is that there must be no divorce between the message we give and the methods we use. Surely, all must agree that our methods as well as our message are to be controlled by the New Testament and its teaching? Now the crucial passage on this matter will be found in 1 Corinthians 2:1–5, especially the section which reads: 'And I, brethren, when I came to you, came not with excellency of speech or of wisdom, declaring unto you the testimony of God. For I determined not to know anything among you, save Jesus Christ, and him crucified. And I was with you in weakness, and in fear, and in much trembling. And my speech and my preaching was not with enticing words of man's wisdom, but in demonstration of the Spirit and of power: that your faith should not stand in the wisdom of men, but in the power of God.' Here the great apostle goes out of his way to explain to us that he deliberately rejected certain methods, and he did so in order that it might be clear to everybody that the results were not of man but of God. He did everything 'in demonstration of the Spirit and of power'. He deliberately did not use 'enticing words of man's wisdom'. In other words, the apostle deliberately avoided what he knew would appeal to the congregation, what they liked, and what they were accustomed to. He carefully avoided the method of the Greek rhetoricians and philosophers. He became a 'fool',[7] he tells us, and he did it of set purpose. In this statement we have the apostolic pattern and the apostolic authority for saying that our methods must be controlled in a similar manner, and that it must always be 'in demonstration of the Spirit and of power'. Is it not true to say that some have been guilty of giving a message which is controlled by Holy Scripture, while at the same time arguing that any method that the world finds to be successful may be employed, whether or not it is in keeping with New Testament principles? Thereby, I say, we open the door wide to the kind of criticism that we have in the book *Battle for the Mind*. In reply to such a warning, people often will ask, But why should not the Holy Spirit make use of these modern techniques? Why set them in opposition to one another? The answer is that the apostle Paul would never have argued like that, but deliberately avoided all that can be subsumed under the heading 'man's wisdom'. He *could* have argued in that manner about the use of philosophy and rhetoric, but deliberately did not do so.

[7]Since some have misread even this expression it may be necessary to add that what he means is that both his central message concerning the cross, and the direct manner in which he presented it, would sound too simple to the Greeks.

In the second place I think we must avoid anything that leads to a suspicion that in evangelistic activities we are conditioning people in a psychological manner. We must exclude anything which opens the door to criticism of the type we have been considering. It is, of course, not the criticism which it is important to avoid, but the use of any method which God cannot approve. This again suggests that we must avoid any deliberate use of techniques as aids to the gospel. The reader will have noticed how frequently the term 'technique' occurs in Dr Sargant's book, how he imputes to Wesley and others the deliberate application of techniques. Naturally, if what you desire is to produce *psychological* results then, of necessity, you will have to employ the proper psychological techniques, but I am arguing that we are not to do so if we really believe in the work of the Holy Spirit. We are to present the truth, trusting to the Holy Spirit to apply it. I would urge, therefore, that on scriptural grounds we must not of set purpose decide to employ techniques. That is to go over on to the side of, and to the use of, psychology.

Another important principle is that in presenting the Christian gospel we must never, in the first place, make a *direct* approach either to the emotions or to the will. The emotions and the will should always be influenced through the mind. Truth is intended to come to the *mind*. The normal course is for the emotions and the will to be affected by the truth after it has first entered and gripped the mind. It seems to me that this is a principle of Holy Scripture. The approach to the emotions and the will should be *indirect*. Still less should we ever bring any *pressure* to bear upon either the emotions or the will. We are to plead with men but never to bring pressure. We are to beseech, but we are never to browbeat. This, it seems to me, is a vital distinction which every preacher and missioner must always bear in mind.

I would affirm that much of the modern approach to evangelism, with its techniques and methods, is unnecessary if we *really* believe in the doctrine of the Holy Spirit and His application of God's message. I suggest that our techniques and mechanics actually divert the attention of people from *the truth of the message* to some lower, particular, immediate, and practical action which may have the opposite effect from what is intended. The point I am making is that it is surely our business to avoid anything which produces a merely *psychological* condition rather than a *spiritual* condition.

In other words, I am suggesting that this book by Dr Sargant, which has focused attention on the psychological element which exists in religious work as well as in politics, does bring us face to face with the questionable nature of the methods used by some well-meaning people and warns of the danger which is inherent in the increasing tendency to employ various planned 'techniques'. To that extent we can be grateful to him, and nothing would be worse than to dismiss his entire statement without facing up to our own mistakes. While regretting and deploring Dr Sargant's serious misunderstanding of vital aspects of the Christian faith and certain historical events, we can at the same time make use of the thesis which he has put before us so plainly in order to examine and improve our own outlook and practice.

Finally, we must face a radical question: Are we to be primarily and almost exclusively concerned with evangelistic campaigns and with the attempt to make them more efficient by new methods and techniques? Or should we not concentrate more, as the church has done throughout the centuries, upon praying for, and laying the basis of Christian instruction for, revival as it is described in the Bible? Should we not pray with greater earnestness for a visitation of God's Holy Spirit both upon the church and upon ourselves as individuals? The biblical rule has not been abrogated even in this twentieth century and still is 'Not by might, nor by power, but by my Spirit, saith the Lord of hosts' (Zech. 4:6).

Seven

*

Remembering the Reformation[1]

*

Mr Chairman and Christian friends, I would like to say immediately that I regard this occasion as one of the greatest privileges that has ever fallen to my lot. I prize the invitation that I received from the friends of the Free Church of Scotland very highly indeed. This is an historic occasion. We are doing something that I am certain is well-pleasing in the sight of God and which I trust, under God's benediction and blessing, will prove to be of value and of benefit to our souls and, let us hope, to the whole cause of God in this nation and in all nations at this present time. I always say, when I have the pleasure of coming to Scotland, that I am interested to come, not only because of my concern about the gospel, but because of the deep feeling of admiration which I have always had within me for you as a nation and as a people. And there is certainly nothing in your long history which is more glorious and more remarkable than that great movement of God which took place four hundred years ago, and which we are met tonight to commemorate. Therefore, for every reason I was very ready to come here to Edinburgh once more.

Now our Chairman has very rightly put to you one of the questions that I also felt should be put, because it is a question which does arise, apparently, in the minds of some people. Why, they wonder, should we consider the Reformation in Scotland at all at a time like this, with the world as it is and with the multiplicity of problems that are pressing in upon us on all sides? Why turn back and consider what happened four hundred years ago?

As I understand it there are two main objections to doing this. The first is a general objection to looking back, a feeling that the past has

[1]The report of an address given in the Usher Hall, Edinburgh on 5 April, 1960, in commemoration of the Reformation in Scotland.

nothing to teach us. For, after all, we are the people of the twentieth century, the people who have split the atom, who are encompassing all knowledge and have advanced to such giddy heights as our forefathers could not even have imagined. Why then should we, of all people, look back, and especially look back four hundred years? The whole climate of opinion today, and indeed during the last hundred years, has been governed by the evolutionary theory and hypothesis, which holds that man advances from age to age and that the present is always better than the past; this whole climate of thought is inimical to the idea of looking back and learning from previous history. That is one objection.

The other objection is that we should not hold a meeting like this because the Reformation was a tragedy. Now this is a view which is gaining currency very rapidly at present. We are told that what we should be considering today is unity, and that if we spend our time considering the disruption and division in the church which took place four hundred years ago, we are doing something sinful. There is, alas, an increasing body of opinion in Protestant circles which is saying, openly and unashamedly, that the Protestant Reformation was a tragedy and that it is our business to forget it as soon as we can and to do everything possible to heal the breach, so that we shall be one again with the Church of Rome, and there shall be one great world church.

Those are the two commonest objections, as I see the situation, which are brought against what we are engaged in doing this evening. Why then are we doing it? How do we justify a gathering such as this, and the other gatherings that are to follow? Well, let me say quite frankly that there are wrong and false ways of doing what we are doing here tonight. There are people who are interested in the past merely in an antiquarian sense; history happens to be their great interest in life. They like delving into the past and reading about the past, not that they are interested in it in any kind of active philosophic or religious sense; they just like burrowing in ancient history. There are people who do this in other realms; some like collecting old furniture, and the glory of anything to them is that it is old. They are not interested in a chair from the standpoint of something to sit upon; what they are interested in is the age of the chair. Now that is antiquarianism, and it is possible for us, of course, to be governed by a purely antiquarian or historical motive. But there is no value in that; the times in which we are living are too urgent and too desperate for us to indulge a mere antiquarian spirit.

Now the last time I stood at this desk, I said that I could not speak without having a text. Well, I am still the same. And it seemed to me that there were two texts which would not be inappropriate for this meeting, and for our consideration this evening. There is a right way and a wrong way of viewing a great event like the Reformation and the great men who took part in it. The first, the right way, we are told of in the Epistle to the Hebrews, chapter 13, verses 7 and 8: 'Remember them which have the rule over you, who have spoken unto you the word of God: whose faith follow, considering the end of [or, the outcome of, their lives and of] their conversation. Jesus Christ the same yesterday, and today, and for ever.' That is the right way to do it; we look at these men in order that we may learn from them, and imitate and emulate their example.

But there is a wrong way of doing this, and we find it in Matthew, chapter 23, verses 29–32. These are terrible and terrifying words: 'Woe unto you, scribes and Pharisees, hypocrites! because ye build the tombs of the prophets, and garnish the sepulchres of the righteous, and say, If we had been in the days of our fathers, we would not have been partakers with them in the blood of the prophets. Wherefore ye be witnesses unto yourselves, that ye are the children of them which killed the prophets. Fill ye up then the measure of your fathers. Ye serpents, ye generation of vipers, how can ye escape the damnation of hell?'

Now those are the words of the Lord Jesus Christ and He was addressing His own generation, His own contemporaries. He said, in effect, You are paying great tribute to the memory of the prophets; you are looking after and garnishing their sepulchres and you are saying what great men they were – How noble, how wonderful, we must keep their memory alive – and you say what a terrible thing it was that your forefathers should have put these men to death. If you had been alive then, you maintain, you would not have joined them in those wicked deeds; you would have listened to the prophets, you would have followed them. You hypocrites, says our Lord, you would have done nothing of the sort.

How, then, does He prove it? Well, He does it in this way. He tests their sincerity by discovering what their attitude is at the present to the successors to the prophets. What is their reaction to the people who are still preaching the same message as the prophets? He says, You say that you are admirers of the prophets and yet you are persecuting and trying to compass the death of a man like myself who is the modern representative of the same message, and the same school of prophecy. Ah, says our Lord, it is one thing to look back and to praise famous men, but that can be sheer hypocrisy. The test of our sincerity this evening is this: What do we feel about, and how are we treating, the men who, today, are preaching the same message as was preached by John Knox and his fellow reformers?

So, you see, this meeting is a very important one for us. You cannot do a thing like this without examining yourself, without coming under scrutiny. Our presence indicates that we are admirers of these great prophets of God, but I wonder whether we are in reality? So it is a good thing, it seems to me, that we should come together, if only so that we can examine ourselves in the light of this word of our Lord and Saviour Jesus Christ.

Why then are we doing this? How do we justify our action? Our Chairman has already dealt with one of the answers. The fact is that you simply cannot understand the history of Scotland unless you know something about the Protestant Reformation. It is the key to the understanding of the history of your great country in the last four hundred years. What Scotland has been she has been, directly and unmistakably, as a result of the Protestant Reformation. So if we had no other reason, that is enough.

You are a nation of people famous for education, for knowledge, for culture. Everybody knows that. The peasants of Scotland were cultured and able, intelligent and intellectual people. What accounts for that? It is not merely a matter of blood, because before the Protestant Reformation they were woefully ignorant, backward, and illiterate. What is it, then, that has caused your nation to be regarded, perhaps by the whole world, as supreme in her interest in education and the pursuit of knowledge? The answer is, the Protestant Reformation. So, apart from any religious considerations we have this mighty and all-important consideration.

And then I want to add a third reason. Why are we considering the Reformation of four hundred years ago? Well, if I am to be quite honest, I must confess that this is my main reason: because of the state of affairs today. I am primarily a preacher, not a lecturer, not a historian, very fond of history, but not an antiquary, as I have said. No, I am interested in this because, as a preacher I am concerned about the present state of affairs which is increasingly approximating to the state of affairs that obtained before the Protestant Reformation. You are aware of the state of the morals of this country, and of Great Britain in general, before the Reformation: vice, immorality, sin were rampant. My friends, it is rapidly becoming the same again! There is a woeful moral and social declension. We are being surrounded by the very problems that were most obvious before the Reformation took place. The moral state of the country, these urgent social problems, juvenile delinquency, drunkenness, theft and robbery, vice and crime, they are coming back as they were before the Protestant Reformation.

But it is not only a matter of moral and of social problems. What of the state of the church? What of the kirk? What about the numbers who are members of the church? How many even attend? We are going back to the pre-Reformation position. What about the authority of the church? What about the state of doctrine in the church? Before the Reformation, there was confusion. Is there anything more characteristic of the church today than doctrinal confusion, doctrinal indifference – a lack of concern and a lack of interest? And then perhaps the most alarming of all, the increase in the power, influence, and numbers of the Church of Rome, and the romanizing tendencies that are coming into and being extolled in the Protestant church! There is no question about this. This is a mere matter of fact and observation. There is an obvious tendency to return to the pre-Reformation position; ceremonies and ritual are increasing and the Word of God is being preached less and less, sermons are becoming shorter and shorter. There is an indifference to true doctrine, a loss of authority, and a consequent declension, even in the matter of numbers. I wonder, Christian people, whether I am exaggerating when I suggest that at the present time we are really engaged in a great struggle for the very life of the Christian church, for the essence of the Christian faith? As I see the situation, it is nothing less alarming than that. We are fighting for an heritage, for the very things that were gained by that tremendous movement of four hundred years ago. That to me is the most urgent reason. We cannot afford the luxury of being merely antiquarian; we should be concerned about this because of the state of affairs in which we find ourselves.

But, somebody might say, why go back for the answer to that? Why don't you do what is being done everywhere else, and in every other realm of life? I read an article in a supposedly evangelical weekly paper not so long ago, which said, 'Why does the Church stand still?' The man went on to say something like this: 'I see in business and everywhere else that people are making experiments, they are employing the backroom boys and the experimenters, and they are trying to discover new methods, new machinery, new everything – Why doesn't the Church do this? The Church always seems to be looking back.' They regard that as something which is wrong. Now the answer to that, as I see it, can be put like this. I am not at all sure but that the greatest of all the lessons which the Protestant Reformation has to teach us is just this, that the secret of success in the realm of the church and of the things of the Spirit, is to go back. What happened in essence four hundred years ago was that these men went back to the first century, they went back to the New Testament, they went back to the Bible. Suddenly they were awakened to this message and they just went back to it. There is nothing more interesting, as one reads the stories of Luther and of Calvin, than to notice the way in which they kept on discovering that they had been rediscovering what Augustine had already discovered, and which had been forgotten. Indeed I suggest that perhaps the greatest of all the lessons of the Protestant Reformation is that the way of recovery is always to go back, back to the primitive pattern, to the origin, to the norm and the standard which are to be found alone in the New Testament. That is exactly what happened four hundred years ago. These men went back to the beginning, and they tried to establish a church conforming to the New Testament pattern. And so, let us be guided by them, as we look at them this evening and as we try to garner certain lessons from them.

What, then, happened four hundred years ago? Well, whatever your views may be, you will have to admit that it was one of the most remarkable historical phenomena that have ever taken place. It is no exaggeration to say that the Protestant Reformation changed and turned the entire course of history, not only the history of the church but secular history too. There is no question about this, and it is granted by historians, that the Reformation laid the foundation of the whole democratic view of government. That is a fact of history. All the nations of the world at present are looking to the United States of America. How did the United States of America ever come into being? It would never have come into being were it not for the Protestant Reformation. The Puritan fathers who crossed the Atlantic in the *Mayflower* were men who were products of the Reformation, and it was the desire not only for religious liberty, but also for democratic liberty, that drove them to face the hazards of crossing the Atlantic at that time and to establish a new life, a new state, and a new system of government in the New World. You cannot explain the story of the United States of America except in terms of the Protestant Reformation.

The Reformation gave life-blood to the whole democratic notion in the realm of politics, and the consequences, as judged from a social and from a moral standpoint, simply baffle description. This country of yours, from being a dissolute, drunken, and illiterate country, became famous throughout the world for her sober, righteous, able, intelligent people. And it was the Protestant Reformation that led to it.

My difficulty on this occasion is to know what not to say. The theme as you see, is endless. But let me interject this before I proceed, for it is one of the greatest lessons which need to be learned at the present time. Everybody today is aware of the moral problem, and they are trying to deal with it along various lines: acts of Parliament, prison reform, psychiatric treatment in the prisons, and the various other expedients which are advocated. But they do not seem to be very successful, do they? Why not? For the reason that you cannot have morality without godliness. The tragedy of the last hundred years has been due to the fallacy of imagining that you could shed Christian doctrine but hold on to Christian ethics. That has been the controlling notion. But it cannot be done. There is one verse in Paul's Epistle to the Romans, chapter 1, verse 18, which should have put us right on this once and for ever: 'For the wrath of God is revealed from heaven against all ungodliness and unrighteousness of men.' You notice the order – ungodliness first, unrighteousness second. If you do not have a godly people, you will never have a righteous people. You cannot have righteousness without godliness. And the Protestant Reformation is the most striking proof of this that the world has ever known. Once you have godliness, righteousness and morality follow. We are today trying to have morality, righteousness, and a good ethical conception without the godliness, and the facts are proving, before our eyes, that it simply cannot be done. So if you are a sociologist in this meeting, if you are a politician, if you are just interested in the moral problem, then I say to you, go and read the history of the Reformation. There you will see that the only way to exalt your nation, is to put godliness first, and righteousness will then follow.

As I have said, the Reformation was not purely a religious movement. It was a general movement and it was witnessed, not only in Scotland, but in England, France, Holland, Switzerland, Germany, and various other countries on the Continent. It was a great movement of the Spirit of God in which your country was given her share and portion.

Well, what do we find as we look at it? I can only give you some headings. If you want the details, I commend to you very warmly and happily the book by our Chairman, which has already been mentioned to you. It gives a clear, succinct account of what actually happened, and it is a thrilling and moving story. Buy it, read it, and digest it. He gives you the general setting and shows you the peculiar features in Scotland. The one excellence, of course, which we who come from south of the border have to grant you is that your reformation was a pure reformation. In Scotland, there was no question of a king trying to get out of his matrimonial difficulties and entanglements. You were free of that. It was a pure reformation and the result was, I believe, that you had a purer church. But, generally speaking, what happened here was the same as what happened in most other countries.

What do we see then? Well, of course the first thing that attracts our attention is the men, the men that God used. Look at them, Patrick Hamilton, George Wishart, John Knox, Andrew Melville, John Welsh, and many others. Here are men worthy of the name! Heroic, big men, men of granite! Our Chairman need not apologize for being a history worshipper, I am a hero worshipper! Think what you like of me, I like to look at and to read of a big man! In an age of pygmies such as this, it is a good thing to read about great men. We are all so much alike and of the same size, but here were giants in the land, able men, men of gigantic intellect, men on a big scale in the realm of mind and logic and reason. Then look at their zeal, look at their courage! I frankly am an admirer of a man who can make a queen tremble! These are the things that strike us at once about these men. But then I suppose that the most notable thing of all was the fact of the burning conviction that dwelt within them; this is what made them the men they were.

What were these convictions? We have already been referred to some of them; let me add some others. What did these men believe? What did they teach? What were their characteristics? Here is the first, obviously: their belief in the authority of this Book. The pre-

Reformation church was moribund and asleep under a scholastic philosophy that displayed great cleverness, with intellectual and critical acumen. But it was all in the clouds and dealt with vague generalities and concepts, while the people were kept in utter ignorance. The men who did the teaching and the lecturing argued about philosophic concepts, comparing this view with that, and indulging in refinements and minutiae. But, in contrast, the great thing that stands out about the reformers was that they were men who went back to the Bible. They said, nothing matters but this. This, they said, is the Word of God in the Old Testament and in the New Testament, this is not theory, supposition, or speculation, this is the living God speaking to men: He gave His Word to the prophets, they wrote it; He gave it to the apostles, they recorded it; and here it is for us. Here we have something which is in a category of its own, the living Word of God speaking to men about Himself, about men, about the only way they can come together and live together. They stood for the authority of the Bible, not for scholastic philosophy.

You see, my friends, the importance of looking back at the Reformation. Is not this the greatest need at the present time, to come back to this Word of God? Is this authoritative or is it not? Am I in any position to stand above this Book, and look down at it and say, That is not true, this or that must come out? Is my mind, is my twentieth-century knowledge the ultimate judge and decider as to the veracity of this teaching? It is since the time, a hundred years ago, when that notion began to creep in, that the church has been going down. But the reformers based everything upon this Book as the Word of God to man, which they were not to judge but to preach. And you and I have got to return to this. There can be no health, there can be no authority in the church, until she comes back to this basic authority. It is idle to talk about this as the Word of God in a sense which still allows you and me to decide that certain things in it are not true! The Book hangs together, the Lord Jesus Christ believed the Old Testament. After His resurrection, He took His disciples through the books of Moses and the Psalms and the prophets. He says, I am there, let me show you myself there. Read them, why have you not understood them? Why have you not believed all that the prophets have written? That was their trouble, it has always been the trouble of the church in periods of declension, and we must come back to the Protestant reformers' position and recognize that we have no authority apart from the authority of this Word of God.

In this Book they found also the mighty doctrine of the sovere[ignty] of God, which taught them not to approach their problems ___ __ subjective manner as you and I are prone to do. Their concern was not, how can I get a bit of help, how can I get some physical healing, how can I get guidance, how can I get happiness and peace, how can I get a friend who will help me in my loneliness? No, they saw themselves before this almighty, sovereign God and the one question was, How can a man be just with God? They bowed before Him! They were godly men; they were God-fearing men. God was at the centre of their thoughts, the controller of their activities and their lives. The sovereignty of God! They did not talk much about free will, as I read them, but they knew that God was over all, and He was to be worshipped and to be feared.

And then there was the great central doctrine of the Lord Jesus Christ and His perfect finished work. They did not feel sorry for Him as they looked at Him on the cross, they saw Him bearing their sins, they saw God laying on Him the iniquity of us all, they saw Him as a substitute, they saw God putting our guilt upon Him and punishing Him for our guilt. The substitutionary atonement! They preached it; it was everything to them. The finished, complete, atoning work of Christ. They gloried in it! And that in turn, of course, led to the great pivotal central doctrine of which we were reminded in the reading, justification by faith only.

Now, I may be mistaken, but as I see the contemporary situation, the greatest battle of all, perhaps, at the moment is the battle for justification by faith only. 'Works' have come back! I was reading a religious newspaper a fortnight ago which carried the words 'Saint Gilbert' as a heading to a paragraph. The writer of the paragraph was of the opinion that this man whose Christian name was Gilbert was undoubtedly a saint and we must accord him the name and the dignity of a saint. Then he went on to say this: 'Of course I know that in actual practice he called himself a rationalistic agnostic.' Though this man Gilbert called himself a rationalistic agnostic, a so-called Christian paper says that nevertheless he was a saint. And they justified their assertion on the basis of his life: he was a good man, he was a noble man, he had high and exalted ideals, he gave much of his life to the propagation of the League of Nations union, and to uplift the human race, he tried to put an end to war, he made protests against war; therefore, the argument goes, though he denied the being of God, though he did not regard the Bible as the Word of God, though he did not believe in the Lord Jesus Christ, nevertheless, he was a saint. What makes a man a saint? Oh, his works, his life!

We are confronted again by a generation that no longer believes in justification by faith only we are told that 'the greatest Christian' of this century is a man whose belief in the deity of Christ, to put it at its mildest, was very doubtful, who certainly did not believe in the atonement, whose creed seemed to be what he calls 'reverence for life' – yet we are told that he is the greatest saint and Christian of the twentieth century! Look at his life, they say, look what he has done; he gave up a great profession and he has gone out to Central Africa, look what he has suffered, look what he has given up, he might be wealthy, he might be prosperous, but he is living like Christ, he is imitating Christ, he has done what Christ has done! You see, it does not matter what you believe. According to this teaching, it is the life that makes a man a Christian. If you live a good life, if you live a life of sacrifice, if you try to uplift the race, if you try to imitate Christ, you are a Christian, though you deny the deity of Christ, though you deny His atonement, though you deny the miraculous and the supernatural, the resurrection and many other things, nevertheless you are a great Christian and a great saint!

My friends, John Knox and other men risked their lives, day after day, just to deny such teaching and to assert that a man is justified by faith alone without works, that a man is saved not by what he does but by the grace of God, that God justifies the ungodly, that God reconciles sinners unto Himself. It is all of God and none of man, and works must not be allowed to intrude themselves at any point or in any shape or form. The battle for justification by faith only is on again! And if this meeting and these celebrations do nothing else, I trust that they will lead us to a rediscovery of the absolute centrality of the doctrine of justification by faith only.

These reformers were also men who believed in possessing assurance of salvation. Now I am somewhat more controversial, am I not? Do you believe in assurance of salvation as the Protestant reformers did? I have known people who have paid great tribute to the memory of John Knox and others, who deny the possibility of assurance and regard it as almost an impertinence. I know that the Westminster Confession of Faith is careful to say that a man can be saved without assurance of salvation, that saving faith and assured faith are not the same thing, and I am happy to agree with the Westminster Confession. But let me say this: The Protestant reformers were so against the Roman Catholic Church which teaches that a man can never be certain, that they did not draw that distinction, and they would have been equally against a modern movement, which likes to claim itself as reformed, but which denies the possibility of assurance. These Protestant reformers said that a man was not truly saved unless he had assurance! Without going all the way with them, we must notice this, that whenever the church is powerful and mighty and authoritative, her preachers and ministers have always been men who speak out of the full assurance of faith, and know in whom they have believed. It was for that reason that the martyrs could smile in the face of kings and queens, and regents and local potentates, and go gladly to the stake; they knew that from the stake they would wake in heaven and in glory and see Him face to face! They rejoiced in the assurance of salvation!

Then, to make my little list complete, I must add a few more of their main convictions. They were men who believed in the universal priesthood of believers. They held to simplicity of worship. Away with idols, away with vestments, away with forms and ceremonies. A simple service! And not least important, a pure church. The three marks of the church that they taught are these: it is a place where the pure gospel is preached, where the sacraments are administered, and where discipline is exercised. A pure church! No room for all and sundry; no room for men who are doubtful, no room for men who show by their lives that they love the world and its ways and its sin. No! A pure church, because the church is the body of Christ! Those were their convictions, those were the doctrines which they held.

The other thing I want to note about them is this: their power in prayer. We must not think of these reformers only in terms of doctrine, though we must start with that. This other thing was equally notable and remarkable about them, they were men of prayer. Did not Mary Queen of Scots fear the prayers of John Knox more than she feared the English soldiers? Of course she did! Why? Because he was a powerful man in prayer. Have you read about the prayer life of John Welsh, the son-in-law of John Knox? There was a man who spent nights in prayer; his wife would wake up at night and find him on his knees almost stone-cold. What was he doing? Praying for the townspeople to whom he was ministering, asking for power, asking for authority. These men, every one of them, were men of great prayerfulness; they spent hours of their lives in prayer, knowing that in and of themselves, though their doctrines were right and orthodox, they could do nothing. I like to hear that story of another of these men, Robert Bruce. We read that when he was praying with some ministers one day, he felt they were lifeless and dull. He cried to God that the Holy Spirit might come down upon them but nothing seemed to be happening. Then as he began banging on the table they were all conscious of God coming among them and thereafter men spoke of Bruce as one who knocked down the Holy Ghost among them! Is not that the kind of man we need today? Where is the power, where is the influence, where is the authority? These reformers were only men like us but they knew these things. They were men of prayer, who lived in the presence of God and who knew they could do nothing without Him.

This brings me to the last point: their preaching. We have been reminded that the reformers re-introduced preaching and that they put preaching at the centre instead of ceremonies and sacraments. Yes, but let us remember that there is preaching and preaching. Merely to speak for twenty minutes is not necessarily preaching. Though you may have taken a text and divided it up very cleverly, it is not necessarily preaching. Oh, there is preaching and preaching! What is the test of preaching? I will tell you; it is power! 'Our gospel came unto you', says the apostle to the Thessalonians in the First Epistle, chapter 1, verse 5, 'not in word only, but also in power, and in the Holy Ghost, and in much assurance'. Who had the assurance? The preacher! He knew something was happening, he knew God was using him, he knew that he was the vehicle and channel of divine and eternal grace. 'Much assurance'! And that was the sort of preaching you had from the Protestant reformers. It was prophetic preaching, not priestly preaching. What we have today, is what I would call priestly. Very nice, very quiet, very ornate, sentences turned beautifully, prepared carefully. That is not prophetic preaching! No, what is needed is authority! Do you think that John Knox could make Mary Queen of Scots tremble with some polished little essay? These men did not write their sermons with an eye to publication in books, they were preaching to the congregation in front of them, anxious and desirous to do something, to effect something, to change people. It was authoritative. It was proclamation, it was declaration.

Is it surprising that the church is as she is today; we no longer believe in preaching, do we? You used to have long sermons here in Scotland. I am told you do not like them now, and woe unto the preacher who goes on beyond twenty minutes! I was reading in the train yesterday about the first Principal of Emmanuel College in Cambridge, Chadderton, who lived towards the end of the sixteenth century. He was preaching on one occasion, and after he had preached for two hours he stopped and apologized to the people: 'Please forgive me, I have got beyond myself, I must not go on like this.' And the congregation shouted out, 'For God's sake go on!' You know I am beginning to think that I shall not have preached until something like that happens to me. Prophetic! Authoritative! Proclamation! Declaration! Their view of preaching was certainly not our modern idea of having a friendly discussion. Have you noticed how we have less and less preaching on the wireless programmes? Instead we have discussion. Let the young people say what they think, let us win them by letting them speak; and we will have a friendly chat and discussion, we will show them that after all we are nice, decent fellows, there is nothing nasty about us; and we will gain their confidence; they must not think that we are unlike them! If you are on the television you start by producing your pipe and lighting it; you show that you are like the people, one of them! Was John Knox like one of the people? Was John Knox a matey, friendly, nice chap with whom you could have a discussion? Thank God he was not! Scotland would not be what she has been for four centuries if John Knox had been that kind of man. Can you imagine John Knox having tips and training as to how he should conduct and comport himself before the television camera, so as to be nice and polite and friendly and gentlemanly? Thank God prophets are made of stronger stuff! An Amos, a Jeremiah, a John the Baptist in the wilderness in his camel-hair shirt – a strange fellow, a lunatic, they said, but they went and listened to him because he was a curiosity, and as they listened they were convicted! Such a man was John Knox, with the fire of God in his bones and in his belly! He preached as they all preached, with fire and power, alarming sermons, convicting sermons, humbling sermons, converting sermons, and the face of Scotland was changed: the greatest epoch in your long history had begun!

There, as I see it, were the great and outstanding characteristics of these men. What was the secret of it all? It was not the men, as I have been trying to show you, great as they were. It was God! God in His sovereignty raising up His men. And God knows what He is doing. Look at the gifts He gave John Knox as a natural man; look at the mind He gave to Calvin and the training He gave him as a lawyer to prepare him for his great work; look at Martin Luther, that volcano of a man; God preparing His men in the different nations and countries. Of course, even before He produced them, He had been preparing the way for them. Let us never forget John Wyclif and John Hus; let us never forget the Waldensians and all the martyrs of these terrible Middle Ages! God was preparing the way; He sent His men at the right moment, and the mighty events followed.

Shall I try to draw certain lessons for ourselves? The conclusion of all this is that righteousness, and righteousness alone, exalts a nation, and there is no righteousness without a preceding godliness. The times are cruel; the world is in a desperate plight; there is an appalling moral breakdown before our eyes. Marriage is breaking down, home life disappearing, little children not knowing home and loving parents. It is a tragedy! Can nothing be done? Is there no hope? To me the main message of the Protestant Reformation of four hundred years ago is to point us to the one and only hope. Things were bad in Scotland when God called John Knox and sent him out as a burning flame and the others with him. Our position is not hopeless, for God remains, and with God nothing shall be impossible! The conditions could not have been worse than they were immediately before the Reformation; yet in spite of that the change came. Why? Because God was there and God sent it. So the only question we need ask is the old question of Elisha face to face with his problem: 'Where is the Lord God of Elijah?' And I want to ask that question this evening: Where is the God of John Knox? Our meeting will have been in vain if we do not ask that question. If we stop with John Knox it is not enough; the question is, Where is the God of John Knox, He who can give us the power, the authority, the might, the courage, and everything we need, where is He? How can we find Him? I suggest to you that the answer is to be found again in the Epistle to the Hebrews, in chapter 4 this time, in verses 14 to 16. They seem to me not inappropriate as I end this evening.

How can we find this God? Here is the answer: 'Let us hold fast the confession.' It does not actually mean there, of course, the Westminster Confession, though in reality it does! Hold fast the old Scots Confession. You will never find the God of John Knox without that. 'Seeing then that we have a great high priest that is passed into the heavens, Jesus the Son of God, let us hold fast the confession'. What is the confession? It is the confession about 'Jesus the Son of God', our great high priest; the Scots Confession, the Westminster

Confession, the faith of these Fathers. We must have it because without it, who dares go into the presence of God? As it is put there in Hebrews 4:16: 'Let us therefore come boldly unto the throne of grace.' What is the 'therefore'? The knowledge that we possess, that we have got this great high priest that has passed through the heavens, Jesus the Son of God, and that He is 'touched with the feeling of our infirmities, but was in all points tempted like as we are, yet without sin'. Where is the God of Elijah? How can we find Him? How can we receive the power that we need? We must go back to the confession, go back to the faith, go back to the Word, believe its truths, and in the light of it go with boldness, confidence, assurance, to the throne of grace; to obtain mercy and find grace to help in time of need. We are living in an appalling time of need, sin and evil rampant; the whole world is quaking and shaking. Is the end upon us? The times are alarming – 'time of need'. The one thing necessary is to find this God, and there seated at His right hand, the One who has been in this world and knows all about it, has seen its shame, its sin, its vileness, its rottenness face to face; friend of publicans and sinners, a Man who knew the hatred and the animosity of the Pharisees, scribes and Sadducees, the doctors of the law, and Pontius Pilate. The whole world was against Him, and yet He triumphed through it all; He is there, and He is our representative and high priest. Believe in Him, hold fast to the confession. Let us go in His name with boldness unto the throne of grace, and as certainly as we do so we shall obtain the mercy that we need for our sinfulness and unfaithfulness, and we shall be given the grace to help us in our time of need, in our day and generation. The God of John Knox is still there, and still the same, and thank God, Jesus Christ is the same yesterday, today, and for ever. Oh, that we might know the God of John Knox!

Eight

*

How Can We See a Return to the Bible?[1]

*

As we are met together on this great and interesting occasion, it seems to me that there are two main things which we need to do. The first is to remember and commemorate the printing of the Authorized Version of the Bible in 1611. The second great purpose of this gathering is to call back the people of this nation to the Bible.

I will take the second purpose first. Why should we come together in this manner and call the men and women of this country back to the consideration of this book which we call the Bible? There are many answers that can be given to that question. But what I regard as the most urgent reason of all is simply that the conditions in which we find ourselves at this very moment are, in the main, due to the departure of men and women from the Word of God.

This is true, in the first place, with regard to the Christian church herself. We are here, I take it, to be honest and to search ourselves. These are no days for coming together just to enjoy ourselves. The times are evil; the times are out of joint. I trust we are all here animated with a desire to do something, and to discover what we have to do, in order to deal with the appalling conditions which prevail round and about us. I say that the condition of the church herself is due to her departure from the authority of the Bible. The Christian church in this country is in a deplorable condition. The statistics tell us that only some ten per cent of the people of this country claim to be even nominally Christian; ninety per cent of the population is entirely outside the church! It was not always thus.

[1]An address given at the National Bible Rally, organized by the Evangelical Alliance, at the Royal Albert Hall on 24 October, 1961.

What has been the cause of this; why the difference in the condition of our churches today as distinct from what they were a hundred years ago? I know there are many explanations put forward. People point to the world wars, and I do not dispute that they did contribute to it. They also point to the wireless, the television, the motor car, and all these other agencies that are militating against the work and the appeal of the church. I am prepared to grant to such causes a certain amount of influence, but when you come to examine this question seriously and soberly, there is only one adequate answer for the fact that the masses of the people are no longer attending places of worship. It is due to the loss of the authority of the Scriptures. And to what is that due? Without question, it was the devastating Higher Critical movement, so called, which began in Germany around the 1830s, and which subsequently came and infected this and most other countries. This meant the substitution of the mind of men and of what is called 'philosophy', for divine revelation. It was claimed that this Book must be regarded as every other book, and examined in the same way as every other book is examined. Added to this, there was the Darwinian teaching which came in 1859 and immediately became so popular. Then psychology played its part. And in these ways men began to look at this Book, not as they had hitherto looked on it throughout the centuries as the Word of the living God, but as a human word. They began to talk more and more, not about the power of the Holy Spirit in the preacher, but of his scholarship, of his knowledge of philosophy and the sciences, and of psychology. Human reason was put upon the throne, and the very pulpits of the church herself were engaged in undermining the faith of the masses of the people in this Book as the Word of God.

It is time we face these facts. We are trying to do all we can to improve the existing condition. But, if this is the major problem, is it not obvious that nothing except a rectifying of *this* can deal with the situation that confronts us? There is no question about the reason for what has happened. Men began to talk about 'the assured results' of scholarship and of criticism, and the masses of the people believed these 'great experts'. Tonight, of course, we know that 'the assured results' are not quite as assured, and increasingly, we find the scholars having to abandon the positions which were put with such dogmatism before the people at the end of the last century and in the first fourteen years or so of this century. Not only so, we know that liberalism, the modernism, so called, which was so popular up until

1914, has become utterly outmoded. The First World War shattered it; the confidence in man and in man's own ability ended with that war. The old liberalism which emptied our churches is as dead as the dodo and utterly discredited.

Unfortunately, that does not mean that people have returned to the Book. They seem to be prepared to do everything except come back to the Book and submit themselves to it. Some of them are cleverly trying to say that you must take the message of the Book, but not the facts. Others say that God speaks in the Book through great acts, but not in propositions and not in teaching. In other words, they still will not submit to the authority of the Book. It is they who decide what to accept and what to reject, what to believe and what not to believe, so that though the old liberalism and modernism are utterly discredited, the position in reality is no better. I am here to assert that this is one of the main causes, if not indeed the main cause, of the decline of the Christian church.

There is one other cause of present conditions which I add with regret, and that is statements made by Christian ministers from Christian pulpits, which are nothing but blank contradictions of the basic teaching of the Bible. We hear the ridicule that is poured on the doctrine of sin, the rejection of the miracles and of the precious blood of Christ, and, to cap it all, recently, a statement to the effect that we can 'expect to meet atheists in heaven'. If this is true, if we are to expect to meet atheists in heaven, if a man who does not believe in God can go to heaven, why should we ask him to believe in the Bible? Why should we have a Christian church at all? If an atheist who lives a good life is to go to heaven, there is no need for the Christian church and all the organizations, and there is absolutely no need for the Scriptures. The masses of the people are outside the Christian church because they have been given the impression that the Christian church herself no longer believes in the Book as authoritative.

I say that this is the explanation not only of the state of the church, but also of the world in general, and conditions in general in this country. Look at our industrial problems which are so acute at the moment and so dangerous. Look at our social and moral problems, to which reference has already been made. What are these due to? It seems to me that there is only one adequate answer: it is that the whole notion and concept of law and of duty, of punishment and retribution, has gone. As men have ceased to believe in the Bible, they have ceased to believe in law, in justice, and in righteousness. So the whole notion of punishment and retribution is derided and dismissed. Indeed, I am afraid we can go a step further and say that one of the major problems in this country tonight is this, that the whole idea of responsibility is disappearing rapidly. We are approaching a state in which a prisoner standing in the dock in a law court will be examined in terms of disease, or what they call 'diminished responsibility', rather than in terms of crime. The whole notion of crime is going out. A man behaves as he does, it is argued, because of the odd combination of the ductless glands in his body, or because he was not well at a particular moment. Today it is a case of diminished responsibility; there is no such thing as a crime, there is no such thing as a criminal; it is all a problem for the doctors. So with the disappearance of the law of God goes the disappearance of belief in any law, in the notions of punishment, correction, and discipline. Thus – and I could elaborate so easily – the state of the church and of the world in general is due to this one major cause: there is no authority, no ultimate sanction, to which men feel compelled to bow.

If that is so, the question that should be uppermost in our minds here tonight is how to get the people back to the Bible? How can we bring them back again to this Book? There are many suggestions put before us on this subject, and I want to look at one in particular. We have been reminded tonight, and very rightly, of the part that this Book has played in the history of the life of this country. There is no question about it; the true greatness of this country was laid down and established, whatever you may think of it politically, in the Cromwellian period and by men in the House of Commons who believed this to be the Word of the living God. You do not understand the history of this country if you do not know something about the influence of this Book.

However, I do not hesitate to say tonight that it is not the appeal to history that is needed. There are people who are so ignorant that they are not interested in the past, or in the past glory of this country. They think they have got something better. Others – and the statesmen particularly are very fond of doing this – talk about the Bible and praise it as literature. Of course, as literature, it is incomparable, but merely to tell people that this is 'great literature' is not going to make them submit to its message. Look, they say, at the influence it has had upon the great masterpieces of our literature. Perfectly true, but the average man is not interested in that sort of thing; he is out for his bingo, or whatever he may chance to call his pleasure. That is not the way to bring them back.

What else can we do? Well, there are many who are engaged in a kind of defence of the Bible. That is sometimes called apologetics. I am not here to say a word against it. Archaeology comes into that department, and we thank God for it and for Professor Wiseman as one of the distinguished people who are practising in this realm. But that is not going to be enough either. I agree with what Spurgeon said about this: 'You don't defend a lion, you just let him loose', and the same is true of the Bible. Apologetics are all right as far as they go and they can be helpful in strengthening the faith, but we are living in a period when we need something much more. Still less must we fall back upon any tendency to accommodate the teaching of the Bible to modern learning and to modern views. Sometimes, I fear, I see a tendency to do that, even among evangelical people. Why should we be afraid of the scientist? He has no facts which interfere with this Book. We must not accommodate them; we must not try to placate people and please them. That is not the way to handle this Book.

And now I must say a word – and I do so with considerable hesitation and trepidation – but it seems to me that, if we are to face the facts, this is unavoidable. I suppose that the most popular of all the proposals at the present time for bringing people back to Scripture is this: Let's have a new translation of the Bible. We have had one in this year, 1961.² The argument is that the people are not reading the Bible any longer because they do not understand its language, its archaic terms. 'What does your modern man, what does your modern Teddy boy know about justification, sanctification, and all these biblical terms?' That is the question. No, they say, it is no good; they cannot understand the Bible. And so we are told that the one thing necessary is to have a translation which Tom, Dick, and Harry will understand. I began to feel about six months ago that we had almost reached a stage at which the Authorized Version was being dismissed, to be thrown into the limbo of things forgotten, no longer of any value. Need I apologize for saying a word in favour of the Authorized Version in *this* gathering? Well, whatever you may think, I am going to do it, and I am going to do it without any apology.

As I read the Christian periodicals earlier this year – and I am sorry to have to add, even the evangelical ones – and all the articles about

²*The New English Bible.*

this new translation, I almost began to think for a moment that the letters NEB stood for New Evangelical Bible. Everybody seemed to have succumbed to the ballyhoo, the propaganda, and the advertising. I began to wonder whether evangelical people really had lost the vital spark; but, thank God, by tonight I think I see signs of a recovery and a return to sanity.

We must examine this for a moment. Let us, first of all, be clear about the basic proposition laid down by the Protestant reformers that we must have a Bible which is, as they put it, 'understanded of the people'. That is common sense; that is obvious. We all agree too that we must never be obscurantist; we must never approach the Bible in a mere antiquarian spirit. Nobody wants to be like that, nor to defend such attitudes. But there is a very grave danger incipient in much of the argument that is being presented today for these new translations. There is a danger of our surrendering something that is vital and essential.

Look at it like this. Take the argument about the terms that the modern man does not understand, the words 'justification', 'sanctification', and so on. I want to ask a question: When did the ordinary man ever understand those terms? I am told the modern Teddy boy does not understand them. But consider the colliers to whom John Wesley and George Whitefield used to preach in the eighteenth century. Did they understand them? They had not even been to a day school, an elementary school. They could not read, they could not write. Yet these were the terms which they heard, and the Authorized Version was the version used. This is a very specious argument, but it does not hold water. The common people have *never* understood these terms. However, I want to add something to this. We must be very careful in using such an argument against the Authorized Version, for the reason that the very nature and character of the truth which the Bible presents to us is such that it is extremely difficult to put into words at all. We are not describing an animal or a machine; we are concerned here with something which is spiritual, something which does not belong to this world at all, and which, as the apostle Paul in writing to the Corinthians, reminds us, 'the princes of this world' do not know. Human wisdom is of no value here; it is a spiritual truth; it is something that is altogether different. This is truth about God primarily, and because of that it is a mystery. There is a glory attached to it, there is a wonder, and something which is amazing. The apostle Paul, who probably understood it better than most, looking at its contents, stands back and says, 'Great is the mystery of godliness' (1 Tim. 3:16).

Yet we are told, It must be put in such simple terms and language that anybody taking it up and reading it is going to understand all about it. My friends, this is nothing but sheer nonsense! What we must do is to educate the masses of the people *up* to the Bible, not bring the Bible *down* to their level. One of the greatest troubles in life today is that everything is being brought down to the same level; everything is being cheapened. The common man is made the standard and the authority; he decides everything, and everything has got to be brought down to him. You are getting it on your wireless, your television, in your newspapers; everywhere standards are coming down and down. Are we to do this with the Word of God? I say, No! What has always happened in the past has been this: an ignorant, illiterate people in this country and in foreign countries, coming into salvation, have been educated *up* to the Book and have begun to understand it, and to glory in it, and to praise God for it. I am here to say that we need to do the same at this present time. What we need, therefore, is not to replace the Authorized Version with what, I am tempted at times to call, the ITV edition of the Bible.[3] We need rather to teach and to train people up to the standard and the language and the dignity and the glory of the old Authorized Version.

I am here to suggest that we ought to protest against the dropping of great words like 'propitiation' and 'redemption' which are very essential to a true understanding of our gospel. And I protest against a translation that translates 2 Timothy 3:16 like this: 'Every inspired scripture has its use for teaching the truth.' That is an obvious statement but it is not what the apostle Paul wrote. The correct translation is '*All* Scripture is God-breathed and is profitable'. Paul does not speak of 'every Scripture that is inspired' because every Scripture *is* inspired. The translators have perpetuated the error of the Revised Version, which even the Revised Standard Version of America has corrected and brought back to the translation of the Authorized Version.

As I leave this aspect of the matter, my only remaining comment upon this new version, which is so popular, is to quote two statements, first from the *Times Literary Supplement* of the

[3]In 1961, ITV was the only British television channel financed by advertising.

24 March. This is not a Christian publication, but it is a very scholarly one, and a very learned one, and this is what a contributor says: 'What then is lost in this new translation is dimension in depth and in time, and with dimension, beauty and mystery. In short,' he goes on, 'insofar as religion is rational, social, simple, communal, historical, the new Bible may help. Insofar as religion touches and satisfies men's deepest aspirations and needs, it is almost all loss.' Such is the opinion of the *Times Literary Supplement*. It is not the view of some ignorant evangelical like myself, or of Mr Terence Brown[4] who has been so vilified. Here is a learned writer in the *Times Literary Supplement*. But let me also quote to you an Archbishop of the Anglican communion, the Very Rev Philip Harrington who is the Anglican Archbishop of Quebec, a learned, scholarly man and the author of two massive volumes on the early Christian church. This is how he writes: 'The intelligent reader will find much of it that is helpful and even illuminating, but he must keep his old Authorized Version by his side in order to find out what the apostles or prophets actually said, if that is what he wants to know.' I am free to confess that I came nearer to becoming an Anglican when I read that than ever in my life! But the Archbishop does not stop at that point – there are archbishops and archbishops it seems to me! – he adds: 'When the old and new differ in meaning, King James, at least in the Revised Version of 1881, will be correct ninety-nine times out of a hundred.' That is the opinion of the Anglican Archbishop of Quebec, writing this year on the New English Bible.

Very well, my friends, let me say a word for the old book, the old Authorized Version. It was translated by fifty-four men, every one of them a great scholar, and published in 1611. And here is another thing to commend it to you: this Authorized Version came out at a time when the church had not yet divided. I mean by that she had not yet divided into Anglican and Nonconformist. I think there is an advantage even in that. They were all still as one, with very few exceptions, when the Authorized Version was produced.

Another important point to remember is this. The Authorized Version was produced some time after that great climactic event which we call the Protestant Reformation. There had been time by then to see some of the terrible horrors of Rome and all she stood for. The early reformers had too much on their plate, as it were; Luther may have left many gaps; but when this translation was produced,

4The General Secretary of the Trinitarian Bible Society.

there had been time for men to be able to see Rome for what she really was. These translators were all men who were orthodox in the faith. They believed that the Bible is the infallible Word of God and they submitted to it as the final authority, as against the spurious claims of Rome, as against the appeals to the Church Fathers, and everything else. Here, I say, were fifty-four men, scholars and saintly, who were utterly submitted to the Book. You have never had that in any other version. Here and here alone you have a body of men who were absolutely committed to it, who gave themselves to it, who did not want to correct or sit in judgment upon it, whose only concern and desire was to translate it and interpret it for the masses of the people.

In view of all this, my argument is that the answer does not lie in producing new translations; they are coming out almost every week, but are they truly aiding the situation? No, and for this reason: men no longer read the Bible not because they cannot understand its language, but because they do not believe in it. They do not believe in its God; they do not want it. Their problem is not that of language and of terminology; it is the state of the heart. Therefore what do we do about it? It seems to me there is only one thing to do, the thing that has always been done in the past: we must preach it and our preaching must be wholly based upon its authority.

We must not come to the Bible to find out whether it is true or not; we must come to find the meaning of the truth that is there. That has been the fatal error of this so-called Higher Criticism, that has come to the Bible to find which part is true and which part is not. The moment you do that you are already wrong, irretrievably wrong! We do not come to the Bible to discover whether it is true; we come to discover its meaning and its teaching. And therefore I say the only hope is that we preach its message to the people. We must preach it to them as the Word of God. Yes, this Book is the very thing that it claims to be. Look at its original writers! Did any one of them say it was his own idea? No, they are all unanimous in saying that it was given to them. Some of them did not even want to write it. Isaiah, given his commission, says, 'I am a man of unclean lips'; I am not fit to do this. It is not a question of a great man, a great philosopher, a great thinker, who has got to tell the people what to do. No, Isaiah is given a mission and a commission. He says, I am not fit. Jeremiah says, 'I cannot speak: for I am a child.' Ezekiel, when he was given his commission and message, sat stunned and amazed for seven days, and it needed the Holy Spirit to put him on his feet again. Amos said, I am a herdsman, a man tending sycamore trees. I am no prophet, nor the son of a prophet. That is what they all say. They say it is not *their* message. Well, what is it? Oh, they say, it is 'the burden of the Lord', the message of the Lord; the burden of the Lord came unto me. Jeremiah did not want to speak, but he could not refrain; it was like a fire burning in his bones. God had given him a message and was sending him out with it. You and I must come back to this: 'No prophecy of the scripture is of any private interpretation. For the prophecy came not in old time by the will of man: but holy men of God spake as they were moved by the Holy Ghost' (2 Peter 1:20–21). That is the authority. Look what our Lord says about it. He refers to the Scriptures using phrases such as 'It is written'. He believed the Old Testament; He believed it all. He says, 'the scripture cannot be broken' (John 10:35): who are we to dispute it? And the apostles – look at their attitude to Scripture; they constantly refer to it and quote it. For them it is the final argument; it settles all disputes.

We must present the Bible as the Word of God, not the words of men, but the Word of the living God: God speaking about Himself; God speaking about men; God speaking about life; God telling us what He is going to do about a fallen world. That is what we need to preach with certainty, with assurance. Let us tell the people about its marvel, that though it contains sixty-six books, written at different times and in different centuries, there is only one message in it. Let us tell them about fulfilled prophecy. Let us point out to them how things prophesied and predicted hundreds of years before the events were actually verified in the fullest and minutest detail. Let us *tell* them: they do not know it. It is for us to proclaim the Word of God, and especially at this critical time in our history. Let us tell people something about its message. It is the only book that explains life. It is the only book that explains the world as it is tonight. We have been told now for nearly a century that the world is advancing, that man is becoming more and more perfect, that with more and more education and scientific knowledge there will be no more war. The problem was, they said, that people did not know one another. They did not meet. If only they met they would all love one another and embrace one another; but now that we are meeting so constantly, we cannot live together for even a few seconds! You see, there is no explanation except the explanation that is given in this Book.

'There is no peace, saith my God, to the wicked' (Isa. 57:21). You can be clever, you can be mighty and great and strong, you can be a great philosopher, and be very wealthy, you can own the whole world – but you will never know peace, either as an individual or among men and nations, while you are wicked. The Bible alone has the explanation. It is man's sin, man's rebellion against God. You see, you must come back to theology; you must seek the Book and discover its message, its theology, its doctrines. If you evangelical people are against doctrine you will never get people back to the Bible. It is not enough just to read a few verses. You must dig down and get the doctrine, the doctrine of a wholly absolute God, who is the creator of the ends of the earth, and who is the judge of the whole earth. Man is not something that came out of some primeval slime, but a creature made in the image of God, given something of the stamp of the eternal Lord of creation, meant to live in communion and correspondence with his creator! But man has fallen into sin, has asserted his own will-power, has said that he is autonomous, that he can arrange his life, that he does not need God, he does not need God's direction and God's Word: that is why the world is in trouble.

This is what we must tell people; we must try not just to defend the Bible but to preach its truth. Tell men that they are in their present state because the world has turned its back upon God. That is why this twentieth century is so appalling. It is the century of all centuries that has asserted itself and its own will and its own understanding over and against God and His truth and His eternal will. We must tell them this, we must tell them very plainly and without any apology that the wrath of God has been revealed from heaven 'against all ungodliness and unrighteousness of men' (Rom. 1:18). We must tell them that the very history of this century, with its two awful wars and all its present horrors, is due to the same thing. These things are a part of the judgment of God. The apostle Paul puts it thus in Romans 1, that one way in which God punishes men is, that He abandons people to themselves. He 'gave them over to a reprobate mind' (verse 28). I believe this is what is happening tonight; it is to me the only explanation of this present century. God is saying to us, Very well, you said you could live without me; you said you could make a perfect world without my laws, without my Word, without my truth – get on with it, see what you make of it! And this is what we have made of it: man a creature of lust, self-centred and selfish, fighting all others. War is inevitable while man is in that condition. The Bible alone explains this. And when you turn to the future it is exactly the same thing: there is no light for the future anywhere except in this Book. There are people who, in the name of Christianity, are still saying that if we only preach this message we can put an end to wars. Never! The Bible asserts that there shall be wars and rumours of wars right to the end. While man is evil and sinful and the creature of lust, there will be wars. Christianity has not come into the world to put an end to war; it has not come to reform the world. What has it come for? It has come to save us from the destruction that is coming to the world. This Book asserts a judgment, an end of history. God in Christ will judge the whole world in righteousness, sending those who have turned their backs upon Him, refused His offer of salvation in Christ, to everlasting perdition, and ushering the saints into the glory of 'new heavens and a new earth, wherein dwelleth righteousness' (2 Pet. 3:13).

Christian people, we must proclaim to the world that we are not afraid of the morrow. We are not afraid of what the nations may do. We know that an evil world is under condemnation, and that the only course of safety and of wisdom is to come in penitence and contrition to the Son of God, our blessed Lord and Saviour, who came out of eternity, who died for our sins, and who will come again to receive His own unto Himself. That, it seems to me, is the thing to which we are called. We must preach the Bible's message without fear or favour and with the holy boldness of the apostles of old, not merely to say it, but to have the Holy Ghost upon us as we do so. Pray for power to proclaim it so that it shall become like 'a hammer that breaketh the rock in pieces' (Jer. 23:29). Or in the words of the apostle Paul, the message must be seen to be 'mighty through God to the pulling down of strong holds; casting down imaginations, and every high thing that exalteth itself against the knowledge of God, and bringing into captivity every thought to the obedience of Christ' (2 Cor. 10:4, 5).

That is our calling.

> *O Word of God incarnate,*
> *O wisdom from on high,*
> *O truth unchanged, unchanging,*
> *O light of our dark sky!*
>
> *O make thy Church, dear Saviour,*
> *A lamp of burnished gold,*
> *To bear before the nations*
> *Thy true light as of old.*

Nine

*

The Basis of Christian Unity[1]

*

Introduction

No question is receiving so much attention at the present time in all branches and divisions of the Christian church as the question of church unity. It is being written about, talked about, and preached about. Now we are all agreed, surely, that the Christian church should be one, that she was meant by God to be one. And therefore, we must agree, further, that it is a tragedy that division ever entered into the life of the church. In addition, we must all regard schism as a grievous sin. That is common ground. But having said that, one must also point out that there is obviously great confusion, and much disagreement, as to what constitutes unity, as to what the nature of unity is, and as to how unity is to be obtained and preserved.

I. SOME CURRENT VIEWS

There are many divergent views with regard to this. The Roman Catholic solution to the problem, of necessity, and in spite of what appears to be greater friendliness at the present time, is simply absorption into her institution and organization. *Semper eadem* is her great slogan: the church is 'always the same'. From her standpoint, and on the basis of her definition, it must be. Therefore it is quite logical that her notion of unity should be that all other sections of the church should return to her who is 'the one and only true church of Christ'. The so-called 'Orthodox' churches, Greek and Russian, hold a similar view.

[1]The substance of two addresses given to the Westminster Ministers' Fellowship in June, 1962 and first published by the Inter-Varsity Press in December, 1962.

But there are other views, some of which contrast sharply with this in their looseness. The commonest of these maintains that what is desired is a visible unity and coming together of all who call themselves Christian in any sense whatsoever. Unity means that all sections of the Christian church, anybody, everybody claiming the name of Christian, should meet together, have fellowship together, and work together, presenting a common front to the enemies of Christianity.

One other view must be especially mentioned at this point as it seems to be becoming fairly popular in evangelical circles. This regards unity in terms of coming together to form a kind of 'forum', where various views of the Christian faith may be 'discussed' and people may present their different 'insights', hoping that as a result they may eventually arrive at some common agreement. There are other views, but let that suffice as a broad classification.

2. THE LIMITS OF THIS STUDY

This subject is exceedingly complex and many volumes have been written about it. My objective in this paper is a very limited one; it is to examine the two passages of Scripture which are most frequently quoted in this connection. I refer, of course, to John 17 and Ephesians 4, and in particular to John 17:21 and Ephesians 4:13. These are the verses that are so frequently quoted today and used as slogans, statements which apparently settle the matter once and for all and place it beyond any dispute or discussion. It is essential, therefore, that we should examine them very carefully.

I propose to examine them in the light of certain questions. First: What is the nature or the character of true unity? Secondly: What is the place of doctrine and belief in this matter of unity? Thirdly: How does unity come into being?

Attention is focused mainly on the third question because of its practical character. The majority view holds that the way to produce unity is not to discuss and consider doctrine, but rather to work together and to pray together. The slogans are that 'doctrine divides', but that as we 'work together' and 'pray together' we shall arrive at unity.

This becomes serious when it is applied to the question of evangelism. The commonest argument used to press upon us the vital and urgent importance of this question of unity is that evangelism is impossible apart from it, that the divided church is an offence to the world, and that while we are divided the world will not listen to us. Therefore, we are told, it is urgently essential that we should come together in order that we may evangelize. We have been told frequently that at this point of evangelism we can surely all be one. During an evangelistic campaign in London a few years ago a weekly paper, now defunct, calling itself *The Christian World*, carried the heading, 'Let us have a theological truce during the Campaign'. A well-known evangelistic leader has also committed himself to this: 'We can all at any rate be ecumenical in evangelism.' That it is only after the stage of evangelism that you begin to consider doctrine is a very common and prevailing view.

All this obviously makes it of vital importance that we should be clear in our thinking on these questions which I have raised with regard to the basis of Christian unity. It is essential, therefore, that these key passages should be carefully studied. It is also my aim to show that the general tenor of New Testament teaching supports and confirms the proper interpretation of these two passages. This will be dealt with in Part III.

Part I: The Teaching of John 17

Verse 21 of this chapter is the one which is so frequently used as a slogan. In it our Lord prays, 'That they all may be one; as thou, Father, art in me, and I in thee, that they also may be one in us: that the world may believe that thou hast sent me.'

How do we interpret it? We do so, first of all, by taking it in its context and setting. This is a principle which should always govern scriptural exposition. The charge that has been so frequently hurled against evangelicals is that they are fond of using 'proof-texts'. That is the criticism brought against the Westminster Confession and, indeed, most of the confessions. They are based, it is said, on proof-texts. We are told that we must never do that, that we must take the general tenor and sense of Scripture and not base our position upon particular texts; but advocates of the ecumenical movement have done precisely that with regard to this verse. They have taken it entirely out of its context and then proceeded to use it as a slogan. Over against this we assert that it is *always* wrong to take a text in isolation. The first rule of interpretation is that a text should always be considered in its context, and, in addition, compared with other texts. If ever that canon of interpretation was important it is in connection with this particular statement.

1. THE CONTEXT ANALYSED

We start, therefore, by giving a general analysis of the seventeenth chapter of John's Gospel. It falls into obvious sections. The first section consists of the first five verses, where our Lord is praying chiefly for Himself. The second section consists of verses 6 to 10 in which He gives a description of His people, for whom He is praying, and offers a general prayer for them. Then in verses 11 and 12 He offers the fundamental prayer that they may be kept as one. In verses 13 to 16 He prays in particular that they may be kept as one against the subtle attacks of the evil one who is always anxious to disrupt this essential unity. In verses 17 to 19 He prays for their sanctification, again in order that they may be kept in the truth and in this unity. In verses 20 to 23 He takes up what He has already prayed in verse 11 and elaborates it in order to define in more detail the nature of the unity. And in verses 24 to 26 He gives expression to His ultimate desire for His people, that they may be where He is, that they may behold the glory which the Father has given Him. That is the general analysis of the whole section.

2. PRINCIPLES OF UNITY

As we come to a more detailed consideration of this question of unity we notice that the first specific mention of it is in verse 11. Our Lord says, 'And now I am no more in the world, but these are in the world, and I come to thee. Holy Father, keep through thine own name those whom thou hast given me, that they may be one, as we are.' That is the fundamental text, and in that one statement we have all the essential principles stated.

(a) Its restricted reference
First, we notice that He is praying for particular people whom He designates as 'these'. They, and they alone, are the subject of this unity. Who are 'these'? In the chapter itself there are many answers to this question. 'These' are the people of whom He has said right at the beginning that they have been given to Him by God. That is a fundamental statement, which He goes on repeating. There are

certain people who belong to God, whom God the Father has given to Him, and for whose sake He has come into the world and has done what He has done.

Another thing He says about them is that they are people who have been separated from the world. 'I pray for them: I pray not for the world, but for them which thou hast given me; for they are thine', He says in verse 9. That is a very important statement. Here are people who have been taken out of the world, separated from it; and it is for these, and for these alone, that He prays. There is no 'universalism' in this chapter. There is nothing here to suggest that the work that our Lord did in this world was done for everybody, and that though there may be some who do not realize it and do not know it while they are in this world, it is nevertheless true of them, and ultimately all are to be saved. On the contrary, there is a clear-cut division and distinction between those who are still in the world and those whom He has called out of the world.

We have a still more interesting and important definition as to who 'these' are in verses 6 to 8: 'I have manifested thy name unto the men which thou gavest me out of the world: thine they were, and thou gavest them me; and they have kept thy word. Now they have known that all things whatsoever thou hast given me are of thee. For I have given unto them the words which thou gavest me; and they have received them, and have known surely that I came out from thee, and they have believed that thou didst send me.' This is of crucial importance. So much so that our Lord brings out the same idea again in verse 20, where we have: 'Neither pray I for these alone, but for them also which shall believe on me through their word.' These have believed on Him and His Word; others are going to believe on Him through the same Word which these are now going to speak in the world. The emphasis is the same. He repeats it again in verse 25; this is the final definition of these people: 'O righteous Father, the world hath not known thee: but I have known thee, and these have known that thou hast sent me.' This is a most important statement because it further defines who these people are.

What, then, are the characteristics of these people? Again we must emphasize the element of separation and distinction. Our Lord does not pray for the world; He prays only for these people who have been given to Him. Indeed He says specifically in verse 19: 'And for their sakes I sanctify myself, that they also might be sanctified through the truth.' That is a reference, of course, to His giving Himself, setting

Himself apart for His death, for the work of atonement and reconciliation; and there He specifically says that He does not do that for everybody, He does it for 'these' people only. Again, a most important statement.

In other words these people who are the subjects of the unity of which our Lord is speaking are not those who happen to have been brought up in a certain country, or who happen to belong to a given race or nation or a particular visible church. They are those who have 'received' His Word, His teaching, and particularly His teaching concerning Himself. They have known who He is, that He has been sent by God, and that He has been sent to do this work for them. They have 'believed' and have 'received' that Word. That is His own definition of these people. In other words, the unity of which He is speaking applies only to those who receive and believe this Word, what we now would call the gospel message.

(b) Its origin

The second principle which He lays down in the eleventh verse concerns the origin of the unity. You notice that He uses the word 'keep'. 'Holy Father,' He says, 'keep through thine own name those whom thou hast given me.' Nowhere in this chapter is there an exhortation or an appeal to produce a unity. Our Lord is saying that the unity is already there, already in existence. It is the unity of those who, in contradistinction to all others, have believed the truth concerning Him and His work. Our Lord, knowing that He is now about to leave the world and that they are going to be exposed to the attack of the evil one and all the forces of temptation of sin and evil, is praying to His Father to keep them in the unity that already exists. That, I repeat, is a very important point and principle. Our Lord is not dealing with something at which we should aim. Indeed our Lord does not address His disciples at all in this chapter. It is a prayer to God to keep the unity that He, through His preaching, has already brought into existence among these people.

(c) Its nature

The third point which our Lord raises is that of the nature of the unity: 'That they may be one, as we are.' This is the fundamental text, as it were, on the subject, but as our Lord elaborates it in verses 20 to 23, let us now proceed to consider them: 'Neither pray I for these alone, but for them also which shall believe on me through their word; that they all may be one; as thou, Father, art in me, and I in thee, that they also may be one in us: that the world may believe that thou hast sent me. And the glory which thou gavest me I have given them; that they may be one, even as we are one: I in them, and thou in me, that they may be made perfect in one; and that the world may know that thou hast sent me, and hast loved them, as thou hast loved me.'

Here we have what is undoubtedly one of the most exalted statements to be found anywhere in the whole of the Scriptures. We notice at once that the essential character of the unity about which our Lord is speaking is that it is comparable to the unity that exists between the Father and the Son. It is also comparable to the unity between the Son and the people for whom He is praying.

Light is thrown on this in certain verses of John 14. For instance, in verse 20 our Lord says: 'At that day ye shall know that I am in my Father, and ye in me, and I in you'; and in verse 21: 'He that hath my commandments, and keepeth them, he it is that loveth me: and he that loveth me shall be loved of my Father, and I will love him, and will manifest myself to him.' Verse 23 continues: 'If a man love me, he will keep my words: and my Father will love him, and we will come unto him, and make our abode with him.' Now whatever else may be said of the verses we are examining in chapter 17, it is quite obvious that this statement is not one to be handled lightly, glibly, or loosely, as if its meaning were perfectly clear and self-evident. Our Lord is dealing here with the mystical union which subsists between the three persons of the blessed Holy Trinity. It is the highest mystery of the Christian faith. And yet this is the term, the verse, that is being bandied about as if its meaning were obvious, and indeed as if it had but one meaning, namely, some external organizational unity. Everything about the statement indicates the exact opposite. It is concerned with a unity of essence. That is the whole mystery of the Trinity. There are three persons and yet but one God. The same essence and yet the distinctions in the persons. But what makes them one is the unity of essence. That cannot be excluded. Of course, in addition to that, there is the unity of outlook and of thought and of purpose, the mutual love, and everything else that follows of necessity from it. Now that is the way in which our Lord Himself defines this unity which already obtains among His people and which He prays God to preserve and to keep after His return to glory.

We deduce from this that the unity which is to obtain in the church is something which involves this unity of essence, of being. This is, of course, only another way of putting the doctrine taught so plainly in the New Testament that the Christian is a man who is 'born again', 'born of the Spirit', a 'partaker of the divine nature'. All that is implicit here. We must be careful because the subject is difficult. We must never teach that the Christian is made divine, but the scriptural phrase as used by Peter is that we are made 'partakers of the divine nature' (2 Pet. 1:4).

There is no unity at all in our Lord's sense apart from this fundamental operation of the Holy Spirit of God, who creates within the believers of the truth this new nature. And that in turn leads, by the same analogy, to an identity of view, of object, of love, and so on.

In other words, the unity that our Lord is talking about is a unity that clearly can obtain only among those who are regenerate or born again. It is not something, by definition, that one can decide to go in for. It is not like a number of people deciding to form a coalition or a society in order that certain objects and purposes should be carried out. I am not saying that there is anything wrong in that. My concern is to show that that is not what our Lord was talking about. It is not even a matter of friendship. It is deeper than that. It is like a family relationship. You have no choice about it and what it involves. You are born into a family. Though you may disagree with members of your family you cannot get rid of the relationship. It is a matter of blood and of essence. So is the unity of the church. It must never be thought of, therefore, as something voluntary. It is something which is inevitable because it is the result of being born into a given family. Christians are brothers and not merely an association of friends.

3. SUMMARY

To sum up the teaching of this passage before we turn to the other: our Lord is praying here that this unity which He has brought into being, and which He has Himself preserved while He was still with the disciples, may be continued. Incidentally, it is interesting to notice that He mentions that extraordinary exception, the case of Judas. Here is one who belonged to the company but who shows quite clearly that he is not truly 'of' it. Verse 12 says: 'While I was with them in the world, I kept them in thy name: those that thou gavest me I have kept, and none of them is lost, but the son of perdition; that the scripture might be fulfilled.' You may give the appearance of belonging, but if there is not this new life and this new birth there is no real unity; and it must eventually show itself.

So we find here that the whole of our Lord's statement is not an exhortation to us to do anything, but is a prayer to His Father asking Him to preserve this unity that is already in existence. Moreover that unity is essentially spiritual, is produced by the operation of the Holy Spirit in the act of regeneration, and shows itself in a common belief and reception of the teaching concerning our Lord's person and work. Any 'unity' which lacks these characteristics is not the unity of which our Lord speaks in John 17.

Part II: The Teaching of Ephesians 4

The second crucial passage with which we are concerned is Ephesians 4:1–16. In many respects it runs parallel to the one we have already looked at, the one big difference being that it is an exhortation addressed to Christian believers rather than a prayer which is offered to God. For this reason we shall devote the major part of our space to its consideration.

1. Does Fellowship or Doctrine Come First?

What does this passage teach? There are many who think that the teaching here is that we are exhorted to have fellowship with one another, whatever our views of the Christian faith may be, in order that ultimately we may come to a unity of faith and belief. Some years ago a well-known evangelical preacher put it like this: 'I always used to think that you could not have fellowship with a man unless you were agreed with him about doctrine. My position had always been that first of all you must have agreement about truth and your view of truth, and then, on that basis, you could have fellowship with people.' But he went on to say that he had made a great and startling discovery from reading again this fourth chapter of the Epistle to the Ephesians. He had observed for the first time in his life that the apostle starts by exhorting to fellowship: 'Endeavouring to keep the unity of the Spirit in the bond of peace' (verse 3). He said, 'I discovered that there you start with fellowship and it is only later, in verse 13, that the apostle says, "Till we all come in the unity of the faith, and of the knowledge of the Son of God, unto a perfect man, unto the measure of the stature of the fulness of Christ."' So in the light of that he was now proposing to have fellowship with people who disagreed with him theologically, those who were liberal in their doctrinal outlook, and others. He was going to do this because he believed it was through such fellowship that he could hope to arrive ultimately at doctrinal agreement. It was a complete reversal of the position that he had before held. He felt convicted, he felt he had been sinful. And now he exhorts Christian people to put his new view of the teaching of Ephesians 4 into practice. It is through working together, evangelizing together, praying together, and having fellowship together, he declares, that we shall ultimately arrive at the unity of the faith.

The crucial question we must consider is whether this section of Scripture teaches that or not. Again the context is absolutely vital, and we must therefore begin by making a general analysis of the passage. The theme, quite clearly, is the unity of the church. Indeed that has been the theme of the apostle right from the beginning of the Epistle. In many ways the key verse to an understanding of the whole letter is 1:10: 'That in the dispensation of the fulness of times he might gather together in one all things in Christ, both which are in heaven, and which are on earth; even in him.' The apostle proceeds to show how God has been doing this by bringing the Jew and the Gentile together in this one new body, which is the church, and then calls attention in particular to this theme in the section we are examining.

A general analysis of the section reveals the following: in verses 1 to 3 Paul makes a general appeal for unity; in verses 4 to 6 he describes the nature of the unity; in verses 7 to 12 he describes the variety in the unity and the means which God has taken to preserve it; finally, in verses 13 to 16, he describes the unity perfected, or its ultimate full realization and flowering. This he presents both positively and negatively.

The key to the whole exposition of chapter 4 is the word 'therefore' in verse 1. It points us back to the first three chapters of this great Epistle, and emphasizes that the theme of unity is something which follows as a consequence of what has gone before. This, of course, is typical of the New Testament method of dealing with matters of conduct and practice. Its essential teaching is that conduct is always the outcome of truth and of teaching. Practice and behaviour are the result of the application of doctrine which has already been laid down. And that is precisely what the apostle does here. 'Therefore', he says, 'I therefore, the prisoner of the Lord, beseech you that ye walk worthy of the vocation wherewith ye are called.' The exhortation that follows is made in the light of all that he has been saying in the first three chapters.

It is clear, then, that anyone who interprets this section as saying that the apostle starts with fellowship and then goes on to doctrine is fundamentally wrong: his entire exposition is vitiated at the outset for the simple reason that he starts with verse 3 and ignores verses 1 and 2. The doctrine expounded in chapters 1 to 3 is already the basis and the background of everything the apostle has to say about unity. He does not start with unity and then proceed to doctrine; he takes up unity because he has already laid down his doctrine.

2. The Context of Ephesians 4

The apostle makes this abundantly clear in his opening exhortation that we are to 'walk worthy of the vocation wherewith ye are called'. Now the word 'worthy' brings together two main ideas. One is 'equal weight', 'balance'. In other words he is saying, You have already heard what the doctrine is, now you must balance that with your practice and conduct. You have exactly the same thought in Hebrews 6:11: 'And we desire', says the writer there, 'that . . . you do shew the same diligence.' They had been showing diligence in their practical works of helping one another, so he says, in effect, We exhort you now to show the same diligence in the matter of the full assurance of hope to the end. In other words it is again a matter of balance, balance between doctrine and practice.

The second notion in this word is the idea of something that 'becomes' or 'fits in with' something else. Philippians 1:27 conveys exactly the idea: 'Only let your conversation be as it *becometh* the gospel of Christ.' You have your doctrine, Paul says; now be careful that your conversation *becomes* it, that it corresponds to it, that it does not clash with it, that it fits in with it, that it shows it out still more in its glory and in its perfection. Another well-known phrase in the letter to Titus puts it like this: 'adorn the doctrine' (Tit. 2:10). That is what conduct and practice are meant to do. We must not think of them apart from doctrine. To talk about unity apart from doctrine is like talking about a woman's clothing as if it had no connection with her person. The business of the clothing is to adorn the person. So it is with practice and doctrine. One is to adorn the other. This is quite fundamental in all approaches to this question of unity.

Then to make it still more specific the apostle says that we are to walk worthy of the vocation, or calling, wherewith we are called. What does he mean by this repetition of the word 'call'? He is referring here to the whole plan of salvation as he has already outlined it in the earlier chapters. It is not simply a matter of 'living up to your calling' as the New English Bible puts it. It involves the whole doctrine of the 'call', and to understand what is in the apostle's mind we must go back to the earlier part of the Epistle.

3. A SUMMARY OF EPHESIANS I TO 3

Briefly we can put it like this. In verses 9 and 10 of chapter 1 the apostle outlines the plan and the purpose of salvation in the general statement: 'Having made known unto us the mystery of his will, according to his good pleasure which he hath purposed in himself: that in the dispensation of the fulness of times he might gather together in one all things *in Christ*, both which are in heaven, and which are on earth; even *in him*.' That is the great eternal purpose of God which, as Paul has already told us in verse 4, has been planned 'before the foundation of the world': 'According as he hath chosen us *in him* before the foundation of the world.' This purpose has been carried out through everything that has happened in and through our Lord and Saviour Jesus Christ. (Notice the repetition of the words 'Jesus Christ', 'Christ', 'in him', throughout this entire section in the first chapter.) In particular, salvation is through the blood of Christ, 'in whom we have redemption through his blood, the forgiveness of sins, according to the riches of his grace' (verse 7).

That is the great doctrine stated in general. There is no unity, there can be no unity, apart from the person of the Lord Jesus Christ, apart from His work and especially apart from the redemption which is 'through his blood'. That is essential to the only unity in which the New Testament is interested, and which it defines so clearly.

The question now arises, How does anyone ever come into this unity? The apostle tells us in 1:4–6: 'According as he hath chosen us in him before the foundation of the world, that we should be holy and without blame before him in love: having predestinated us unto the adoption of children by Jesus Christ to himself, according to the good pleasure of his will, to the praise of the glory of his grace, wherein he hath made us accepted in the beloved.' That is the great source of all unity. That is how men enter into it, and it must never be thought of apart from this great, high, and exalted doctrine. Paul expresses the same thought in verse 11 'In whom also we have obtained an inheritance, being predestinated according to the purpose of him who worketh all things after the counsel of his own will.'

In practice and experience we enter into this unity through the process described in 1:12, 13. In verse 12 he talks about the Jews: 'That we should be to the praise of his glory, who first trusted in Christ.' That is how the Jews came in; they had placed their trust in Christ. Then in verse 13 he turns to the Gentile Ephesians: 'In whom ye also trusted, after that ye heard the word of truth, the gospel of your salvation', and 'in whom also after that ye believed . . .'. In practice we come into it as the result of hearing this word of the gospel of the Lord Jesus Christ and believing it, trusting it, putting our faith utterly and entirely in it and in Him. That is the essential message of the first chapter.

In the second chapter the apostle elaborates all this, putting it still more plainly. Who are these people whom he is exhorting to continue in unity? They are those who have realized that by nature they were dead in trespasses and sins. That is the vital statement in verse 1. They realize further that they are under the dominion and the control of the devil, 'the prince of the power of the air', and rebels against God (verse 2). They realize also that they are the slaves of their own lusts and passions. And still more important and significant, they realize that they are under the wrath of God, that they, like everybody else, are 'the children of wrath' (verse 3). In other words, these people believe in the fact and the doctrine of the fall of man. They realize that they are spiritually dead, under the condemnation of God and His holy law, and that they can do nothing about their salvation and reconciliation to God. They realize, furthermore, that they are now Christians, members of God's church, solely because of what God has done to them through the Holy Spirit: 'you hath he quickened'. They realize that God has quickened them by the Spirit, put new life into them, given them the ability to see the truth as it is in Christ Jesus, and to believe it.

Furthermore, Paul tells us that they are people who are united to Christ. They have been 'quickened together with Christ', they have been 'raised together' with Him, and they have been 'made to sit together in heavenly places in Christ Jesus' (verses 4–7). And in order to make the thing clear beyond any doubt he goes on to say, 'For by grace are ye saved through faith; and that not of yourselves: it is the gift of God: not of works, lest any man should boast. For we are his workmanship, created in Christ Jesus unto good works, which God hath before ordained that we should walk in them' (verses 8–10).

In other words the people whom the apostle is exhorting to 'keep' this unity of faith are those who have been 'regenerated', who are God's 'workmanship'. They are what they are as the result of what God has done to them and in them.

But he does not leave it even at that. In 2:13–16 he reminds these Ephesian Christians that they are people who have realized that all their own good works, all their good living, all their activities, their nationality, their religion, and everything they had before, are entirely useless, and that they are made Christian, and brought into this unity which is in the church, entirely by the action of the Lord Jesus Christ, and particularly by the shedding of His blood upon the cross: 'But now in Christ Jesus ye who sometimes were far off are made nigh by the blood of Christ. For he is our peace, who hath made both one, and hath broken down the middle wall of partition between us; having abolished in his flesh the enmity, even the law of commandments contained in ordinances; for to make in himself of twain one new man, so making peace; and that he might reconcile both unto God in one body by the cross, having slain the enmity thereby.'

These, and these alone, are the subjects of the unity of which he speaks in chapter 4. That is how these people have been brought into the unity. It is entirely wrong to start with unity as a separate concept. It is something that results from all that has gone before. As we have already pointed out, the word 'therefore' in 4:1 points back to all these matters which are elaborated in such detail in the second chapter. These people are those who have been 'bought' into God's kingdom and family at the cost of 'the precious blood of Christ'. No-one can ever belong to this family, and participate in its unity, unless he believes that.

The apostle then goes on to say that it is only because of this that we can pray. 'For through him we both have access by one Spirit unto the Father' (2:18). There is only one way in which any man can pray and that is 'through' the Lord Jesus Christ 'by' the Holy Spirit. A man cannot have access to the Father except 'by the blood of Christ'.

Hebrews 10:19 teaches us the same thing. It is the teaching of the whole of the New Testament: 'God heareth not sinners' (John 9:31). It is only by relying upon the blood of Christ, by believing that His blood was shed for us and for our sins, that God 'made him to be sin for us, who knew no sin' (2 Cor. 5:21), and punished our sins in Him, that we have access to the Father. And it is the Holy Spirit who enables us, in the light of it, to have this access to the Father.

The apostle ends this chapter by saying that the people whom he is exhorting to continue in this unity are those who, as the result of all this, are now fellow citizens, and members together of the household of God, and are established together and 'built [together] upon the foundation of the apostles and prophets', which means the teaching and the doctrine of the apostles and prophets. And because they are on this foundation they have become 'a habitation of God', who dwells in them. That is a summary of the teaching of the second chapter.

The third chapter tells us how this great plan and purpose of God had been revealed to the apostle and includes his prayer that these Ephesian believers should enter more fully into an understanding of all this. It is a glorious chapter. It is not essential to our present purpose that we should go into it in detail. His prayer for the Ephesians is that they, together with all other saints, may be led by the Spirit into an even fuller understanding of what God has made possible for them in and through the Lord Jesus Christ.

So he starts this fourth chapter which we are considering. That is the calling wherewith they are called, nothing less than that. It is not simply that a man thinks he is a Christian or decides to be a Christian. He is a man who has been called effectually by the Spirit of God into this position and relationship through believing the truth which has been presented to him. The apostle is concerned, as he has said in 1:18, that the Holy Spirit may 'enlighten the eyes of the understanding' of these people in order that they may enter into a fuller and deeper comprehension of this wonderful truth.

4. The Unity of All who are 'In Christ'

That, then, is the character of the people who are the subjects of the unity which the apostle now proceeds to consider. He is writing to such, and to nobody else. What is his appeal to them? We have it in verses 2 and 3: 'with all lowliness and meekness, with longsuffering, forbearing one another in love; endeavouring to keep the unity of the Spirit in the bond of peace.' He says that we should show 'great diligence eagerly'. To what end? Not to produce a unity, not to create a unity, not to try to arrive at a unity, but to 'keep the unity'. Again, it is the same fundamental point which we noticed in our exposition of the passage in John 17. The unity is already in existence. It is the unity of all those who have believed the message expounded in chapters 1 to 3. As our Lord had prophesied in His prayer recorded in John 17, there were to be people who would believe the message of the apostles whom He was sending out. And here is one of the apostles writing to Ephesians who have believed, who have 'received' that message. And because of that they are in this body, they are one with all others who believe the same message; and the exhortation is that they should 'keep', should preserve, this unity.

That is the way in which the New Testament always puts it. The unity itself is inevitable among all those who have been quickened by the Holy Spirit out of spiritual death and given new life in Christ Jesus. What they have to be careful about is that they do not allow anything to disrupt it or in any way to interfere with it. The emphasis is entirely upon the word 'keep'.

In order that this may be abundantly clear the apostle again reminds us that it is 'the unity *of the Spirit*'. In other words, it is a unity which is produced by the Holy Spirit and by Him alone. Man cannot produce this, try as he may. Because of the nature of this unity, because it is a spiritual unity, it can be brought into being only as a result of the operation of the Holy Spirit. The apostle rejoices in this staggering fact, that these people who were once Jews and Gentiles are now one in Christ Jesus. They not only share the same life, they are agreed about their doctrine. They believe the same things, they are trusting to the same person, and they know that He has saved them all in the same way. The middle wall of partition has gone. The Jews no longer pride themselves that they are Jews and that they had the law given to them, whereas the Gentiles were ignorant and were not in the unique position of being the people of God. All these differences have gone, and they are one in seeing their lost estate and condition, their utter hopelessness and helplessness. They are united in their common trust in the Lord Jesus Christ, the Son of God, who has purchased them at the cost of His own precious blood. So they are ready to listen to this exhortation which urges them to maintain with great diligence, to preserve and to guard, the unity into which they have been brought by the operation of the Holy Spirit of God.

5. THE NATURE OF SPIRITUAL UNITY

That leads us to our next question: What, then, is the nature of the unity produced by the Spirit? The answer is supplied in verses 4 to 6: 'There is one body, and one Spirit, even as ye are called in one hope of your calling; one Lord, one faith, one baptism, one God and Father of all, who is above all, and through all, and in you all.' Notice again the exalted way in which the unity is described. This is not just a question of friendliness or fellowship, of good nature, or of desiring to do good together. It is something, once more, which lifts us up into the realm of the blessed Holy Trinity, the Spirit, the Son, the Father! The unity must always be conceived of in this exalted way and never merely in terms of human fellowship, or co-operation, or organization.

Observe that the word 'one' is used seven times in these three verses. At the beginning of verse 4 the Authorized Version translators have supplied the words 'There is'. The words in the original are, 'endeavour to keep the unity of the Spirit in the bond of peace. One body. . .'. The apostle puts it baldly because the thing is beyond dispute. The translators rightly supplied the words 'There is' because that helps to emphasize that fact. 'There is but one body', and it is this body that has been produced by the Holy Spirit. Unity is already there, he says. We must get rid entirely of the notion that the Ephesians are being exhorted to produce or to arrive at something. '*There is*', he says; you are already enjoying it; all you have to do is to preserve it!

The first thing we are told about the nature of this unity is that it is the kind of unity that is found in a physical body. That is clearly the apostle's favourite analogy in this connection. He has already used it in 1:22 and 23. He has reminded us of it again in 2:16. We shall find it again in 4:16. He works it out *in extenso* in Romans 12 and in 1 Corinthians 12.

Why is this such a good analogy? For the obvious reason that it emphasizes the vital and organic character of the unity. It is not just a loose grouping, or a mechanical or external attachment. The whole marvel and mystery of the human body is that, while it consists of so many different parts, all with their various functions, they are all one; they are bound together in a vital manner. It is not a question of fingers being stuck on to hands, and hands to forearms, and so on. It is all one. All the parts come out of an original cell, as it were, an original germ of life, and they are all extensions and manifestations of this. The unity in the church is like that and, whether we like it or not, we have to face this fact.

Paul goes on to compare this with the unity that characterizes the life of the blessed Holy Trinity, the mystical union between the Father, the Son, and the Holy Spirit. 'There is one body,' he says, 'and one Spirit . . . one Lord . . . one God and Father of all.' Three in one, one in three. That is the kind of unity about which the apostle is speaking, and he now proceeds to indicate in greater detail the character of the unity in terms of the part played by the three persons in its production.

(a) 'One Spirit, even as ye are called in one hope of your calling'
It is the peculiar work of the Spirit to 'call' us into this unity. He does so, of course, by convicting us, by quickening us, by enabling us to believe. He enters into us. He baptizes us into the body of Christ (1 Cor. 12:13). He then enlightens our understanding and leads us on. We enjoy His fellowship.

The apostle is particularly concerned to emphasize the 'calling' of Christians, the results of this call worked by the Holy Spirit, and the effectual character of this work. He does so in many places. In 1 Corinthians 2, for example, he tells us that 'The natural man receiveth not the things of the Spirit of God: for they are foolishness unto him: neither can he know them, because they are spiritually discerned' (verse 14). How then does anyone believe? He says, 'God hath revealed them unto us by his Spirit' (verse 10). And again, 'We have received, not the spirit of the world, but the spirit which is of God; that we might know the things that are freely given to us of God' (verse 12). It is the Spirit who does this work, and it is an effectual work. He does the same thing in each one of us, though there may be minor and unimportant differences in detail. The result is that He produces an identity of belief and of outlook, and especially of hope. In other words, these people are all looking in the same direction. The verse of a hymn sums it up for us:

> *One the object of our journey,*
> *One the faith which never tires,*
> *One the earnest looking forward,*
> *One the hope our God inspires.*

One the gladness of rejoicing
On the far eternal shore,
Where the one almighty Father
Reigns in love for evermore.

'One hope of your calling'! These people are 'strangers and pilgrims' in this world. They are new men with an entirely new outlook, and they are all looking towards the same eternal home. They have 'one hope of their calling', the blessed hope of the coming of our Lord, the final judgment of sin and evil, the setting up of His eternal kingdom, and their reigning with Him in the glory everlasting. 'One Spirit'! The one work of the one Spirit is that it always leads to 'one hope of your calling'

(b) 'One Lord, one faith, one baptism'

First we must emphasize the fact that there is only 'one Lord'. This was the very essence of apostolic preaching. Peter states it unequivocally and boldly when he and John were arraigned before the authorities. 'There is none other name under heaven given among men, whereby we must be saved' (Acts 4:12). There is no other! There is no second! You cannot put anybody by His side. He is absolutely unique. He is no mere man, teacher, or prophet. He is the Son of God! He is the Lord of glory who has taken to Himself human nature! 'One Lord – Jesus Christ,' and there is no other. Paul puts it thus in a memorable statement: 'For though there be that are called gods, whether in heaven or in earth, (as there be gods many, and lords many,) but to us there is but one God, the Father, of whom are all things, and we in him; and one Lord Jesus Christ, by whom are all things, and we by him' (1 Cor. 8:5–6). He expresses the same truth again in 1 Timothy 2:5: 'There is one God, and one mediator' – and only one – 'between God and men, the man Christ Jesus.'

Now, in the matter of Christian unity this is essential. The unity is the unity of those who believe that there is only 'one Lord', and that He is so perfect, and His work so perfect, that He needs no assistance. There is no co-redemptrix such as the Roman Catholics claim the virgin Mary to be. There is no assistant needed. The Christian does not need the supererogation of the saints, and does not need to pray to them. There is only one mediator, and He is enough. He is complete in and of Himself, and nothing must be added to Him and His perfect completed work. The only unity known to the New Testament is that of people who believe this truth. It is an essential part of the definition of the unity. We look to this unique Lord, and we look at no-one but Him. He is the first and the last, the Alpha and the Omega, the beginning and the end; He is the all and in all. 'He that glorieth, let him glory in the Lord.' 'One Lord'!

Paul reminds us also that there is but 'one faith'. What does this mean? This is more difficult. There are those who say that it is a reference to our subjective faith, to our belief, or to the quality of our faith. That is included, I believe; but it seems to me to stop far short of the real emphasis of the apostle at this point. There is surely an objective element here. Does this mean that we must subscribe to a certain complete and full confession of faith or to a particular creed? It cannot be that, because there have always been differences in such confessions at certain points and with respect to certain details. That is the thing to which we come eventually, as he points out in verse 13. But he says here that there is already this 'one faith'.

What is this one faith? It seems to me that there is only one answer to the question. It is the great essential New Testament message concerning justifying faith. That was the very nerve and centre of apostolic preaching. It is stated perfectly by this same apostle in the words, 'I am not ashamed of the gospel of Christ: for it is the power of God unto salvation to every one that believeth; to the Jew first, and also to the Greek. For therein is the righteousness of God revealed from faith to faith: as it is written, The just shall live by faith' (Rom. 1:16–17). This was the kernel of apostolic preaching, that it is by faith a man is justified, not by the deeds of the law, nor any righteousness of his own.

We have a classic statement of it in Romans 3. Having reminded us that as Christians we are now in a new position, in the words, 'But now the righteousness of God without the law is manifested' (verse 21), Paul goes on to say, 'Being justified freely by his grace through the redemption that is in Christ Jesus: whom God hath set forth to be a propitiation through faith in his blood, to declare his righteousness for the remission of sins that are past, through the forbearance of God; to declare, I say, at this time his righteousness: that he might be just, and the justifier of him which believeth in Jesus. Where is boasting then? It is excluded. By what law? of works? Nay: but by the law of faith. Therefore we conclude that a man is justified by faith without the deeds of the law' (verses 24–27).

That is the great central message of the gospel. It is through this faith in the Lord Jesus Christ and His work that we are justified. That is the meaning of this 'one faith'. It is, of course, the whole argument of the Epistle to the Galatians. This is the gospel, and there is no other gospel, says the apostle. And the gospel is that God justifies the ungodly who believe in Jesus. This 'one faith' is something that is set over against every other teaching with regard to the way of salvation. It is this 'one faith' over against 'baptismal regeneration'. It is this 'one faith' over against 'transmissible grace'. It is against all notions that we can justify ourselves by works or actions, our own, or those of others. It is the teaching that it is Christ alone who saves, and that we become participants in this salvation through faith. So we have 'one Lord, one faith'.

This brings us to the phrase 'one baptism'. Here again is something which we must look at carefully. I remember reading a comment on this 'one baptism' in a Christian weekly paper. The writer was happy to dismiss it with the words, 'Of course, this means water baptism by immersion.' But, surely, in the whole context we cannot regard this as just a reference to the mode of baptism.

You notice that it is put under this heading of 'one Lord'. What is the significance of that? He is the one Lord in whom we believe by faith, and by whom we are saved through faith. But, furthermore, we have to realize that we are incorporated into Him. That is the apostle's theme at this point. He has been talking about the 'one body', and he will tell us in verse 15 that Christ is the head of this 'one body'. So the obvious interpretation of this 'one baptism' is that it is a reference to our baptism into Christ. Not merely a baptism into His name, because that again calls our attention to the physical act of baptizing, whereas the apostle here is concerned rather with the question of the mystical union which is symbolized by that act. It seems to me, therefore, that this is a reference to our being baptized into the Lord Jesus Christ. I am suggesting, in other words, that it is just another way of putting what the apostle says in 1 Corinthians 12:13. There he is talking about the 'one body' as he is here in Ephesians 4, and this is how he puts it: 'For by one Spirit are we all baptized into one body, whether we be Jews or Gentiles, whether we be bond or free; and have been all made to drink into one Spirit.'

The unity we have to 'keep' is unity in the 'one Lord'. Faith is the instrument which points us to Him; but furthermore, we are incorporated into Him, we are baptized into Him, we are 'in Christ'.

It is exactly the same idea as we found in the second chapter, where Paul says that everything that happens to us happens because of our union with Christ: quickened with him, raised with him, seated with him in the heavenly places. It is exactly the same teaching as is found in Romans 6:3–5: 'Know ye not, that so many of us as were baptized into Jesus Christ were baptized into his death? Therefore we are buried with him by baptism into death: that like as Christ was raised up from the dead by the glory of the Father, even so we also should walk in newness of life. For if we have been planted together in the likeness of his death, we shall be also in the likeness of his resurrection.' This is the great and exalted teaching about the union of the believer with the Lord Jesus Christ. Or as it is put in Romans 5, we who were 'in Adam' are now 'in Christ', and we receive all the benefits of His person and of His work. 'One Lord, one faith, one baptism.'

(c) 'One God and Father of all'

The third big assertion is this glorious statement about the Father: 'One God and Father of all, who is above all, and through all, and in you all.' This is the end and the ultimate in the matter of salvation. We do not stop at the Lord Jesus Christ, the Son of God. He came and He died, as Peter reminds us, to 'bring us to God' (1 Pet. 3:18). Here we arrive at the ultimate source of all union, the God, the only God, who has created all things, by whom all things are kept going, the God who planned this great salvation and who sent His Son. We are 'His people'. We all go to Him together and worship Him as 'our Father'. 'This is life eternal,' says our Lord, 'that they might know thee the only true God, and Jesus Christ, whom thou hast sent' (John 17:3). The knowledge of God! That is the ultimate goal, the *summum bonum*. There is only one God, there is only one knowledge, and we know Him as 'our Father'.

'Ye have not received the spirit of bondage again to fear; but ye have received the Spirit of adoption, whereby we cry, Abba, Father. The Spirit itself beareth witness with our spirit, that we are the children of God: and if children, then heirs; heirs of God, and joint-heirs with Christ' (Rom. 8:15–17). This is the thing that makes us one. We are 'children' of the same Father. We know that He has a great inheritance prepared for us. And the unity that obtains among us is the unity of those who are 'joint-heirs with Christ', who are waiting for the final consummation and their entrance into the presence of God. 'Blessed are the pure in heart: for they shall see God' (Matt. 5:8). He is over all and 'above all, and through all, and in you all'.

That is the account which the apostle gives of the nature of this unity, and the point that he is making is, of course, that there is no unity unless we are agreed about these things and participating in them. Paul's teaching here is exactly the same as we found in the teaching of our Lord in John 17. Unity is not something which exists, or of which you can speak, in and of itself. It is always the consequence of our belief and acceptance of this great and glorious doctrine of God who has provided in His Son the way of salvation, and who mediates it to us through the operation of the Holy Spirit. That is the basis and the nature of Christian unity. It must never be thought of except in terms of this great background, this essential doctrine.

6. GOD'S GIFTS TO THE CHURCH

We saw in our analysis of the whole section that in verses 7 to 12 the apostle teaches that God has appointed certain means to preserve and to develop this unity. This is of course of great importance, but as our present objective is a limited one we cannot go into it in detail. It is wonderful to realize that, though we are all one in the fundamental sense of which we have been speaking, we are not all identical. To 'every one of us is given grace according to the measure of the gift of Christ'. There is diversity in this great unity, as is illustrated, of course, by the analogy of the body to which Paul has already referred and with which he deals in greater detail in verses 15 and 16.

In verses 8, 9 and 10 the apostle turns aside to indicate how the Lord is in the position of being able to give these gifts according to the measure of His grace. He rejoices in the one who has ascended up on high, and has received gifts which He can then give to men. Who is this? He is the one who 'descended first into the lower parts of the earth'. The whole marvel and miracle of the incarnation is essential to this giving of gifts. It is the one who came from glory, who humbled Himself, and came 'in the likeness of men' and 'of sinful flesh', became a servant, came right down to earth and lived our life and died our death. This is the same one who has 'ascended up far above all heavens, that he might fill all things'. It is He who now dispenses these gifts.

Why does He give these gifts? For the sake and the good of His people. 'And he gave some, apostles; and some, prophets; and some, evangelists; and some, pastors and teachers.' What for? They are there for the benefit of the church. He has planned the church and brought her into being, and He has provided these offices and officers in the church 'for the perfecting of the saints'. It is in order that we who have become believers, and are in this 'one body', and sharing in this glorious unity, might be taught and trained.

Verses 13 to 16 deal with the subject of what we are being trained for. Here we are looking at what I described earlier as the ultimate goal: 'Till we all come in the unity of the faith, and of the knowledge of the Son of God, unto a perfect man, unto the measure of the stature of the fulness of Christ.' Then negatively: 'That we henceforth be no more children, tossed to and fro, and carried about with every wind of doctrine, by the sleight of men, and cunning craftiness, whereby they lie in wait to deceive; but speaking the truth in love, may grow up into him in all things, which is the head, even Christ: from whom the whole body fitly joined together and compacted by that which every joint supplieth, according to the effectual working in the measure of every part, maketh increase of the body unto the edifying of itself in love.'

7. THE HEART OF THE PROBLEM

It is at this point that we come to the heart and centre of the common modern misunderstanding. The popular idea is that, having decided to have fellowship together, though we may disagree fundamentally about doctrine, by meeting together, by being kind and friendly to one another, by working and evangelizing together, and by praying together, we eventually can hope to arrive at an agreement even about doctrine. Of course, we must not start with doctrine, because according to the accepted slogan, 'doctrine always divides'. And it is claimed that the verses we are considering teach that. Our object is to show that the teaching here is actually the exact opposite of that.

(a) Unity and faith in Ephesians 4
Notice that in verse 13 the apostle says 'we all': 'Till we all come . . .'. Now that refers to the same people we have already defined, those who have believed and received 'the gospel of salvation'. 'We all', are the people referred to in 1:12 and 13, the Jews who have received and

believed the message, the Gentiles who have done the same thing. In other words, they are the people who have already accepted the doctrine. He says, 'Till we all arrive at the unity of the faith'. The New English Bible has here, 'the unity inherent in our faith', and that is surely right. In other words, you cannot have the unity without the faith.

The question that arises is, Does this allow for present disagreement about doctrine? Does it look forward to an ultimate agreement as the result of our fellowship together? The apostle himself answers the question by telling us that what he is dealing with is the 'perfecting' of something that is already in existence. He is not teaching that we are going to 'arrive' at something which was non-existent before. What he is saying is that what is in existence already is going to grow and develop and ultimately will be perfected. I argue thus because he says in verse 12 that the whole object of providing apostles and prophets and evangelists and pastors and teachers is 'the perfecting of the saints', that they may be useful in ministering to the building up of the body of Christ.

This interpretation may be further substantiated. Paul says, 'Till we all come in the unity of the faith, and of the knowledge of the Son of God.' Now, to translate the word used by the apostle by the word 'knowledge' is quite inadequate. What the apostle wrote was *epignosis*, which means 'full knowledge'. In other words, we already have knowledge, but the function of the officers in the church is to bring us to '*full* knowledge'. In the same way we have faith, and believe the faith, already. What is needed is the 'full' perfection of that. He is not envisaging a gathering of people who differ with regard to basic doctrine but who, through meeting together and through fellowship, may ultimately arrive at the same basic doctrine. That is entirely foreign to what the apostle is saying. He is writing to people who are already one in their doctrine, and one in their knowledge of the Lord Jesus Christ; but it is not perfect, or fully developed, as yet.

Now that, I suggest, is the key to the understanding of this passage. If there were any doubt about it he settles it once and for all by his use of the negative in verse 14: 'That we henceforth be no more children, tossed to and fro, and carried about with every wind of doctrine, by the sleight of men, and cunning craftiness, whereby they lie in wait to deceive.' His desire is that his readers should become adult men, that they should not remain as children. Surely that puts the matter entirely beyond dispute. Even as 'children', incomplete, not fully developed, they are one. They stand as an acorn does in relation to the full-grown oak. The moment we grasp that, we see that the current popular use of this passage is entirely false to the apostle's teaching. He is not hoping or trying to produce agreement; his concern is that the understanding, the agreement, the knowledge, and the faith which they already have should grow and develop into its ultimate completeness and fullness.

(b) New Testament teaching on maturity

This is teaching which is found very frequently in the New Testament. The apostle Peter realizes that we need to 'grow in grace, and in the knowledge of our Lord and Saviour Jesus Christ' (2 Pet. 3:18), but before we can grow we must be born. It is only a living child who can grow. There can be no growth where there is no life. The very notion of growth and development and perfection presupposes a life already in existence. Exactly the same point is made by Paul at the beginning of I Corinthians 3. He complains that the Corinthians are still babes, that he cannot write to them as men because they are not yet in a condition to receive it. But remember, they are already Christians, 'called saints'; they are born again, they have believed in 'Jesus Christ and him crucified'. They are on the one and only foundation already; but that does not mean that they are complete. They need to be taught. This knowledge needs to develop and to grow; there are aspects of it they have not yet understood.

At the end of Hebrews 5 the author makes the same complaint about his readers that he cannot feed them with 'strong meat' but can give them only 'milk'. He would like to tell them about the wonderful doctrine of Christ as Melchisedec, but he cannot. Yet the life is there: they have believed the truth; they have laid hold of the 'first principles', the elements of the gospel of Christ. The writer's concern is that they should not 'slip away' by believing false teachers. At the same time he wants them to 'go on unto perfection'.

Much the same thought is expressed in 1 Corinthians 13:12: 'Now we see through a glass, darkly; but then face to face: now I know in part; but then shall I know even as also I am known.' The fact that we now see in a glass darkly does not mean that we do not see at all or that we do not see certain things clearly. That statement in no way allows or makes provision for disagreement about the fundamentals of Christianity among Christians. No, what Paul is saying is that all of us who are agreed about these things are only seeing the glorious thing itself as in a glass darkly now, but then we shall see it face to face, in all its fullness; then shall we know even as we are known now.

That is precisely the idea we have here. From all these illustrations and parallel passages we see that the apostle is concerned about the *development* of that which is already in existence, rather than about arriving at something which is hitherto non-existent. There is no question about this. The foundation is always there, and must be there, that is, 'Jesus Christ, and him crucified' (1 Cor. 2:2). It is 'the foundation of the apostles and prophets' (Eph. 2:20), their fundamental teaching.

Perhaps the clearest statement of the point which the apostle is making here is found in Philippians 3:10, where he says that his greatest desire is 'that I may know him'. Does he mean by that, that he did not know Him at all, and that he is longing to have a knowledge of Christ? Of course not. What he is saying is this: I do know Him, but I want to know Him much more. I want to have a deeper knowledge. He longs for an 'increase' and for the perfecting of the knowledge he already has.

To put the matter finally beyond dispute we may turn to the paradoxical statement of Philippians 3:12–15. Paul begins, 'Not as though I had already attained, either were already perfect'; and then continues, 'Let us therefore, as many as be perfect, be thus minded' (verse 15). What does he mean? There is no real contradiction, of course. What he means is that all true Christians already have the knowledge essential to salvation and are perfect in that sense. So he says, 'Let us therefore, as many as be perfect, be thus minded.' Then he goes on to say, 'If in any thing ye be otherwise minded, God shall reveal even this unto you.' There are still aspects of the faith and of the truth which we do not yet know; they will be revealed to us. As regards the faith we have, and our present position on the foundation, Christ Jesus, there is a sense, therefore, in which we are already perfect. But we must also go on to perfection. We have not arrived, have not 'already attained' (verse 12). We are now growing in this knowledge that we have. We are now coming into it. It is because we are in it already that we can grow and develop in and through it.

The apostle Peter teaches the same thing: 'Desire the sincere milk of the word, that ye may grow thereby: if so be ye have tasted that the

Lord is gracious' (1 Pet. 2:2–3). It is to the people who have 'tasted that the Lord is gracious' that he writes, but they are to go on drinking in the 'milk of the word' in order that they may 'grow thereby'.

In all of these instances the basic assumption as shown by the context is the very opposite of the modern idea of a loose association of people, in disagreement about the elements of the Christian faith, but hoping to reach agreement through fellowship together.

8. THE DANGERS OF FALSE DOCTRINE

Having clearly established the harmony of our interpretation of the Ephesian passage with other New Testament teaching on Christian growth and development, we return now to verse 14 which is also very important in another way. Paul calls upon his readers to 'be no more children, tossed to and fro, and carried about with every wind of doctrine'. This presupposes just such an essential faith, belief, and knowledge, even in the youngest and most undeveloped Christian, as we have been discussing. How otherwise could these young Christians be exhorted to avoid false teaching and to hate it? Unless they had a knowledge of true teaching by which to test and examine everything else such exhortation would be futile.

We must examine this still more closely, since it is germane to the whole question of unity as it is now being presented to us. The apostle says that we must 'be no more children'. It is interesting to notice what he says about children. What are their characteristics? They are unstable, fickle, ignorant. They like novelty, dislike work but like play. They dislike being made to think and to reason; they like entertainment and excitement. Children, unfortunately, are very susceptible to showmanship and to that which is plausible and meretricious. These are their obvious characteristics. But, above all, they are liable to be deceived by that which is false. They are liable, in fact, by their very nature to be 'carried about with every wind of doctrine' because their understanding is not fully developed. They are 'children'; they have the essential life, but they need to develop, to grow, to be perfected, in order that they may be able more effectively to recognize and guard themselves against that which is false.

What, then, are the characteristics of false teaching? How important it is, in these days when scarcely any standards are recognized, to observe the detailed instruction which the apostle gives about this. 'Sleight of men' is a reference to dice-playing, a reference to deceit, trickery, and cheating. 'Cunning craftiness' is self-explanatory; it depicts the cunning man, the crafty man, the clever man, the subtle man. Paul says that they 'lie in wait'; the picture in the word is of someone following another, tracking him down as a wild animal tracks its prey. He says that there is an element of deliberate planning, of system in this false teaching. It is not something haphazard; it is organized and planned; it is laid down as traps are laid down, or as the beast of prey cunningly plans his method of procedure. The apostle sums it all up in Ephesians 6 by using the word 'wiles' – 'the wiles of the devil' (verse 11).

To what is he referring? He is dealing with sham and pretence and dishonesty. But what has this to do with the life of the Christian church? There are many instances one could give. One thinks of professors of theology telling their students, 'Now this is the real truth in this matter as discovered by scholarship; but do not preach it yet, the people are not in a position to receive it. You must introduce this carefully and slowly.' This has happened many times during the past hundred years. One thinks, too, of the practice of using such terms as 'Saviour' and 'salvation' while evacuating them of their meaning. There is also the man who takes an oath of subscription to the articles of a church or who accepts its credal basis but makes mental reservations as he does so. Is not this 'cunning craftiness'? He appears to be taking the oath, but he has his reservations. Or it could apply to the practice of issuing a document but allowing such liberty in its interpretation that those who subscribe to it may hold completely contradictory beliefs as to what the document teaches. It may even amount to being orthodox on paper, and deliberately using phrases to give the impression of orthodoxy, but at the same time attaching a private meaning and significance to the phrases used.

The apostle warns these Ephesians that they are going to be confronted with that kind of thing, that teachers will come along who will be plausible, attractive, nice and ingratiating and entertaining, who will give the impression that they are Christians, but who are not Christians! It is deceitfulness, it is 'cunning craftiness', it is akin to the tactics of the beast of prey. It is done quite deliberately to serve their own ends.

The apostle's point is that if we are to maintain the unity of the church we must beware of that kind of thing and avoid it as we avoid the very plague itself. This surely, therefore, is a most important statement for us at the present time. He is concerned about these young Christians who have 'received' the truth and have 'believed' it and subscribed to it. He is concerned that they should not be deluded, that they should not be led astray by some specious, plausible teaching which masquerades under the name of Christianity, but which is nothing but a lie and the deceit of Satan himself.

9. TRUTH AND LOVE

In verse 14 Paul has given us the negative aspect. In the following verse we have his positive teaching: 'Speaking the truth in love, [we] may grow up into him in all things, which is the head, even Christ.' Here again is a much-quoted text, but unfortunately it is not always quoted accurately. Frequently the emphasis is put entirely upon the 'love' and not at all upon the 'truth'. Indeed the position is sometimes such that we are almost told that you cannot have the two together, and that the trouble with evangelicals is that they are so concerned about the truth that they forget the element of love. Let us be honest and admit that the charge may sometimes be true, but let us add that the sin is not one-sided. We all fail in this matter of love and charity.

What the apostle is saying is not that we should avoid doctrine, or minimize doctrine, or suppress doctrine in the interests of love. What he is saying is that we should 'speak the truth in love'. Indeed it is not even just 'speaking the truth'; what he actually says is much stronger. Some say that the translation here should be 'truthing' it, that the whole of our life should be in terms of truth. We should have the truth, we should hold the truth, we should walk in the truth, we should speak the truth: 'Truthing it in love.'

In other words you cannot be truly loving unless it is in terms of truth. Let us put the emphasis on the two words. The apostle is not just telling us that we have to be nice and affable and friendly, and that in the interests of fellowship we must be prepared to accommodate, or even suppress, the truth. No! If you truly love a man you want him to know the truth because that alone can save him. But at the same time Paul warns us of the danger of becoming partisan, mere party men.

The truth is to be held in love, and it is to be presented in love. We must not be merely negative or critical, nor must our only concern be to win an argument. So let us put full emphasis upon the two aspects which are mentioned by the apostle. What he is urging is not that we should join together in a 'quest for truth'; he is not talking about searching for truth. He tells us to hold to the truth we have and to represent it and manifest it in the whole of our life, and especially in our speech, in a loving manner.

In other words, we must always contend for the truth in the right spirit. Not in a party spirit, but with a compassionate desire that men and women should come to know this glorious God who is over all, this 'one Lord' who bought us even at the cost of His own precious blood, and the gracious operations and fellowship of the Holy Spirit. And if we hold this doctrine truly, surely it is something which will in and of itself compel us to preach and to present this truth in such a spirit of love.

Let me now attempt to summarize the apostle's teaching in this chapter. The only unity of which this passage speaks is an already existing spiritual unity which then expresses itself externally. Certain things are essential to it. First and foremost, a fundamental spiritual experience of regeneration or rebirth produced by the Holy Spirit. Unity is never considered except in terms of this 'new nature' and 'new life', which express themselves always in a belief of certain fundamental truths: the 'word' or 'words' of which our Lord speaks in John 17; the 'teaching' or 'doctrine' of which the apostle speaks in Ephesians.

What are these truths? That man is lost and helpless and hopeless because of sin and the fall. That the Lord Jesus Christ, who is the Son of God, saves us by His perfect life of obedience to the law and by His death, which was the result of His bearing our guilt and the punishment meted out upon it by the law of God. That salvation becomes ours by faith alone; it is apart from any works or any merit in ourselves, and solely as the result of God calling us effectually by His Spirit. That is the faith, without which there is no unity.

Now this is not the whole or the fullness of truth; much more remains for us to grasp and to learn. Otherwise these New Testament Epistles would never have been written. The new-born babe in Christ has not a full understanding; he needs to grow, he needs to be instructed, he needs to be warned and guarded. Hence, again, the New Testament Epistles, and hence the offices appointed in the church. There are many things about which this babe may even be wrong for the time being, or at any rate he may be muddled and confused in his understanding of them. I emphasize again that he possesses the essential truth, without which there is no salvation at all; but having that he may be very unclear about many other matters. For instance, he may be Calvinistic or Arminian in his understanding of what we may call the mechanism of salvation; but that does not mean that he has not the essential truth. He may know nothing about the doctrine of the final perseverance of the saints; he may be very lacking in his understanding of the doctrine of the union of the believer with Christ; he may be very confused about a good deal of prophetic teaching, and uncertain about some aspects of the sacrament of baptism and about the final glorious hope. But though all that may be true of him, he nevertheless is a 'child', he is born again of the Spirit. He has received this fundamental message of salvation, the only way of salvation through the Lord Jesus Christ and His work. He needs to grow in his understanding of the many things of which he is at present relatively ignorant, but such matters are not essential to salvation. They are a part of this perfecting, this full knowledge, at which we shall arrive only when we are in the glory itself.

My contention is that the teaching of the New Testament is quite clear about this, that there is an absolute foundation, an irreducible minimum, without which the term 'Christian' is meaningless, and without subscribing to which a man is not a Christian. That is 'the foundation of the apostles and prophets': the doctrine concerning 'Jesus Christ, and him crucified', and justification by faith only. The passages we have considered teach that apart from that there is no such thing as fellowship, no basis of unity at all.

How easy it is to say, Well, it does not matter how much we disagree, let us pray together. But the question arises at once, How does one pray? One man says that he can turn to God whenever he likes, that he has only to sit down and relax, and he is already listening to God and talking to God. The other says that there is only one way of entry into 'the holiest of all', and that is 'by the blood of Jesus'. How can those two men pray *together*? True fellowship in prayer is not possible unless we are clear as to the way of access into the presence of God. That is why this is so constantly repeated in the New Testament. For instance, Paul says in Romans 5:1–2: 'Therefore being justified by faith, we have peace with God through our Lord Jesus Christ: by whom also we have access by faith into this grace wherein we stand.' We have no such access without Him. But the other man claims that he has, that a man can pray to God apart from the Lord Jesus Christ, and apart from the influence and the work of the Holy Spirit. What is the point of talking about unity in prayer when it is clearly impossible unless we are agreed as to how one prays?

In the same way the idea that you can evangelize together without bringing doctrine into it is surely the height of folly. If you call upon men to come to Christ certain questions at once inevitably arise: Who is He? Why should one come to Him? How does one come to Him? Why is He called the Saviour? How does He save? From what does He save?

In other words the teaching is that there is no fellowship among people who are not agreed about the one Spirit, 'one Lord, one faith, one baptism, one God . . . who is over all'. There is no real fellowship and unity in a group of people where some believe in the wrath of God against sin and that it has already been 'revealed from heaven' (Rom. 1:18), and others not only do not believe in the wrath of God at all, but say that it is almost blasphemous to teach such a thing and that they cannot believe in a God who is capable of wrath. Fellowship exists only among those who believe, as the result of the operation of the Holy Spirit, these essential truths concerning man's lost estate, that we are all 'by nature the children of wrath' (Eph. 2:3), and the action of God in Christ Jesus for our salvation and restoration. There is no fellowship between people who believe that and those who believe something else, which they may call a gospel but which, as Paul tells the Galatians, is not a gospel (Gal. 1:6–7). How ridiculous it is to suggest that there can be fellowship and unity between those who believe that they are saved and have access into God's presence solely because in His great love He made His own Son 'to be sin for us' (2 Cor. 5:21) and spared Him not 'but delivered him up for us all' (Rom. 8:32), and those who believe that the death of Christ was a great tragedy, but that God forgives us even that, and that ultimately we save ourselves by our obedience, good works, and our practice of religion. Those are the conclusions to which we are driven by our examination of the two passages which are so frequently quoted today. They agree entirely with each other; they say precisely the same thing. But let us turn now to look at some of the supporting evidence elsewhere in the New Testament. We shall soon find that this is not some isolated emphasis.

Part III: New Testament Corroboration

1. CAUSES OF DISUNITY

The New Testament teaches that certain things break this unity. What are they? One is that people, instead of looking at Christ tend to form factions around men, and say, as they did at Corinth, 'I am of Paul; and I of Apollos; and I of Cephas.' The question Paul puts to such people is, Have you been baptized into any of these? He answers by reminding them that they have been baptized into Christ alone and that He cannot be divided (1 Cor. 1:10–16). The moment you take your eyes off Him and look at anybody else you are already causing a disturbance in this unity and threatening to disrupt it.

Still more important is false teaching. What does this include? Among other things, philosophy, or 'the wisdom of this world'. Paul was terrified, as he tells us in 1 Corinthians 1:17, 'lest the cross of Christ should be made of none effect' through philosophy, through turning it into a notion and an idea instead of believing the stark reality of the fact of what happened there, that God was making 'him to be sin for us, who knew no sin' (2 Cor. 5:21), that God was smiting Him with the stripes that we deserve. The apostle foresees the danger of philosophizing or turning the cross into nothing more than a beautiful picture. He says that this destroys the unity completely. The same idea is taught in Colossians 2, where he warns against substituting philosophy, this same wisdom of men, for the facts reported in the gospel and the true meaning of those facts.

John says the same thing in his First Epistle with regard to the antichrist. The antichrists he exposed were those who denied the reality of the incarnation and the work of Christ. Some denied that He had really come in the body and said that He had but a phantom body, and so on. Others denied His deity and regarded Him as but a man. These are the things that cause division because they all interfere with the doctrine concerning the one Spirit, the one Lord, the one Father, and all that is involved in the content of the doctrine.

Others who cause division are those who fall back upon 'the works of the law'. Those were the people who in the early church said that you must be circumcised, that you must keep the law in addition to believing in Christ. That was the heresy which Paul had to deal with in his letter to the Galatians. It is the theme likewise of the Epistle to the Hebrews. Those people did not realize as they should have done that Christ is pre-eminent and all-sufficient, and they were beginning to look back to the old Jewish religion. Those are the people who caused disunity. These Judaizers were obviously in the mind of the apostle as he wrote the third chapter of the Epistle to the Philippians. He has them in mind also in writing 1 Timothy 1. These people always want to go back under the law, and are ever ready to rely on 'endless genealogies' and other things for their salvation. The apostle's teaching is that the law is all right when it does its own work, but that it is never a means of salvation. Neither law nor angels nor any other agency can save. There is but one message of salvation: 'This is a faithful saying, and worthy of all acceptation, that Christ Jesus came into the world to save sinners' (1 Tim. 1:15). To suggest anything else or to modify that is to cause division.

Then, of course, any attempt to add to Christ and His work has the same effect. Was not that the chief point under discussion in the council at Jerusalem reported in Acts 15? The decision was that no yoke of law must be put upon Christians, that no addition must be made, that Christ is sufficient. The same thing in a different form is dealt with in Colossians, where the apostle denounces talk about intermediaries because they are not necessary, and all the various angels and hierarchies that were supposed to come between man and God. He denounces that because it causes disunity. Why and how? Because it interferes with the fundamental faith and belief which makes a man a Christian at all.

The third group of things which cause disunity is anything that exalts self and not Christ. Some in the early church were glorying in their spiritual gifts. But they are reprimanded because that again detracts from Him, takes our eyes off Him, and all the truth as it is in Christ Jesus. Anything that has that effect is always disruptive. Self leads to jealousy and rivalry and disputation and so Christ is 'divided'.

2. DOCTRINE CAN BE DEFINED

Let us now look at it positively. The New Testament everywhere insists upon true doctrine. I emphasize this because, as we have seen, the whole tendency today is to discourage talk about doctrine and to urge that we work together, pray together, and evangelize together, because 'doctrine divides'. Doctrine is being discounted in the interests of supposed unity. The fact is, however, that there is no unity apart from truth and doctrine, and it is departure from this that causes division and breaks unity.

The first thing the New Testament emphasizes is that doctrine can be defined. If this were not so Paul would never have written his Epistle to the Romans. He had been unable to visit them, so he writes to them a summary of his teaching. It is a great doctrinal statement in which the cardinal doctrines of justification, atonement, union with Christ, assurance, the final perseverance of the saints, and so on, are set forth. Let us remind ourselves again of 1 Corinthians 3:11: 'Other foundation can no man lay than that is laid.' The apostle had already laid it: Jesus Christ and Him crucified; there is no other. That is an absolute. What is the purpose of 1 Corinthians 15? Is it not to say just this: that belief or disbelief in the literal physical resurrection is not an immaterial or unimportant point? The apostle says that it is as important as this, that if it had not happened, 'then is our preaching vain, and your faith is also vain . . . ye are yet in your sins' (verses 14, 17). But the whole tendency today is to say that it does not matter whether a man believes in the literal physical resurrection or not. The apostle Paul says it is an absolute and that there is no gospel apart from it: 'Ye are yet in your sins'! The same argument is found in 2 Timothy 2. Nowhere, perhaps, is it stated more clearly than in the first chapter of the Epistle to the Galatians. He 'marvels' that they are so soon turned away from the gospel which he had preached to them: 'I marvel that ye are so soon removed from him that called you into the grace of Christ unto another gospel: which is not another . . .' (Gal. 1:6–7). How can he say that if you cannot define the gospel?

But that is far removed from the modern attitude and the way in which the subject of unity is being presented today. We are told that the Christian faith cannot be stated in propositions, that it is something mystical which cannot be analysed or put down in a series of definitions stating what is right and what is wrong. By saying that, they are not only running counter to the practice of the church in the early centuries when she drew up her creeds and confessions of faith; they are also denying the teaching of the New Testament itself which maintains that truth can be so defined that you can say that a man has departed from it. For how can you say that a man has departed from something if you do not know what the thing itself is? The whole presupposition is that it can be defined and described accurately. Nothing is so interesting as to contrast the ecumenical councils of the first centuries of the Christian era with the World Council of Churches today. The great concern of the former was doctrine: definition of doctrine and denunciation of error and heresy. The chief characteristic of the modern movement is doctrinal indifferentism and the exaltation of a spirit of inclusivism and practical co-operation.

But the apostle goes even further than that. He says to the Philippians, 'Brethren, be followers together of me' (Phil. 3:17). He does not hesitate to put it like that. He appeals to them to follow him and his teaching and example. That follows what he has already said: 'Nevertheless, whereto we have already attained, let us walk by the same rule, let us mind the same thing' (verse 16). They were to think the same thing, and to go on preaching and teaching the same thing. In 2 Timothy 2:8 he talks about 'my gospel'. He is contrasting it with 'other gospels'. He is not saying what I once remember reading in a sermon on this text: 'The important thing is that you should have an experience, that you should be able to say "my gospel". Of course, it may not be the other man's gospel, but the thing is, can you say "my gospel"?' According to that interpretation the important thing is to have an experience, to be able to say that something has happened to you. The precise cause of the experience was regarded as being unimportant. But the apostle, surely, is teaching the exact opposite of that. He is saying that his gospel alone is the true gospel, not because it was his, or because of what it had done for him, but because of what God had done in Christ. The context in which he makes his statement is the false teaching of others. He says, 'Remember that Jesus Christ of the seed of David was raised from the dead according to my gospel.' There were other teachers who said that 'the resurrection is past already', and they were overthrowing 'the faith of some' (verse 18). Do not listen to them, he says. The gospel that he, Paul, preached was the only true gospel, and any teaching that contradicted it was a lie.

In other words, he not only defines it, and says that it can be defined, but he says, This is it, and every other is wrong. The same truth emerges in Hebrews 4:14–16: 'Seeing then that we have a great high priest, that is passed into the heavens, Jesus the Son of God, let us hold fast our profession' – our confession, the faith which we believe concerning Him, 'Jesus the Son of God'. The remedy for the unhappiness of those Hebrew Christians was not to cultivate a vague general spirit of fellowship, but to hold fast the cardinal doctrines.

What are they? The doctrine of the person of Christ. The incarnation. Christ as our high priest who has offered His own blood as an atonement for sins, as the writer goes on to explain in chapters 7 to 10. That is the only way in which we can enter into 'the rest' that God has provided for His people. We must know the doctrine and hold on to it and reject all false teaching. It is also the only way in which we can approach 'boldly unto the throne of grace, that we may obtain mercy, and find grace to help in time of need'.

Everywhere in the New Testament, as we have seen, there is an insistence upon true doctrine in contradistinction to false doctrine. That is only possible because doctrine can be defined and stated in terms and propositions. We have an objective standard by which we can test ourselves and others.

3. False Teaching Condemned

This becomes even clearer when we note the way in which false teaching is denounced in the New Testament, and the language which is used with regard to false teachers. In particular, observe the way in which our Lord Himself does this. For the whole climate of opinion today is utterly opposed to this. I find it amusing to notice in the reviews of books that a point which is almost always emphasized is whether the writer has been entirely positive or not. We must never be negative; we must never be critical of other views. That is regarded as sub-Christian. It is the spirit that matters. So we must never criticize, still less must we denounce anything. Views which are totally divergent are to be regarded as valuable 'insights' which point in the direction of truth.

The fact is, of course, that in our misunderstanding of the New Testament and its teaching we are exalting a kind of niceness and politeness, which are not to be found there, not even in the Lord Jesus Christ Himself. Look, for instance, at what He says in Matthew 7:15–27. He says that there are false teachers whom He can compare only to 'wolves in sheep's clothing'. No severer castigation than that can be imagined. He is referring to men who themselves are deniers of the truth but who give the impression that they are preaching it. He warns us against them. They are 'false prophets', 'false teachers', people who claim that they belong to Him and say, Lord, Lord, have we not done this, that and the other in thy name? He says that they are liars and that at the great day of judgment He will say to them, 'I never knew you'! They have never been His at all. One cannot imagine any stronger teaching than that.

Or take what He teaches in Matthew 24:24–26. There, He issues a most important warning to His followers and to all Christian people throughout the centuries: 'For there shall arise false Christs, and false prophets, and shall shew great signs and wonders; insomuch that, if it were possible, they shall deceive the very elect. Behold, I have told you before. Wherefore if they shall say unto you, Behold, he is in the desert; go not forth: behold, he is in the secret chambers; believe it not.' Here He is warning us against false and deceitful teachers. The language once again is very strong.

We have already seen the same thing in Ephesians 4. Here is this great apostle, filled with the spirit of love, and, let us remember, 'speaking the truth in love'; but the language he uses, as we have seen, is, 'Be no more children, tossed to and fro, and carried about with every wind of doctrine, by the sleight of men, and cunning craftiness. . .'. That is 'speaking the truth in love'. It includes denouncing these false teachers in the church and making clear the sort of people they are and the kind of thing they do. He describes them as predatory beasts lying in wait 'to deceive'. To speak the truth in love includes a clear exposition of error, and everything that can be harmful to 'babes in Christ'.

Even stronger language is used by the apostle in his farewell address to the elders of the church at Ephesus: 'Take heed therefore unto yourselves, and to all the flock, over the which the Holy Ghost hath made you overseers, to feed the church of God, which he hath purchased with his own blood. For I know this, that after my departing shall grievous wolves enter in among you, not sparing the flock. Also of your own selves shall men arise, speaking perverse things, to draw away disciples after them. Therefore watch, and remember, that by the space of three years I ceased not to warn every one night and day with tears' (Acts 20:28–31). That is the language! 'Wolves'! 'Grievous wolves'! In 2 Corinthians 11:13–15 he calls them 'false apostles' who are like the devil, who 'himself is transformed into an angel of light'. In Galatians 1:8 he says, 'Though we, or an angel from heaven, preach any other gospel unto you . . . let him be anathema', that is, let him be accursed.

All that comes under the heading of 'speaking the truth in love'. Why is such speech abominated today and regarded as sub-Christian? Because the notion of truth as something which can be defined has gone, and we are replacing it by a flabby, sentimental notion of unity and of fellowship. In Philippians 3:18–19 the apostle writes, 'For many walk, of whom I have told you often, and now tell you even weeping, that they are the enemies of the cross of Christ: whose end is destruction, whose God is their belly, and whose glory is in their shame, who mind earthly things.' Such people were in the church and represented themselves as teachers of the truth of the gospel, but the apostle does not hesitate to denounce them as 'enemies of the cross of Christ'. Why? Because they were denying this essential doctrine at some point.

We must speak the truth in love about such people in order that the 'children' in the faith may be protected from their nefarious influence. The terms used about such people are extraordinary in their strength and variation. He talks about 'philosophy and vain deceit'; 'the traditions of men' (Col. 2:8); 'profane and vain babblings' (1 Tim. 6:20); words which 'will eat as doth a canker [cancer]' (2 Tim. 2:17). The apostle Peter in equally strong terms speaks of 'wells without water' (2 Pet. 2:17). They appear to have something but in reality have nothing. What is in their gospel, what is its content? They stand and talk glibly about love; but what is the love of which they are speaking? Where is their salvation? What is the meaning of the terms which they are employing?

Look also at the language used by Jude. Look at the language used in the letters to the churches in Revelation 2 and 3. The New Testament talks about people being carried away with 'strong delusion', and people believing 'a lie' (2 Thess. 2:11). The false prophets are referred to as 'dogs', as those who teach and speak 'damnable heresies', whose ways are pernicious and who are 'liars'. It refers to false teaching as a canker, a cancer that eats away at the vitals of life. That is New Testament teaching. But all that is abominated today and is regarded as being a complete denial of the spirit of love and of fellowship, indeed of the spirit of Christ.

In other words, this modern teaching about unity has departed so far from the New Testament that it dislikes any polemical element at all in the preaching and the teaching of the truth. As I say, we are told that we must never be negative, that we should always be positive. The man who is admired is the man who says, I am not a controversialist, I am simply a preacher of the gospel! Some evangelists and others who are evangelical in their own views are praised by those who are very liberal in their theology on the grounds that they do not 'attack' liberalism and modernism. That is what is admired. Any polemical element is regarded as a negation of the Christian spirit. We must never criticize; we must always be kind and friendly. I agree that we must always be kind and friendly, we must always 'speak the truth in *love*'. But we must always 'speak the *truth* in love'. We must, as the New Testament itself does, 'contend for the faith'. We must expose error and denounce it and not be men-pleasers only. The New Testament is full of that, as I have just proved.

That is what was done at the time of the Protestant Reformation. That is what is always done in times of revival and renewal because at such times there is a return to the New Testament. Error is unmasked, exposed, and denounced. It was done, likewise, in the time of the Puritans. Let us remember in these days when 'niceness' and 'friendliness' and 'fellowship' are exalted to the supreme position and at the expense of truth, that the exhortation addressed to the New Testament teachers and believers was not that they should be ready to agree with anything for the sake of unity and fellowship. The exhortation addressed to them in 1 Corinthians 16:13–14 is: 'Watch ye, stand fast in the faith, quit you like men, be strong. Let all your things be done with charity.' We are to be men, we are to be strong, we are to stand fast in the faith which we have believed. We are to know that we have a foundation beneath our feet and we must know what it is. We are not to be riding on clouds; we are not to be in the air; we are to be 'standing fast' on a solid, recognizable, definable foundation. We are exhorted to 'earnestly contend for the faith' (Jude 3).

In 2 John we are told that we are not to receive into our house, or to 'bid God speed' to, a false teacher and that to do so is to be 'partaker of his evil deeds' (verses 10–11). In 2 Thessalonians 2:15 the apostle uses these words, 'Therefore, brethren, stand fast, and hold the traditions which ye have been taught, whether by word, or our epistle.' Traditions taught by word and in writing! Something definable, something concrete, something clear, something which is unmistakable. That was written to people such as the Thessalonians, to young Christians in the faith. And we are to contend for it earnestly, with all our might and power.

In Titus 3:10–11, the apostle sums it all up again in a most important statement: 'A man that is an heretick after the first and second admonition reject; knowing that he that is such is subverted, and sinneth, being condemned of himself.' We are not to be 'nice and friendly' to him. If he persists in being a heretic after the first and second admonition we are to reject him. He is a danger to the church and we must put him out. That is the plain and explicit teaching of the New Testament everywhere. All this, of course, is quite inevitable in view of the nature of the truth concerning salvation, and the nature of the unity that obtains in the church. But it is far removed from the popular teaching of today which not only tolerates the doctrine of men who deny the plain New Testament teaching concerning our Lord's person and work, but even exalts them and praises them as outstanding Christians worthy of the emulation of young believers.

Part IV: Conclusions

It may be helpful to summarize and list the conclusions we have arrived at.

1. Unity must never be isolated or regarded as something in and of itself.

2. It is equally clear that the question of unity must never be put first. We must never start with it, but always remember the order stated so clearly in Acts 2:42, where fellowship follows doctrine: 'They continued stedfastly in the apostles' doctrine and fellowship, and in breaking of bread, and in prayers.' That, as we have seen, is precisely the order in which they are placed in both John 17 and Ephesians 4. The present tendency to discount and to depreciate doctrine in the interests of unity is simply a denial and a violation of plain New Testament teaching.

3. We must never start with the visible church or with an institution, but rather with the truth which alone creates unity. Failure to realize this point was surely the main trouble with the Jews at the time when our Lord was in this world. It is dealt with in the preaching of John the Baptist, who said, 'Bring forth therefore fruits worthy of repentance, and begin not to say within yourselves, We have Abraham to our father: for I say unto you, That God is able of these stones to raise up children unto Abraham' (Luke 3:8). Our Lord teaches the same thing in John 8:32–34. The Jews had objected to His saying 'the truth shall make you free', their argument being that they were Abraham's seed, and were never in bondage to any man. He draws attention to their rejection of His Word and their

attempts to kill Him, and concludes: 'If ye were Abraham's children, ye would do the works of Abraham. . . . Ye do the deeds of your father. . . . Ye are of your father the devil' (John 8:39, 41, 44). Their fatal assumption was that the fact that they were Jews guaranteed of necessity their salvation, that membership of the nation meant that they were truly children of God. As John the Baptist indicated, the notion was entirely mechanical; God could produce such people out of stones.

The apostle Paul also deals with this confusion when he says in writing to the Romans: 'For he is not a Jew, which is one outwardly; neither is that circumcision, which is outward in the flesh: but he is a Jew, which is one inwardly; and circumcision is that of the heart, in the spirit, and not in the letter; whose praise is not of men, but of God' (Rom. 2:28, 29). He repeats this in the words, 'For they are not all Israel, which are of Israel' (Rom. 9:6). This is further enforced by the statement, 'Know ye therefore that they which are of faith, the same are the children of Abraham' (Gal. 3:7). And also, 'And if ye be Christ's, then are ye Abraham's seed, and heirs according to the promise' (Gal. 3:29).

The same mistake of starting with the visible institution rather than with truth was also made at the time of the Reformation. What Luther was enabled to see, and what accounted for his courageous stand, was this self-same point. He refused to be bound by that mighty institution, the Roman Catholic Church, with her long centuries of history. Having been liberated by the truth of justification by faith he saw clearly that truth must always come first. It must come before institution and traditions, and everything – every institution, even the church – must be judged by the Word of truth. The invisible church is more important than the visible Church, and loyalty to the former may involve either expulsion or separation from the latter, and the formation of a new visible church.

4. The starting point in considering the question of unity must always be regeneration and belief of the truth. Nothing else produces unity, and, as we have seen clearly, it is impossible apart from this.

5. An appearance or a façade of unity based on anything else, and at the expense of these two criteria, or which ignores them, is clearly a fraud and a lie. People are not one, nor in a state of unity, who disagree about fundamental questions such as (a) whether we submit ourselves utterly to revealed truth or rely ultimately upon our reason and human thinking; (b) the historic fall, and man's present state

and condition in sin, under the wrath of God, and in complete helplessness and hopelessness as regards salvation; and (c) the person of our Lord Jesus Christ and the utter, absolute necessity, and sole sufficiency, of His substitutionary atoning work for sinners. To give the impression that they are one simply because of a common outward organization is not only to mislead the world which is outside the church but to be guilty of a lie.

6. To do anything which supports or encourages such an impression or appearance of unity is surely dishonest and sinful. Truth and untruth cannot be reconciled, and the difference between them cannot be patched over. Error is always to be exposed and denounced for truth's sake, and also, as we have seen, for the sake of babes in Christ. This is also important from the standpoint of the statement in John 17:21, 'that the world may believe that thou hast sent me'. Nothing so surely drives the world away from the truth as uncertainty or confusion in the church with respect to the content of her message.

That is undoubtedly the main cause of the present declension in religion. The world will not be impressed by a mere coming together in externals while there is central disagreement about the fundamentals of the faith. It will interpret it as an attempt on the part of church authorities to save their institution in much the same way as it sees business men forming combines and amalgamations with the same object and intention. The question the world is still asking is, What is Christianity? What is your teaching? Have you anything authoritative and powerful to offer us? It is interested in this rather than in organizational matters, and rightly so. It is also ready to respond to it.

7. To regard a church, or a council of churches, as a forum in which fundamental matters can be debated and discussed, or as an opportunity for witness-bearing, is sheer confusion and muddled thinking. There is to be no discussion about 'the foundation', as we have seen. If men do not accept that, they are not brethren and we can have no dialogue with them. We are to preach to such and to evangelize them. Discussion takes place only among brethren who share the same life and subscribe to the same essential truth. It is right and good that brethren should discuss together matters which are not essential to salvation and about which there is, and always has been, and probably always will be, legitimate difference of opinion. We can do no better at that point than quote the old

adage, 'In things essential unity, in things indifferent liberty, in all things charity.'

Before there can be any real discussion and dialogue and exchange there must be agreement concerning primary and fundamental matters. Without the acceptance of certain axioms and propositions in geometry, for example, it is idle to attempt to solve any problem. If certain people refuse to accept the axioms, and are constantly querying and disputing them, clearly there is no point of contact between them and those who do accept them. It is precisely the same in the realm of the church. Those who question and query, let alone deny, the great cardinal truths that have been accepted throughout the centuries do not belong to the church, and to regard them as brethren is to betray the truth. As we have already reminded ourselves, the apostle Paul tells us clearly what our attitude to them should be: 'A man that is an heretick after the first and second admonition reject' (Tit. 3:10). They are to be regarded as unbelievers who need to be called to repentance and acceptance of the truth as it is in Christ Jesus. To give the impression that they are Christians with whom other Christians disagree about certain matters is to confuse the genuine seeker and enquirer who is outside. But such is the position prevailing today. It is based upon a failure to understand the nature of the New Testament church which is 'the pillar and ground of the truth' (1 Tim. 3:15). In the same way it is a sheer waste of time to discuss or debate the implications of Christianity with people who are not agreed as to what Christianity is. Failure to realize this constitutes the very essence of the modern confusion.

8. Unity must obviously never be thought of primarily in numerical terms, but always in terms of life. Nothing is so opposed to the biblical teaching as the modern idea that numbers and powerful organization alone count. It is the very opposite of the great biblical doctrine of 'the remnant', stated, for instance, so perfectly by Jonathan to his armour-bearer as they faced alone the hosts of the Philistines, in the words: 'Come, and let us go over unto the garrison of these uncircumcised: it may be that the Lord will work for us: for there is no restraint to the Lord to save by many or by few' (1 Sam. 14:6). Still more strikingly, perhaps, is it taught in the incident of Gideon and the Midianites, where we read of God reducing the army of Israel from 32,000 to 300 as a preliminary to victory (Judg. 7).

God has done His greatest work throughout the centuries through remnants, often even through individuals. Why is it that we forget Micaiah the son of Imlah, and Jeremiah, and Amos, John the Baptist, the mere twelve disciples; and Martin Luther standing alone defying some twelve centuries of tradition and all the power of a mighty church? This is not to advocate smallness or exclusiveness as if they had some inherent merit; but it is to suggest that the modern slavish attitude to bigness and organization cuts right across a central biblical emphasis. Indeed it suggests ignorance of, and lack of faith in, the power of the Holy Spirit.

9. The greatest need of the hour is a new baptism and outpouring of the Holy Spirit in renewal and revival. Nothing else throughout the centuries has ever given the church true authority and made her, and her message, mighty. But what right have we to pray for this, or to expect that He will honour or bless anything but the truth that He Himself enabled the authors of the Old Testament and the New Testament to write? To ask Him to do so is not only near blasphemy but also the height of folly. Reformation and revival go together and cannot be separated. He is the Spirit of truth, and He will honour nothing but the truth. The ultimate question facing us these days is whether our faith is in men and their power to organize, or in the truth of God in Christ Jesus and the power of the Holy Spirit. Let me put it another way: Are we primarily concerned about the size of the church or the purity of the church, both in doctrine and in life? Indeed, finally it comes to this: Is our view of the church Roman Catholic (inclusivist, organizational, institutional, and hierarchical) or reformed, emphasizing the universal priesthood of all believers and the need for keeping the church herself constantly under the judgment of the Word?

Ten

*

'Consider Your Ways'
The Outline of a New Strategy[1]

*

It seems to me that at least once a year it is a good thing for us to review our position. The danger with all of us is that we simply go on doing our work and become so immersed in it that we are in danger of missing the wood because of the trees. It is a good thing therefore, as far as we can, to stand aside for a moment and look at the whole situation, and particularly as we ourselves stand in relation to it. It was in order that we might do that that I asked Mr Caiger[2] to read us that first chapter of the book of the prophet Haggai.

I do not propose to give an exposition of this chapter. I do not intend to do what I did last year, which was more or less entirely exposition. But I think that Haggai chapter one sets before us the present situation, as I see it, and that the words of verse 5, repeated in verse 7, are particularly relevant: 'Now therefore thus saith the Lord of hosts; Consider your ways.' The position as described by the prophet is very much the same as it is at the present time, a period of transition, of reconstruction, of new beginnings. Haggai addresses these people in that situation, points out to them their failure, indicates to them what they are doing, and what they are not doing, and in the midst of it there comes this great appeal, 'Consider your ways'. Now that is what I am hoping to do, but not, as I say, in the form of a verse-by-verse exposition. I am rather

[1]An address given to the members of the Westminster Fellowship of Ministers at their annual outing to Welwyn on 19 June, 1963. As usual, Dr Lloyd-Jones announced no heading. The above heading, and the subheadings which follow, have been added by the publishers.
[2]The Rev John Caiger, Secretary of the Ministers' Fellowship.

[164]

taking that general exhortation and applying it to our situation at the present time.

Or to put it in a different form, I am going to try to 'draw out' in the Puritan manner, the lessons which come inevitably, as I would have thought, from what I was trying to say last year.[3] All I was able to do then was to ask certain questions in the light of the exposition of the two passages, John 17 and Ephesians 4. Now I want to carry that a stage further and to enter into a little more detail. Present circumstances, as I see them, demand that we should 'consider our ways' in the light of our present position. There are certain unique features, I think, which compel us to do this and I am going to note some of them.

The Present Situation

One feature is that we happen to be living at a time when everything in connection with the church, her life, and her activity, once more seems to be in the melting pot. I do not think it is an exaggeration to say that the position in which we find ourselves is more similar to that which obtained at the time of the Protestant Reformation than anything that has happened since. I know there have been upheavals, there have been times of crisis, but I think I could demonstrate that there are features in the present situation which have not obtained since the time of the Reformation.

What I mean is this: that until comparatively recently the Reformation was taken for granted and, generally speaking, was accepted; it was not queried. There were these two great positions, the Roman Catholic and the reformed (using that term in its most general form). There they were, and everybody recognized them; but we are now in a position and a period when that is no longer the case. Everything is once more being queried. There is a kind of fluidity in the current situation such as has not been the case since the time of the Protestant Reformation. So if we had no other reason for considering our ways and examining the whole situation, this feature, I would have thought, is enough in itself. With the ecumenical movement, and still more the new relationships between the Church of Rome and the other churches, and the whole changed atmosphere, particularly in an emotional sense, we are at a point when people obviously entertain the hope of something quite new. The old landmarks are being taken down and everybody seems to be

[3] See chapter nine, 'The Basis of Christian Unity'.

agreed that we have got to think anew and afresh, and take nothing for granted. Very well, we are related to this situation, and therefore it behoves us to know exactly what our position is.

A second feature which calls for consideration is that actual unions are taking place between different sections of the Christian church. We have had them in South India; there are proposals in this country, and so on. Whether we like it or not, many will be involved in movements for amalgamation of the denominations to which they belong.

Then, as a third reason, there is the situation on the mission field and the whole question as to the future of foreign mission work as it relates to young churches and young countries. A new nationalism presents us with something quite different; until comparatively recently these other countries were prepared to receive missionaries from the so-called colonial powers. There was no difficulty about it. Other countries were ready for us to impose our patterns upon them, not only in terms of our beliefs but even in our church order and other things. But with the new nationalism that is arising they are no longer prepared to do that. Undoubtedly, they are going to think out the whole problem of the church for themselves; and that in turn compels us to do the same, because if we fail to do so, and to relate ourselves to what is happening among them, they will not listen to us at all and it will be the end of the missionary enterprise. There, I think, is another urgent reason for us to consider the whole situation.

Another reason, upon which I am not going to dilate, concerns what has been happening among the Exclusive Brethren. I am myself very deeply impressed by this, as I know many of you are. I feel that it creates a new situation for us. Here are numbers of people who have come out of the bondage in which they have been held for so long, and they are scattered all over the country, not quite knowing what to do nor where to turn. They are a body of people who in many respects have unique qualities, and I feel that it is a challenge to us to determine our relationship to them.

Then another and a very urgent matter, of course, is the blatant unbelief that is manifesting itself now in the official churches. We have known that it was there, but this unbelief is now coming into the open, declaring itself with rejoicing and not hesitating to do so; and, attracting so much publicity, it has become a matter of great interest to the general public. We are related to this and we are called upon to say something. We cannot just stand by as if nothing were happening.

I would put under this same heading what seems to me to be very real evidence of a subtle and yet rapidly increasing change in emphasis, even in evangelical thinking. This is something which has been happening in the United States for a number of years. We had a talk on the subject some two and a half years ago, if I remember rightly, by Dr Marcellus Kik, who spoke to us about the so-called 'new evangelicalism'. The fact is that there is a new movement, which has been going for a number of years now, which, while still claiming the name evangelical, is adopting positions, and prepared to make concessions, which evangelicals, until ten years ago, were not prepared even to consider. I must not go into this in detail because it will take too much time, but we note their different attitude, for instance, towards the early chapters of Genesis, towards the flood, indeed, even towards the whole question of miracles. The tendency now is to say that a miracle is purely a question of timing, in other words, that you can more or less explain miracles in terms of natural phenomena, and that what has happened is that God timed the natural phenomena to happen at a given point. But they still claim the name evangelical!

Over and above this movement in the United States there are particular instances which those who read *Christianity Today* will have observed. For example, a man who is on the faculty of a well-known and thoroughly evangelical Bible college and institute has recently published a book in which he manifests this new evangelicalism in his attitude towards the question of inspiration. The book seems to me to depart from the traditional evangelical attitude to the doctrine of inspiration. Even the Southern Baptist Church in America, which has been regarded as a pillar of evangelical orthodoxy, has an acute problem arising in one of its colleges, and for the first time, they are having to fight liberalism coming right into the heart and centre of their denomination. Coming to our own country, I think that there are evidences of the same things happening here. It is evident in a good deal of the book-reviewing that goes on; there is a new tendency to praise books which are not evangelical at all, and the caveat that is entered is mild and merely slipped in at the end. In other words, there seems to be a new attitude which takes the view that though there may be some very real poison in a book, 'nevertheless . . .'! The policy seems to me to be almost inciting the readers of these journals to read such books, as though, on the whole, they were all right and their faults almost trivial. It is as if the fact that there are merely a few minims of deadly poison in a bottle of medicine is irrelevant to the value of the remainder.

All this, it seems to me, is something which is increasing in this country. There is a tendency to be a little critical of the old emphasis upon doctrine, and one hears increasingly of people in evangelical circles saying, Well, is doctrine after all as important as all that? Now, when evangelicals begin to talk in that way, it is a very serious matter indeed. I do not think that anybody can dispute that. There has been a change, quite a striking one, during the last five years, in well-known evangelical periodicals and journals. Their whole tone is mildly critical of what evangelicalism has always stood for. There is also this tendency to gloat over scholarship. I think it is part of the inferiority complex of evangelicals – the great thing now is to prove that we are 'scholars'.

That was how it began in the United States, and it seems to me that the same thing is happening here. We are more concerned about getting a good word from so-called scholars who are not evangelical, than we are about our strict adherence to the truth. The causes of all this are very difficult to arrive at. I have my own ideas about them, but I am not going to weary you with them. All this has been going on for about ten years and I think it is beginning to show itself now in a very open manner. Here then is something that demands our attention.

Then the next reason I would give is this: the whole moral condition of the country, and the need of a clear statement, an authoritative prophetic statement. I need say no more about that for it is a thing that we are all agreed about, I am certain; but it is an appalling thought that in the present state of this country and its morals – the whole condition of society – somehow or other *we* are failing. When we contrast ourselves with what our forefathers did in such times, I think we should put on sackcloth and ashes and feel utterly ashamed of ourselves. We seem to be living in our 'cieled houses' and to be ready to believe that everything is all right as long as everything is all right with us. The whole general situation seems to pass by default as far as we are concerned.

The next thing that I would emphasize is the tremendous need of preaching the gospel in an evangelical manner up and down the country. I have a feeling that we who meet under these auspices, who belong mainly to the Greater London area, are in a very false position with regard to this, and perhaps in a very misleading one. It is a well-known fact that evangelicalism, speaking generally, is concentrated in the Greater London area. What is happening in industry is happening in evangelicalism; everything is crowding into the south-east of England. You have these great derelict areas, the north of England, the Midlands, the eastern part, and the south-west of the country, and Wales, which are virtually derelict. Our danger, it seems to me, is that because we are in the Greater London area where there are so many evangelical churches, and so many which are well attended (particularly in the outer rim of Greater London), our tendency is to say that all is well. We are in our 'cieled houses'; everything is all right with me; my church is flourishing; everything is going well; and we tend to forget the conditions that prevail in the greater part of the country. I am increasingly appalled at this and troubled about it: faithful evangelical people all over the country cannot get fellowship, cannot get spiritual food, and are at their wits' end as to what is to be done in their areas. This is a tremendous challenge to us.

In other words, to sum it all up, it seems to me that there is not only a great challenge that comes to us at this time, but a unique opportunity. The bodies which are not evangelical are failing; they have no message to offer. They are preaching ecumenicity, or they are preaching against it, and the people are not given the gospel, they are not given the message. It is we alone who can give them this message and there is this unique opportunity calling to us. But in this very situation we seem to be silent; we seem to be ineffective; we seem to be doing nothing; our voice is not really being heard. In this tremendous period of change and crisis, with people looking for a lead, waiting, wondering what is going to happen, there is no clear statement emanating from the evangelicals. We do issue statements now and again, but I think that we will all agree, even those of us who put our names to them, that they are very tepid and harmless; there is no challenge in them. They are so carefully worded that in the end they achieve practically nothing. Such is the situation in which we find ourselves, and it is in the light of it that I say, 'Consider your ways'.

Let me make it clear before I proceed any further that what I am going to say applies to all of us, to all evangelicals, to evangelicals in every section of the Christian church. It applies to some more than others but I would make it quite clear that I have no one particular denomination or section of the Christian church in mind. I say, 'Let a ,nan examine himself' (1 Cor. 11:28). I am not here to throw stones at any particular section of the church. I believe that evangelicals in all the major denominations are in precisely the same position at the present time. When people come to me, whether they are ministers or not, and say, I am unhappy and in trouble in my denomination; what shall I do? – the one obvious thing is that there is not much point in changing denominations because precisely the same position exists in one major denomination as in another.

Here, then, is the call, 'Consider your ways'. Why are we in this parlous, ineffective position? Why are we counting for so little? Why are we so silent? Now I must try to answer these questions. I think that the one big explanation of our condition as evangelicals is that we are so divided up among the major denominations that our witness is diluted. On top of that, we have evaded the problem by contenting ourselves with 'movements'. The situation seems to me to demand a threefold analysis, and what I propose to do is chiefly to ask questions. I believe that we are at the stage when that is the thing to do. In other words it is, 'Consider your ways'. I have not come here with a cut-and-dried programme; I have not got a blueprint for the future. I do not think we are in a position to do that. What we need is to think, because the gravamen of my whole position here is that we have not been thinking and that in various ways we have indeed almost deliberately avoided thinking. Now let me put that to you in connection with three subjects.

The Evangelical Commitment to Movements

First, I would raise the question of the legitimacy or, if you prefer it, the scripturalness of movements. Now this question of movements is, of course, the predominating one in evangelicalism. The characteristic form which evangelicalism has taken for the last hundred years has been one of movements and I do not think it is at all difficult to trace the genesis of this idea. The movements arose during the last hundred years, because of the new factor which had come into the denominations in the shape of what we have called Higher Criticism, liberalism or modernism.

Prior to that the position was that men who were generally agreed about certain things might fall into error with regard to particulars, or it was sometimes that there was a general deadness or lifelessness, and a failure to apply and live up to what was more or less tacitly believed and accepted, but with the coming of the Higher Critical movement in the 1840s and following, and various other movements like Darwinism and Marxism, and then psychology, of course, the whole situation took a new turn and evangelical people recognized this. Here, it seems to me, is the crucial question. Our forefathers, our grandfathers in particular, decided to meet this by forming movements. They did not meet it on the church level. They decided that the thing to do was to form movements in which like-minded believers could come together, movements and societies in which they could find the fellowship they could not find in their churches, in which they could strengthen one another's faith and make protests against what was happening. So you had the coming into being of large numbers of movements and societies among evangelical people. But the time has come for us to ask this fundamental question, Was that a scriptural procedure? Can we find a warrant for that in the Bible itself?

Now I think that one can justify movements and societies for the purpose of taking action of a social or a semi-political nature. Here you are not in the realm of doctrine but you are confronted by practical circumstances in which certain things need to be done as, for instance, the Clapham Sect with regard to the abolition of slavery. I do not think that there is any difficulty about justifying that. Most of us would grant the same to the temperance movement which followed later. In these instances a body of Christian people came together for the purpose of taking action which was chiefly semi-political or social in its ambit. But – and here is the big question – is the same thing legitimate when you come to the realm of doctrine and the essentials of the faith? It seems to me that there are certain objections to it at this level and I am going to note them in order that we may discuss them. Immediately you begin to defend the faith in terms of movements, it seems to me, you begin to atomize the truth. You no longer take it as a whole but you become concerned and interested in particulars.

We are familiar, of course, with some of the particular movements which came into being, and are still in being, for doctrinal reasons, the movement to teach sanctification, for instance. I am querying the scripturalness of that procedure – of forming a movement round one doctrine only. Is it not the case that this procedure does something that is not only dangerous but unscriptural? The inevitable tendency is to lose the balance of Scripture and 'the whole counsel of God'. One truth is being treated in isolation. A foundation is laid for a movement which is not big enough, not wide enough. To isolate any one doctrine and form a movement round it seems bound to lead to a dangerous lack of balance. I can illustrate this from the realm of medicine. In a sense, the same thing is being done in medicine now as has been done by evangelicals during the last hundred years, and with the same danger. The notion of a physician who is a general consulting physician and more or less competent with any kind of illness or affliction which affected any part of the body has gone out. You now have experts. You get a man who is interested only in the chest and not in abdominal conditions, and so on. Now there is a real danger here, for the body is one, and you may get a pain which is abdominal in its location, yet has been caused by something in the chest. So if you have your 'chest man' only, and your 'abdominal man' only, you can see the obvious dangers that arise for the patient.

I suggest that this has been happening in evangelicalism as the result of its formation of movements with regard to particular doctrines. I have mentioned sanctification as an illustration, but as another instance of the same thing, take the whole question of prophecy: is it right to have a movement or a series of movements given over to prophetical teaching? Is it right to take this out of the Scriptures and to say, Here we only deal with prophecy? I think that it is a matter for discussion whether the mere doing of that is something which, in and of itself, has taken us out of the realm of scriptural teaching. Or take another subject, evangelism. Should evangelism be in the hands of movements for evangelism? Is that scriptural? Is it right to isolate evangelism? I will go further and include missionary societies and movements in the same question.

It is an interesting thing that only evangelicals have formed interdenominational missionary societies. The others have always done it through the church as a part of the church's activity. It is evangelicals alone, as far as I am aware, who have detached it from church life, and have based it on societies and movements which are not churches, and they have been very careful to emphasize that they are not churches. This of course is another form of the question whether evangelism should ever be based on anything but a church, whether it is ever right to base it upon a movement, or upon a society, or any particular organization which is not the church.

Where the Movement Strategy Has Failed

The result of evangelicals having done these things in this way is that there is no guarantee of progressive teaching. A particular movement says, I am concerned only about evangelism. The converts are left without any guarantee of further teaching, without means and methods for their growth, and the result is that you have immature Christians, and, still worse, perhaps, self-appointed leaders arising because there is no authority to control them. The society which brought them into being, as it were, under God, has finished what it was supposed to do. These people are left at that point, and they may become self-appointed leaders and teachers. I think that a part of the chaos with which we are familiar is more or less directly the result of that.

That, then, is one criticism with regard to this whole question of movements, but I suggest that there is a second criticism of the way in which we as evangelicals have faced our position in terms of movements and societies. It is that our testimony has been inconsistent, and I would argue that it has inevitably been inconsistent. As evangelicals we have criticized those in the churches who have been in error, we have denounced them for their false teaching, and yet we have continued to belong to these same churches. We have not only denounced them drastically; we have even at times said that they are not Christian in their teaching; but still we acknowledge them as members and officials and dignitaries in the churches to which we belong. It applies to all the main denominations, not to one but to all.

I suggest that this more or less nullifies our criticism, because people say, Ah well, they talk very powerfully but what do they do? They write very powerful letters but what do they *do* about it? What is the value of a powerful letter if you are still a brother of this man, and are members of the same denomination? Now I am simply putting the question, Does this procedure not inevitably nullify the effect of the protest that we are making? How can we denounce dishonesty in statesmen if there is dishonesty among ourselves? I think we have got to face these things. When there is dishonesty, intellectual dishonesty, rampant in the Christian church, how can the church speak to the nation, to the politicians, and to the statesmen?

Let me give you a word from John Owen on this question of

criticizing, while still belonging to the same denomination as, those we oppose. Owen says:

> Now although we do not lay the weight of refraining from their communion on this consideration, yet there is enough in it to warrant any man in his so doing; for a man in his conforming thereunto, makes it a part of his religious profession, not only that the church wherein he is joined is a true church, but that there is in its state and actings a due representation of the mind of Christ, as unto what he requireth of his churches, and what he would have them to be.[4]

Owen is dealing with the whole question of belonging to churches which are teaching error, and no longer propagating that which is the truth, and he says that by remaining with them, or belonging to them, our own testimony becomes inconsistent.

There is a further form of inconsistency which seems to me to be important, and it is that we are advocating, in practice, a wrong kind of independency. Now I am particularly concerned about this. When it is pointed out that we belong to denominations where people are propagating error blatantly, and we are asked, How can you belong to that; how can you associate yourself with that? We tend to answer: In my own church I can do what I like, I have got absolute freedom, nobody restricts me here; I am not prevented from preaching the truth, I can criticize as much as I like; in my own church I am absolutely free. And yet at the same time the evangelicals who say that belong to, and jealously guard their relationship to, the larger denominational body. Now I call that a false idea of independency. You are isolating yourself from the body to which you belong, and yet you still belong to it. That to me is utterly inconsistent. You cannot belong to a church and yet contract out of it.

Is that attitude not the very thing that the prophet Haggai had in his mind? You are living in your 'cieled houses'. You say, It is all right, here am I, everything is going well. Look at my local church, there is no restriction, no prohibition, no restraint, I can say what I like: my 'cieled house'! But what about the whole church? The thing is surely utterly inconsistent. It is a wrong kind of independency. Yet while we are asserting this independency we still claim to belong to the body of which we are acting independently.

[4] *The Works of John Owen* (reprinted Banner of Truth Trust, 1965-68), vol. 15, p. 353.

Or take this matter of inconsistency as it relates to our attitude to the authority of the Bible. We stand for the Bible but when it comes to the question of the church, we so often depart from it. I read recently a letter to a newspaper, by a well-known evangelical layman dealing with the question of the relationship of church and state, and he made this statement: 'Of course it is no use going to the Scriptures with regard to this question. The problem had not arisen then, therefore it is not dealt with there.' In other words he was saying, the Scripture does not help you there at all; so you have got to decide the question on extra-scriptural grounds. I think we could easily show the fallacy of his scriptural interpretation apart from anything else. Because the subject is not explicitly dealt with as a problem, he says, you cannot get any help from the Scripture and he seems to be happy in making that statement. He does not realize that he is putting himself virtually into the Roman Catholic position. The difficulty, he says, is something which has happened since the end of the New Testament canon, so we face it from the standpoint of tradition and history, and we have no help and guidance in the elucidation of our problem from what we assert, in every other respect, is our only authority in all matters of faith and of practice. It is sheer inconsistency! But I suggest that we are very guilty of it.

What makes these three aspects of the inconsistency in our testimony still more serious perhaps is that they are things which are true only of evangelicals. Whatever we may say about the liberals you have got to grant that they are more or less consistent; they do say the same thing at all levels. We do not. Among us, for instance, there are evangelical leaders who say that at the student level there must be absolute separation; they argue strongly and hotly that the IVF should have nothing to do with the SCM at all, should never co-operate with them in any respect but maintain complete isolation and individuality. But when you come to the church level they are advocating the exact opposite, and are saying that we should go into the World Council and the ecumenical movement to try and influence it from the inside. Now that is sheer inconsistency. If a thing is right on one level should it not be right on another level? This is the kind of inconsistency in which we find ourselves because we have approached this whole problem in terms of movements and societies instead of in a different way; and, as I say, it makes our position almost untenable when we are dealing with these others, the liberals and the ecumenical people, because they have a consistent line. There is no contradiction or inconsistency in their position; they say the same thing on all levels and they put into practice what they believe. That puts us in a very difficult, not to say parlous, position.

Another consequence of trying to deal with this problem in terms of movements is that it renders discipline more or less impossible, and I would have thought that the main trouble with us as evangelicals at the present time is the sheer indiscipline of our position. But it is inevitable. What authority does a movement possess? What executive authority has it got? What power has it got? What status or standing has it got? These are voluntary associations; they cannot discipline and they do not discipline. So what we are confronted by is this: there are leaders who have been discredited in public and because of that have had to leave one evangelical movement, yet they emerge as leaders in another movement and there is nothing to stop them. If you have the necessary gifts and influence and the kind of power which counts, you can do that. There is no discipline. You can pass from movement to movement and nobody can do anything at all about it. There is no cohesion between the movements; each one is independent, and thus any power of discipline has already vanished altogether. So what we find is, that not only are there these tendencies showing themselves in the realm of doctrine, but also in the realm of practice there is an increasing tendency to chaos. Evangelical people are no longer unanimous in matters of moral conduct and behaviour; what we see on the other side is beginning to percolate to our side also, and it is all due to a lack of central authority.

This brings me to my last point under this heading which is the crucial one; all these other points have been leading up to it. It is that while evangelicals have tried to solve their problem and get out of their difficulties by forming movements, they have evaded, avoided, and bypassed the whole question of the nature of the church. That would be my fundamental criticism of our grandfathers, and those before them, during the last century. The moment they began to meet the situation by forming movements they had already gone wrong. I think it is there that they departed from the Scripture. Surely these are matters that should be decided and determined in terms of the church, and in the realm of the church, but they allowed the position to develop in the church, and then they went out of it, as it were, and met in their little conclaves. All their concern was about the safeguarding of their own experiences, the 'cieled house' again. It

was as though they thought that so long as they could meet tog
as evangelicals, all was well. But what was happening to the v._
church?

I think it is a simple fact that from 1870 onwards, evangelicals
more or less retired from the church situation, and became concerned only about themselves and their own experiences. It was the
'cieled house' rather than concern for the house of God. I do not
want to be unfair; I think the reasons why they did this are quite
obvious, and they still obtain today; that is why I am putting this
whole matter before you. It is such a desperately serious matter. They
avoided the question of the church for the obvious reason that they
were afraid of causing disharmony and disagreement in the movement. It happened like this. Here are evangelicals and there is
liberalism with its attack upon the faith. Very well then, we
evangelicals must come together from all the denominations in order
to safeguard what we have got and to fight for our heritage. So we
meet together and we rejoice that we are 'all one in Christ Jesus'; but
you must not bring up the question of the nature of the church,
because the moment you do, denominationalism will rear its head. If
you raise the question of the church you are going to produce
disharmony; indeed not only that, you may be offending somebody.
If you give your view of what the Scripture seems to you to teach
about the nature of the church you will be told, Now look here, you
are offending these others; you will wreck the movement; the whole
thing will collapse – you cannot do that. The result is that in our fear
of causing division, or in our natural love towards our brethren, and
our desire to avoid putting them, as we say, on the spot, and in a
difficult position, we have left the whole doctrine of the nature of the
church unconsidered; we have just evaded it. I think you will all have
to agree that this is a simple statement of fact and I have given you the
reasons why I am pointing it out. Surely the doctrine of the church is
central; it is foundational. All these other matters arise out of the
church and it is because we have been evading the doctrine of the
church in this way that we find so many of our present difficulties.
The church is 'the pillar and ground of the truth' (1 Tim. 3:15); all
activity should be church activity, and if we are uncertain as to the
nature of the church how can there possibly be a true unity, or a true
activity?

Such are the points that I feel should be raised with regard to this
whole question of the legitimacy or the scripturalness of movements.

What I am questioning has been the peculiar characteristic of evangelicals, the characteristic of those of us who claim that we are Bible men and women. Has not the time arrived when we must re-examine the whole thing and particularly in view of the general situation in which we find ourselves? Many of the evangelical movements, if not most of them, are running to seed; we are aware of that. They were started in the Victorian era, they have run on their own momentum for a given length of time, but I believe that by now everybody is beginning to see that we have got to think afresh. Here is a unique opportunity for us to examine the whole situation once more and to see whether we can justify what evangelicalism has been doing for, more or less, exactly a hundred years, or whether we have not got to start anew and afresh.

The Major Question: The Nature of the Church

In the light of what I have been saying it is obvious that it is the nature of the church which has become the major question and problem. What is the Christian church? What is the real nature of the church? How do you decide that? We are all agreed in saying that you can only decide the question by the Scripture, but, as I have already hinted, when it comes to the realm of practice and the realm of actual decisions so often we are influenced more by tradition and history than we are by purely biblical exposition. We are so influenced by the need to maintain the *status quo* that we start with that rather than with the scriptural teaching. I mentioned that as one of my questions a year ago. I am repeating it in order that we may take it up, because I think it is one of the crucial issues.

The argument is that throughout the centuries certain things have happened and developed so that we find ourselves confronted by an existing situation. That is all right as an actual historical statement but if we make the traditional 'existing situation' our starting point, we face a very grave danger. Antiquity is of value, but it is no guarantee of truth. The case for tradition is that the early church was, after all, the early church, and that the New Testament canon ended when the church was still in a very inchoate, almost primitive condition and at a time when many problems had not arisen. But, it is argued, the Holy Spirit was still guiding the church and, under the influence of the Holy Spirit, the church saw that certain things were expedient and that certain things should be done for the safeguarding of the truth, the ordering of the life of the church, and the propagation of the gospel. There, it seems to me, is where the danger comes in. If you accept this argument, the case comes to rest not so much upon the scriptural teaching, as upon what the church found to be expedient, particularly in the third and fourth centuries. In some quarters this is almost taken for granted and regarded as something which must not be queried. But, I maintain, it is a false argument. Consider it in this way. Supposing we accept that argument for a moment, the argument that the church, under the guidance of the Spirit, has the right to do what is expedient in its own day and time and generation. If that was a true principle in the third and fourth centuries, then it is equally true today; therefore it does not follow that what was expedient then is still expedient now. The very argument for tradition on the grounds of changed circumstances and conditions leads to this conclusion! I say the circumstances and conditions have changed again. We must therefore query that whole approach, and start *de novo* and discover from Scripture what is right and best for this generation. Whatever way you take it, it seems to me that it is a wrong and an unscriptural position to be in, that is to be governed more by antiquity, by history, and by tradition, than by the teaching of the Scripture itself. So we would lay it down as a principle that we must go back to the Bible itself and particularly, of course, to the New Testament teaching.

With that established, let us proceed to the great question, What is a church? What is the nature of the church? (To me there is no point in considering particulars until we are clear about this.) All the reasons I have been adducing surely compel us to come right back to this. At all costs, we must come back to this and face it. What is the New Testament picture of the Christian church? Is it not something like this? It is a gathering of saints; it is an assembly of true believers; it is a gathering of men and women who have believed the preaching of the gospel. More, it is a gathering of people who have been 'born again'. It is the association of people who are the body of Christ and members in particular. It is those who are 'in Christ'. That is how the New Testament regards them; that is how it always addresses them. They meet together, conscious of His presence in the midst, conscious that they are a spiritual society with the Holy Spirit as their companion, as the one who leads them, and the one who inspires them, as the one who has been given to them to lead them into all the truth.

Now I could quote many Scriptures to establish what I am saying. Let me give just one or two which are perfectly familiar. We start in the second chapter of the book of the Acts of the Apostles, and here are a number of statements. Verses 41–42: 'Then they that gladly received his word were baptized: and the same day there were added unto them about three thousand souls. And they continued stedfastly in the apostles' doctrine and fellowship, and in breaking of bread, and in prayers.' Verse 44: 'And all that believed were together, and had all things common.' Verses 46 and 47: 'And they, continuing daily with one accord in the temple, and breaking bread from house to house, did eat their meat with gladness and singleness of heart, praising God, and having favour with all the people. And the Lord added to the church daily such as should be saved', or, if you prefer it, 'such as were being saved'. Now that is the church. The people who are being saved, who believe the truth, are conscious of this change in their lives; they have been taken out of the world, and are conscious of a new life and a new outlook, and have the desire to be with others who are the same; and the others gladly receive them.

There are many other statements which come to much the same thing. Take for instance that great statement of Ephesians 2:19–22: 'Now therefore ye are no more strangers and foreigners, but fellow-citizens with the saints, and of the household of God; and are built upon the foundation of the apostles and prophets, Jesus Christ himself being the chief corner stone; in whom all the building fitly framed together groweth into an holy temple in the Lord: in whom ye also are builded together for an habitation of God through the Spirit.' You have got almost exactly the same notion in 1 Peter 2:4–9, where Peter uses very much the same analogy: 'To whom coming, as unto a living stone, disallowed indeed of men, but chosen of God, and precious, ye also, as lively stones' – they are *living* stones – 'are built up a spiritual house, an holy priesthood, to offer up spiritual sacrifices, acceptable to God by Jesus Christ', and so on, leading up to, 'But ye are a chosen generation, a royal priesthood, an holy nation, a peculiar people; that ye should shew forth the praises of him who hath called you out of darkness into his marvellous light.'

I sum up by reading again from John Owen on this matter. Here is a very good summary of what I have been trying to say. It is from his *Brief Instruction in the Worship of God and Discipline of the Churches of the New Testament*:

Question: *What is an instituted church of the gospel?* Answer: A society of persons called out of the world, or their natural worldly state, by the administration of the word and Spirit, unto the obedience of the faith, or the knowledge and worship of God in Christ, joined together in a holy band, or by special agreement, for the exercise of the communion of saints in the due observation of all the ordinances of the gospel.[5]

Then Owen adds to that the next question:

Question: *By what means do persons so called become a church of Christ?* Answer: They are constituted a church, and interested in the rights, power, and privileges of a gospel church, by the will, promise, authority and law of Jesus Christ, upon their own voluntary consent and engagement to walk together in the due subjection of their souls and consciences unto his authority, as their king, priest, and prophet, and in a holy observation of all his commands, ordinances and appointments.[6]

I suggest that that is a fair statement of the New Testament picture of what a 'gospel church', as John Owen calls it, is.

I know it is not complete, it is inadequate, but for the sake of brevity and of time I leave it at that to proceed to the second question which is, What, then, are the marks of a true church?

This is the thing that becomes the crucial question if we are agreed about what I have already said. It has been generally believed among evangelicals that there are three main marks of the Christian church. The first is that the gospel, or the true doctrine, should be preached. If the true doctrine is not preached it is not a church. It is only by the true doctrine of Christ, that unadulterated milk of the Word, that we can grow. This is primary, this is fundamental, this is the great thing argued for in the New Testament, the thing I tried to deal with a year ago. All the apostles were preaching the same thing. The apostle Paul uses that argument more than once. It was *his* gospel, yes, but it was also the gospel of the others. They were all preaching this same fundamental message.

Secondly, the church is a gathering where the sacraments are faithfully administered. Here again I do not think there would be any disagreement among us. We would all be equally opposed to the doctrine of transubstantiation and all that is indicative of sacerdotalism. The sacraments 'faithfully and truly administered', leaving out

[5]Ibid., p. 479.
[6]Ibid., p. 486.

all that is magical, or that claims to be miraculous in the wrong sense. We are all agreed about that.

Thirdly – and this is perhaps a point on which we are not all so much agreed – the church is a gathering where discipline is administered. Now this is a very important point. Can we evade the conclusion that the New Testament in its doctrine of the church definitely and specifically teaches that discipline is to be administered? Is it not implicit in what happened at Cæsarea Philippi and our Lord's statements made there in this very connection? 'Jesus answered and said unto him, Blessed art thou, Simon Bar-jona: for flesh and blood hath not revealed it unto thee, but my Father which is in heaven. And I say also unto thee, That thou art Peter, and upon this rock I will build my church; and the gates of hell shall not prevail against it. And I will give unto thee the keys of the kingdom of heaven: and whatsoever thou shalt bind on earth shall be bound in heaven: and whatsoever thou shalt loose on earth, shall be loosed in heaven' (Matt. 16:17–19). Surely that carries with it the whole notion of discipline and that the church is given this power to exercise the discipline of admission and of excommunication, without which you have no guarantee whatsoever of the purity of the life of the church, both as regards her doctrine and her practice.

Then you have exactly the same thing taught in the twentieth chapter of John's Gospel in verses 21 to 23: 'Then said Jesus to them again, Peace be unto you: as my Father hath sent me, even so send I you. And when he had said this, he breathed on them, and saith unto them, Receive ye the Holy Ghost: whose soever sins ye remit, they are remitted unto them; and whose soever sins ye retain, they are retained.' We must again elaborate and assert the evangelical exposition of these words. We have tended to avoid it, and have allowed the Roman Catholics to claim that as their great text. It is ours! And its importance is related to this whole question of the exercise of discipline. Or take what you find in Matthew 18:15–20: 'Moreover if thy brother shall trespass against thee, go and tell him his fault between thee and him alone: if he shall hear thee, thou hast gained thy brother. But if he will not hear thee, then take with thee one or two more, that in the mouth of two or three witnesses every word may be established. And if he shall neglect to hear them, tell it unto the church: but if he neglect to hear the church, let him be unto thee as an heathen man and a publican. Verily I say unto you, Whatsoever ye shall bind on earth shall be bound in heaven: and whatsoever ye shall loose on earth shall be loosed in heaven. Again I say unto you, That if two of you shall agree on earth as touching any thing that they shall ask, it shall be done for them of my Father which is in heaven. For where two or three are gathered together in my name, there am I in the midst of them.'

It is this doctrine which we find put into practice when we come to the Epistles. My first example of that is in 1 Corinthians 5, where the apostle is dealing with this terrible case: 'It is reported commonly that there is fornication among you, and such fornication as is not so much as named among the Gentiles, that one should have his father's wife. And ye are puffed up, and have not rather mourned, that he that hath done this deed might be taken away from among you. For I verily, as absent in body, but present in spirit, have judged already, as though I were present, concerning him that hath so done this deed, in the name of our Lord Jesus Christ, when ye are gathered together, and my spirit, with the power of our Lord Jesus Christ, to deliver such an one unto Satan for the destruction of the flesh, that the spirit may be saved in the day of the Lord Jesus' (verses 1–5). Now that is clear instruction. It ought to have been carried out, you notice, by the church. The church is to exercise discipline in this way.

The same thing is indicated in Galatians 5:12: 'I would they were even cut off which trouble you.' Paul is concerned about these false teachers, these Judaizers. Then you have another statement of it in 2 Thessalonians 3:6; 'Now we command you, brethren, in the name of our Lord Jesus Christ, that ye withdraw yourselves from every brother that walketh disorderly, and not after the tradition which he received of us.' The last quote is from Titus 3:10–11: 'A man that is an heretick after the first and second admonition reject; knowing that he that is such is subverted, and sinneth, being condemned of himself.' The heretic has got to be 'rejected' and that is what did happen; such discipline was the practice of the church up to a certain point in history. There are other references that I could quote, such as are to be found in the Second and the Third Epistles of John.

Here is this whole subject of discipline, but the question is, Do we believe any longer in it, do we exercise it? Is this teaching concerning discipline compatible with a view which justifies what we are doing by saying, Ah yes, the church, the denomination to which I belong is a wonderful place to fish in, by which we mean, Oh I know that many of the members of the church are not Christians, but I get a wonderful opportunity to evangelize them. Is that compatible with

the teaching of the New Testament concerning discipline? Should
the Christian church be a good place to 'fish' in evangelistically? I
am, of course, not referring to our public services which are meant
to evangelize those who are outside; my criticism is of the argument
which justifies remaining in a church because its *members* need to
be evangelized; they are the fish that, it is hoped, will be caught. Is
that compatible with the biblical teaching concerning the administration of discipline?

Or consider another question: Is the popular interpretation of the
parable of the tares, which applies it to the church, the true
exposition of that parable? In the popular interpretation 'the field'
where the seed is sown is made the church, and on that ground we
are told that we must not exercise discipline lest we destroy the
wheat while we are uprooting the tares; thus the absence of
discipline in the church is justified. But our Lord says, 'The field is
the world' (Matt. 13:38). The popular interpretation is not only
misinterpreting the parable of the tares; it is making the parable of
the tares contradict the plain teaching of those Scriptures which
speak of putting certain people out of the church on the grounds of
their heresy or their immorality. So this third mark of the church
again faces us with one of the primary and fundamental questions
we have got to consider: Is a church truly a church if she does not
administer the discipline that the Scripture indicates?

For what causes should we administer discipline? On this point
there is a useful summary in John Owen. These are the five main
headings under which he lists the scriptural reasons for excluding
'offending persons' from the church:

1. *Moral evils*, contrary to the light of nature and express commands or
prohibitions of the moral law, direct rules of the gospel, or of evil report
in the world amongst men walking according to the rule and light of
reason. And, in cases of this nature, the church may proceed unto the
sentence whereof we speak without previous admonition, in case the
matter of fact be notorious, publicly and unquestionably known to be
true, and no general rule lie against their procedure. 1 Cor. 5:3–5;
2 Tim. 3:2–5.

2. Offences against the *mutual love* which is the bond of perfection in
the church, if pertinaciously persisted in, Matt. 18:16, 17.

3. *False doctrines* against the fundamentals in faith or worship,
especially if maintained with contention, to the trouble and disturbance
of the peace of the church.

4. Blasphemy or evil speaking of the ways and worship of God in the church, especially if joined with an intention to hinder the prosperity of the church or to expose it to persecution.

5. Desertion, or total causeless relinquishment of the society and communion of the church; for such are self-condemned [what about a man who only turns up in church once a year? M. L-J] having broken and renounced the covenant of God that they made at their entrance into the church.[7]

We have been looking at this whole question of the biblical teaching on the Christian church. There are many other questions that arise, but it seems to me that the thing on which we have to concentrate is our fundamental conception of the nature of the church. What is the church and how do we know that she is really functioning truly? Is it not about time we asked that again? We are allowing ourselves, I think, to be dragged into a vague consideration of current church life which is not interested in this fundamental question. Is it right for us as evangelicals to do that? Ought we not to insist rather that we first be agreed with regard to the whole nature of the Christian church? As I have said, we are presented with a unique opportunity for doing this, and to me it would be tragic in the extreme if we allow this opportunity to go by default because we are afraid of upsetting people or of causing division. Have we a right to do that? Surely we must come back to the New Testament and face some of these primary and fundamental questions.

Such is the second great point that I have tried to put before you. It follows of necessity, as you can see, from what I have been saying with regard to the whole question of the legitimacy or the scripturalness of movements. We must come back and start with this basic question that we have evaded and avoided.

The True Nature of Schism[8]

We come now to the third and the last matter which is the whole question of schism. Schism is the charge that has always been brought against those who have urged the importance of going back to the New Testament ideal of the church and who have queried and questioned the *status quo*. Throughout the centuries it has been

[7]Ibid., pp. 522–23.
[8]Dr Lloyd-Jones resumed his address at this point in the afternoon session of the Westminster Fellowship.

hurled at such people that they are guilty of this terrible sin of schism, so we must address ourselves to that subject. Furthermore the doctrine of schism has a more positive and direct application to us than we sometimes imagine. Indeed I am raising the question of schism not so much to defend ourselves against it but to try to indicate that we may perhaps be guilty of it in a manner that we have never suspected.

I do not want to go into this in any detail; I am simply raising it as an issue, as I tried to do with the other matters. Schism is the charge that the Church of Rome brings against the whole of Protestantism, but I am not concerned to deal with that. It is such a fatuous charge that it need not detain us. In any case we are all agreed about that and can see this aspect of the matter quite clearly; at least I hope we can, but nowadays one cannot be sure of anything. Again, it is a charge that has been brought against people who have objected to an imposed uniformity. It was the charge brought against those Puritans who believed in separation in the sixteenth and seventeenth centuries, and they were able to refute it. John Owen and others did so, it seems to me, very successfully. To protest against man-made and unscriptural additions to the church, or the life of the church, is not to be schismatic. It is the very opposite. However, such charges are not our present interest.

What is important for us is to arrive at some kind of positive notion as to what schism really is in its New Testament connotation. The First Epistle to the Corinthians is the *locus classicus* with regard to this matter and we can define schism as being 'division in the true visible church about matters that are not sufficient to justify division or separation'. The definition is really important because we must agree that schism is a grievous sin. There is nothing to be said for schism. There has been a lot of it in the church and there still is, unfortunately. The things that have caused it, at least many of them, are enumerated in the First Epistle to the Corinthians: divisions in the church over persons and personalities; groups forming round personalities because they like them, because they appeal to them, and so on. To divide the church solely over persons is schism always, and to do it in terms of learning, or ignorance, or in terms of the strong and the weak brethren, is the same thing. To divide the church over such matters as the observation of days or the eating of meats, and similar things, has to be put into the same category. And then, the other big thing in Corinth was the division over the variations in the spiritual gifts which the different members of the church had been given, the tendency to elevate some gifts at the expense of others, and to divide the body of Christ in terms of the possession or the lack of particular gifts.

Now those are the main things indicated in the New Testament itself, which constitute the sin of schism; but the really important thing for us to observe is that, in the church at Corinth, which had been guilty of schism in those various ways, there was no actual separation. While the church at Corinth was guilty of schism, the church had not actually and in practice divided up into rival groups which did not meet with one another. They were still meeting with one another and this is surely a very important and vital point. It shows there can be schism without an actual rending or sundering of the various parties from physical contact with one another, or from alignment with one another in terms of organization. I am emphasizing that for this reason, that if schism, as so defined and as it obtained in the church at Corinth, is a grievous sin, how much greater is the sin of those who actually divide even in a physical sense and who belong to different alignments in the church?

From our immediate standpoint that is the important point. I work it out like this. The church consists of those who believe the truth, who are born again, who are regenerate, the new men and women in Christ Jesus, and who gather together for worship, fellowship, mutual edification, for the propagation of the gospel and upbuilding, and so on: that is the church. Therefore all of us who are agreed about the essentials and fundamentals of the Christian faith should constitute the church. We should be one, because we are agreed about the faith, we are agreed about the sacraments, we are agreed about the need of discipline. We, who gather together in this particular way and manner, seem to me to conform to everything that I have tried to say about the nature of the church, and the marks of the church; and therefore it seems to me that we are entitled to ask the question: On what grounds are we separated from one another in the matter of church affiliation and alignment? The people who believe the same truths and share the same experience are one, and, as I understand the New Testament teaching, the sin of schism occurs when *such people* allow themselves to be divided from one another for inadequate causes and reasons.

I do not know whether you agree with my argument but that seems to me to be the New Testament argument. As I said, in the church at Corinth they were said to be guilty of it though they had not actually parted from one another and did not belong to different organizations. They were still in the same organization, the same institution, if you like; but they were condemned for this, and they were condemned for it because they were allowing subsidiary things to interfere with their fellowship, to affect the atmosphere of love and the community of belief, of spirit, and of activity which belongs to the church. That is the charge brought against them.

The Question To Be Answered

What then of us, who are agreed about all the fundamental things, but who, nevertheless, are divided and separated; and to make it worse, who are not only divided and separated from one another, but are joined to people who often deny the truth, which we all hold in common, who are erroneous in their view and administration of the sacraments, and who have no discipline at all?

This is surely a very relevant matter for us, and that is why I think there is nothing more urgent at the moment than this definition of the whole matter of schism. Am I right in my interpretation of it in the New Testament or not? In other words, is it right for us – who are agreed about these essential matters that constitute a church and which make us members of the church – is it right that we should allow ourselves to be divided by tradition, by an inherited position, by what is often nothing but the sheer accident of birth? Can it be right to allow a feeling of dislike for any interference with our present positions to come before what we all agree is the teaching of the New Testament in this connection?

I do not want to give a list of the things which we adduce as reasons for being separated from one another because they are not really the important thing, but I must mention one factor which affects our thinking because I think it may be a potent one, namely, the fear of consequences. We have got to face this. Men who have tried to conceive of the church, and to function in the church, in New Testament terms have generally had to pay for it, and have had to pay for it very dearly at times. It seems to me to be almost a universal rule – that it may involve suffering.

There is the further argument that to adopt this approach to the present scene may diminish our usefulness and opportunity, and I think a good deal can be said for that argument. It has also to be granted that there have been people who have been over-ready to divide, but when they have done so they have only landed themselves in a wilderness where they have been more or less useless. They have not been able to do anything at all. In other words, I grant that this is a big subject and I am not going to go into it here. There is a true and a false division. There are people who divide, I would say, over matters that do not justify division. But without going into details I am emphasizing this big question: Can we absolve ourselves from the charge of schism? In other words, if we do agree with what I have attempted to lay down as a definition of the church, if that is our view of the church, the New Testament church, then can we absolve ourselves from the charge of schism? The trouble has been always that men have tended to approach schism in terms of the existing state of the churches instead of taking it right back to the New Testament conception of the church and asking, Are we dividing that? We have allowed the opposition to govern our thinking on this question of schism, and thereby, it seems to me, we have put ourselves into a false position. What I should ask myself is this – not, Am I guilty of dividing the visible church as I know it, but, Am I guilty of dividing the truly spiritual New Testament church? Surely that is the question that should be most urgent and uppermost in the minds of those of us who are evangelical.

I leave it at that in order that we may proceed to discuss it together at another time. I like the spirit of a statement of John Owen's which I will read to you. He ends his treatise on schism with these words:

> I am not so vain as at this time to expect the reduction of Christian religion unto its primitive power, purity and simplicity; nor do I reflect blame on them who walk conscientiously in such a church state, and order, as they approve of, or suppose it the best that they can attain unto; only I think it lawful for all Christ's disciples, at all times, to yield obedience unto all his commands, and to abstain from being servants of men in what he hath not enjoined.[9]

I think that we will all agree with and accept the spirit of that.

A New Strategy for a New Situation

Let me, now, try to sum all this up, and bring it to some kind of a conclusion. We have been looking at evangelical movements, at the nature of the church, and at the question of schism, in the light of the

[9] John Owen, ibid. *Inquiry Concerning Evangelical Churches* p. 373.

present situation, this unique situation in which we find ourselves. It is an astounding thing that we should be in the world at just such a time as this. We know that it is a period of transition and of change in almost every realm. It has fallen to our lot – God have mercy upon us! – to be in an age in which we see the breaking down of things that were regarded as immovable and impregnable. We are witnessing the collapse of things, in many, many realms, that people would have asserted a hundred years ago could never collapse. We are witnessing that in the whole realm of the church and of the Christian faith about which we are so concerned.

Now there are two ways of reacting to that. One is to be depressed, to wring our hands, and to say, Alas that I should ever have been born into such an age, into such degenerate times! And then decide just to get on as best we can, doing our own work in spite of what is happening around us, and saying, Well, as far as my particular church is concerned, at any rate, everything is all right. Now it seems to me that Haggai ought to put us right on that, once and for ever. We cannot contract out of this situation. It is sinful to do so. Why? Because, surely, what is at stake at the moment is the essence of the gospel. Nothing less than that. The issues at the present time are not about refinements of the Christian faith and of our belief; the whole of the gospel is involved, and we are fighting at the present time for the whole notion of revelation. The prevailing thought seems to be doing away with it altogether, and we are reverting to philosophy, to human reason. That is what is at stake! Not only that: the great Protestant doctrines that have made us what we are are being questioned and queried. Some of you may have heard a man saying on the television a few weeks ago, that in his particular denomination he was quite sure that ninety per cent of the people did not believe in justification by faith any longer. There is no doubt about it, that is the situation and the position. Therefore I argue that we have no choice at all, that, as those who believe this faith and who have been called to be its custodians and guardians, we must arise and not only defend it but assert it. We are to stand together, as Paul puts it to the Philippians, 'in the defence and confirmation of the gospel' (1:7), and the need is tremendous. My appeal therefore is, that in the light of these present conditions we must subordinate everything to this one supreme idea, and free ourselves from everything that hinders or hampers us in the defence and proclamation of the gospel. Some of those hindrances we have considered. I argue that the supreme thing before us should be this notion of the church, the true church, which is God's own appointed instrument for the doing of His work. We must rediscover that and recapture it, give ourselves to it at all costs. That does not mean, of course, that we should be agreed about everything, but, as I say, when our concern is about the fight for the very fundamentals of the faith we surely should be one, and we should get rid of all hindrances and obstacles and restraints. There will be discussions among us but they will be discussions among brethren, among those who are agreed about the fundamentals, which has always been to me the glory of this particular gathering. We do not have to waste our time here arguing about fundamental matters. We are agreed about them; so we can proceed to the particulars and we can discuss them together as brethren, and in a true and right Christian spirit.

At the moment, however, we have got to be clear in our minds about the big grand objective, and we must keep our eyes concentrated on that. If we do not, we are going to lose everything. In other words I am arguing for a great overall strategy rather than for particular tactics at the moment. The time for tactics will come, but what we need at the moment is a strategy. It is the whole situation that is involved, and I am pleading that we must subordinate everything to that, and refuse to allow ourselves to be divided and side-tracked and negatived by matters that are of lesser importance, though inherently they may be important. I believe this is the only way in which we can repudiate in an authoritative manner those who deny the truth. Do you not think the time has arrived when we must say quite openly that these people who reject revelation and who seem to cast doubt on a personal God, the deity of Christ, the miraculous, the atonement, and the resurrection – the physical resurrection – do you not think the time has arrived when we must say quite plainly that they are not Christians, and that we do not belong to them, that we regard them as enemies of the truth and of the faith? We must repudiate them; but how can you repudiate them if you belong to them? What is the value of expressing criticisms if in practice and in action you are saying, We are one with them after all; we belong to the same church and we recognize them as brethren in the church? It seems to me that if we are to have any impact upon the world and society around us at the present time, we must be in a position where we can state this openly and quite plainly, and tell the people, This is not Christianity; this is 'another gospel' which is not a gospel; it is a lie. And we must free ourselves to be able to say so.

In exactly the same way it is only thus that we can speak with authority on the whole question of morals. If a church is lacking in dicipline herself, what right has she to talk about the indiscipline of society? If the church is dishonest in the matter of her own belief, if men say quite openly, as they seem to be beginning to do, that they are going to do something which is dishonest because they are required to do so, then what right have we to express an opinion on the veracity of statesmen and politicians? Not only that; how can we evangelize effectively and build up the converts, how can we put an end to this utter confusion and lawlessness which has come in among us, people not knowing what to believe, not knowing where to turn and nobody seeming to be responsible? That is the position. As a result of that, nobody takes responsibility, and no authority is manifesting itself.

In this unique position at which we have arrived, there is the opportunity for a most powerful testimony and witness. I would say that it is a day of opportunity in a most remarkable manner. We know that those who disagree with what we are saying have got nothing to offer the people. Their churches are proving that on the whole, and will do so more and more. They have no message; they cannot expect the Holy Spirit to bless it, even if they believe in the Holy Spirit. They are entirely bankrupt. The people are in ignorance and in sin. I believe that if a body of people stood together and said, We have been careful before reaching a decision, we have allowed this situation to develop, but the time has come when we can see that we have got to state what we believe and what is the truth. If we all did this together, I am suggesting, there would be such a powerful witness that the whole country would know about it. I believe we would be entitled to expect the Holy Spirit to bless it and to honour it and to set His seal upon it. But how can we do that while we are guilty of our present inconsistency – inconsistency at various levels, inconsistency with ourselves – and the evasion of this fundamental matter, namely the doctrine of the church?

There is another factor which I could have mentioned this morning. I am told, on very good authority, that the Student Christian Movement has now, through its new general secretary, who was recently the Bishop of Johannesburg, issued an official statement, in which it says that the SCM from now on is going in for 'secular activity', that they are not going to bother any longer about prayer meetings and too much Bible study. They are taking up the

Bonhoeffer idea of the secularized church, this religionless Christianity. They are to go out among the people and to live among them 'quite deliberately'. In a sense they are themselves almost repudiating the church. They have always hurled that as an argument against us, that we are not interested in the doctrine of the church, and I have been more or less admitting this morning that there is a great deal of truth in what they said. But now, if we come back to the true doctrine of the church, they, at the same time, seem to be abandoning the whole thing. Well, here is a heaven-sent opportunity, and I believe that it is an occasion and an opportunity that has not confronted evangelical people for a very, very long time.

Other Questions for Discussion

I close by putting certain questions for discussion. For instance, Is there anything spoken of in the New Testament apart from the local church? We will have to consider Acts 9:31. The Authorized Version reads: 'Then had the churches rest. . . .' There is a claim, supported by some manuscripts, that the word 'church' should be in the singular, not the plural. That is largely a question, of course, of the priority which we give to the variant readings, but in examining that point let us remember the unquestioned wording of Galatians 1:22 where we are told that Paul 'was unknown by face unto the churches of Judæa which were in Christ'. There is the same plural as in the Greek text underlying the A.V. translation of Acts 9:31. It occurs again in 1 Thessalonians 2:14: 'For ye, brethren, became followers of the churches of God which in Judæa are in Christ Jesus. . . .' My interest is in the broad principle: Is anything spoken of in the New Testament apart from the local church? Have we any right to talk about the holy Catholic church in the sense of a visible institution? In terms of the New Testament, is it right to speak of the holy Catholic church in any sense except the invisible? I think it is an acute problem. It may be a part of the solution to many of our difficulties.

Then, secondly, I suggest that we must go thoroughly into the question of the first two centuries of the Christian era. The danger, as I indicated earlier, is to concentrate too much on the third and fourth centuries. Are we not tending to forget the first two centuries and what obtained then? We know that from the very beginning of the church, erroneous ideas tended to come in, and heresies and disputations. They are partly dealt with in the New Testament, and the church continued to have to deal with them; but it is surely of importance to us, if we do believe in going back at all, to go right back and to give more attention to the first two centuries before the position began to harden into the condition which eventually became the papacy.

This brings me to my third point, that we need to re-examine the history of Constantine and the supposed conversion of the Roman Empire, because there we are face to face with this issue of the relationship between the state and the church. We have to be bold enough, in the light of the New Testament teaching, to query the most honoured names among us. We have to venture to question and to query Martin Luther and John Calvin. It would be a pathetic condition if we found ourselves saying that Calvin could never be wrong. We have to question everybody, not that we think we are perfect – we know we are not – but we recognize that these men were fallible as we are. We thank God for them; we revere their memories; but we do not believe they were perfect. And, after all, they were men involved in such a fight and conflict that they could not possibly cover the whole field, and they tended to take certain things over. To me, one of the tragedies of the Reformation was the way in which Luther, Calvin, and Zwingli tended to take over the notion of the state church. They did it in different ways, but I think they all did it.

There has been a great deal of wonderful research in the last forty years on the whole Anabaptist movement. I am not interested in it from the standpoint of Anabaptism but I am very interested in it from the standpoint of the doctrine of the church, and it is interesting to see the grounds on which the major reformers tended to oppose these men. However, I am simply saying that there is a whole field here for examination and for study. We must not take these things for granted.

Once more let us be clear that these questions do not apply only to the Anglican Church. It was a fact about the Puritans of the seventeenth century, as I tried to say in an address I gave to the Conference last December at Westminster,[10] that they all believed in a state church up to a given point. Their differences were about what form it should take. We must examine whether they were not all wrong; whether their belief can be justified from the New Testa-

[10] This address, 'Puritan Perplexities: Some Lessons From 1640–1662' is published in *The Puritans: Their Origins and Successors* by D. M. Lloyd-Jones, Banner of Truth Trust, 1987.

ment; and whether they were not guilty of accepting an inherited position.

The last question I have is this: When does a church become apostate? When do you decide that a church is apostate? Is it when the majority, and the controlling powers, in particular, are teaching error? Is it when they no longer exercise any discipline and are not even concerned about discipline and the reformation of the church? What are the conditions which should decide whether a church is apostate? I would suggest that the above is the very minimum, that when the main teaching, the prevailing, controlling teaching, and the power in the church has passed into the hands of those who teach error, who deny the truth, the essential truths, such a church is apostate, whatever it is, whatever it has been in the past, and whatever its own professed standards are. I think the latter is a most important point. We have got to examine the argument which says that as long as the standards are correct then all is well, the church is not apostate. Is it right to say that, when the majority no longer believe in those standards but openly ridicule them and express their disagreement with them? Is that a valid position for us to take up, especially when it is accompanied by an utter lack of discipline, so that men, in the name of the church, can deny the essentials of the faith and nothing happens? They are allowed to go on in their positions of leadership and importance. This again is something that applies to every single denomination. It all comes back, I think, to this: what is our ultimate conception of the church?

There is also this whole question of the exercise of gifts in the church. I mentioned our ex-Exclusive Brethren this morning and I did so deliberately in order that it might focus our attention on this particular point. Here are men who have come out of their bondage but are bewildered and confused; they do not know what to do. They have certain major difficulties, one of which is the so-called 'one-man ministry'. We have our views about that, but I feel the time has come for us to examine even questions such as these. It does not mean that you necessarily abandon that ministry, but it does focus attention on this: are we giving the members of the church an adequate opportunity to exercise their gifts? Are our churches corresponding to the life of the New Testament church? Or is there too much concentration in the hands of ministers and clergy? You say, We provide opportunity for the gifts of others in week-night activities. But I still ask, Do we manifest the freedom of the New Testament church? In other words, this is another reason why we must come back and consider the whole doctrine of the nature of the church, and the marks of the church. By doing so we shall be solving, in detail, many of these particular points and problems which need to be reconsidered among us.

When one looks at the New Testament church and contrasts the church today, even our churches, with that church, one is appalled at the difference. In the New Testament church one sees life and vigour and activity; one sees a living community, conscious of its glory and of its responsibility, with the whole church, as it were, an evangelistic force. The notion of people belonging to the church in order to come to sit down and fold their arms and listen, with just two or three doing everything, is quite foreign to the New Testament, and it seems to me it is foreign to what has always been the characteristic of the church in times of revival and of reawakening.

Positive Thinking: The First Need

Now you may ask me, Are you proposing anything? Well I said at the beginning, this morning, that I have not come here with a blueprint, I have not come here with a cut-and-dried scheme, for the good and simple reason that I have not got one. I do not think the time has come for that, but what I do think is that the time has come when it behoves us, indeed it is our bounden duty – because we are who and what we are and because of the grace of God to us – to face this question, of the nature of the church, together.

We cannot just go on in the position we have inherited, which we have inherited from mid- and post-Victorianism and Edwardianism. The machine is still running so many of these things, but is it running to any good purpose? It is for us to call a halt and to stop.

I am not suggesting that what we need is something like a number of Bernard Levins[11] writing to the religious press week by week, sniping and criticizing; that does not get us anywhere. We need positive, constructive thinking. We need to approach these things scripturally and theologically, and my suggestion is that we do that together. I have increasingly had a feeling recently, that the thing is so urgent that we may even have to change the form, the traditional form, in which we have conducted our meetings together, and perhaps take a whole series of meetings to discuss some of these

[11]A well-known columnist in *The Times*.

points which I have tried to put before you; that we appoint men to look into different aspects of this and to read us papers which we then discuss. We may have to meet more frequently. If I am right in my diagnosis, the position is moving very rapidly and unless we do something, it may be too late; or we may be so overwhelmed in disaster that it will only be out of a terrible wreckage that we may gradually crawl out into a new position. I say the alternative is to recognize that it is time for us to act, to clarify our own minds. Surely we need not be afraid of discussing the question of the church? I think we have been afraid to do so. Even in our last meeting, you remember, the question was raised by somebody about the possibility of our discussing the report on the Methodist–Anglican conversations, but immediately there was a reaction against our doing so, for the reason I gave this morning – Ah, but that is going to divide us! Now we must get rid of that; we must get rid of the spirit of fear. The position is too serious. I am not laying down any proposals; all I am asking is that in honesty, in submission to the Word, and to the guidance and the leading of the Spirit, and in brotherly love, we work out these questions together. Then, if we arrive at a measure of agreement, the time will come for us to begin to ask, What do we do about it? But surely the first thing is to clarify our minds and to discover what we really believe. The time of avoidance and evasion of this central doctrine has gone. We will become guilty of a dereliction of duty if we do not bestir ourselves and take it up without any further delay.

Eleven

*

The Weapons of Our Warfare[1]

*

I should like to say that I regard it as a very great privilege to be asked to give the last lecture in this series. There are many things that I could say, indeed I could spend the whole of my time, and very much more, in giving personal reminiscences of Dr Campbell Morgan. I did that, in a sense, when we held a memorial service to him here. That is now in print in his official biography. But I could very easily supplement that, and I would be very happy indeed to do so. Our association here is something that I constantly look back to with very great pleasure. He and I, as I need scarcely say, were two very different men; and yet there were certain things about us which were so much alike, and we had so much in common, that our association together was one which was supremely happy. I thank God for those years that I was privileged to be with him.

I am afraid I must leave it at that, because it would be his will, I know, that I should do what I am indeed compelled to do by the terms of the Lectureship, namely, to expound the Scripture to you and deal with a particular aspect of its teaching.

My subject is 'The Weapons of Our Warfare'. I derive this title, of course, from that well-known passage in the Second Epistle of Paul to the Corinthians, chapter ten, verse 4, where he says, 'The weapons of our warfare are not carnal, but mighty through God to the pulling down of strong holds.'

Here, again, is a point in which I am reminded of a characteristic which I shared with Dr Campbell Morgan. I cannot speak without a text; and he could not. Neither of us was any good at giving what is

[1]This address was given as the sixteenth and last lecture in the Campbell Morgan Memorial Bible Lectureship series, at Westminster Chapel on 10 June, 1964.

called a talk or an address. He was supremely an expositor of the Word, and he did his work, and said what he wanted to say, by means of expositions of the Scriptures. And I tonight am doing exactly the same thing, because there is a sense in which I feel, as he always felt, that a preacher should be incapable of doing anything except expound the Word of God.

Now the subject matter of this lecture is, I feel, a most appropriate one in a Campbell Morgan Memorial Lecture because he was a man who in his time in this church, and elsewhere, was very much engaged in a warfare in this great 'fight of faith'. I am referring particularly to his first period here from 1904 to 1917 when there was a tremendous battle going on in this country over what was then called the 'new theology'. The chief proponent of that teaching was Dr R. J. Campbell, who was then the minister of the City Temple; and the battle raged right until 1914 and the outbreak of the First World War. It was, perhaps, one of the most extreme forms taken by the Higher Critical movement which had started around the 1840s in Germany, and which came over and influenced the life and the thinking of the Christian church in this country.

Dr Campbell Morgan was actively engaged in that battle. His method of fighting was to expound the Scriptures. He did not enter, as it were, openly into the conflict by using names and by writing articles or letters to the periodicals; but he was heart and soul in the controversy, his method being the teaching and the exposition of the Word of God.

I remember very well something that was said to me many years ago by a man who lived in the middle of the Rhondda Valley in Wales, a very intelligent layman. He told me that, through reading a paper called *The Christian Commonwealth* which in those days was published weekly and contained a sermon by Dr R. J. Campbell, he and others had been influenced by this new theology and were, indeed, beginning to be shaken. But then, he said, 'Dr Campbell Morgan came down, and for a week held a series of meetings here in the centre of the Rhondda. He just expounded the Scriptures in a series of addresses on the person of the Lord Jesus Christ, his general theme being 'Who is this Son of Man?', and I was put right immediately and have remained right ever since.' That, I say, was one of the great characteristics of his ministry from 1904 to 1917. He was here to answer this attack upon the faith, and his method of doing so was the positive exposition of the Scriptures.

But there is another interesting fact. Twelve volumes appeared around 1911 or 1912, bearing the title *The Fundamentals*. They were published in Chicago in America in order to remind people of the fundamentals of the Christian faith, especially in the light of this liberal-modernistic new theology attack upon the truth. Dr Morgan was one of the contributors to that notable twelve-volume series, and so you see he was very much involved in, and in the very forefront of this fight for the faith. In other words he was concerned about this whole question of 'the weapons of our warfare'. I suggest therefore that it is not inappropriate for us in this final lecture in the series to consider together this same subject.

It is right that we should do this not merely that we may thus pay our tribute once more to the memory of Dr Morgan, but also that we may meet our own situation at the present time. I can think of nothing that is more urgently necessary, and especially among those of us who are evangelicals – to whom Dr Morgan belonged as most of us here tonight belong – nothing is more necessary than that we should consider this vital and all-important subject. But there is one great difference between the situation today and that which obtained from 1904 to 1917, and that is, that whereas then the lines were fairly clearly drawn and the issues were perfectly plain, the chief characteristic of our age is unutterable confusion and the blurring of lines.

THINKING THAT THERE IS NO WARFARE

I suggest that there are three main aspects of this subject, or three lines, if you like, along which we should consider it. There are three main dangers, as I see it, confronting those of us who are evangelical. The first is, to think that there is no warfare any longer. Now this is one of the main causes of the confusion. We are being told endlessly about the changed climate; we are being reminded how the old liberalism, the new theology, and all I have been referring to, was killed once and for ever by the First World War; and we are being reminded that we live in an age in which biblical theology has been restored. As a result of all this we are told that we are therefore all one, and that we must all come together.

Another argument is that our situation is quite new because there has been a great change also in the realm of science. For a hundred years and more there has been a great fight going on between science and religion; but we are now told that even that has changed. We are told that the post-Newtonian mechanistic theory has been rejected, that it has been exploded by Einstein in particular, and by others. Further, as the post-Newtonian mechanistic theories have been rejected and we have in their place a dynamic view of reality as a result of the new atomic physics and what is called microphysics, science and religion have drawn much nearer together, and therefore the faith is finding itself in a more advantageous position now than it has done for many long centuries. We are told that the old antagonism has gone, and that this new vital view of reality has changed the entire situation. There, then, is a second reason suggested for saying that we need not talk too much at the present time about a warfare.

Then there is a third reason – and we are hearing this more and more – that even Roman Catholicism is changing. Here was something, people thought, that would never change. The conflict and the fight between Protestantism and Roman Catholicism was assumed to be something that was permanent; whatever changes might take place within Protestantism there would always remain a fundamental difference between the Roman Catholic and the Protestant outlook. But we are told that even that is changing now, that Rome is changing. Was not this quite obvious in the appearances of the late Pope John on the television screens? What a fine, kind, and benevolent looking man; and all he said was full of such a loving Christian spirit! Moreover the Roman Church, we are told, is now advising and urging her people to read the Bible. We must give up those old ideas of conflict; we are all becoming one, and those old differences are no longer there; so we must not talk any longer about a warfare. This, I think you will agree, is an increasing body of opinion, that there is no longer a warfare to wage.

That, in and of itself, would be more than sufficient matter for a lecture; but as I am trying to give a comprehensive picture of the whole situation, I will have to content myself with just some few passing remarks concerning it.[2]

The answer to all that, it seems to me, is this. First we have got to examine this new 'biblical theology' and discover whether it is truly biblical, or whether it is not just philosophy using and twisting certain biblical terms to suit its own mood and thinking. We have got to face this whole question as to what is really taught by great men

[2]For arguments based on changes in science, see Dr Lloyd-Jones's *Approach to Truth: Scientific and Religious*, Tyndale Press, for Christian Medical Fellowship, 1963.

like Karl Barth and Bultmann in Europe, and Tillich in America, let alone our notorious friends on the South Bank here in London. Has that really changed the situation? I need scarcely say that as far as I, at any rate, am concerned, the battle is as fierce and as strong as it has ever been, and that we are called upon more than ever to fight the good old fight of the faith.

The idea that Roman Catholicism is changing is, perhaps, the most subtle and dangerous thing of all. I do not want to go into that. Of course we all agree that in her outward behaviour she is changing. She has done that many times before. It suits her at times to be militantly persecuting; it suits her at other times to be pleasant and ingratiating. If she can win us into the fold by being kind and pleasant she is ready to do so. But the fundamental question is this: Is there any evidence whatsoever of any change in fundamental doctrine in the Church of Rome?

I would have thought that one single book which has been published this year ought to be in and of itself sufficient answer to that question. It is a book called *The Problem of Catholicism* written by an Italian of the name of Subilia who is a professor in the Waldensian College in Rome. Now what is unusually interesting to me about this book is that it has not been published by an evangelical firm of publishers, but by the Student Christian Movement Press. I have never read anything that shows more clearly the difference between Roman Catholicism and Protestantism, or establishes more clearly beyond any doubt that there has been no change whatsoever in any fundamental doctrine and that there can be no such change, than this very book, studded as it is with quotations from the late Pope John, the present Pope, Hans Küng, and other leading Roman Catholic writers. It is interesting to observe that this book has had very little publicity. It has not even been reviewed by many of the religious weekly papers. Here is a book, not published by evangelicals, which shows that the old conflict between Romanism and Protestantism is as acute as, if not more acute than it has ever been before. There, then, is one of the dangers, to feel that there is no warfare, that there is no fight to be fought.

AVOIDING THE WARFARE

The second great danger is the danger of avoiding the warfare. This is different. The man who avoids a war does recognize that there is a fight, but he avoids it.

Now there are many ways in which this is done. One way, of course, is to retreat into a kind of pietism. That is what many evangelicals did in the last quarter of the last century. They said, Now, we are not going to touch this new teaching; we are not going to read their books; we are not going to do anything about them. If we are to preserve our faith, we must turn our backs on all that, and we must cultivate our own religious life. So they wrote, and they read, devotional books, and they tried to build themselves up in this devotional manner. They had no contact at all with the great fight that was raging outside.

There are many still who adopt the same attitude. Sometimes today it takes the form of saying that you must always be positive. Such people have a strong dislike of the negative. They do not like people who point out to them what is wrong and what must not be done. Always be positive, they say. Why can you not just give us the positive message? Why must you always be exposing error and demonstrating that it is wrong?

Or such people delight in the fact that they are not controversialists. Indeed, they are very nice people who never offend anybody at all, and they are well spoken of by everybody! But the Scriptures tell us that a man who is well spoken of by everybody is in a very dangerous condition. 'Woe unto you when all men speak well of you.' We should not desire certain people to speak well of us. They did not speak well of our Lord, and there is something seriously wrong with His followers if they speak well of them.

The third danger in connection with evading and avoiding the warfare is the danger of retreating into a kind of orthodox scholasticism. What do I mean by that? It is the danger of saying, I cannot be bothered with all that these people are saying. It is all wrong. I am able to read the grand old writers, and I am going to give all my time to that. And so you can become a little coterie turning round in your own circle and making no contact with the man in the street, the man of the world, and with the masses of people in this country who are outside the Christian church. It is a very comfortable life. There is no more happy life than the life of a scholar, of a man who spends his time reading and then discussing the subject matter of his reading with friends who are of a like mind. But while you and I may be doing that, the world is going to hell! There is this terrible danger of avoiding the warfare.

FIGHTING WITH THE WRONG WEAPONS

Thirdly – and this is our subject tonight – there is the danger of fighting the war with the wrong weapons. 'The weapons of our warfare', says the apostle, 'are not carnal.' The apostle, you notice, believed in negatives! He says that they are 'not carnal'. Many today would like to say to the apostle Paul, Why are you not always positive? Why need you say that they are 'not carnal'; why don't you tell us what they are? We are not interested in knowing what they are not, we want to know what they are. That is the kind of thinking and speaking, as I am trying to say, that has so often sold the pass. My friends, we are in this war, and we must know what we are doing. It is vital in this connection that we should realize what are the wrong weapons. This is, perhaps, the greatest danger of all. As I see things, it certainly is the greatest danger at this present time.

There is nothing new in all this. There is a great deal about the question of how you fight this battle in the New Testament itself. We have it here in 2 Corinthians 10. It is in many places in these polemical argumentative Epistles of the apostle Paul. The church had to begin this fight almost immediately, and this apostle is particularly concerned about it. Indeed in these two Epistles to the Corinthians he gives a great deal of space and attention to this one matter of how we fight the battle for the faith.

I must not weary you with a long list of the wrong weapons, and the things we must not do; but the apostle mentions some of them in the context, so I just note them. He says that we must not fight this battle with our personalities. 'Now I Paul myself beseech you by the meekness and gentleness of Christ, who in presence am base among you.' He is referring there to the way in which some people criticized him in Corinth. Because he was not of a striking personal appearance, they said, 'his bodily presence is weak, and his speech contemptible'. There were people in the church at Corinth who were interested in what today are called 'big personalities'. They made these offensive remarks about the personal appearance of the great apostle who apparently was not a handsome man, but probably, according to all accounts, a short man with a bald head who suffered from an inflammation of the eyes.

The apostle does not enter into that at all except to say that he does not fight in that sort of way. The battle is not to be fought by men's appearances, by the sort of impact (as the modern jargon puts it) that they make upon the congregation. A man should not be interested in that at all, says the apostle; that is carnal. Too much interest in the preacher and his personality is always one of the hallmarks of carnality. That was the great trouble in the Corinthian church – 'I am of Paul; and I of Apollos; and I of Cephas' – following persons. Alas, the cult of personality is still with us, and, perhaps, more so than ever.

Then there is the question of methods. The apostle had been dealing with that in the First Epistle – 'not with enticing words of man's wisdom' (1 Cor. 2:3–5). He did not use the rhetoric of the Greeks; he did not use any tricks; he would never employ methods which belong to the world rather than to the realm of the Spirit. He was never a man-pleaser, he keeps on saying. He was as scrupulous about his methods as he was about his message. He did not say, The end justifies the means, or, Anything we can do to interest and to attract people and to bring them to listen is perfectly legitimate; we may not like it but if it leads to good results we must do this. The apostle was one who abominated that; he would describe those methods as being 'carnal'.

I wonder how the Christian church faces up to this particular negative of the apostle at the present time? There is a tendency today to put great emphasis upon methods; they are even advertising the Christian church. I mean by that setting up publicity departments to advertise the church, paying the papers, etc. in an attempt to sell the church to the public as you would present a play or sell soap or some other commodity. The apostle, it seems to me, condemns all this as being carnal. This is man's method, human wisdom, human knowledge and understanding, human trickery. Our methods, says the apostle, 'are not carnal'.

But the church has often gone even further than that. In her attempt to defend the truth and the faith, the church has, at times, made the mistake even of invoking the help and the aid and the power of the state and of the law. That came in, of course, as the result of the conversion, so called, of the emperor Constantine and of Christianity becoming the official religion of the Roman Empire; and it has continued since then. Men have used the state and acts of Parliament to defend the faith, and whoever, therefore, did not conform could be thrown into prison, his goods could be taken from him, and he might perhaps even be put to death.

Here is a subject on which we might easily enlarge, but we must avoid the temptation, and content ourselves with confessing with sorrow and shame that even men like Luther and Calvin were not completely successful in avoiding that particular trap. You cannot defend the Christian truth by the power of the state; and it is no part of the business of the state to defend Christian truth. The church and the state are complementary but essentially distinct spheres. To hide behind acts of Parliament, and to try to defend your position by shielding yourself behind such acts, seems to me to be guilty of trying to fight the great fight by methods which are entirely carnal.

But more serious perhaps than all these is the question with which the apostle has to deal so frequently in his Epistles, and which I feel is supreme at the present time. It is the danger of trying to fight this fight, and to war this warfare, by means of what we may call Hellenism. What I mean by Hellenism is the Greek outlook and mentality, or, if you prefer it, 'the wisdom of this world', or, again, philosophy. This was the thing that the Corinthians wanted the apostle Paul to do. They complained that he was so simple, and that he simply preached 'Jesus Christ, and him crucified'. There was no philosophy in his preaching, they said. He did not reason things out, and bring in these great theories of the masters who had lived among them. He did not do that, so they said that his speech was 'contemptible'. It was on those grounds they were criticizing him. That is why the apostle has to take up that matter at the very beginning of his First Epistle, in the very first chapter, in verse 17. He says, 'Christ sent me not to baptize, but to preach the gospel: not with wisdom of words, lest the cross of Christ should be made of none effect.' They had expected 'wisdom of words'; and after he had gone they said that he had no 'wisdom of words'. There was no philosophy in his preaching; it was so simple. Anybody could listen to that and accept it and believe it. There was nothing involved and intellectual about it, involving the handling of the great philosophic theories. They criticized him because he did not behave as a Hellenist, as a Greek, because he did not use 'worldly wisdom' and philosophy.

What has this to do with us? Well, unless I am seriously mistaken, this is the greatest danger threatening the evangelical position in the Christian church at this present hour. What is it? Its motive is a very good one; its idea is to make Christianity acceptable to men. Those who think in that way are out to evangelize, out to help. They want to make the gospel acceptable; and they say that you can only do this if you can make it intellectually respectable. We are living, they say, in an educated age, in a scientific age, so we must show that our message is a reasonable one. It is an attempt to make the gospel reasonable in the sight of men.

THE TENDENCY SEEN IN CHURCH HISTORY

There are various reasons why people try to do this. It is very interesting to notice its history in the long story of the Christian church. It is the simple truth to say that from the very beginning the Christian church has had to guard herself against this very tendency, the tendency to wage the warfare with this particular carnal weapon. As I have already indicated, it had arisen even in New Testament times. The apostle deals with it not only in the Corinthian Epistles, he deals with it also, particularly, in the Epistle to the Colossians. It is to be found in the Pastoral Epistles, particularly the First Epistle to Timothy. And as you read the subsequent history of the Christian church you will find the same thing.

It is quite easy to understand how and why this happened. It occurred in this way. When the gospel was first preached in Palestine, it was the common people who heard it gladly; but it began to spread into the great Roman Empire and into the Greek world. Among others, certain able, intelligent, educated Greeks were converted and became adherents of the Christian faith. Now this is what tends to happen. Once a man like that believes the gospel, the first thing he wants to do is to reconcile his new faith with his old learning and knowledge. He feels that he must not live in two compartments; that he must not be one man on Sunday and a different man when he is out in the world as a philosopher or scientist or something else during the week. So he tries to reconcile the two. That is where the danger comes in.

One of the first to do this was a man by the name of Clement, the famous bishop of Alexandria. He was one of the first to show this tendency to bring in philosophy to help Christianity, or to bring in philosophy in the presentation of Christianity. He did it first of all to put himself right in an intellectual sense.

Then a second reason arose, and that was persecution. There was terrible persecution of the early church, not only in the first century but still worse in the second century. They were persecuted, among other things, for being atheists. Why were they thought to be atheists? Well, for this reason: the Greeks worshipped a great multiplicity of gods, and because the Christians did not do so they were called atheists. So the Christians were driven to show that they were not atheists, and that they were not barbarians either though they did not believe in Greek philosophy. So you have the great martyrs and confessors. The leading one was a man called Justin Martyr. His whole object was to show that Christianity was not only not dangerous to the state and was not atheism, but also that it was not opposed to Greek philosophy, that it was really teaching very much the same thing.

A third reason was that heresies arose. Whenever a heresy arises it has to be answered; and the danger always is to put something of your own wisdom into the answer. Much of this confusion in the Christian church arose simply as the result of the conflict with heresies.

Then fourthly, there was the motive of evangelism: how could they present this gospel to the Greek world? The Greeks were learned people, they were interested in thought, in trying to understand life. How could this simple gospel be presented to them? Well, some of these men – and I am thinking now of a man like Origen in Alexandria, in Egypt, and Clement of Alexandria – felt that the thing to do was this. They said in effect: You cannot expect educated Greeks to accept the Old Testament as it is, they cannot accept the facts of the Old Testament. Very well, we must show them that they are not really facts but rather, allegories, or pictures; they did not really happen, but they convey important truth. So they introduced that whole fanciful, allegorical method of interpreting the Scriptures. Their motive in doing so was to help to evangelize their fellow men and women.

That is what happened in the first three to four centuries; and it is extraordinary to notice how this tendency has persisted ever since. Even after the Protestant Reformation, when Luther and Calvin and others discovered the old essential faith and truth, before a hundred years had gone this same element had come in. Great teachers began to rationalize the Christian faith, and to work it up into a great system and dogmatic body of truth. So you had what is called the scholasticism or the orthodoxy of the seventeenth century which became the kind of counterpart of medieval orthodoxy. It tended to be hard and dry as dust and purely intellectual; and it provoked a reaction which became known as pietism and which emphasized the importance of experience and feeling.

Again you notice that the motive was a good one. They were anxious to defend the faith against Roman Catholicism, and against some of the excesses of some of the wilder sects that arose; but in doing that they introduced so much of the element of philosophy and human wisdom that it became a rigid and lifeless system.

After the great Evangelical Awakening of the eighteenth century the same thing tended to obtrude itself again; and during the whole of the last century this philosophical element came in more and more. Let us be honest and admit that you cannot even absolve a man like Charles Hodge of this particular charge. Philosophy comes in! Too much philosophy comes in, and you tend in the end to have an intellectualist system rather than the dynamic living faith and preaching which we see in the New Testament, and which we see in every period of reformation and of revival.

THE DANGERS TODAY

That then, is, the way in which this tendency comes in; and those are the reasons which explain it. Why should we be concerned about this? We should be concerned about it because of the terrible dangers that are involved. What are the dangers? The lessons of history, in addition to the teaching of the Scriptures, show this quite plainly. By the time that Constantine brought the Roman Empire into the Christian church around AD 325 you could say that Christianity had become Hellenized. It was very difficult to recognize it as the same thing that had started in the first century, the church of the New Testament. It had become Hellenized, so permeated with the influence of Greek philosophy that it had almost become the exact opposite of what it was originally.

Now there were certain people who saw this danger clearly. There was a great man in the Christian church round about AD 200, a little before and a little after, called Tertullian. He focused this problem, this danger, by putting what became a very famous question. It was this: What has Athens to do with Jerusalem? What has the academy to do with the church? That is the great question: What has Athens, the centre and home of philosophy, to do with Jerusalem, the home of the church? What have the academy and the porch, the places where the philosophers taught, to do with the Christian church? If only the church in those days had paid attention to that question! But are we paying attention to that question today? What is happening today, as I see it, is that 'Athens' is coming back into evangelicalism, the academy is coming back into the church and Christian organizations. It is always one of the most dangerous things that can happen, if not indeed the most dangerous of all.

Why is that the case? For one thing, it indicates a wrong spirit. It indicates a spirit of fear. Why should there be this tendency to bring back philosophy and intellectualism and worldly wisdom into the realm of the gospel? The ultimate reason is that educated Christian people are a little bit afraid of not being regarded as intellectual, because they are Christians. They do not want to be looked down upon, they do not want people to think that they are Christians simply because they are not intellectual. Now that is a spirit of fear.

Or, sometimes, they are afraid of being proved wrong. They say, If we take the Bible as it is and then suddenly one day science proves something to be a fact, which we have denied, where are we then? They are afraid of being proved wrong. That, again, is the spirit of fear.

In addition to fear there is pride, pride of intellect, pride of knowledge. Keep your eye at the present time on the word 'scholarship'. Scholarship! There is a very real danger of our worshipping scholarship. Do not misunderstand me. I am not out to defend obscurantism; I have already described it as one of the dangers. It is not the business of a Christian to bury his head in the sand and to say, As long as I have got my faith I don't care what people think or say. Apart from other considerations, you are your brother's keeper; you have a duty to others. If a man has a brain he must use it, and if you have knowledge it is excellent. I am not out to advocate obscurantism, but I do say that we are in grave danger of worshipping scholarship.

I came across an instance of this this very week in a religious paper I was reading. I quote it because it illustrates this tendency very plainly. I was reading an article by a man who was explaining why he did not believe in the virgin birth. He not only does not believe in the virgin birth, he does not believe in the infallibility of the Scriptures, and he is very much opposed to the infallibility of the Pope. But this is what he actually said. He was quoting a statement by that famous New Testament scholar, the late Professor T. W. Manson. Now what I am saying has nothing to do with Professor Manson himself. I am sure he would be the first to discount the kind of statement I am going to quote. Here is a very able man, trained not only in Oxford, but also in the famous Union Theological Seminary in New York City. He writes this: 'Disagreement with a critic as able and as learned as Manson is impossible.' You must not believe in the infallibility of the Bible, you must not believe in the infallibility of the Pope, but you must believe in the infallibility of the late Professor Manson. Why? Ah, he was a scholar! All honour to the late Professor Manson and many other great scholars, but none of them is infallible.

This man writes quite seriously. He and those who belong to that outlook charge us with being bibliolaters. They say that we make an idol out of the Bible, that we worship an idol, and that you must not worship idols. I quite agree, but the time has come when it is our duty to point out that scholarship can also be made into an idol, and that you can so worship scholarship that it drives you to say that you cannot and must not disagree with a man like this because he is so able and so learned. That is the situation which is creeping in among us. We are so anxious to be thought intellectually respectable and afraid of being charged with not being intellectual, that we are in grave danger of worshipping scholarship in a wrong sense, and of being guilty of intellectual pride.

It not only leads to a wrong spirit but it leads also to wrong actions. What do I mean? I mean that the moment you begin to think along those lines you will soon be anxious to use big names, and, to use a biblical expression, you will be much too ready to 'lay hands' upon certain people hurriedly. Have you not noticed a tendency creeping in among us to lay hold on any man who is prominent in any sphere of life, who even vaguely hints that he is a Christian, and particularly if he has gained distinction in one of the learned professions or has high academic honours? If he makes a statement even vaguely Christian we lay hands upon him, and ask him to be the chairman at the next public meeting.

We do not seem to trouble any longer as to whether the man really holds our conservative evangelical position. He is a great name – that seems to be the great consideration. That is one of the things to which this attitude leads; and this in spite of the fact that it is prohibited specifically in the Scripture itself.

Another thing to which it leads is what I am constrained to describe as the 'degree mania'. Again, I am not against degrees; they have a value. There is nothing wrong in having degrees, but if you are going to estimate a man as a Christian, and his effectiveness in the church, by means of his degrees, well, the first thing you must do is to put out the man whose memory we are honouring here tonight, and many others whom I could mention. The thing is monstrous and even unintelligent quite apart from the contrast it presents to the unlearned and ignorant men of Acts 4:13.

A further terrible danger – and it is a very serious one in this country today – is that this tendency to worship scholarship is landing us in a position in which the whole training for the ministry is determined by secular universities. I can imagine nothing which comes so directly under the category of fighting this warfare with carnal weapons.

The third thing it does, and this is the most serious of all, is that it compromises the truth. The moment you begin to think in terms of worldly wisdom and knowledge, and intellectual understanding and scholarship, you will not be quite as careful as you should be in the translation of Scripture. You will be more interested in the fact that scholars have done it, and that it is new and up to date, than in its accuracy and its spirituality. Are these not living issues among us? What is our acid test of a translation? Is it that it is new? Must it be right because it is new, and because it is the result of the latest scholarship? Is that the guarantee? These are some of the effects and results of thinking in the wrong way.

Another thing it does is to tend to make us go beyond the Scriptures. In our desire to explain everything, in our desire to accommodate those who are outside, we make statements that go beyond the Scriptures; instead of saying quite simply and honestly, I do not know; I cannot understand everything nor explain everything; this is all I know. There is a tendency today to attempt to explain things that cannot be explained.

A further danger is that of granting too much to modern knowledge and to modern theories and speculations, granting so much that eventually you contradict some of the vital doctrines of the Bible and of the Christian faith. I am thinking of things like granting too much with respect to the early chapters of Genesis, granting too much to the theory of evolution. Why do I say that this is dangerous? For the reason that it involves the whole doctrine of man, and the doctrine of the fall. That, in turn, involves the doctrine of redemption and of salvation, and, indeed, of the person of the Lord Jesus Christ Himself. These are some of the terrible dangers.

Another is the danger of explaining things away. There was a striking example of this not so long ago when a man published a book under some such title as *The Bible Is True*. It was a best-seller. Why? Because in the book this man was saying that he was now able to believe so much of the Bible that he could not believe before. He could now believe some of the things reported as miracles. One example was the incident when Moses struck the rock and the water gushed out. He said that he had always been in trouble about that, but now he was able to believe it. Why? Well, because a British soldier in the last war in Palestine was using a pickaxe, and accidentally, in lifting up his pickaxe to strike, it just happened to touch a rock behind him, and a little water trickled out. So, you see, the Bible is true; miracles now can be accepted! I remember a man once telling me with great excitement that his minister had pleased him tremendously the previous Sunday night because he now believed in the destruction of Sodom and Gomorrah as the Bible teaches it. The minister had read in an article that geologists had discovered that there were certain substances in the ground, geologically, in that part of the world which now enabled one to understand how the destruction of those cities had happened. What such people do not realize is that by explaining miracles you explain them away. You sound very learned, you sound as if you can still be scientific and at the same time believe in miracles, but what you have actually done is do away with miracles. It is exactly as the apostle says with regard to the preaching of the cross. If you try to explain the cross in terms of something beautiful, or some wonderful illustration of pacifism, you have made it 'of none effect' by your philosophy.

WHY IT IS SO WRONG

Those are some of the dangers. Why is all this so essentially wrong? For the reason that this attempt to make the gospel accept-able to men is already wrong in and of itself. The Bible tells us that man is in a state of sin, that man is blinded by the god of this world, that 'the carnal mind is enmity against God: for it is not subject to the law of God, neither indeed can be' (Rom. 8:7), that 'the natural man receiveth not the things of the Spirit of God: for they are foolishness unto him: neither can he know them, because they are spiritually discerned' (1 Cor. 2:14). This modern tendency forgets all that. This idea that you can take the gospel, and, because of modern knowledge, present it in such a way that it is going to be easier for modern man to believe it, is a denial of the gospel. 'The offence of the cross' (Gal. 5:11) has gone, the scandal of Christianity has evaporated, the 'foolishness' of preaching or of the thing preached is no longer true. It is altogether wrong.

But let me add to that: it is also so foolish. If I need modern knowledge to help me to believe the Bible, how did people believe it in the past? If I have to rely on microphysics and thank God for it because it now makes it easy for me to believe the gospel, what about the people who accepted the theories of Isaac Newton? In other words if you put this modern attitude to the test of history you find the whole thing becomes ridiculous at once.

A further reason is this: There is nothing more dangerous than to be controlled by modern knowledge. Why? Because what is modern knowledge today will be out of date tomorrow, or at least in ten years, or certainly in fifty years. Where are 'the assured results' of the Higher Critics against which Dr Campbell Morgan had to contend when he was here before the First World War? So many of them have vanished into thin air. You have not got 'assured results'. Nothing is so precarious as to base any part of your position upon modern knowledge or modern science. In the same way nothing is so dangerous as the modern tendency to confuse theories and facts.

Finally, consider this. The modern conservative evangelical who thinks along these lines does all this because he wants to win people. But consider what an American author by the name of Hordern, writing in 1959 in *The Case for a New Reformation Theology*, says. He is not a conservative evangelical, he espouses what is called the 'new reformation' theology. He says, 'The new conservative theology of today in its desire to be up to date, intellectual, and relevant, is in grave danger of conforming too closely to the modern age to be able to bring a word to that age.' What he means is that you can so modify your message, your belief, or your method, that the man you are trying to win says, Well, I don't see much difference between what you are saying and what I have already believed. You will no longer be able to help him. In your over-desire and over-anxiety to help him you are frustrating your own effort and endeavour.

Do I mean, then, by this that there is no place at all for apologetics? I do not, but it is vital that we should realize what exactly is the place of apologetics. It is this: The chief business of apologetics is to buttress the faith of the believer. It does not make him a believer, but it helps to support and to buttress his faith. The business of apologetics is to show the wrongness and utter inadequacy of every other view apart from the biblical view. Apologetics, the use of modern knowledge, is excellent as an introduction to the sermon but it does not go any further. It is very good in the work of demolition, but it does not help you to put up the building. It helps you to pull down the old, it does not help you at all to erect the new. It can never bring a man to salvation. Any use of modern knowledge, modern argumentation, or any such carnal implements and weapons will never bring a man to faith in Christ.

THE TRUE WAY

What is the true way? This can be stated briefly. It is the traditional evangelical position of the centuries. We only need to be reminded of it. The main need of evangelicals at the moment, I feel, is the negative warning already given. Let me therefore turn, briefly, to the positive. What is it? Listen to the great apostle: 'For though we walk in the flesh, we do not war after the flesh: for the weapons of our warfare are not carnal, but mighty through God to the pulling down of strong holds; casting down *reasonings*, and every high thing that exalteth itself against the knowledge of God, and bringing into captivity every thought to the obedience of Christ.'

How are we to fight? Let us before everything put our emphasis on this – the spirit in which we fight. That is what is so tragic about this modern tendency. As I have tried to show, it produces a spirit of fear, instead of the spirit of confidence, such as we find here glowing in the words of the great apostle. How are we to fight modern unbelief, modern philosophy, modern science, modern anything you like?

Let me put it as tersely as I can in this way: not by trying to fight Goliath in Saul's armour – never! That is never the way. You will only stumble. You will look an impressive figure when you come out of your tent, but you will stumble and you will be defeated. Let David fight in David's way! Let him be a fool, let him be ridiculous, let him just pick up those stones and use his sling. Let him appear to be a lunatic in the sight of the giant, and perhaps of his own people also. That is God's way!

Let us actually look at the great words that were used by David. It will do us good just to read them together and to hear them again. This is the way in which God teaches us to fight. 'David spake to the men that stood by him, saying, What shall be done to the man that killeth this Philistine, and taketh away the reproach from Israel?' Then listen to this! 'For who is this uncircumcised Philistine, that he should defy the armies of the living God?' (1 Sam. 17:26). That is the way to fight. All the Israelites were cowering and terrified. They had not got a man who was big enough, and the armour was not adequate, and so on. Then this stripling of a lad comes along, with his stones and his sling, and he says, 'Who is this uncircumcised Philistine?' That is the way to fight the battles of the Lord! But let David go on speaking to us. 'Then said David to the Philistine' – who was insulted by the very sight of David – 'Thou comest to me with a sword, and with a spear, and with a shield: but I come to thee in the name of the Lord of hosts, the God of the armies of Israel, whom thou hast defied. This day will the Lord deliver thee into mine hand; and I will smite thee, and take thine head from thee; and I will give the carcases of the host of the Philistines this day unto the fowls of the air, and to the wild beasts of the earth; that all the earth may know that there is a God in Israel' (1 Sam. 17:45–46). That is the way to fight.

Or let me put it in this form. How are we to handle the 'ark of the Lord' that has been committed to our care? How are we to do so? Well, we must not do it by means of what I would call the 'new cart' philosophy. You remember when the children of Israel were going to move the ark back to its rightful place, instead of carrying it according to the instructions that God had given, which was that they should carry it on poles, they made a 'new cart'. It seemed so much better than the old poles. And they made this marvellous new cart and they had oxen to draw it, you remember. But then it began to shake and that poor man Uzzah put his hand upon it to steady it, and he fell dead the next moment. Quite right! What was God doing there? God was just saying that His ark had to be handled in His way, not in man's way. The new cart is not superior to the old poles. Let us get rid of the 'new cart' philosophy. Let us adopt the philosophy, if you must have the term, of a man like Gideon who, again, was told that he was not to fight with great battalions but with a mere handful of people who could be trusted. They were to go with only pitchers in their hands with lights in them, just a handful of them, three hundred against the great hordes of the enemy, and all they had to do was to shout, 'The sword of the Lord, and of Gideon.'

That is the instruction that is given to us. We must get rid of this spirit of fear, this lurking pride, this inferiority complex, this tendency to apologize for the Word of God and its blessed truth. We must get back into the position of these giants of the faith and say, 'Though we walk in the flesh, we do not war after the flesh: for the weapons of our warfare are not carnal, but mighty through God to the pulling down of strong holds.'

CONFIDENCE IN THE WORD

We must have confidence and assurance! In what? In the Bible as the Word of God. Why? Because it is God's Word, because it is God's revelation; because it is not the theories and the ideas of men with respect to truth; because it is not what men have discovered and arrived at as the result of their great study and scholarship and meditation. It is what the living God has revealed to men, has shown them, and has commanded them to preach. Let us remember Martin Luther's contrast between philosophy and revelation. He puts it like this: 'Philosophy has to do with what can be known by human reason. Theology has to do with that which is "believed", with that which is apprehended by faith.'

This is God's Word, this is God's truth. This is from heaven, not from men and it is therefore invincible. We must learn to say what this great apostle said in his Epistle to the Galatians in the first chapter: 'Though we, or an angel from heaven, preach any other gospel unto you than that which we have preached unto you, let him be accursed' (verse 8). 'I marvel that ye are so soon removed from him that called you into the grace of God unto another gospel: which is not another; but there be some that trouble you, and would pervert the gospel of Christ' (verse 6). 'I certify you, brethren, that the gospel which was preached of me is not after man. For I neither received it of man, neither was I taught it, but by the revelation of Jesus Christ' (verses 11–12). 'A dispensation of the gospel', he says to the Corinthians and to others, has been 'committed unto me' (1 Cor. 9:17). This was his whole position and it must be ours. This is the Word of God! This is revelation! This is infallible because it is God's. This is the first weapon of our warfare. This is something which is to be proclaimed; not to be defended, but to be proclaimed; to be spoken with a holy boldness; to be 'declared' unto men. We do not need 'dialogues', we need declaration.

And what is its message? Well, what I would emphasize particularly is that we must have the full message. We must, like this great apostle, deliver the whole counsel of God. I believe that much of our present position is due to the fact that we have not done that. We have only preached parts of it. We have been afraid of offending. We have been superficial. We have been so interested in getting visible results that we have kept back certain vital aspects of the truth. It must be the whole counsel, the full gospel.

What is that? It starts with the law. The law of God. Preaching starts with the law; it must start with the holiness of God, the law of God, the demands of a righteous God, the wrath of God. That is the way to bring men and women to conviction; not by modifying the truth, not by presenting it with an apparent learning which dilutes it. We must confront them with the fact that they are men, and that they are fallible men, that they are dying men, that they are sinful men, and that they will all have to stand before God at the bar of eternal judgment and give an account of the deeds done in the body, and with the fact of the wrath of God, which has already been revealed 'against all ungodliness and unrighteousness of men' (Rom. 1:18). We must preach it without fear or favour, with the holy boldness that characterized the first apostles.

And then we must present to them the full-orbed doctrine of the grace of God in salvation in Jesus Christ. We must show that no man is saved by the deeds of the law, by his own goodness or righteousness, or church membership, or anything else, but solely, utterly, entirely by the free gift of God in Jesus Christ His Son. We must tell them that the eternal Son of God came from heaven into this world, was born miraculously and uniquely of the virgin, was born under the law, and gave a perfect obedience to that law, that He took upon Him the guilt of our sins, and received our punishment, and that thereby alone we are saved. We must tell them that He died, that He was buried in a grave, that He literally rose in the body, manifested Himself to chosen witnesses, ascended into heaven, sat down at the right hand of God, and that He is waiting until His enemies shall be made His footstool; that He will come again, riding the clouds of heaven, surrounded by the holy angels, that He will destroy all His enemies, and set up His glorious and eternal kingdom. We must preach the full-orbed doctrine leaving nothing out: conviction of sin, the reality of judgment and hell, free grace, justification, sanctification, glorification.

We must also show that there is a world-view in the Bible. We must demonstrate that here alone you can understand history: past history, present history, future history. Let us show this great world-view, and God's eternal purpose. Let us preach it to the people. Let us forget about their science and learning and scholarship. Let us say to them, This is history, this is what has happened, and this is what must happen; God has said so. Let us give them the full-orbed gospel and its message.

Let us at the same time be very careful that we are giving it to the whole man. What do I mean? I mean that the gospel is not only for a man's heart, but that you start with his head and present truth to it. Truth comes first to the mind and to the understanding. Let us expound the truth. Let us not imagine that to evangelize is just to tell stories, to amuse people, and to use certain psychological techniques. Let us show that it is a great message given by God which we in turn pass on to the mind, to the heart, to the will. There is ever this danger of leaving out some part or other of man's personality. Some are purely intellectual in their approach, some are entirely emotional or sentimental, some are always urging people to decide or to surrender – all emphasis on the will. They are all wrong. 'God be thanked,' says this great apostle in Romans 6:17, 'that ye were the servants of sin, but ye have obeyed from the heart that form of sound words which was delivered unto you.' Let us be certain that we address the whole man: his mind, his emotions, and his will.

Lastly, let us realize that the weapons of our warfare are not carnal, but mighty through God, powerful in the power of God. Let us realize that we can be orthodox yet dead. Let us realize that we can be highly intellectual and theological and yet useless. Let us realize that even our proclamation of this Word in our own strength and power is finally null and void. 'Mighty through God!' Through the power of God! This is the thing upon which the great apostle so constantly insists. That is why he says in 1 Corinthians 2: 'I was with you in weakness, and in fear, and in much trembling. And my speech and my preaching was not with enticing words of man's wisdom, but in demonstration of the Spirit and of power' (verses 3–4). If ever a man could have used his brain, his reason, his logic, and relied upon them it was this man; but he didn't. He trembled lest he might do that. The power and the authority and the demonstration were to be 'of God': 'That your faith should not stand in the wisdom of men, but in the power of God' (verse 5).

Listen to him again in 1 Corinthians 4:19–20. He says, 'I will come to you shortly, if the Lord will, and will know, not the speech of them which are puffed up, but the power. For the kingdom of God is not in word, but in power.' It is the mighty power of the Holy Ghost; and apart from this we can do nothing. 'Our gospel', he says to the Thessalonians, 'came not unto you in word only, but also in power, and in the Holy Ghost, and in much assurance' (1 Thess. 1:5).

This is as essential as orthodoxy and correctness of doctrine and of belief. Without this we can do nothing. At the beginning of the eighteenth century certain orthodox men could see the position falling away and they said, What can we do to safeguard the truth? They decided to set up what are called The Boyle Lectures. What were they? They were designed to defend the Christian faith. A great bishop, you remember, wrote a book which we know as *Bishop Butler's Analogy*. He was going to defend the Christian faith. And another man called Paley did much the same thing.

But these books were not what saved the situation, good as they were. What saved the situation? I can tell you. It was the Holy Ghost coming upon George Whitefield at his ordination. It was John Wesley's heart being 'strangely warmed' in Aldersgate Street on 24 May, 1738. It was the outpouring of the Spirit of God. It was the power! 'Mighty through God'! For here is the very power that had floored and humbled, and convinced the apostle Paul himself, the proud self-righteous pharisaical Saul of Tarsus. He had to be knocked down, he had to be humbled, he had to be floored; and it is only the power of God, the power of the risen Christ, that can do it through the blessed Holy Spirit. The same happened to the great St Augustine, the same to Luther, the same to Calvin, the same to Blaise Pascal. It is the same thing with all of them with their giant intellects, and learning and understanding. And it is as true tonight as it has ever been throughout the centuries.

You and I must not tremble in a wrong way for the ark of the Lord. The future is assured. This is not complacency; this is Christian faith; this is Christian optimism; this is Christian assurance. This is our position. This is what God, I believe, is saying to us tonight out of Isaiah 41:10–14: 'Fear thou not; for I am with thee: be not dismayed; for I am thy God: I will strengthen thee; yea, I will help thee; yea, I will uphold thee with the right hand of my righteousness. Behold, all they that were incensed against thee shall be ashamed and confounded: they shall be as nothing; and they that strive with thee shall perish. Thou shalt seek them, and shalt not find them, even them that contend with thee: they that war against thee shall be as nothing, and as a thing of nought. For I, the Lord thy God, will hold

thy right hand, saying unto thee, Fear not; I will help thee. Fear not,
thou worm Jacob, and ye men of Israel; I will help thee, saith the
Lord, and thy redeemer, the Holy One of Israel.'

Christian people, when we realize that the weapons of our warfare
are 'not carnal', and that they are at the same time 'mighty through
God to the pulling down of strong holds', of every 'reasoning', and of
'every high thing that exalteth itself against the knowledge of God' –
when we realize that, we shall be ready, I think, to agree with Charles
Wesley when he says:

> *Jesus the Saviour reigns,*
> *The God of truth and love;*
> *When He had purged our stains*
> *He took His seat above.*
>
> *His kingdom cannot fail;*
> *He rules o'er earth and heaven;*
> *The keys of death and hell*
> *Are to our Jesus given.*
>
> *He sits at God's right hand*
> *Till all His foes submit,*
> *And bow to His command,*
> *And fall beneath His feet.*
>
> *Rejoice in glorious hope;*
> *Jesus the judge shall come,*
> *And take His servants up*
> *To their eternal home.*
> *We soon shall hear the archangel's voice,*
> *The trump of God shall sound, rejoice!*

Twelve

*

The Centenary of Westminster Chapel 1865–1965[1]

*

We are here to celebrate the hundredth anniversary of the opening of this building. We are not celebrating the anniversary of the formation of the church, but we are specifically and primarily concerned about the building. Of course we cannot confine ourselves to that, because the importance of the building after all lies in what has happened and has taken place in it. But we must try to be accurate about these things.

Now some of you may have noticed that my way of announcing and referring to this meeting on Sunday seemed to contain an element of hesitation in it; and that was perfectly true. I was not attempting to conceal the hesitation. The question occurs to me, as it may do to many of you tonight, as to whether we are doing a right thing tonight. Should we as Christian people be celebrating the opening of a building? An interesting theological point arises in connection with that, and I want to say just a few words about it before I give some of the interesting and notable facts in connection with this building, and what has taken place in it, during this long period of time.

I will explain in a moment my reasons for having some hesitation with regard to this. My first instinct was to make some reference to this event in a purely domestic church meeting in September. We generally have a meeting in September when I return from my holidays, in which we meet together for fellowship and talk about certain matters – my first instinct was to do just that. But I was persuaded that we ought to go beyond that and have the kind of meeting that we are having here tonight.

[1]An address given at Westminster Chapel on 6 July, 1965.

[222]

I have many reasons for this kind of hesitation. I am not really a believer in anniversaries at all, especially in connection with churches. I think that one of the regrettable developments in connection with free church life has been to multiply these special occasions – anniversaries, half-yearly anniversaries, etc. Some even have quarterly anniversaries and all sorts of other days and commemorations. Well, instinctively, all that does not appeal to me, and that is why we never have any anniversary meetings here.

However, I was somewhat helped by something that I read in a newspaper yesterday morning. The paper happens to be the *Western Mail* of Cardiff. This is what I read in the *Western Mail* for yesterday. There was an account in it of the centenary of the opening of a most interesting and fascinating 'light railway' known as the Talyllyn Light Railway. That was opened a hundred years ago yesterday, so the occasion was being celebrated. But this is what I read: 'The Talyllyn Railway has operated continuously since its inception and claims to be the first narrow-gauge railway in the world to be able to celebrate a century of steam operation with the two original engines still working.' You may wonder what this has got to do with our meeting tonight – but wait a minute. The report goes on, 'It is now operated on a non-profit making basis and attracts tens of thousands of holiday-makers every year.' Now listen: 'At St. Cadfan's Church, Towyn, yesterday [that is to say, last Sunday] a United Churches' Service of Thanksgiving was held in connection with the Railway centenary anniversary. A hundred year old railway truck, a stoker's shovel, a sledge-hammer, and a locomotive sign bearing the words "The Centenarian" occupied a place of honour in the transept of the church. Thanksgivings were offered by the Rev David Williams, pastor of Towyn Congregational Church, and the sermon was preached by the Rev W. V. Awdry of Wisbech, a member of the Preservation Society and author of several popular children's books on trains and railways.'

Well, having read that, I was put a little bit at ease with regard to what we are doing tonight!

Now, what is the cause of this hesitation that I had in my mind, and partly, perhaps, in my spirit? Well, it is, of course, ultimately, one's whole attitude as a Christian to buildings, to what are called 'religious' buildings. I am free to confess that this is not an easy subject; in fact I have always found it an extremely difficult one. Read the Old Testament and you will find that a great deal of attention is paid to this. Think, for instance, of what we read about Solomon building that first great temple and how it was to be 'exceeding magnifical'; and all the details and all the expert artistry and all the care and attention that went into the building of the temple. The temple as a building was regarded with very great seriousness; all the best should be put into it, and it should be great and wonderful and magnificent in every respect because it was the house of God.

The Old Testament, as you know, is full of that kind of attitude towards buildings in which God was worshipped; but when you turn over to the New Testament you tend to find something different. You find our Lord preaching sitting in a boat, or sitting on the side of a mountain. You read about the church in so-and-so's house. The whole picture seems to have changed completely, and therein, I think, the problem arises.

As you come down the history of the centuries you find that a development took place. From that simplicity that is so characteristic of the New Testament a tendency arose and developed to go back, as it were, to the Old Testament idea until you arrive at the great medieval churches and abbeys and cathedrals and so on. There arises this interesting question, this problem: How do we reconcile these things?

Then, you remember, when you come to the seventeenth century, and the Puritan movement becomes powerful, you get a new attitude again appearing with regard to these buildings. You get a reaction coming in against cathedrals and ornate buildings and painted windows and all the rest that is so characteristic of the cathedral, and that type of architecture and furnishing. You find the Puritans going in for simplicity and plainness in buildings as well as in worship. Indeed they did another thing which perhaps, to me at any rate, is still more important; they stopped referring to the place of worship as the 'church', and they would refer to it as the 'meeting house'.

That is the Puritan tradition – that the building is just a meeting house. Those of you who have read any of the history of Quakerism will know how George Fox, in particular, used to denounce those 'steeple houses' as he called them. That was in general the tendency of all the Puritans. They reacted against all the medieval development which was taken over by the Church of England, and continued by it; and they went in for 'meeting houses'. All you needed was a building where men and women could meet together to pray, to listen to the preaching of the Word and have fellowship together, and above all, of course, to meet with God.

I must not detain you with all this tonight, because we have announced that what we are going to do chiefly is to give a little bit of the history. But I could not do that without trying to justify what we are doing.

Is there some way of reconciling these things that I have put before you? Well, it seems to me that the best we can say is something like this, that there is no absolute rule in these matters, and that the problem is not as simple as it sometimes appears to be. You get the two extremes in this matter, but I feel that both extremes are wrong. All we can safely say, I think, is this, that there is a danger always in externalizing our worship. It not only applies to buildings, it applies to music, it applies to art, it applies to many other things in connection with our worship of God. The danger is, I say, to go to one extreme or the other. That arises, of course, because we are still in the flesh, and because it does seem to be a rule as far as one can tell from a reading of the history of the church, that externalizing and spirituality seem to be opposites, and that they are inversely proportional to each other. As people attach more and more significance to the externals and to the forms, they tend to pay less and less attention to the living spiritual element in worship.

Now I am not making absolutes of these; I am simply saying that it behoves us to be careful. We can go wrong at both extremes because the Holy Spirit of God can work anywhere, and He has worked in places that some of us with a puritanical outlook would be amazed to hear about. There is no limit to God's power and to what is possible with Him. Nevertheless I think it is fair to say that generally speaking you have not found Him working in great revival power in cathedrals and abbeys, but you have found Him working in such power in the little bethels, the plain unadorned conventicles that have so often been despised, and often in sheds, often in caves, often on mountain tops. I do not want to press this too far, but I think it is something that it behoves us to bear in mind.

The next general remark I want to make is this: We cannot possibly meet together like this this evening without having a great contrast in our minds, and that is the contrast, of course, between 1865 and 1965. What a contrast! It is very difficult to imagine a greater contrast. You see, this building had to be built in 1865 because their previous building, as I am going to tell you, had become too small! And do not forget this: this building was built in 1865. It was in 1861 that Spurgeon's Metropolitan Tabernacle was built and opened. You see, within four years of one another this great building and that still greater building there to the south of the River Thames were built.

Now that gives us in a picture the conditions prevailing in 1865 and the mid-Victorian era. They were years of crowded churches and chapels, years of great religious success, years when almost everybody went to a place of worship, and everybody was talking about building bigger buildings. But today the whole position has changed. The big buildings have become a problem, and when rebuilding takes place today they are very careful to build smaller buildings. The rebuilding of the City Temple illustrates this – the maximum that it can seat now is 1,400. And it is the same with Spurgeon's Tabernacle rebuilt after the last war. It is the exact opposite of what obtained in 1865.

I was tempted sorely to spend the whole evening on the contrast between 1865 and 1965. I am not going to do so. But it is interesting to me in this way. I have often said from this pulpit that I am very glad that I am preaching here now and not a hundred years ago. People have sometimes been very surprised at that. Surely, they say, you would not deliberately choose these difficult, dark, discouraging days in which we live; you would not sooner have that, surely, than the halcyon days and that great condition of religious prosperity which you have just been reminding us obtained in the sixties of the last century? Well, I resolutely say that I would deliberately choose to be here now rather than a hundred years ago.

Why? That raises the whole question of one's view of the Victorian era. It is an era of which I am a critic. I believe that one of the first and most urgent things the Christian church has to do today is to forget the Victorian era, and go back to the previous century, the eighteenth century, and perhaps also to the one before that. The Victorian era always seems to me to have been a very artificial era. It seemed so prosperous, it seemed so wonderful. And the people of that age were convinced that it was. They were sure that they were advancing towards perfection. Even those who rejected the biological theory of evolution as such seemed to assume it in a religious sense. The church was expanding and the missionary societies were growing and developing – the whole world was going to become Christian. They held their great conferences and they did not hesitate to say that they could produce a plan to evangelize the whole world within a given period of time.

How pathetic it all was! They did not realize that even in 1865 the canker had already entered the body. They did not realize that the Higher Critical movement, about which they were beginning to hear, and which had come from Germany in the thirties and the forties, was already beginning to undermine the whole situation. They went on in their false optimism – and they went on, indeed, until 1914. And then, or soon after, it began to be obvious to most people that it was quite artificial, that there was a rottenness at the centre. But by today that is obvious to everybody; and that is why I prefer to be here now rather than a hundred years ago. We now know exactly what we are facing, what the position is. We have got no illusions. I trust at any rate that this is true of all of us who are here tonight. We are facing reality and not some artificial painting which really was rotten, in a sense, at the very centre.

So we could have spent our time very profitably, I think, in drawing and pointing the contrasts, the great contrasts between 1865 and 1965. Let us keep that in our minds as we now come to the actual facts of the history in connection with this place.

The history of the origin of this church, for some extraordinary reason, is enshrouded in a kind of mystery. I do not know why. I have read many times of a Nonconformist place of worship in Westminster in the eighteenth century, but it is very difficult to discover where exactly it was. So all we know is this – that a church was formed here on 6 May, 1841. Actually the church was incorporated a little before that. But at any rate they built a chapel here which was opened on 6 May, 1841. That chapel seated 1,500 people. That was their first chapel. It is said that it was built here on the site of the old Westminster Hospital. Again, people are in considerable doubt as to what that means. Some think that it was the present St George's Hospital, which was originally called the Westminster Hospital. However, it is a fact that there was a hospital on this site, and it was known as the old Westminster Hospital. On that site, then, a building was opened here on 6 May, 1841, and it seated 1,500 people.

At that point the church had not got a minister; but in the next year, 1842, they called a minister whose name was Samuel Martin. He was a minister, a Congregational minister, in Cheltenham. He had a good reputation as a preacher, and they therefore called him here. He was a very active man, full of ideas. He immediately started a day school and Sunday schools, a ragged school, as it was then called, for children in certain parts of Westminster, and meetings for people described as 'down-and-outs', beggars and tramps, etc. He was full of that kind of activity. Proof of that is found in what we call the Intermediate Hall at the back, the foundation stone of which was laid in 1843, after he had been here just about a year.

Dr Samuel Martin was obviously a good preacher, and he was also an excellent pastor, and full of this kind of activity. The result was that under his ministry the church grew, grew rapidly, and grew to very large proportions; so much so that by 1863 the building had become too small. As was the prevailing custom at that time, pews and seatings were allotted, and by 1863 there was a waiting list of four hundred people who could not get seatings in the building. So it was decided in 1863 that they must have a larger building. That is how they came to plan this present building. I could tell you many details about this and how they proceeded to do it; but I do not propose to weary you with that. The fact is that on 6 July, 1865 – exactly one hundred years ago today – this present building was opened.

This building was planned to seat 2,500 people. The previous one, you remember, seated 1,500. They felt they must be able to accommodate a further 1,000 people. Those are the figures that were given. Sometimes in the subsequent history the figure is put higher than that, sometimes it is put lower. I have almost been persuaded at times, as I have read different people writing on this matter, that buildings can expand and contract, and that they seem to do so in terms of the particular man who happens to be the minister at the time! However, I must not enter into that. The building was erected to seat 2,500 people, and it undoubtedly can seat 2,500 people if they are closely packed together. The cost of the building itself was £13,484, but as they had also bought an extra bit of land the total cost came to £18,000. Now that was a lot of money a hundred years ago, but that is what it cost them.

We must pause here to emphasize a most important point. You see the building, you are familiar with it, and you see its character. What do we say about it? What we must say about it, of course, is this – that it is typically Victorian, and typical of Victorian Nonconformity. It illustrates perfectly what was happening to Nonconformity at that time. This is where Nonconformity, it seems to me, went so wrong. Nonconformity began to develop an inferiority complex. Nonconformists had not shown any evidence of that until, say, the twenties or the thirties of the last century. Prior to that Nonconformity had been proud of itself; it knew it had life as over against the established Church; it knew the Spirit of God was in it, and it experienced His power. And they rejoiced in it. But somewhere in the thirties, forties, and fifties of the last century a very subtle change took place in Nonconformity. Nonconformity began to feel that she looked rather drab and shabby. There they were with their little buildings: and they looked at the great churches, the great cathedrals, and the great abbeys, and they felt that they must do something about this. After all they were now educated people, and no longer just common, ignorant people. They were now becoming prosperous financially and in other respects, and were being educated, and they really must show that they were equal to the Church of England in every respect, including their buildings. So you begin to find a new phrase emerging, you begin to hear about 'Nonconformist cathedrals'. And this is one of them!

Now to me a 'Nonconformist cathedral' is a contradiction in terms, and it is, at the same time, an abomination. I am not saying that this building is an abomination to me, but I am saying the whole concept is. I say that because it is indicative of a carnal spirit coming into Nonconformity, a desire to be respectable, a desire to look big in the sight of the world and so on. There is no doubt whatsoever but that the whole design of this building is the result of this inferiority complex showing itself in an attempt to produce a 'cathedral' that can stand comparison with Westminster Abbey. Nonconformist cathedral!

I am always interested when I read this story to observe this, that even in the time of Dr Samuel Martin they very rarely had to use the top gallery. It was built for him because of his successful ministry, and to give this extra room, but it was not very much used even in the heyday of those successful years, and under the ministry of Dr Samuel Martin himself. One other interesting thing is that Mr Spurgeon preached here, and various other famous preachers of that age preached here also.

Now Dr Samuel Martin was undoubtedly a remarkable man; and he had a great impact upon the City of Westminster. He very rarely travelled; he believed it was his duty to spend his time here in these various activities. By about 1875 he was beginning to fail and they had to call a man to act as co-pastor with him. The man they called was the Rev Henry Simon. He was an uncle of the man who is best known to us, perhaps, as Sir John Simon, who afterwards became Lord Simon, Lord Chancellor of England. He came from Pembrokeshire, that part of Pembrokeshire which is sometimes called 'Little England beyond Wales'. I do not acknowledge him as a Welshman, because he came from that part, but he did actually, geographically, come from Pembrokeshire!

The Rev Henry Simon joined Samuel Martin here as co-pastor in 1875. In 1878 Dr Samuel Martin died. There is something I want to emphasize about that. When he died, Dr Samuel Martin was only sixty-one years old. Why do I emphasize that? I do so for this reason, that I am persuaded in my mind that it was this building that killed him. He had continual trouble with his voice and throat. It is not surprising. It is a difficult building to speak in. I will make a few remarks about that later on, but I am sure that this man died at the age of sixty-one very largely because of this building. He had been ailing and failing a great deal years before that and eventually he died, as I say, in 1878. The famous Dean Stanley of Westminster Abbey spoke at his funeral, as did also another famous Dean – Dean Farrar. He was very friendly particularly with A. P. Stanley, and to those of you who know anything about Dean Stanley and his works, that will be a very significant thing. The bust you have often noticed in the vestibule is that of Dr Samuel Martin. It was put there in memory of him.

After his death the Rev Henry Simon became the pastor, the sole pastor of the church. In 1879 they decided to commemorate the memory of Samuel Martin, in addition to the bust in the vestibule, by installing this organ which is here behind the rostrum in the first gallery. It was built in 1879, in memory of Dr Samuel Martin, by a very famous organ builder, one of the greatest of all times, I understand – Mr Henry Willis, often called Father Willis because he had a son who was also expert at the same work. The cost of the organ, if I remember rightly, was about £1,500, which in those days, of course, was a tremendous sum of money. They were acting again on the same principle, to have one of the best organs in London. You see, everything now had to be the very best. You were competing with the Church of England which had had a start of so many centuries over them. But you were not to be outdone, so you get the very best possible. So Henry Willis built this organ. The organ was reconstructed and enlarged in 1920 and has been here functioning ever since. We are now having it cleaned and reconditioned at a cost of over £2,000. The people who look after it for us, Messrs Rushworth & Dreaper, told us when we decided to do the present work that we ought to start putting money aside now because in ten years' time this organ will have to be completely reconstructed at an estimated cost of £15,000.

I mention that fact for this reason. I shall probably not be here then, but let me say this for the guidance of those who will be here. If you do that, well then, I say that you are forfeiting every right to expect God to bless you. To spend £15,000 on reconstructing an organ in an age like this I regard as nothing but grievous sin. However, that is for other people to face. I am simply reminding you that this organ was built, and that it is a part of the whole Victorian attitude to public worship.

To return to the story, you remember that the Rev Henry Simon came here first in 1875. He became sole pastor in 1878 and he continued here until 1887. Then he resigned and left, and went to a church in another part of London. Why did he go? Well, it seems to me that it was the same reason again; it was the building. He was tired, he was feeling the strain. It was not so much the congregation and the work, I think, as the building. He was, it is true, also contending with another factor, another element which is interesting for us to notice. Just about the time when he was here the trend of the middle classes to move further out from the centre was taking place, and taking place very rapidly. Anybody who could afford to do so was pressing out to the suburbs. Mr Spurgeon had to face the same problem, but, of course, because of his outstanding qualities his people still tended to come in. They used to come in by trains in great crowds. There was a train which was always known as 'The Tabernacle Special', crowded with people going to listen to Mr Spurgeon.

Here, they had not got a man of the magnitude of Mr Spurgeon, and they were undoubtedly feeling the effects of this trend out to the suburbs. As a result of that, but still more on account of the first reason I have given you, the strain of the building, the Rev Henry Simon resigned. He was able to thank God, he said, that in spite of this trend to the suburbs the congregations had been holding up very well.

He went in 1887. From 1887 to 1894 this church was without a pastor at all. They tried many men, but not a man would accept the invitation. Why not? Surely the explanation is still the same – this building. Men had known what had happened to Dr Samuel Martin, and they knew what had happened to the Rev Henry Simon. They saw the strain upon one's physical resources, and also this trend to the suburbs. The result was that many famous preachers who were invited here, and on whom considerable pressure was put to come here, would not come. The result was that for seven years the church was without a settled pastor.

However, in 1894 a man of the name of W. E. Hurndall accepted the invitation and became the pastor here. He seems to have been a remarkable man, and he would undoubtedly have done very well here; but unfortunately within a year he was killed in an accident. That again left the church without a pastor.

Then in 1896 they called another man who accepted the invitation – the Rev Richard Westrup. He seems to have been a remarkable man, a strange man in many ays. The descriptions of him tell us that he held very advanced socialistic views. As far as I can make out, his position was very similar to that of Dr – I beg his pardon, I mean Lord – Soper today. He at that time seemed to hold similar views and he preached them, and did his utmost to put them into practice here. He was here until 1902. But it was not a successful ministry. In spite of his attempt to appeal to the man in the street, the modern man, with his political preaching, it was not a success and his ministry here ended in 1902.

From 1878 onwards there was a good man working in connection with this church, and doing an excellent work, whose name was A. W. Hewitt. He was the father of the Misses Hewitt who are here tonight, and Mrs Caiger, and the father-in-law of Mr A. W. Caiger, our one-time treasurer. He was the official evangelist in this church and he did great work here in the City of Westminster in connection with mission work and so on, the kind of work that you would expect such an evangelist to do. He was here from 1878 until 1916 and was a man who was honoured by all who knew him. There is a photograph of him hanging on the wall in the Institute Hall where he richly deserves to have his place with the various men who have been ministers of this church. However, in spite of his work, and in view of the other things I have been describing to you, this place went from bad to worse. A most serious and alarming decline took place. We read that the services were attended by just a handful of faithful old saints, and that young people were absent almost entirely. I read that only 185 members were to be found in regular communion.

By 1903 this place was described by Dr A. E. Garvie, the principal of one of the Congregational theological colleges, as the 'white elephant of Congregationalism'. The place was described as 'dirty, dilapidated, and almost deserted', and there was a very strong body of opinion in the Congregational Union that this building should be sold, and that with the money they would get for the site they would be able to build a number of chapels in the suburbs. It was felt that it was wrong to go on maintaining such a building as this. It had had its day, it had served its purpose, and it was wrong to continue with it. That was the official view. However, there were still some who felt that this must not happen. But it very nearly did happen; and it undoubtedly would have happened but for one thing. It was felt that there was only one man who could do anything at all here and that one man was George Campbell Morgan. He came here, and preached, and it was still more evident that he was the man. So they invited him. He accepted the invitation to come, but was not able to do so, owing to commitments in America, for six months. He eventually came here and started his first pastorate in November, 1904.

Now Dr Campbell Morgan was a man who had many advantages in many ways apart from his outstanding natural gifts as a speaker and as a teacher. He was very well known. He had been associated with the work of D. L. Moody, particularly in America, and had become, in a sense, a world-famous person. So that when he came here people knew about him. He not only preached here, he also began his famous Bible School which he held on Friday nights.

When he came he decided at once that the whole place must be reconstructed, and it was reconstructed. It was he who ordered this particular rostrum. The previous pulpit was a smaller one, but he wanted this large rostrum. Why? Well, in his Bible School he used to have a blackboard here in the rostrum, and he used to put his main headings on that board. He wanted room for that. He also liked having people with him in the pulpit. His idea was that Westminster Chapel should be a great evangelical centre, so he planned everything accordingly.

A friend of his became his colleague, the Rev Albert Swift. They not only preached and had a Bible School on Friday nights, they started a kind of institute in the premises at the back where there were thriving meetings of all descriptions. There were lectures and classes on literature and art and drama – almost everything. A highly organized institutional church was brought into being which obviously appealed to many young people; and it was a very flourishing effort. All that went on right until the outbreak of the First World War in 1914.

I report the following fact because to me it is a very interesting point in connection with church work. Dr Morgan told me more than once that if he had his time over again he would never have started the Institute. 'Why?' I asked. 'Well,' he said, 'it produced a church within a church.' But he did it, and he did it with great thoroughness. They also appointed a large number of 'sisters' here, deaconesses, who did various works, teaching, visiting in the area, holding meetings for women, etc. It was a place of thriving activity, a hive of activity. All this went on until the outbreak of the First World War.

That of course raised many very great problems, but Dr Morgan continued. He unfortunately got an attack of typhoid fever which, of course, laid him low. There was very little that could be done for typhoid fever in those days. He was seriously ill. He eventually recovered, but he never seemed to recover his strength fully, and that, plus again, I have no doubt at all, this building, even with his extraordinary voice – a naturally powerful voice – meant that the work became a burden to him and a strain, with the result that in November, 1917, he resigned from the pastorate of the church. In other words he had been here for thirteen years. This in no way does justice to Dr Campbell Morgan's unique ministry here. But as I say we are concerned only with a general review of the story of this building.

In 1918 a successor was invited and called who accepted the invitation. He was the famous Dr John Henry Jowett. He had been famous as minister of Carr's Lane in Birmingham, and after that had become still more famous as minister of the Fifth Avenue Presbyterian Church in New York City. I again give you a detail which will give some indication of how times change. When Dr Jowett was called here, in addition to the call sent him by the church, King George V sent him a personal message pleading with him to come back to this country. That was done, of course, at the suggestion of the then Prime Minister, Mr Lloyd George, who himself was a Nonconformist. It was felt that the return of Dr Jowett would be a good thing for the whole country. You see, the lesson had still not been learned. There was a feeling abroad that after the war we really were going to make a new world, 'a world fit for heroes to live in', and Dr Jowett was felt to be just the man for that great task. He was very interested in politics, and he was a great favourite with politicians. So the call and invitation from the church was reinforced by a word from King George V. And Dr Jowett came here.

Now Dr Jowett, I read in his biography, did not like this building at all. In fact he disliked it very much. He compared it to Charing Cross Station. I do not agree with him in that; but he disliked it and he disliked this rostrum in particular. He disliked it so much that he had them drape it in with a kind of curtain right round. He said that when he stood in this pulpit as it is now he felt exactly as if he were standing naked in the middle of a field. You good friends have no idea as to what it is like to stand in this pulpit. It can be a most terrifying place. Well, that is how Dr Jowett reacted, and he got them to drape it in. He also got them to cover in the windows at the back. He was troubled by seeing late comers standing in the vestibule during the early part of the service. He was also greatly troubled by the empty top gallery. Of course, at first when he came, with all the excitement and publicity, the top gallery was filled. But it did not remain full; after some months it became empty. All that, remember, was in 1918–19. People have often said to me, 'Why cannot we get this top gallery full?' Well, remember that Samuel Martin did not fill it, nor Dr Jowett, nor even Dr Campbell Morgan, even in those days.

Well, there it was. He came but, unfortunately, he soon began to suffer from pernicious anaemia, and the result was that he had to resign in 1922. Again the pastorate was vacant.

The next man invited was a Scotsman of the name of Dr John A. Hutton. He came here in 1923 and remained here until 1925. I often listened to him. I think I listened to him most of the Sunday mornings that he was here. I was a young medical man at the time and this man's preaching appealed to me tremendously. He could be a most effective preacher, but his congregations went down and down. Why? Largely because people could not hear him. He had a bad habit of dropping his voice at the end of a sentence; and if you do that in this pulpit without the aid of microphones and a loud-speaking system you just cannot be heard. After being here for only two years Dr Hutton was invited to become the editor of the *British Weekly* in 1925, and he accepted. So again the church was without a pastor.

The next man invited was Dr Hubert L. Simpson, another Scotsman. He came here in 1928. He was not able to build up the congregation again, but he held Dr Hutton's congregation and perhaps added to it somewhat. But he, again, soon became a sick man. Whether it was the building again or not I do not know, but that is a fact.

Towards the end of 1932 Dr Campbell Morgan was invited to come back here and to join Dr Simpson in the pastorate. They became co-pastors or associate pastors of this church at the beginning of 1933. Dr Morgan had been in America since about 1919, but in 1933 he came back and they had this joint ministry. It was felt at once that the entire premises must be renovated. A Restoration Fund of £7,500 was raised and this building was put in order once more.

Dr Simpson's health finally failed altogether, and he had to resign in 1934. So during 1935 Dr Campbell Morgan was here alone again as the sole pastor of the church. But his strength now also began to fail. He began to have trouble entering the pulpit owing to rheumatism, and various other evidences of weakness began to appear. The result was that he was no longer able to preach more than once on a Sunday, so they had to invite other men to take the second service. They went on like that until 1938 – September, 1938. In September, 1938, it was my privilege to come here.

There are one or two points in connection with my coming here which will interest you. I mention these things because they have obviously played a large part in my life. I do not pretend to be able to understand one of them. I shall never forget reading in a newspaper at breakfast one morning at the end of 1932, in just a little paragraph, that Dr Campbell Morgan was coming back from America to join Dr Hubert Simpson in the pastorate of Westminster Chapel and that he was going to start at the beginning of 1933. I read that quite casually, but as I read it I had a strange and curious intimation. It was more than a kind of intuition, I call it an intimation. It was so definite that I called the attention of my wife and I read the paragraph out to her. I said, 'Now, you may think that I am going mad but I am telling you here and now that this has got something of vital importance to do with me.' Well, the thing, of course, appeared to be sheer lunacy. I had never met Dr Campbell Morgan, and there was nothing further from my mind than the idea of leaving the church where I was ministering in South Wales.

However, as I read the paragraph that is what happened. My wife is a witness to this. That was at the end of 1932.

I was taking part in a meeting in the Albert Hall in December, 1935. Strangely enough it was the night when the old Crystal Palace was burnt down. That night proved to be a turning point in my story. Dr Campbell Morgan had come to the meeting. I shall never forget how he frightened me before the meeting. It was a typical December night, about 6 December if I remember rightly, and there was quite a nasty fog about. He came on to me in the speakers' room before the meeting and said, 'I tell you in the presence of my Maker that no one and nothing would have made me come out on a night like this but you.' Well, of course I was already feeling nervous about speaking in the Albert Hall; and how I survived that remark I do not know. However, that is how it happened. The sequel was – that was a Tuesday night – that on the Thursday morning I had a letter from Dr Campbell Morgan asking me if I could preach here on the last Sunday of that year, 1935. I accepted, and I came, and I preached for the first time in this pulpit on the morning of the last Sunday of December, 1935. I preached both morning and evening.

The next interesting link between us happened in June, 1937. I was in America giving some addresses at the General Assembly of the Presbyterian Church in the USA and they had arranged a preaching tour for me. One day I arrived to preach in the city of Philadelphia. There was a heatwave on, unfortunately for me. I had been driven in a car most of the day from a place called Scranton and I was feeling completely exhausted. I arrived at the house of a minister, and as he received me this is what he said to me: 'Well, I don't know what sort of a congregation we can expect tonight. It is very hot as you know and people are away.' He then said, 'I don't know what sort of a congregation we are going to get, but this I do know; I can tell you who will be the most distinguished person in the congregation.' I said, 'Who is that?' He said, 'Dr Campbell Morgan.' He went on, 'He arrived last night from England with his wife. They are staying with his son Howard, and the moment he heard that you were preaching here tonight he said, "I am going to be there".' We went into the meeting at the appointed time and there he sat in front of me. He was the last man I wanted to see! But he did a thing which was very characteristic of him, and which somehow put me right. As I was taking my text I could see him through the corner of my eye taking out his watch. I saw that he was going to time me. And that somehow or another helped me and stimulated me. (Incidentally, and as I believe I said in his memorial service, he was the best listener I have ever known.)

Well, that proved to be an important night in this way. When I had finished preaching and went down from the pulpit he was the first man to come to speak to me. Then, having spoken to me he turned to leave the building. A number of other people were there speaking to me. As I was talking to them I could see him walking up an aisle on the side of the building. I noticed that he would stop every now and again and turn back and look at me. Then he would walk on, and then he would stop again and look at me. I knew exactly what was happening, and I was right! He decided there and then that I was to be the man eventually to join him here. He was only able to preach once a Sunday now and could see that the real solution was to find an associate pastor.

He sent a message back home to Mr Marsh, secretary here for over fifty years, and I preached here again in July, 1937. But there was still no thought of my ever coming here. However, towards the end of 1937 I myself was a little bit overtired through sheer overwork. Not only that, there was a proposal in the denomination to which I belong, the Presbyterian Church of Wales, to appoint me to give lectures on preaching and pastoral work in their postgraduate college. However, the post at the college would not be open until the session beginning in September, 1939. I felt disposed to accept this invitation but I also felt I needed a little bit of rest. Dr Morgan somehow or another heard all this and he sent me an invitation along these lines. He said, 'While you are taking a bit of a rest why not come and join me? We will share the ministry. You preach one end of the day and I will preach the other.' Well, this suited me very well, so I accepted; and I came here as a kind of permanent 'pulpit supply'. That was all, and I never intended it to be anything more than that. However, after I had been here a very short time Dr Morgan engineered (I use the word deliberately) that the church meeting should extend to me an invitation to join him in the joint pastorate, and I was given that invitation in October, 1938. I did not accept it until April, 1939, as I was not clear as to my duty. However, I did so in April, 1939. Dr Morgan and I went on together exactly as before, except that I was now officially associate pastor or joint-pastor. We each preached once on Sundays alternating from morning to evening each month.

Then in September, 1939, war came again; and it was a period of very great trial. We had no protection here at all against possible bombing, nothing underneath such as they have in many buildings. In addition there was a mass evacuation and people were scattered all over the country. Dr Morgan was most troubled. He said 'I have brought you here, and this is what I have brought you to.' He was very troubled about this and, one day, he said, 'Of course we are almost certain to be bombed completely to the ground. We are so near Buckingham Palace, it is only a matter of days probably until this building will be completely demolished and you and I will be out of work and without a pastorate.'

Once more, one of these extraordinary things happened. I am not one of those people who is given to what are called hunches or intimations – I am not 'psychic'. I am not that kind of person at all, but when Dr Morgan said that to me I was able to answer him with complete confidence. I said, 'This chapel will not be bombed.' He said, 'You are very sure, are you not?' I said, 'I am absolutely sure.' He said, 'How do you know?' 'Well,' I said, 'I cannot explain it to you, but I have received an intimation that this chapel is not going to be destroyed.' He was most impressed by this, by the fact that I was so sure, so confident that this was going to be the case.

Well, on we went, and we had that first period of bombing, and nothing happened here. But I shall never forget a certain morning, Sunday morning, 11 May, 1941. I had travelled up to Oxford the day before (10 May) because I was due to preach in the chapel of Mansfield College on the Sunday morning. Then I was going to travel back in the afternoon and preach here at night. I was staying with the then principal of Mansfield, Dr Nathaniel Micklem. We had gone to bed on the Saturday night, and the next thing I remember is that I was awakened in the morning by Dr Micklem who had brought me up a cup of tea. As he handed me the cup of tea he said, 'Look here, I am going to announce this morning in the service that you will be preaching at night as well as in the morning.' I said, 'But you mustn't do that, I am preaching in Westminster Chapel tonight.' 'My dear man,' he said, 'you will not be preaching in Westminster Chapel tonight.' 'Why not?' I said. He said, 'There is no Westminster Chapel.' I said, 'What do you mean?' 'Well,' he said, 'there has been a terrible raid last night, the worst we have ever had.' (And it was actually the last of the great night bombings of London.) He said, 'I have heard on the wireless that the whole of Westminster is practically flattened, so why not preach here tonight?' I said, 'Listen to this. I am telling you that Westminster Chapel has not been demolished, and that I shall be preaching in it tonight.' He was amazed at this, and especially at my certainty. He said, 'But it's ridiculous.' I said, 'I am telling you this, and I am sure of it.'

So I did not allow him to make the announcement that I would be preaching at night also. I preached in the morning, and after lunch got my train for London. I shall never forget this. I remember travelling up from Ealing Broadway to Paddington. I could see fires burning in places on both sides of the line. I got out of the train and found a great queue of people waiting for taxis. At last I got one. 'Where for, sir?' said the taxi-man. I said, 'I want a chapel called Westminster Chapel halfway along Buckingham Gate, Westminster.' 'I'm afraid, sir,' he said, 'you cannot get into Buckingham Gate.' 'Why not?' 'Oh, terrible bombing last night,' he said, 'everything flattened.' I said, 'Look here, you get down in the direction of Victoria and I will guide you.' I had decided to bring him along Palace Street and then to turn in here into Castle Lane. While all this was going on he was telling me about what he had seen; but I was still absolutely certain that I would be preaching in this chapel. I will never forget it. We came round the corner from Palace Street into Castle Lane. I looked, and here was this old building standing as if there had not been a raid at all. I believe I am right in saying that two window-panes on the left side from the pulpit were cracked; and that was all that had happened. I preached here and took the service as usual.

However, in 1944 when the flying bombs came we did have a little bit of trouble. A bomb dropped on that block of flats on the Buckingham Palace side of us one morning and it blew off half the roof of this building, and shattered all the windows on that side. But this was the remarkable thing; as regards the building as an auditorium it was perfect, and the organ was entirely undamaged. The only thing that had happened was that all those windows were out, and that wall had been moved an inch and a half out of position, and the main joists had been moved, and half the roof was off. The result of that was we had to go and worship in the Livingstone Hall, which was kindly loaned to us for fourteen weeks. After that we came back. All the empty windows were boarded over, we had rubberoid instead of slates put on the roof; and we were able to continue with our regular worship.

Eventually the war ended in May, 1945. The great thing to me was that this building was still standing. The City Temple had gone, Spurgeon's Tabernacle had gone, but this was here – still here. The intimation I had been given, I am certain, was of God Himself.

Eventually, of course, we had to face the question of putting this building back into order – our great war-damage reconstruction. The total cost of that was roughly £24,000. Many of you will remember how for thirteen months we worshipped here regularly Sunday by Sunday with scaffolding inside the building. It was most extraordinary. The first Sunday I shall never forget. I seemed to be looking at people in cages, such was the extraordinary effect produced by the scaffolding that was inside here. But however I may have felt about it on the first Sunday that I preached with it, that was nothing in comparison with my feelings the first Sunday after the scaffolding was taken away! That was a most desolating feeling. I felt I was in a strange place and that the people were on top of me, and no longer in the distance in cages. However, we survived it all, the scaffolding was removed, and we have continued like this ever since.

We have made some improvements since then. We have made great improvements outside. We have a new kitchen, we have put the old almshouses into serviceable condition, and we have spent a lot of money in doing so and in the general maintenance of the fabric.

That brings us to the end of the story as regards this building, and some of the things that have happened in it. Will you permit me just a few reflections before I close?

What do we learn from all this? One of the things we learn, I think, is this. We must never be governed by the spirit of the age. I believe the people who built this building were governed by the spirit of the age. That was Victorianism! It was not Christianity. How subtle this is, how it creeps in. The devil comes in and brings in carnal elements without our knowing it. 'Nonconformist cathedral!' But what is the value of a Nonconformist cathedral if you have got it at the expense of the Spirit and loyalty to the truth! Let us remember that the church is ageless, and that we are to be governed not by the trend of the age, not by 'the development of thought', but by the New Testament principles, by the teaching of the Word of God.

Now let me say something about this building. What have I to say about it? Well, I have already said that I do not agree with Dr Jowett's description of it. It is an extraordinary building; it is a building that grows on you. Of course it is too big. The real mistake they made, I think, was in the excessive height and head-room. That is why the acoustics are so difficult. If only they had put a flat ceiling from the top of the windows from one side to the other I believe this would have been a perfectly easy building to speak in. But, instead, they had that curve, and that is always fatal. Then that alcove facing the pulpit is thoroughly bad acoustically. All these things are a hindrance. The best chapels to speak in, the best buildings acoustically, are always square buildings with flat ceilings – and they must be absolutely flat. Any variation from that always leads to trouble, however slight the variation. The Methodist central halls up and down this country are always difficult to preach in, just because they have rounded and curved all the ceilings.

I have always been very interested in this. I have had to preach in many chapels which have been built since the last war and it is very interesting to observe that I cannot think of a single new building that has been put up since the last war but that its acoustics are hopeless. They all have to introduce microphones – even in small buildings. Why? Because they have never realized that a flat ceiling is absolutely essential as a sounding board. The moment you vary that you ruin the acoustics. I think that is the main trouble here.

Let me add a personal note here. You notice that I have been in this pastorate longer than anybody apart from Dr Samuel Martin. He was here altogether about thirty-six years. It was not fully that, because of his weakness and illness and forced absences. But on the whole we can describe it as thirty-six years. Dr Campbell Morgan was here in his first ministry thirteen years, then when he came back, the second time, he was here altogether ten years, five of which he shared with me and two of which he shared with Dr Hubert L. Simpson. Adding his two periods together, it comes to twenty-three years. To my utter amazement and astonishment I am just finishing my twenty-seventh year here. Actually, in this building, I have preached longer than anybody, because as it was only opened in 1865 Dr Samuel Martin only preached in it for thirteen years. My reason for mentioning this is that I am absolutely certain I would not have been here for anything like this time, even half of it, were it not for this microphone. Fortunately for me even Dr Campbell Morgan, owing to his weakness, could not be heard, and they had to provide a loud-speaking system before I came here. I have thanked God for it ever since. This building, you see, has killed men. It would have killed me beyond any doubt whatsoever, but, fortunately, this thing has been invented, and it enables me, and has enabled me for twenty-seven years, to exercise my ministry as best I can by the grace of God.

But I must say this. In spite of the fact that the acoustics are so difficult, it is a wonderful pulpit to preach from. Though the place is so big the congregation is nevertheless near the preacher. It is almost unique, in my experience, in that respect.

I will never forget something Dr Hutton said to me on one occasion just after I had come here. He said it in his characteristic manner. He said, 'You know, that pulpit of yours in Westminster Chapel is the most wonderful and the greatest pulpit in the world to preach from as long as you are prepared. But if you are not prepared,' he added, 'it is the most awful place in the universe.' Well, he was speaking from experience; and those who remember him and who remember his quaint characteristics, will know that he was really speaking from experience!

However, I agree with his general proposition. When the preacher enters it with a message this pulpit is a great place to occupy. But if a man attempts to speak here without adequate preparation, he will find, as Dr Hutton said, that truly it is indeed a terrible place.

However, the question that arises in one's mind is this: what is to be the future of a place like this, or similar places? The cost of the upkeep of these premises and fabric is alarming. It is going up year by year. It is quite astonishing and amazing. 'Hitherto the Lord has helped us', and we have been enabled to do our work without trouble. We thank God, and praise Him for it, for the way He has blessed us and helped us and sustained us. But it must of necessity become a great and an increasing problem in the years that lie ahead.

I put out a question for your meditation: what is the future to be? The only justification, it seems to me, for a place such as this is that it is a place for evangelical witness. My firm conviction is that God preserved this building during the last war for the sake of its evangelical witness. I have no doubt about that. And I think He will continue to do so as long as it witnesses to that faith.

Has this building always been a great place for evangelical witness? It would be wrong, it would not be true, to say that it has. I find it difficult to place Dr Samuel Martin theologically. His friendship with Dean Stanley puts him into a category, and likewise his friendship with Dean Farrar. He was one of those men who, influenced by the idea of the all-importance of learning and scholarship, began to compromise the truth. Not very much, perhaps, but quite definitely. I do not know enough about his immediate successors to say anything, but I think I am justified in saying that there have only been two ministers here of whom it can be said without any hesitation that they have stood for the evangelical faith unadulterated. Those two are Dr Campbell Morgan, and the present minister. It would be wrong to give the impression that this has always been a great evangelical centre. It has not. But I do believe, for the reasons that I have been giving you, that it was God who brought Dr Campbell Morgan and your humble servant together, and gave me that unmistakable leading with regard to what my duty was.

I was certain that I was called to minister in Wales. I used to refuse automatically every invitation that came from England. I did not even consider them. I was called to Wales, and I refused all invitations with scarcely any thought. But when that invitation came to speak at that Bible Witness Rally in the Albert Hall, to my own amazement – they had written to me many times before – on this occasion I felt I had to accept it. And I have told you the remainder of the story.

I believe, I say, that God has preserved this edifice for that one reason; and He will keep this place open, I am certain, while this testimony to the infallible character of this Book is proclaimed and pronounced from this pulpit. And while that evangelical faith, which alone is true Christianity, is proclaimed, God, I am certain, will not only honour the preaching of it, but He will preserve the building in order that that may be continued.

I trust that these rambling remarks of mine have been of some profit and value to you. I started by querying whether we should do this at all and raised the question of the place of buildings in worship. We have not solved this problem, but God is very tender and condescends to our low estate. 'He remembereth that we are dust.' The place in which you have met God frequently becomes a place that is very dear to you.

> *We love the place, O God,*
> *Wherein thine honour dwells.*

Not bricks and mortar; but this place in which God has met with us! I think that God expects us to feel an affection for the very precincts of the place because He has been pleased to meet with us here, and has honoured us by His presence. We in our measure know something of the feeling of the psalmist when he was prevented from going to the house of God! Oh, how his soul longed to be there with the people of God! Why? Well, grace and glory had been manifested there, and he wanted to be with them. That is the wonderful thing about meeting in a place like this! You never know when God is going to be here in some unusual power. That is why I have never understood Christian people who think that they can afford to miss a single service. You may miss the greatest thing in your whole life. You never know.

Here is the beloved place in which He has been pleased to meet with us so often, and He has promised 'never to leave us, nor forsake us'. We therefore praise Him, and worship His great and holy name, and thank Him for allowing us for so many years to sing His praises together, and to expound 'the exceeding riches of his grace' through Jesus Christ His Son, our blessed Lord and Saviour.

> *O make thy church, dear Saviour*
> *A lamp of burnished gold,*
> *To bear before the nations*
> *Thy true light as of old.*
> *O teach thy wand'ring pilgrims*
> *By this their path to trace,*
> *Till, clouds and darkness ended,*
> *They see thee face to face.*

Thirteen

*

Evangelical Unity: An Appeal[1]

*

My subject is church unity, and I am speaking on this at the request of the Commission to which reference has been made.[2] I think that is important, lest anybody should think that I am taking advantage of the kindness and generosity of the authorities in inviting me to speak here tonight, to foist my own views upon you. I had the privilege of being called as a witness to appear before this Commission and I made a statement of my attitude with regard to these matters. It was the members of the Commission themselves who asked me to state in public here tonight what I am now proposing to say to you. So it is really their responsibility. They have already heard it, and they asked me to repeat it to you.

But I am not apologizing for this. I am very glad indeed of the opportunity because I believe we are considering tonight what is incomparably the most important question that Christian people can be considering and facing at this present time. Had I my way, I would have given the whole of this conference to this one subject. That is not to say that the other subjects are not important. Of course they are. But I believe that this is the key to the solution of all our other problems. The difficulty confronting me at this moment is to deal with such a subject in a short space of time.

[1]The opening address at the Second National Assembly of Evangelicals, organized by the Evangelical Alliance in London on 18–19 October, 1966. This was the last time Dr Lloyd-Jones spoke for the Alliance.
[2]The First National Assembly of Evangelicals had set up a Commission 'to study radically the various attitudes of evangelicals to the ecumenical movement, denominationalism and a possible future United Church' (i.e., a United Evangelical Church). Further on this subject see *David Martyn Lloyd-Jones: Volume Two of the Authorized Biography*, Iain H. Murray, Banner of Truth Trust, 1989.

[246]

Now why is this subject, as I say, such a vitally important one? Well, for one thing, the question of the church is always important. Look at the prominence given to the doctrine of the church in the New Testament itself. Most of the difficulties in the early church seem to have arisen because people had a defective idea of the nature of the Christian church, and many of the particular problems are solved simply by coming to a correct view of the nature of the church. Then there is the question of the unity of the church. That has been dealt with by everyone who has spoken so far, so I need say nothing by way of general introduction, except this, that I want to underline what has been said, that the unity, while it is spiritual, must also be visible. Our Lord prayed, 'that they may be one, that the world may know' – that the *world* may know! Unity is something that is to be visible, as well as spiritual. So I say that we should consider this matter because the New Testament compels us to consider the church and the unity of the church.

In addition to this, there is a most urgent reason why we should be doing what we are now doing and what the Congress will be doing tomorrow morning in its discussion of the Report.[3] It is the present position, the state of the world – the alarming state of the world and the state of our own country, morally and in so many other respects. More than that, there is the condition of the church as such. How little she counts! The world can afford to neglect us, to make fun of us, and to ridicule us. We do not seem to count as the church once counted in this country. Therefore, I say, it is of vital and most urgent importance that we should be considering this question together.

Now, we are met here as evangelical Christians. The word 'evangelical' is a limiting term. It carries a special meaning and connotation, and we do have a special position in this whole matter. Let me remind you very briefly of just a little bit of history. Evangelicals have been in trouble on this question for over a hundred years. Take this very society under whose auspices we are meeting tonight, the Evangelical Alliance. It came into being in 1846. Why? Because John Henry Newman and others had gone over to Rome. The trend to Rome was the cause of the beginning of this Alliance; evangelical people saw the danger signs and felt that they must come

---

[3] *Report of the Commission on Church Unity to the National Assembly of Evangelicals*, London, October, 1966. This report found, 'There is no *widespread* demand at the present time for the setting up of a united evangelical church on denominational lines' (p. 10).

together. After that there came the liberal or the modernistic movement, the Higher Critical movement, or whatever you may like to call it, which increased the difficulties and problems of evangelical people.

How did they meet these difficulties? They met them by forming alliances, movements, and societies. Some of us have very definite views as to whether they were right or wrong in doing that, but I think we will all agree that, as a temporary measure, as a temporary expedient, what they did was fully justified. They felt that they should meet together, strengthen one another and encourage one another in the faith, in the light of these terrible tendencies that were surrounding them.

This brings us immediately to our theme tonight. I am here to suggest that we find ourselves in a new situation, which has very largely been caused by the arising and arrival among us of what is known as the ecumenical movement. This began in 1910 but has become an urgent problem for us as evangelicals, especially since 1948 when the first World Council of Churches met at Amsterdam. The essence of my case tonight is that this movement, as I see it, has presented us with an entirely new situation. I want to put it to you that we are confronted by a situation today such as has not been the case since the Protestant Reformation. There was a great upheaval in the sixteenth century. Since then, in spite of changes and movements here and there, the position has remained more or less static, but it is so no longer. Something entirely new has come among us, affecting all the major denominations throughout the world. These denominations are telling us plainly and openly that they are prepared to reconsider their whole position. They are prepared to throw everything into the melting pot, in order that a new world church might come out of it.

This is a great fact which we have got to face. Denominational leaders are prepared, they say, to give and take; they are prepared to reconsider, to make new arrangements and accommodations with others. They feel that the divisions of Christendom are a scandal, that a divided church is an offence to God, and that it is the divisions of the church that account for her weakness and her ineffectiveness. Therefore, they say, we must become one, and promote the idea of one great world church. There is the major fact confronting us. As we all know, certain unions have already taken place; others are on the verge of taking place. You are familiar with what is happening between the Anglicans and Methodists, between the Presbyterians and the Congregationalists, and what the Congregationalists have done during this present year.

In addition to all this there is the new attitude towards Rome. A change, a profound change, has taken place in the attitude of Protestants towards the Roman Catholic Church. The situation is indeed so novel that I am afraid that many of us as evangelicals do not yet quite realize it and are not aware of what is happening. We have tended to live in our own churches, and our own circles, and have not been aware of what has been happening in the wider world round and about us. On top of all this, the position is moving and changing very rapidly. Whether we like it or not is not the question; it *is* moving. Things are taking place and the momentum is indeed alarming to observe.

What then, is our position as evangelicals in this modern situation in which we find ourselves? Like the Chairman, I can only speak for myself. To me there is only one answer to give to the question as to where evangelicals stand in the light of all this. I feel that our position is a pathetic one. Indeed to me it is a tragic one. Why do I say this? My first answer is this. Can we deny the charge that we, as evangelical Christians, have been less interested in the question of church unity than anyone else? I say we cannot deny that charge. Everybody seems to be talking about church unity except evangelicals. Surely, with our view of Scripture and with our knowledge and understanding of it, we, of all people, ought to be the first to preach the vital necessity of church unity; but we are the last to do so. Not only that, the position is that we are confused and divided among ourselves. There are statistics in the Report which will show you what I mean. Perhaps this very meeting in which we are gathered is already showing it. However, the fact is that we are confused and divided, and there is disagreement among us.

The most pathetic thing of all, to me, is that our attitude towards the question of church union is always a negative one. You can be sure that every time you read the report of the annual assembly of any one of the branches of the Christian church in this country you will find that what evangelicals have been doing at these assemblies is make protests. They have been objecting, opposing, delaying. We are always negative; we are always on the defensive; we are always bringing up objections and difficulties. I do not think we can deny this charge. The impression is given that evangelicals are more concerned to maintain the integrity of their different denominations than anybody else in those denominations.

This, to me, is tragic; and added to that is our silence in the light of things that have been happening round and about us. It is to me a tragedy that, as evangelicals, we have been silent several times this very year when certain things have taken place. Certain visits have been paid to certain places. And on many other issues we remain silent. It has been left to some eccentrics among evangelicals to make the protest, and we have said nothing. I say, Shame on us as evangelicals! Our silence is very nearly becoming a criminal silence. Why is this? As I see it, there is only one answer: it is because we, as evangelicals, are divided among ourselves, and scattered about in the various major denominations. We are small groups in these, and therefore we are weak and ineffective.

There is another very important thing, as I see it. How often have we, as evangelicals, discussed the doctrine of the church? I have been associated – as friends have been kind enough to say this evening – with evangelical activities and movements for nearly thirty years here in London, and I have noticed throughout those years that we could never get a discussion on the doctrine of the nature of the church. Why not? Because we have always been happy to act in terms of these movements, and the authorities in the movements have always pointed out, You cannot do that, you will offend this person or that. In other words, if you discuss the doctrine of the church you would cause division. The result has been that, so often, we have neglected the doctrine of the church altogether. So the charge that is brought against us by members of the ecumenical movement and by the liberals has always been: You evangelicals are not interested in the church, you are only interested in personal evangelism. I am here to say that I am afraid that there is far too much truth in that charge. And it is because we have faced our problems in terms of movements and societies, instead of facing them on the church level. Is it not about time that we realized that we are confronted by a new situation, that we have a most remarkable opportunity right before us, if we could but see it? I want to make an appeal to you this evening. I have not come here to debate; my friends here know that I am not opposed to debating, but I have not come here to debate, and I will tell you why. I regard the position as too serious, too urgent. I believe that evangelical people have got an opportunity today such as they have never had and, I fear that we may never have it again. That is why I say we have met together at a most critical moment. Therefore I would put it to you that there are certain things to which we must address ourselves at once.

Now I can only summarize this. I suggest that there are two major questions to which we must address our minds. The first is this: Are we content, as evangelicals, to go on being nothing but an evangelical wing of a church? Without question, the whole tendency at the moment is towards a territorial, comprehensive, national church. That is the view taken by many evangelicals as well as others. So the first question that faces us is, Are we content to be an evangelical wing, making our protests, exerting our influence, hoping that we can gradually infiltrate so that others may come to see the wrongness of their ideas and the correctness of ours? Are we content to go on doing that? To remain in a church in which there are many who may hold views on the sacraments which we regard as entirely wrong, views on the Bible which we deplore, views on the very being of God in some cases – you have heard of 'the death of God' movement. These things are happening in the Christian church. Are we content with just being an evangelical wing in a territorial church that will eventually include, and must, if it is to be a truly national and ecumenical church, the Roman Catholic Church? There will be certain modifications, of course. There are always experts who can produce a formula which will satisfy all the parties – each one, each part, will interpret it in its own way – so your Anglo-Catholics and your evangelicals can both accept it.

Are you content with a kind of paper church, with a formula that people interpret in their own way, you being just an evangelical wing in this comprehensive, national, territorial church? That is the first great question.

The second is this: Where are we to start in this whole matter? Here again is a cleavage which appears among us. Are we content to start with the situation as it is and try to modify it and improve it as best we can, or are we prepared to accept the challenge of the ecumenical movement and the times in which we live and say, Let's start afresh. Let's go back to the New Testament? These other people are saying that. They are prepared to put everything in the melting pot. Let us say, then, Let's start afresh, not merely modify what is already in existence, but start afresh and anew, and discover what the New Testament church is really meant to be.

These, then, are the questions that come before us: the doctrine of the church. What is the Christian church? That is the question. You cannot discuss church unity unless you are clear in your mind as to what the church is. Now here is the great divide. The ecumenical people put fellowship before doctrine. We are evangelicals; we put doctrine before fellowship. We remember that what we read in Acts 2:42 is that 'they continued stedfastly in the apostles' *doctrine* [or teaching] and fellowship, and in breaking of bread, and in prayers'. This is of the very essence of the church. The famous Protestant definition of the church is that it is a place where the true doctrine is preached, where the sacraments are properly and regularly administered, and where discipline is exercised. Surely, as evangelicals, we do not want to go back on that.

What then is this true doctrine? Reference has been made to it already: our view of the Scriptures as the infallible Word of God; our assertion of the unique deity of the Lord Jesus Christ – yes, His virgin birth; the miraculous and supernatural; His atoning, sacrificial, substitutionary death; His literal, physical resurrection; the person of the Holy Spirit and His work. These are the doctrines which are essential to salvation; there is the truth that is to be preached, the message which is the first of the true marks of the church. And a church, surely, is a gathering of people who are in covenant together because they believe these things. Not only do they believe them, but they are men and women who have experienced their power. They are men and women who are born again and born of the Spirit, and who give evidence of this in their daily life. Surely that is the evangelical view of the Christian church.

I think it is important we should face this. The church, surely, is not a paper definition. I am sorry, I cannot accept the view that the church consists of articles or of a confession of faith. A church does not consist of the Thirty-Nine Articles. A church does not consist of the Westminster Confession of Faith. A church does not consist of the Savoy Declaration. A church consists of *living people*. You cannot have a church without living people. You can have a paper constitution with a majority in that church denying that very constitution. That is no longer a church as I see it. The church is not a paper declaration, important as that is. A church must always consist of living people. Sometimes we are told that the church is a place in which a man can 'fish'. Is that a church? Does the church consist of people who are unconverted and who need to be converted? Surely not! A church consists of saints. That is the New Testament view: the 'saints' who are at Rome, the 'saints' who are at Corinth, and so on. So I say we must come back and realize that this is our basic view of the Christian church, and that what we need, above everything else at the present time, is a number of such churches, all in fellowship together, working together for the same ends and objects. They are one already in their views, in their faith, in their ideas, and they must not, as our general secretary so excellently put it, divide upon secondary, subsidiary, and non-essential matters.

Now that brings me to my next point, which is this: the sin of schism. What do I mean by the sin of schism? As I see things, this is one of the most important matters before us at the present time. Of course, the Roman Catholic Church would charge us all as being in schism because we are Protestants, but to leave a church which has become apostate is not schism. That is one's Christian duty and nothing else. What then is schism? As outlined and defined by the apostle Paul, especially in the First Epistle to the Corinthians, schism is a division among members of the true visible church about matters which are not sufficiently important to justify division. Look at the case in Corinth. In general, they were agreed about their doctrine, but they were dividing over personalities: I am of Paul; I am of Apollos; I am of Cephas; and so on. They were dividing the church. That is schism – holding the same doctrines but dividing over persons. They were dividing over meats offered to idols and various other matters. They were going to law against one another, and so on. Now, according to the apostle, that is the essence of schism. It is division among people who are agreed about the essentials and the centralities, but who separate over secondary and less important matters. Surely that is the only definition of schism which can claim to be biblical. I would therefore argue, in the light of that teaching, that the only people I know at the present time who are guilty of the sin of schism are evangelicals. Why do I say this? Well, the others cannot be guilty of it, because they are not agreed about the doctrine. They do not accept the doctrine.

Work it out for yourselves. Study that First Epistle to the Corinthians. Here were people who were agreed about the centralities, about the doctrines. They disagreed not only about the things I have mentioned but about the spiritual gifts and other matters. These were the things that were causing the schisms, the divisions, the rents in the one body of Christ. That is why the apostle denounces them.

So I argue that people who do not believe the essentials of the faith, the things that are essential to salvation, cannot be guilty of schism. They are not in the church. If you do not believe a certain irreducible minimum, you cannot be a Christian and you are not in the church.

Have we reached a time when one must not say a thing like that? Have evangelicals so changed that we no longer make an assertion like that? I venture to say that the truth has not changed, and we must go on saying that.

You and I are evangelicals. We are agreed about these essentials of the faith, and yet we are divided from one another. We meet like this, I know, in an occasional conference, but we spend most of our time apart from one another, and joined to and united with people who deny and are opposed to these essential matters of salvation. We spend our time with them. We have our visible unity with them. Now, I say, that is sinful.

Why are we as evangelicals thus divided? Why are we divided up among the main denominations? I think if we are honest we will have to admit that most of us really do not know. It is an accident of birth. I was born a Baptist, or an Anglican, or a Congregationalist, or a Methodist, or whatever it was, and, because I was born there, I stay there and I am prepared to fight for it. How often is that the case? I am arguing that for us to be divided – we who are agreed about everything that really matters – for *us* to be divided from one another in the main tenor of our lives and for the bulk of our time, is nothing but to be guilty of the sin of schism. And we really must face this most urgently.

Let me therefore make an appeal to you evangelical people here present this evening. What reasons have we for not coming together? I think we ought to be able to give an answer to that question. Many reasons are given. We are told that we will miss an evangelistic opportunity perhaps, or something like that. I do not accept that argument for this reason: Where is the Holy Spirit? Surely He will honour truth if we stand for it together. Why is it, I say, that we have this desire to hold on in this way to the contradictory position in which we find ourselves? That is the position of evangelicals in all the major denominations at the present time; they spend a great deal of their time criticizing their own leaders, but remember, those criticized are still their leaders. You cannot justify remaining in an Episcopal situation, or in a Methodist or a Presbyterian situation, you cannot justify that honestly in terms of your 'independence'. But that is what we tend to do. We say, As long as I am given liberty in my own church I am going on like this. But you cannot dissociate yourself from the church to which you belong.

This is not only a contradictory position; it is, in addition, one which the man in the street must find very difficult to understand. What cogent reason have we for staying as we are when we have this new, and as I regard it, heaven-sent opportunity for doing something new? What are our reasons for rejecting and refusing the need for change?

Let me put it positively. Do we not feel the call to come together, not occasionally, but *always*? It is a grief to me that I spend so little of my time with some of my brethren. I want to spend the whole of my time with them. I am a believer in ecumenicity, evangelical ecumenicity. To me, the tragedy is that we are divided. Is it right that those of us who are agreed about these fundamental things should only meet occasionally and spend, as I say, most of our time when we are among others fighting negative battles, showing how wrong our own leaders are, and so on? Now you and I have been called to a positive task. We are guardians and custodians of the faith, the faith that has been given once and for ever to the saints. Traditionally it has always been we evangelicals who have been the guardians and custodians of the New Testament heritage. We believe the Bible; we take it authoritatively; we do not impose our philosophies and ideas upon it; and we are the only people who are doing this. God, I believe, has given us the solemn charge of guarding and protecting and defending the faith in this present evil age in which we find ourselves.

My friends, we are not only the guardians and custodians of the faith of the Bible; we are the modern representatives and successors of the glorious men who fought this same fight, the good fight of faith, in centuries past. Surely, as evangelicals, we ought to feel this appeal. We are standing in the position of the Protestant reformers. Are we accepting this modern idea that the Reformation was the greatest tragedy that ever happened? If you want to say that it was a tragedy, here was the tragedy, that the Roman Church had become so rotten that it was necessary for the reformers to do what they did. It was not the departure of the reformers that was the tragedy. It was the state of the Roman Church that was the tragedy. We are the modern representatives of these men, and of the Puritans, the Covenanters, the early Methodists, and others. Can you not see the opportunity?

I believe that God is calling upon us to maintain this ancient witness, not occasionally, not haphazardly, but always, and to put it to the people of this country. The need has never been greater, the need of conviction of sin, of new life, of turning to God, and becoming God's people. This is work that the Holy Spirit alone can do. But have we a right to ask His blessing upon churches which spend most of their time in arguing about the essentials and the vitals of the faith? Surely, the Holy Spirit will only bless His own Word, and if those of us who believe it would only come together, stand together as churches, constantly together, working together, doing everything together, bearing our witness together, I believe we would then have the right to expect the Spirit of God to come upon us in mighty revival and re-awakening. I know people talk about the difficulties, and I am not here to minimize them. I am trying to put before you the positive principles. These are the things about which we have got to be agreed. We will then have to work them out.

There are great and grievous difficulties; I am well aware of them. I know that there are men, ministers and clergy, in this congregation at the moment, who, if they did what I am exhorting them to do, would have a tremendous problem before them, even a financial, an economic and a family problem. I do not want to minimize this. My heart goes out to such men. There are great problems confronting us if we act on these principles. But has the day come when we, as evangelicals, are afraid of problems? The true Christian has always had problems. The early Christians had grievous problems, ostracized from their families and the threat of death ever facing them. They were not daunted; they went on; they believed; they knew; they would rather die than not stand for the truth. And it has been so throughout the centuries. Was Martin Luther not confronted by a problem when he saw the truth? Of course he was; but he was not deterred by the problem; and so with all the martyrs and confessors throughout the ages.

My dear friends, we are living in tremendous times. We are living in one of the great turning points of history. I have said already and I say it again, there has been nothing like this since the sixteenth century. It is a day of glorious opportunity. We may be small in numbers but since when has the doctrine of the remnant become unpopular among evangelicals? It is one of the most glorious doctrines in the whole of the Bible. We are not interested in numbers. We are interested in truth and in the living God. 'If God be for us, who can be against us?' Go home and read the story of Gideon again. Go home and read many another example of what God, at times, has accomplished through just one man. Do not be concerned about numbers. If we stand for God's truth, we can be certain and sure that God will honour us and bless us. Therefore, my dear friends, fellow evangelical Christians, let us rise to the occasion. Let us listen to what I believe is the call of God. Let us face these things with charity, with patience, with everything that our friend Mr Prime so rightly emphasized as he commented on that passage from Philippians 2. We shall need great grace. We shall need to be filled with the Spirit. We shall all need to be humbled. But if we have got one objective only, namely the glory of the Lord, and the success of His kingdom, I think we shall be led by the Spirit to the true answer to these varying problems. And who knows but that the ecumenical movement may be something for which, in years to come, we shall thank God because it has made us face our problems on the church level instead of on the level of movements, and really brought us together as a fellowship, or an association, of evangelical churches. May God speed the day.

Fourteen

*

What Is Preaching?[1]

*

The subject allotted to me is 'What Is Preaching?' and let me say that I am conscious of a very real sense of privilege in being asked to come here and to take some part in this conference on this all-important subject.

I am afraid that I have been trying to do so much of what I now have to speak about that I find myself somewhat weary and tired, so I trust that you will bear with me. But quite apart from that, I have always found it extremely difficult to speak on this particular subject, because it is one of the matters which I personally find quite impossible to tabulate in my mind and to get into any order. I have been struggling with this question for the last forty years and I do not think I am any nearer to a solution than I was at the beginning. Perhaps I am even further away.

Why is this? Well, to me preaching is a great mystery; it is one of the most mysterious things of all, and that is why I find it eludes any kind of analysis. I do not know what your experience is but, personally, I find that I never know what is going to happen when I enter a pulpit. I am constantly being surprised – sometimes surprised in the sense of being disappointed, but at other times surprised at the amazing grace of God. Sometimes when I go into a pulpit, thinking I am going to preach in a wonderful way, it is disastrous. Other times, when I go with inadequate preparation because I have been travelling, doing too much, and really feeling that I have no right to be in the pulpit at all, I find unusual ease and facility and am aware of

[1] An address given to a student conference at Westminster Theological Seminary, Philadelphia, in September, 1967, two years before his lectures at the same institution which were published under the title *Preaching and Preachers* (Hodder and Stoughton, 1971).

power. That is my difficulty. There is this mysterious element in preaching that makes it well nigh impossible for one to speak about it.

A Characteristic of True Preaching

There is another element which always makes me feel that this is an impossible task, and that is the element of dread, of terrible responsibility. I do want to emphasize this just a little because to me it is one of the most important things in connection with this subject.

What I mean by that is there is surely nothing which is more serious, nothing which gives one such a tremendous sense of responsibility, as preaching. I think you will agree that this aspect of the question is very largely forgotten or not realized at this present time. I do not know what your situation is in this country, but the situation as regards preaching in Great Britain, and especially in England, has become quite chaotic, and very largely because this element of dread and of responsibility has somehow been lost. People seem to think that preaching is not only simple and easy, but something which anyone is entitled to do, and able to do almost at will. So we have the chaotic condition where men have been recently converted, and the next thing we hear about them is that they are preaching somewhere.

Now I believe I can trace the origin of this. I think that the Brethren are mainly responsible for this deterioration in the true view of, and the true sense of responsibility with respect to, preaching. They, all of them, seem to be preachers. I have often felt that the text that one should preach on if one were addressing a congregation of Plymouth Brethren, and nobody else, should be the first verse in the third chapter of the Epistle of James – 'My brethren, be not many masters'! – because on conversion they all immediately become masters. That kind of influence seems to have percolated through the various sections of the Christian church in Great Britain. It is all, I think, part of the deterioration of the true view of the Christian church and the functioning of the church, owing, of course, to the disastrous Higher Criticism and the liberal and modernistic elements that have come in. There was such a shortage of true believers, true evangelical believers, that there was a corresponding shortage of true evangelical preachers; and thus any man who was evangelical was regarded almost automatically as being one who was competent to preach.

But that, I think, has been a very great fallacy, and it has done very great harm, particularly because it has made people forget the tremendous sense of awe, and of responsibility, which should always animate us as we engage in the great task of preaching.

There are many ways in which I can illustrate this. Take the question which the apostle puts in Romans 10. You are familiar with that passage where he deals with this whole question of the propagation of the gospel: 'Whosoever shall call upon the name of the Lord shall be saved. How then shall they call on him in whom they have not believed? and how shall they believe in him of whom they have not heard? and how shall they hear without a preacher? and how shall they preach, except they be sent?' (verses 13–15).

I was tempted just to expound that one statement to you. I am not going to do so, but I do commend it to you for careful study. 'How shall they preach, except they be sent?' Who *sends* them? With us, I say, the trouble is that people are sending themselves, appointing themselves as preachers. Surely this is entirely wrong. I interpret this statement in Romans 10 as meaning that God sends us, and also that the church sends us. No man has a right just to get up and start preaching, or what he may regard as preaching. There is this element of sending, and we must return to it. It will help us to get hold of this notion of responsibility – you have got to be sent; you have got to be sure that God sends you; you have got to be sure that the church is sending you.

Now I am well aware that someone may get up and say, But what about so and so? – certain great exceptions in history. My answer is that they are exceptions, and the exception proves the rule. You do not make a rule out of your exceptions, although that is what is happening today in our country. There have been times when a man has been so sure of his calling from God that he has defied the authorities, and there are times when we have got to do this; but a man who does that has got to be very sure indeed that God has called him. The ideal and the right way is that the call comes to the man from God and it is confirmed by the church, and I take leave to doubt whether any man has a right to preach except these two elements are present in his particular case. But then, still more important and more serious is what we find the great apostle saying in 1 Corinthians 2:3–4: 'I was with you in weakness, and in fear, and in much trembling. And my speech and my preaching was not with enticing words of man's wisdom'. I am particularly interested in the third verse: 'I was with you in weakness, and in fear, and in much trembling.'

I want to ask some questions: What do we know about this trembling? What do we know about this fear? Why did Paul feel that? Look at this man, this colossus of a man, this outstanding genius. He was 'in weakness, and in fear, and in much trembling'. I wonder whether a man has a right to be in a pulpit at all and even to attempt preaching unless he knows something about this fear and this trembling. Here is the greatest preacher of all and that is how he felt. Why? Because of the responsibility! Paul is standing between God and men. He is dealing with the souls of men and their eternal destiny. He is a guardian, a custodian, a steward of the mysteries. There is nothing in the universe that is comparable to this: the responsibility is almost overwhelming. And yet I think you will agree with me that there is very little evidence of this spirit at the present time.

As I say, it has almost become the rule now that men rush into pulpits and appoint themselves as preachers as though there is nothing to it. They do it so easily. I have often said, as I have seen it, and understood these things over the years, that there is only one thing that is more dangerous than being a preacher and that is being a lay preacher. And that is, of course, for this reason, that there are terrible temptations to the preacher, but there are certain things that tend to keep him in order. He is supported by the congregation, and that is a good thing in that it tends to put a bit of a brake upon him. But the lay preacher enters the pulpit and he is independent, he can say what he likes, he can speak what he likes. He is in no danger of being dismissed or asked to leave, he is in no danger of having his stipend reduced. That is what makes his position alarmingly dangerous. But most lay preachers never realize this danger; they are perhaps of all men the most confident. And that is why I say the most dangerous thing that can ever happen to a man is that he should be a lay preacher.

The Testimony of Preachers

Is it not amazing that people can enter into pulpits with confidence and ease and assurance, with no trouble at all! They can do it as an aside. They can be running a business, or be in a profession, and as an aside they can do this thing which, to these miserable preachers, seems to be so difficult – nothing to it at all! There is only one thing to say about them; they are the direct antithesis of what we find to be true about the great apostle himself. I can give you further examples out of history to substantiate what I am saying. Those of you who are familiar with the life and the journals of the great George Whitefield, one of the greatest preachers of all times, will remember his hesitation about preaching. He was alarmed by it, he was frightened. Preaching was a tremendous thing, and he went through considerable agony of mind and of spirit. He felt he was unworthy, and, surely, a man who does not know something about this sense of unworthiness has no right to enter a pulpit at all. This mighty preacher was a man who hesitated long and seriously and had to be forced.

I can give you another example. There was a man in Wales two hundred years ago called Howel Harris; he was a layman, he was never ordained, and he was one of the exceptions to which I have referred. Yet this man, again, was mightily used of God. He was terrified at the thought of preaching. In fact, what he did was something like this: having had a great experience of the Spirit of God coming upon him in an overwhelming fashion, he felt that he had a duty to his neighbours, but thought that the best way of discharging this duty was to visit them and to read to them out of godly books. He started visiting the sick and he would read from a book called *The Practice of Piety*, which had been published in the seventeenth century. It never occurred to Harris that he had a right to speak, in fact he felt sure that he had not. But he could read out of this book, and he read with such unction that people were converted while he was reading. And then he went on doing this until he had finished reading all the books that he possessed, and still he knew he must tell people about their souls and salvation. So he now felt that he had to say something of his own to them, but the idea that he should be preaching remained so alarming and so terrifying to him that what he did was this: he continued to have a book in front of him, and appeared to be reading out of it, when he was actually speaking his own thoughts! Whatever you may think about the ethics of that procedure, it shows the sense of dread he felt, the sense of fear, the sense of awe.

Now this to me is a very vital and essential part of preaching, and it is because of these elements that I find it so difficult, indeed, well nigh impossible to deal with this subject. If only we could transport ourselves back two centuries and go down into Philadelphia and listen to George Whitefield, we might learn something about preaching. We would see a master preaching. Then, having listened to Whitefield, if we were fortunate enough, we might listen to Samuel Davies also. You people have neglected Samuel Davies; let me put in a word for him. The greatest preacher you have ever produced in this country was Samuel Davies, the author of the hymn, 'Great God of wonders, all thy ways/Are matchless, godlike, and divine', and the man who followed Jonathan Edwards as president of Princeton. His sermons are still obtainable. Here was another obvious master preacher. At that time, or a few years later, we might have listened to him likewise. If we could only sit and listen to these men, we might know something about preaching.

You will forgive, perhaps, just a personal word in passing. I say that I have been wrestling with this subject for forty years and more and I have had two experiences which I shall never forget. I have a feeling that I have only really preached twice in my life, and on both occasions I was dreaming. I still remember the awful feeling of disappointment, on both occasions, when I found I was only dreaming. If only I could preach like that in the pulpit when I was awake! Then I think I could claim that I have preached, but alas, that is the position.

The best, therefore, that I can do to try to help you in this matter is to talk around my subject. I cannot analyse it, I am incapable of doing that. Let me start like this: preaching, I think we will all agree, has been sadly neglected, especially during this century. There has been a decline in preaching. I know that it is true of your country as well as of our country. If you had visited London a hundred years ago and, indeed, until say the beginning of the First World War, your problem would have been which of the great preachers to go and listen to. There were many of them, and the problem was which of them to select. But today the position is entirely different. There is no problem at all. Is there *any* preacher that you want to go and listen to, who is worth your while to go and listen to? It is the same in your country. There is a dearth of preachers. Why? Because, it seems to me, the whole notion of preaching has, somehow or another, slipped into the background and people no longer believe in preaching as they once did.

Why Preaching Has Declined

What is the cause of this? Well, I can analyse it, I think, fairly accurately as regards Great Britain, and I believe it may be partly true here. In Britain, I am sure that one of the major factors has been that we had a prime minister whose name was Stanley Baldwin. He was a man who came into office in 1924. He followed certain men of the type of Lloyd George, who had been prime minister during the First World War and had in his Cabinet people such as Winston Churchill and Lord Birkenhead. All these men were great speakers, they were great orators; and Stanley Baldwin was not. He was a very clever politician and he realized that the only thing a man like himself could do was to say something like this: Now I'm not a great man, I'm not a great orator, I'm just an ordinary, plain, simple Englishman. He was suggesting that oratory is dangerous and that if a man is a good speaker you cannot trust him. The only man you can trust is the quiet, homely man, who cannot deliver a great oration but who can give you a little friendly chat, and you can trust him.

That idea has undoubtedly come into the whole realm of preaching. I have watched the development of a distrust of preaching. You had a man here in this country, who I think, did great harm – S. D. Gordon. Some of you older people will remember his books, and the titles of his books, to me, give the whole case away: 'Quiet Talks on such and such' – *Quiet Talks on Prayer*, *Quiet Talks on Power*. It must always be a quiet talk, like a friendly chat, none of this 'great pulpit oratory', which is dangerous and not spiritual. Quiet *talks*, just a little conversation! These factors you see, have all worked together.

Then came the terrible invention of the radio and the television – they have been a great curse. And they have been a great curse for many, many reasons. One is, of course, that generally you are on a time limit with these things, and that is always destructive of true preaching, as I am going to show you later on. In addition to that, there is the impersonal element. Very often the preacher is alone in a room, which is very bad: he is not in contact with his congregation. And there are various techniques that they talk so much about; there have been several courses on 'television technique' which men have attended. I cannot imagine anything so pathetic as that preachers should allow themselves to be instructed by these little television experts as to how to conduct themselves, even putting on that ridiculous smile, and all the rest of it. Such courses are destructive of the whole concept and idea of preaching. I am here to speak the truth to you and I must criticize things I have observed among you here, as elsewhere. I do not understand this custom of a preacher going into a pulpit on a Sunday morning and looking at the people and saying Good Morning to them. That is the world; the preacher should not do that. They have come to listen to the Word of God and he comes from God. There is no need for that kind of thing, and already I feel it interferes with the essential element of preaching.

Another factor connected with the decline of preaching has to do with the place of reading. As people have become better educated, and have gone in more and more for reading, the whole notion of preaching has tended to be depreciated. The intelligent man feels that he does not want to be harangued by a man standing in a pulpit; he can do his reading at home, he can read the same books as the preacher. Therefore why should he listen to the preacher? It is more intellectual to sit down and read a book for yourself. I think that has done very great harm indeed. The idea has been that our forefathers did not read, they had not got the books, and many of them often could not read, so they had to depend upon this one man who seemed to be an authority. But the modern generation has rebelled against all this, and reading has come in instead of preaching. Well, each one of these points, of course, could be taken up, and one could show the tremendous difference between reading even good books and preaching. There is no comparison between the two. Preaching is God's ordained method and way, and reading can never be a substitute for preaching. There is something peculiar about preaching which reading can never attain unto.

Another factor that has done great harm to the whole question of preaching in our country, and I believe also in yours, has been a bad and a false kind of popular preaching. We had a glut of this especially in my own country of Wales. There were men who turned preaching into entertainment, men who were much more interested in the way in which they said things than in what they said, and men who were experts at what in my considered opinion is an abomination, namely the over-use of illustrations and stories. The whole point of a sermon was to get an effective illustration! They knew it would have its effect upon the people. The notion of the sermon and of preaching became one of entertainment. And so you had a false popular preaching, with which any truly spiritual person, indeed any intelligent person, became almost disgusted.

Again there was a term used which I abominate, the term 'pulpiteer'. You had these great pulpiteers, the Henry Ward Beechers and people like that, who did infinite harm to preaching. These were great masters of assembly, bombastic men who reigned in the mid and late Victorian era. I think they did great harm to the whole concept and notion of true preaching.

Then, just to add another to this list of factors, there is the sacramentarian movement which has had its influence on different sections of the church, particularly the Anglican church in different countries around the world. The same influence has permeated the free churches, the idea that the sacrament is the central service of the church, that it is more important than anything else. Now the history of this in the Anglican Church in England is really very fascinating. The Anglo-Catholic movement began in the 1830s, introducing vestments and new ideas with regard to the sacrament which approximated more and more to Rome. And as all this developed, preaching correspondingly declined. So the sermon became only a triviality. The great thing was the administration of the sacrament.

The very last element that I put into this category of the things that have done much harm to preaching is the whole notion of personal work, which I believe you call 'counselling'. This too has militated against preaching. The idea has been that what is really needed is a personal conversation in which people can put forward their questions and their difficulties and you work it out together. Perhaps preaching is still believed to have some kind of a function, but just as a general introduction to get people to come along and talk to you; the vital thing is going to be done when you are having a private conversation. This is one of the main results of the interest in psychology and the coming in of the psychological element into pastoral work and, indeed, into the whole activity of the life of the church. And as this emphasis on counselling has increased, correspondingly the emphasis on preaching has declined. I could illustrate this again in the case of Wales where, of course, we have always believed in preaching, more than they ever did in England. They believed in preaching more in Scotland and in Wales than they ever did in England, but preaching has gone out in both countries and very largely because of this emphasis on personal work. In Wales the change was almost entirely due to a professor who became principal of one of the colleges of the Welsh Presbyterian Church. He himself could not preach, poor fellow; he was supposed to be a great psychologist, but he never realized his own complex, which was clear to some of us. He resolved his own personal problem by discounting preaching and emphasizing the value of counselling and of personal work. He was such an able and affable man that he influenced two or three generations of young preachers who did not believe any longer in preaching as such. And, of course, they were able to contrast what they were doing with the false popular preaching, and the result was that the whole notion of preaching became depreciated. Well now, there are some of the factors that have militated against a true understanding of preaching and the place of preaching in the life of the church.

Preaching Is Not Lecturing

What, then, is preaching? Let us try and get a little nearer to a definition. Again I can only do it by giving you some negatives. What is the difference, for instance, between preaching and what I was saying just now, namely reading books? What is the essential difference between these two things? Why do we say that people should come to the church and that preaching should go on in the church in preference to the reading of books at home? What is our real reason for saying that? What is this 'peculiar' thing, if you like, what is the differentia of preaching? What marks it off from all these other activities? Well, I am going to try to answer that question. Let me ask another question: What is the difference between preaching and delivering a lecture? I think this is most important. I think I have detected the tendency for people to imagine that giving a lecture is the same thing as preaching, that because you give a lecture from a pulpit it becomes preaching. But it does not. I would draw a very great distinction here. I remember meeting some men during the Second World War, captains in the United States Army, and I remember hearing one of them using an expression which rather alarmed me. He was in a certain part of England and mixing with some of the churches there; and he had come to a conclusion with respect to their condition. He said, 'And then I decided to preach them my sermon on justification.' He told me all about himself as a preacher in saying that. You see, here was a man who deliberately sat down to prepare a lecture, 'a sermon on justification', and he had got another one on sanctification, and on various other subjects. So he had his 'sermon on justification'. To me that man knew nothing at all about preaching. He had obviously prepared the address on justification and then he found one of a number of texts which he could hook it on to, but that is not preaching. That is lecturing on justification, and on these other subjects. I say that is not preaching. There is a place for lecturing. Lecturing is essential. And there must be teaching in the church. But all I am concerned to say is that it is not preaching. You may well come to the conclusion that I have got some odd notion as regards preaching, but I am prepared to justify what I am trying to say.

A Sermon is not a Running Commentary

Let me give you another negative. Some people seem to think that preaching consists of a running commentary on a passage of Scripture. I am not saying that this does not have its legitimate place and function. You take a paragraph and you comment on every single verse as a kind of running commentary. That is not preaching. It passes as such very often, and especially in the Anglican Church in Great Britain, but to me it is quite different from preaching. Or another way of putting it is this: A man may take a verse or a passage, and he may give you his exegesis, he may tell you about its context, he may give you the meaning of the words, he may divide it and open it up; but still I say that is not preaching. I knew a man who was famous, in your country as well as ours, as a 'Bible lecturer'. He called himself that, and it was a correct term. His method was to take a paragraph of Scripture, perhaps a whole chapter, often a whole book, and he would analyse it for you and give it to you in its component parts. In a technical sense what he did was to give a running commentary on a section or on a book, in the course of which he could add illustrations here and there. And I think this is interesting and important because his books were very popular. They had an influence in your country, and in ours, in the direction of making people imagine that that is preaching. Of course, the argument was that this method is more biblical, but I think that was a complete fallacy. One can deal with the words of Scripture and never get down to the doctrine. This lecturer never dealt with doctrine, he was not interested in theology and he used to say so. Yet, because he was all along dealing with the actual letter of the Scripture, he was thought to be more biblical. My idea of being biblical is that you bring out the real message, the treasure of the Scriptures. You may not be so tied to the literal words all the time, but surely it is the meaning that matters ultimately. This is not to say that we must not be interested in the other aspect; we must, but I say that Bible lecturing stops short of where true preaching begins. I could put the whole of that into my introduction and still I have not started preaching when they finish.

Let me put it another way: Do you draw a distinction between a sermon and preaching? I do. And I have a feeling that part of the trouble with regard to preaching is that people do not recognize that distinction.

What is a sermon? What is the difference between a sermon and a Bible lecture or an exposition of a passage? As I see it, it is that a sermon is always a whole, an entity, a message. Take the phrase that is used by the prophet in the Old Testament, 'the burden of the Lord'. The exposition of the Scripture, to me, does not become a sermon until what you have studied, exegeted, and explained, takes the form of a particular message which leads to a particular end. A sermon is more than running comments. It must have form, it is a complete message, and it leads always to a particular end.

Let me say in passing that I am a great admirer of the Puritans and in a little way, perhaps, I have been responsible for a revived interest in them in Great Britain. But the Puritans can be very dangerous from the standpoint of preaching. The Puritans were primarily teachers, in my opinion, not preachers. In the pulpit they would analyse their passage of Scripture and when the time had gone they would say, Well, we will leave it at that for now and we will take it up the next time. In saying that, to me, they were saying that they were not preaching, because they had not got this form, this wholeness, this complete message. I find it very difficult to put this into words, but this is, to me, a very vital point of distinction between an exposition of a passage and a sermon. The preparation of a sermon is a process that goes on inside one's mind and heart and spirit. I do not know how it happens at all, but I think I can illustrate what I mean. I remember how butter was once made. You used to take the cream and put it into a churn. It went in as cream but then you turned the handle or got a horse to work some great pulley, and it was churned and churned until it came out as butter. Nothing was added to the ingredients at all, but what came out was different from what had gone in. It was no longer cream, it was butter. That is the nearest, I am afraid, that I can get to telling you the difference between exposition, exegesis, commentary, and explanation of the meaning of words and a *sermon*. The same ingredients but a different end result!

Now I must add a word of warning at this point, I think – I need it myself, no doubt, very much. I do not know whether you have read a book by a man called Edwin Hatch, who was a dignitary in the Church of England in the last century. He delivered two courses of famous lectures – the Bampton Lectures – dealing with the nature of the New Testament church, and, unless my memory fails me, around 1888 he delivered the Hibbert Lectures in which he dealt with the influence of Greek thought upon the Christian church. In the latter series of lectures, well worth reading, he makes a point which has troubled me considerably. He argues that the whole notion of Christian preaching changed in the second century, and his thesis is that the change took place as a result of Greek influence. You remember how in the second century the Christian church came right up against the Greek world and the apologists came in. They had to do this, of course, but, according to the theory of Edwin Hatch, the Greek influence had a great effect upon Christian preaching and the effect which it had, he contends, was that the preaching of the apostles and of the early church was a kind of inspired prophetic utterance, but owing to the apologetic influence that came in and the desire to present the gospel in a manner that would not be offensive to the cultured Greek mind, the church more and more began to adopt the Greek and, in a sense, the Roman form of an address. The form which had been employed by the great rhetoricians of Greece involved a preliminary introduction of the subject, then a division of the matter, and finally a conclusion. And his case is that this became the form of the sermon from the second century onwards as a result of Greek influence.

I am prepared to agree that what Hatch says is probably very true, but it puts me in a predicament. I believe intensely in what he calls the original idea of preaching. To me that is the important thing, the most important thing of all. At the same time I also feel that the form not only has a legitimate place, but it is in a sense essential if you are to convey the message truly to the people. You see, we are always in this state of tension. How can I have form and yet avoid becoming a lecturer? How can I have this form which I think the sermon must have without allowing it to degenerate into some kind of general address? Well, with that qualification, I make my assertion that we must always remember that the sermon must have this form and this end, if it is truly to function.

The Sermon and Preaching

We now come to this other distinction, the difference between the sermon and preaching. This brings me to the heart of the matter as I understand it. Do we know this distinction? I have a feeling that it is because we have forgotten it that preaching has fallen on evil days. I remember hearing a story, and I introduce it here simply to point my remarks. There was a preacher in Great Britain, Dr J. D. Jones of Bournemouth. He came often to this country. Once he was preaching in a place in Wales when he was an old man, and a number of ministers met with him and put a question that preachers are so fond of putting. They said, 'Tell us, Dr Jones, who is the greatest preacher you have ever heard?' He thought for a while, and responded, 'Well, I don't know, I don't know, but I'll tell you this, the greatest *preaching* I've ever heard was the preaching of John Hutton.'

Now I think that is a very good point. You see, what he was saying was this: he was not saying that Dr John A. Hutton, who was one-time editor of our *British Weekly*, was the greatest man he had ever heard preaching; nor was he saying that Dr Hutton's sermons were the greatest sermons that he had ever heard, but what he was saying – and I know exactly what he meant because I heard Dr Hutton – was that Hutton's preaching was the greatest preaching that he had ever heard. This man, Dr Hutton, who was one of my predecessors at Westminster Chapel, was an extraordinary man and an extraordinary preacher. When I was a student, a young doctor, I used to go and listen to him. I listened to him the whole time he was there, and I came to the conclusion that in fact he only preached really well about one out of every six occasions. What was the matter? Well, it was this: he was a man who did not pay sufficient attention to the sermon. He had got this preaching gift and he tended to rely upon it. At times he would ramble, it was difficult to follow him, and it could be very bad. There was no form about it; but when this sixth occasion came you not only forgave him the other five, you just went hoping that it would happen again. I recall one occasion when, just as he was finishing his sermon, he raised his extended hands and the whole congregation rose to its feet. I was among them. That is a tribute to his preaching.

What is this difference? Let me give you another illustration. I referred earlier to Samuel Davies. Some of you will remember that around 1753 Samuel Davies and Gilbert Tennent were sent over from this country to Britain to collect funds for Princeton College, which had been recently started, around 1746. After a very long and tedious journey they arrived in London. The first question, of course, which they asked when they got there was, 'Is Mr Whitefield in town?' And, to their great delight, they were told that he was, and that he was due to preach in the Tabernacle the next morning, which was Sunday. So they got there early and, with the place crowded out, Whitefield eventually came in and preached. Samuel Davies gives an account of this service and it brings out my present point to perfection. He said that he realized very quickly that Mr Whitefield had obviously had an extremely busy week. It was clear that he had not had time to prepare his sermon. It was disjointed, illogical, oftentimes he was just rambling – there was no form there. But, said Davies, there was such unction upon the preaching, such an effect which he felt, that he gladly would have crossed the Atlantic again, many times, in order to be under this tremendous influence. That is the difference, you see, between a sermon and preaching. That is why I think a man is in a very pathetic condition who says, I then decided to give them my sermon on justification, my sermon on this, that, or the other! What a terrible mistake that is.

I am reminded of another thing which I did not mention in my list of things that have done such harm to true preaching, and that is the publication of sermons. [*laughter*] You laugh at this, but I mean it very seriously. I think that the printing of sermons in the last century was one of the most harmful influences upon preaching, especially on the sermons of Scottish preachers. And I will tell you why I say this. These men of the late nineteenth century were generally great literary men, and when they prepared their sermons they were frequently preparing them with an eye to possible publication. In so doing, they were, in my view, already going totally astray. If you prepare a sermon for publication, you are not going to be a good preacher when you preach that sermon. Your motive is wrong. Your concept is wrong. There is all the difference in the world between these two things.

True Preaching: A Transaction

What is this point, then, about preaching? Well, it is the extraordinary situation in which something is *happening* between the man who is speaking and the congregation that is listening. You know Phillips Brooks's famous definition of preaching, 'Truth mediated through personality'. I think he is right. Whether he put the content into that statement that I would put into it, I do not know, but there is a sense in which he really has put his finger on the essential thing. The whole man is involved in preaching; that is where the difference between the sermon and the preaching lies. It is not merely what the man says, it is the way in which he says it – this total involvement of the man; his body is involved, every part of him, every faculty is involved if it is true preaching, the whole personality of the individual; and, at the same time, as I said, the congregation is also making its contribution. Here are spiritually minded people, they have come prepared and they are under the influence of the Spirit, and so these two things are blended together. There is a unity between preacher and hearers and there is a transaction backwards and forwards. That, to me, is true preaching. And that is where you see the essential difference between listening to preaching in a church and listening to a sermon on the television or on the radio. You cannot listen to true preaching in detachment and you must never be in a position where you can turn it off. What I am trying to say is that there is an element of control, there is an element of compulsion in preaching, and people who are there are gripped and fixed. I maintain that if that is not happening, you have not got true preaching. That is why reading must never be a substitute for preaching. You can put the book down, or you can argue with it. When there is true preaching you cannot do that, you are gripped, you are taken up, you are mastered. And I argue that this is an essential and a vital part of preaching.

Hindrances to Preaching

What are the things that hinder preaching? (I am sorry that I have got to rush now because my time has gone.) There are certain things that are a very great hindrance to preaching. One is professionalism. This is a curse to the work of a minister. Why do you preach on Sunday? Why will you preach next Sunday? Is it simply because you have been announced to do so? I have often gone into the pulpit for that reason, so have you. You have gone into the pulpit because you were expected to do so, because it is your job. In a sense that is right, but in another sense it is very terrible to do it merely because you have got to do it and it is a part of your routine. That militates against true preaching. A man should always go into the pulpit with a sense of romance, a sense of opportunity, and a sense of the tremendous responsibility. There should be an eagerness about it. Professionalism is a curse.

Another thing that militates against preaching is a man's over-reliance on his preparation. All I am saying can be seriously misunderstood. Of course, a man who does not prepare is a fool, yet the man who relies on his preparation is perhaps an even greater fool. He has written his sermon, he is prepared; he has got everything. Poor fellow, he has got nothing! But we do that, don't we? You think you are finished and ready for Sunday simply because you have prepared the sermon. That is not preaching.

Then there is the danger of being led astray in the form of your preparation – this literary notion which I have already denounced, this wish to be literary or learned and to have masses of quotations. I remember a lady journalist writing about preachers in England and praising a particular minister because, she said, 'he always shares his reading with us'. That is abominable, utterly abominable, but it has come in, as you know. We want to be considered learned and well-read men. We had a man in Britain, a popular preacher who wrote a book entitled *The Craft of Sermon Construction*. To me the idea of 'craft' in sermon preparation is prostitution. Craft is what the prostitute uses: she decks herself up, she paints herself, she makes herself attractive in order to attract people. But you would not marry somebody like that. No, we believe in love, and the attraction of love is not meretricious. Certainly, there are elements of organization which are bound to come into our preparation, but it is giving prominence to any idea of craft that I object to. You see, this man to whose book I refer was a great expert at sermon illustration. This is how he did it: he carried a little notebook in his pocket and whenever he heard a good story, out came the book and he wrote it down. He was always collecting. Then, as he tells us in the book, he would classify the stories according to subject. So, by this means, when he wanted to illustrate a particular point he would look up the relevant section, pull out the drawer, and there were his stories and his illustrations. To me, that is utterly reprehensible. I call that sheer prostitution. Preachers who read other people's sermons for illustrations and stories are not fit to enter pulpits.

Let me put it in another way. There was a bishop in Britain called Hensley Henson. He was the Bishop of Durham and he wrote an autobiography, which was entitled *Retrospect of an Unimportant Life*. (But the unimportant life takes three volumes!) I remember reading in one of these volumes of how he was asked to preach a sermon on some great occasion. He tells us how for three weeks he was preparing that sermon. To me, you see, that man knew nothing about preaching. He delivered great orations, and he could do that, but it was not preaching. Three *weeks*! Contrast that with White-field, preaching in this country day after day, five, six times a day, with almost no time for preparation, and yet what preaching! It is the whole notion of preaching which has gone astray today. If a man reads a manuscript in the pulpit it is destructive of true preaching. I query even the rightness of writing a sermon out in full and committing it to memory.[2] I once used to do that. I stopped doing it because I felt that I was too mechanical, I was having to concentrate too much on remembering. It was a sort of recital, it was not true preaching. What I am trying to say is this, that there is an element in preaching which always leaves loose ends; there is something about preaching which you cannot prepare; you prepare your sermon but as regards preaching you prepare yourself. That is the distinction. You prepare yourself for the preaching. You must have your sermon but even when you have got it, if you have not prepared yourself, if this other element is not there, it will avail you nothing.

God in Preaching

Let me come, then, finally to what I would call some of the vital elements in the preaching. The first is our realization of what is happening, that we are sent of God, that we are heralds of this glorious good news, that we have got authority. If we have not got authority we cannot preach. We must have assurance, we must have absolute authority. Above all, we must be aware of our tremendous responsibility – the privilege of what we are doing, the responsibility of what we are doing. We are speaking from God to men.

You know the story about Robert Murray M'Cheyne. It is said that even as he entered his pulpit in Dundee, during the time of revival there, people began to weep before he had opened his mouth. There was something about his face, and in the conviction which his hearers possessed that he had come from God; he was already

[2]It is not the writing 'in full' as such which Dr Lloyd-Jones is here criticizing. Cf. *Preaching and Preachers*, pp. 215–6.

preaching before he opened his mouth. A man sent from God is aware of this burden. He trembles because of the momentous consequences, the issues, that depend upon what he does.

It is this sense of the word from God – this great idea of 'prophesying' – which brings us a little nearer, perhaps, to understanding preaching. Do not misunderstand me; I am not saying that a man has a revelation from God in the sense of receiving some truth; I am not saying that. But to me, when a man is truly preaching, he has been given the message. What he has himself acquired as the result of his study of the Scripture and his understanding of a passage, this is taken up and it becomes a prophetic utterance. He is speaking in the Spirit, 'in demonstration of the Spirit and of power' (1 Cor. 2:4). I think this is an absolutely vital element in true preaching. A man cannot preach in cold blood. It is impossible. He can utter a sermon, he can read or recite an essay, he can give a Bible lecture, but he cannot preach in cold blood. A preacher is taken up; he is in this realm of the Spirit and God is giving a message through this man to the people. It is not an inspired utterance in the sense that the Scriptures are, but in another sense, it is an inspired utterance because the Spirit is giving it and using it. Thus a vital element in preaching is a reliance upon the Holy Spirit. Another element is freedom – we must be free. That is why I say there are generally loose ends about preaching. A sermon which is perfect in its form, its diction, and in everything else, is one that militates against preaching. You know how the apostle Paul in his writings suddenly forgets, as it were, what he had set out to say. Sometimes he interrupts his own thought; he does not complete his own sentences and he never ends them. How do we explain these breaks, these anacolutha, as they call them? Well, this is the freedom of the Spirit. Paul is taken up; he mentions the name of the Lord and off he goes to some great apostrophe. Then he may or may not come back to his argument.

All this, I say, is a very vital and essential part of preaching. It is not only man preaching, as he says to the Thessalonians in 1 Thessalonians 2:13: You listened, he says to them, and you realized it was not merely the word of man but it was indeed what it actually is, the Word of God. This is his preaching, and this should be true of our preaching. So the preacher is a man who is possessed, and he is aware of this. I do not hesitate to make this assertion. I would say that I only begin to know something about preaching on those occasions when, as it were, I am looking on. I am speaking, but I am really a spectator, and I am amazed at what is happening. I am listening, I am looking on in utter astonishment, for I am not doing it. It is true preaching when I am conscious that I am being used; in a sense, I am as much a spectator as the people who are listening to me. There is this consciousness that it is outside me and yet I am involved in it; I am merely the instrument and the vehicle and the channel of all this. And so one has this abandon, this freedom; and thoughts are given and expressions are given, ideas are given, the imagination is inspired and inflamed, and one is just aware that God is possessing one's whole personality and using every little faculty that He has ever given us at the beginning. Now that is as near as I can describe what is meant by preaching. And we are aware of true preaching only when we are aware in this way, so that we can say, Yet not I; I am preaching, yet not I, but I am being used of God: I am being taken up, I am being employed, and God is using even me to speak to these people. I am an ambassador for Christ, I am a sent one, I am aware of this great responsibility – but it is all right, I am enabled to do it because of His grace and the power that He is gracious enough to give me.

Well, brethren, I trust you will forgive these my rambling remarks. What can you do but something like this when you are given such a title, 'What Is Preaching'?

May God so send His Spirit upon us that we shall again really know what preaching is, experience it ourselves and hear it in others. Do not forget how our hearing of others tests us. I never tire of referring to that great occasion when Whitefield first preached at Northampton in Massachusetts for Jonathan Edwards. I think it is one of the most glorious things that I have ever read. There was this genius, Jonathan Edwards, listening to Whitefield who was not in the same sphere, of course, from the standpoint of genius and ability. But as he was listening to Whitefield, Edwards' face, says Whitefield, was shining and tears were streaming down his face. Edwards was recognizing this authentic, authoritative note, this true preaching. Whitefield was in the Spirit, Edwards was in the Spirit, and the two were blended together. The whole congregation and preacher were one in the hand of God. That is preaching. May God enable us to practise it and to experience it.

Fifteen

*

How To Safeguard the Future[1]

*

> Moreover, brethren, I declare unto you the gospel which I preached unto
> you, which also ye have received, and wherein ye stand; by which also ye
> are saved, if ye keep in memory what I preached unto you, unless ye have
> believed in vain. For I delivered unto you first of all that which I also
> received, how that Christ died for our sins according to the scriptures; and
> that he was buried, and that he rose again the third day according to the
> scriptures (1 Cor. 15:1–4).

This is the text to which I should like to call your attention and in the
light of which it seemed to me we could best celebrate this occasion.
You are all aware that we are met together on this occasion to offer
up our praise and our thanksgiving to God for ever having raised up
the Inter-Varsity Fellowship and for His blessing upon this work
during the last fifty years. We are very right in doing this for we have
many, many reasons for doing so. There are many here today who
owe, under God, the greatest thing in life, namely their salvation, to
the work of the IVF, and there are many men and women in various
parts of the country who can testify to the same thing. Here is a work
which has been responsible for sending a countless number of men
and women into the foreign mission field, spreading the gospel,
establishing medical work in hospitals, schools, and in various other
ways bringing light and knowledge to people who have been born
and brought up in paganism and in the darkness of unbelief. In this
country there are so many men in the Christian ministry owing to the
influence on them, under God, of the IVF and its varied activities in
their formative years. There are, furthermore, men holding high,
important, and influential positions in the various professions who

[1]An address given at a Thanksgiving Service during the fiftieth Annual
Conference of the Inter-Varsity Fellowship in 1969.

[278]

would also be ready to testify that this work has been perhaps the major influence in their lives.

You can see that there are many reasons why we should join together in thanking God and in praising Him for ever having brought the work of the IVF into being, and we might very well spend our time in just reviewing the record, emphasizing some of the most outstanding things that have been done. But I am not going to do that for it seems to me that the best way in which we can show our thanksgiving to God for the IVF, and what it has been, is to make sure that this work will go on. This is no time for complacency, for self-satisfaction and mutual congratulation. The world and the church were in a bad condition when the IVF came into being, but I think no-one would disagree with the proposition that whatever may have been true of the condition of the Christian church and of the world fifty years ago it is altogether more serious at this present time. We are, of course, particularly concerned with the universities. I do not want to be controversial – it is no part of our business to be so, particularly on such an occasion as this – but the position and the condition of affairs in the universities is something with which you are all familiar. A new ferment seems to have entered in, an unrest, a turmoil, and I venture to say, a spirit of lawlessness. The problem therefore of evangelizing students in the universities has, I think, become one of the most urgent tasks at this present time. It is those who are in the universities who are going to be the leaders in the various spheres of life and activity, and unless they can be brought under the influence of the gospel and its specific teaching concerning salvation, and the application of that to the whole of life, then the outlook is indeed a very dark one.

The Need for Constant Watchfulness

I say this as a sort of an apologia for doing what I propose to do with you this afternoon. I take it that most of you are familiar with how the IVF came into being. Prior to that time the Student Christian Movement was working in the universities, being an organization which had come out of the Student Pioneer Movement. The Student Pioneer Movement had been started by evangelical men, but with the passing of the years a great change had taken place in its teaching, its outlook, and its influence. A number of evangelical men in that movement began to feel that it had departed so far from the Christian faith that it was no longer a help, but rather a hindrance, to the furtherance of the gospel. They were concerned that the interest of the SCM had become more social than Christian and that it had departed in a very serious manner from the fundamentals of the Christian faith – from the authority, the inspiration, and the inerrancy of Scripture, and from the whole doctrine of salvation.

These men, becoming thus disturbed, decided that there was only one thing to do, and that was to separate from the Student Christian Movement. I think we must be very clear about this. They did not decide to stay in the Student Christian Movement and try to win it from the inside; they felt that was impossible. They believed that the only way in which they could safeguard the gospel and the truth of God was to separate from the SCM. The IVF, in other words, is a separatist movement; their withdrawal was a deliberate act. They set themselves apart and they established this new organization. What we are celebrating this afternoon is the remarkable blessing of God upon that decision and that action. The story is one which has been written, perhaps should be written in yet greater detail, and it is for all this that we thank God.

But the situation now confronting us is such that we cannot be complacent, and if we are to show our gratitude to God for what has happened and what has been done, we should do so by making certain that we still hold the position that was held by the men who began this work and this movement. We must be determined, under God, to continue it in the same way in the years that lie ahead. I feel that we must therefore ask the question, Is the IVF still in the position that it held at the beginning? Is it wrong to ask that question? I want to show you that it is not, that indeed it is imperative we should ask it, and that in doing so we are obeying a well-known scriptural injunction.

I remember many years ago reading a little book by the late Dean Inge on Protestantism. The only thing I remember of that book was the first sentence, which read, 'All institutions tend to produce their opposite', and he went on to show how so much of what was still called Protestantism was almost the exact opposite of what Protestantism had been at the beginning. All those of us who are familiar with the origin of most of the religious denominations in this country today, and who see the state and condition of these denominations at the present time, will recognize that what Dean Inge said of Protestantism in general has become true of these denominations. If the fathers and founders of these various denominations came back they would not believe their eyes. The position has so changed that what they founded has become almost the exact opposite. So there is this testimony from history to the terrible danger of institutions which start on the right lines and excellently, gradually changing, almost imperceptibly, into something which is almost the exact opposite. That fact in and of itself is sufficient cause to examine ourselves on this occasion.

But the need for self-examination arises not only from the reading of history; the same warning note is to be found in the Bible itself. The New Testament has a great deal to say about this danger. Think, for instance, of the Epistle to the Galatians. In a very short time, the churches in Galatia had virtually departed from the essential truth, and the apostle had to ask the question, 'Where is then the blessedness ye spoke of?' (Gal. 4:15). He is surprised that they had turned so quickly and so easily from the gospel 'unto another gospel, which is not another' (Gal. 1:6–7). They were not aware of this; it is he who has to call their attention to it. And we remember how the letters to the seven churches, in the second and third chapters of the book of Revelation, show this terrible danger of forgetting your 'first love', and of falling away from the truth. Indeed a good case could be made out for saying that most of the New Testament Epistles were written because of this very insidious danger of individual Christians and churches gradually slipping away from the truth, without being aware that any change at all had taken place in them.

It is because this whole question is dealt with in the most perfect manner in the First Epistle to the Corinthians that I am drawing your attention particularly to that Epistle, this afternoon. The church at Corinth was a very outstanding church in many respects. The apostle reminds them in the first chapter that they were second to none in their spiritual gifts and understanding. If one may use such a term of a church, it was a very brilliant kind of church, with remarkable people in its membership; but despite its fine beginnings, something had happened there and a sad decline had taken place. The church was in a state of utter confusion, so much so that the apostle has to use this extraordinary phrase in the second verse of chapter 15. He says, 'By which also ye are saved, if ye keep in memory what I preached unto you, unless ye have believed in vain.' The church was in such a state and condition that the apostle thought it incumbent upon him to raise with them the whole question as to whether they had ever been Christian at all. Now this is an amazing phenomenon, that, in such a short space of time from the founding of the church, as a result of the preaching of the great apostle, this same church had got into a pathetic condition, in which even the question of the salvation of some of them has to be raised by the apostle himself.

Because this is the kind of process to which churches, movements, and institutions are prone and subject, and especially in the kind of situation in which we find ourselves today, we are driven to make certain that all is well with us. It is a good occasion for doing so as we celebrate these fifty years and thank God for them. Let us make certain that we are going on into the future in the same way as this work originally began. We would be lacking in a sense of duty if we were not to do what the apostle did so long ago, with this church at Corinth.

Three Causes of Decline at Corinth

As we consider the apostle's teaching with regard to the church at Corinth, and as we apply it to ourselves, the first question we have to face is this: What were the causes of the trouble in Corinth? What were the factors that had led to this degeneration, this decline, this backslidden condition? It seems to me that there were three main causes of the trouble. The first I would describe under the heading of 'carnality', which is the apostle's own term. A 'fleshly' element had come in, and it was manifesting itself in two main ways. The first was this foolish division over men, some saying, 'I am of Paul', others saying, 'I am of Apollos', and others saying, 'I am of Cephas', quarrelling over preachers, forming factions and groups around these particular personalities. Paul says, That is sheer carnality; you have reverted to the old style of thinking.

But there was carnality in another sense. Some of them had fallen into grievous sin. There was the man to whom Paul refers in chapter 5 who had committed such a sin, and was still in it, such a sin, Paul says, that even the Gentiles do not like to mention. Yet he was being tolerated within the membership of this brilliant church, boasting of her gifts. A foul perversion! They were also quarrelling with one another and taking their disputes to the public courts, as is indicated in chapter 6. They were guilty of 'sins of the flesh': fornication, adultery, drunkenness. Paul deals with all that again, in the sixth chapter. Some of them were even going to the communion table partly intoxicated. And in the fifteenth chapter he indicates quite clearly that there had been moral aberrations among many of them. A kind of antinomianism seemed to have entered in, a feeling that as long as their souls were saved it did not matter what happened to the body, the same antinomianism which was also threatening to creep into so many of the early churches.

The one obvious, potent factor in this decline was carnality; but there was a second element in their decline, and perhaps a more serious one. It is certainly the one that the apostle takes up early in his Epistle – what I call intellectualism. This is the theme of the second half of the first chapter, the whole of the second and third, and most of the fourth. Intellectualism. Of course, in a place like Corinth an emphasis on the intellect was quite natural. The Greeks, after all, were the great philosophers. Athens was the Mecca of the philosophers but all these cities boasted the same interest. Corinth was a cosmopolitan seaport town, yet it is clear that its people, as represented in the church, belonged to this intellectual outlook and rather prided themselves on it. So the apostle has to show them the difference between the 'wisdom of men' and 'the wisdom of this world' on the one hand, and 'the wisdom of God in a mystery'. There was the desire to be wise, the desire to think out their Christian faith in philosophical terms; so he has to say even in that very first chapter, at verse 17: 'Christ sent me not to baptize, but to preach the gospel: not with wisdom of words, lest the cross of Christ should be made of none effect.' These people felt that they could 'explain' the cross philosophically, and it is clear from the fifteenth chapter that they were trying to do the same with the resurrection, trying to show how up to date they were, how intelligent, how intellectual! But they were philosophizing away the whole meaning of the cross and of the resurrection. Indeed it is clear that some of them were even despising the apostle Paul; they said, 'His presence is weak, and his speech contemptible' (2 Cor. 10:10). Paul did not indulge in philosophic speculation, neither did he adopt the rhetorical manner of the Greek rhetoricians. He had 'determined not to know anything among [them] save Jesus Christ, and him crucified', and he did not speak and preach 'with enticing words of man's wisdom' (1 Cor. 2:2–4). The result was that they were tending to dismiss him because he was not giving this show of intellectuality or of intellectualism.

The same thing came out in the attitude of some of the abler members of the church towards those who were less gifted intellectually; we find it in the whole dispute between the strong and the weak brother concerning the question of meats offered to idols, which Paul deals with in the eighth chapter. This desire for knowledge was clearly, in many ways, the main trouble in the church at Corinth, and Paul has to remind them that knowledge puffs up, while it is charity that builds up, that edifies. But they were so keen on this knowledge, wanting to be up to date and even explaining away, without realizing it, the very essence of the Christian message. That was another very grievous trouble in the church at Corinth, this curious notion that you can mix human and divine wisdom, that you can present the message of the cross in a manner that is pleasing to the unregenerate intellectual man. Paul regarded this as a fatal mistake and that is why he deals with it so clearly in this letter.

Then there was a third factor which was also causing havoc in the church. It is what I would call an unbalanced spirituality. You remember how at the beginning of the twelfth chapter he says, 'Now concerning spirituals'. The Authorized Version has 'concerning spiritual gifts', but what he is saying is, 'Now concerning spirituals'. Bear in mind how the church at Corinth was being torn again into factions. They were guilty of schism because of their interest – their inordinate, unbalanced interest – in spiritual experiences, spiritual gifts, and there they were vying with one another, those who had the more brilliant gifts boasting of them, and despising those with the lesser gifts, and vice versa. And the whole church was being so torn that the apostle had to tell them that the church is a body and cannot be torn in this way. They misunderstood everything. There was this unhealthy interest in phenomena and in particular gifts, especially the gift of speaking in tongues. That is the theme of chapters 12 to 14.

There, then, are the three main causes of the trouble in the church at Corinth: carnality, intellectualism, and an unbalanced spirituality. What does it teach us? I suggest to you that there are three main lessons which immediately present themselves to us. The first, to which I have already adverted, is the danger of assuming that because a church, or an institution, or a movement, was once right, that it will continue to be right. The same body, the same institution, the same cause, the same movement with the same organization, can move from its position and end up being almost the exact opposite of what it was at the beginning. That is the first and obvious lesson.

The second lesson is, to me, a much more important one, and it is this: it is the danger of allowing secondary and third-rate matters to occupy the centre of attention. In other words, it is the danger of a lack of balance. That was the real trouble in the church at Corinth. They were allowing a number of matters, which were perfectly right and legitimate in themselves, to occupy the centre, and it was because these things were made central that there was trouble in the church. For instance, preachers have their importance; preachers are useful; but if you make them the centre, so that every time you meet you talk about the preacher instead of the Lord Jesus Christ, your preachers are doing harm; indeed you are making them do harm. Now that was the trouble there. Preachers are all right but they are not meant to be in the centre.

Again, the way in which men preach is important. We have to consider methods of presentation. There is nothing wrong in that, but when that becomes *the* thing, is always being talked of, and is in all the papers, then, I say, the balance has been lost. This was partly the trouble at Corinth – their excessive interest in the way in which the message was presented; they were critical of Paul and tended to praise Apollos, and so on. Presentation is an important matter but it is not the only matter. You see the relevance of this at the present time. You open religious journals today and look at them at random, and you would get the impression that the important thing is the *way* in which the message is presented: pop singing, pop stars, etc. This interest seems to be at the centre: it is *the* thing.

The question of meats offered to idols is an important subject. Of course it is; but if you spend the whole of your time, says Paul, arguing about this, you are doing harm to a weaker brother for whom Christ died. It is not that the thing is unimportant but it should not be in the centre; it must not monopolize attention. You must not give the impression that 'the kingdom of God', as he puts it to the Romans, 'is meat and drink', for it is not. It is 'righteousness, and peace, and joy in the Holy Ghost' (Rom. 14:17).

It is the same with this whole question of gifts. The gifts are given by the Holy Spirit, all of them, but if you are always talking about gifts, says Paul, and if you exalt one of them at the expense of others, or if you put gifts and experiences and phenomena into the centre and make them the be-all and the end-all of your lives as Christian people, then your church is in chaos and you have lost your balance.

Parallel Contemporary Dangers

Those were the things that were troubling the church at Corinth. I simply ask the question, Is there not some evidence of this at the present time in Christian work in general in this country? There is a tendency to put certain things into the central position that have no business to be there. I do not blame any non-Christian in this land who has come to the conclusion, for instance, that the Christian message, the central Christian message, is just pacifism. I would not blame them for coming to that conclusion. That is the impression they would get from looking at religious spokesmen on the television, or listening to them on the radio. There are others who have given the impression, and still do so, that the central message of our gospel is certain matters of prophecies; they are always thinking about these, they talk about nothing else, always prophecy. Of course prophecy is of tremendous importance, but you must not make it central.

In the same way I know many at the present time who seem to me to have the idea that if only every church had elders there would never be another problem in the Christian church. Elders – this is the *one* thing. They talk about it, they write about it, and I am quite sure many of them dream about it! Again, the question of elders and deacons is, of course, an important question but it was never meant to be central. The Christian church is not about elders. In other words, you see, it is all a lack of balance.

Then there is great emphasis on the part of some with regard to the implications of the gospel. Certainly there are implications to be drawn from the gospel but the gospel consists not only in its implications. There is the real danger of forgetting the gospel itself because you are so interested in the political and social and cultural implications of the gospel. I recently read a review of a book which exhorted us all to be familiar with modern art and modern literature, and the reviewer was very pleased with this emphasis. He took it up and ended his article by saying that, if only all ministers read this book, he could foresee a great day coming for preaching, because ministers would then be spending their Saturday nights in preparation for Sunday watching theatre on television! He believed that modern preachers were ineffective, because not knowing the sort of life people were living, they did not know how to present their message. So if you are to be a good preacher you have to be an expert in modern art, modern literature, and modern drama; you cannot preach without this. And, to carry it to its logical conclusion, I take it that you should spend most nights in a public house too, otherwise how can you preach to people who spend their time there, unless you know what they talk about and how they talk? Such is the thinking to which an over-concentration on presentation and on methods of evangelism can lead.

What I am anxious to establish is that the lack of balance is serious. It is not the things in and of themselves that are wrong so much as the lack of balance. We must pay attention to these things, but when they are made central, and the impression is given that these are the things that matter, then we are falling, or in danger of falling, into the Corinthian error and position.

My last general lesson concerns the vital importance of self-examination. The apostle presses this upon the Corinthians at the end of his Second Epistle to them. He says: 'Examine yourselves, whether ye be in the faith; prove your own selves' (2 Cor. 13:5). This is something that we should be doing constantly. In the light of the terrible dangers that confront us, our main duty is to examine ourselves, test our institutions, the IVF, and everything else, by the Scriptures, making certain that we are not unconsciously slipping away from the things which are central, and becoming over-preoccupied with things which, though they are good in themselves, were never meant to occupy a central position.

The Apostolic Answer to Spiritual Dangers

There then is the apostle's teaching concerning the church at Corinth and we must examine ourselves in the light of it. What are we to do? What is his prescription for us? How does it deal with these troubles? The answer is summarized in these first four verses of 1 Corinthians 15. Having gone through these problems in his own inimitable manner, he comes back and says, I want to remind you again of the things which are central. He has taken them through this involved argument about gifts and all these other matters, and then he says, in effect, You are in this terrible confusion because you have gone astray in this way; what are you to do? Well, listen, there are certain things you have got to keep in memory: 'Moreover, brethren, I declare unto you the gospel which I preached unto you, which also ye have received, and wherein ye stand; by which also ye are saved, *if ye keep in memory*' – if you hold fast, if you keep firmly. This is the thing! You notice that he does not now go on to argue with them about other possible methods or this or that detail; he says, There is only one treatment for all this; it is to come back to the things that are central and foundational, and to hold on to them, hold fast to them.

What are these things? They are the things which, he says, 'I delivered unto you first of all'. You notice the alternative translation in the reading: 'amongst the first things', or 'amongst the central things'. I believe both are true; he is speaking of the things which are first in chronological order and also certainly first in importance, first in the sense of their being crucial and absolutely essential to the Christian faith. What you have got to do, says Paul, is to come back to this. Stop talking for a moment about the preachers, stop talking about your understanding of things offered to idols, stop talking about your gifts – I do not care what they are. Come back and consider the things which I preached to you when I first came to you, and which I put in the centre and the forefront; this is your only hope. And it is still the only hope for any individual Christian who is in trouble about his or her spiritual life; it is the only hope for a church, it is the only hope for any movement.

As Paul reminds them of the things which he preached to them 'first of all', it is perfectly simple. He sets out one of his amazing summaries of the whole of Christian doctrine.

The Finality of Scripture

Here is the first thing in Paul's summary: the Scriptures! 'I delivered unto you first of all that which I also received, how that Christ died for our sins according to the scriptures; and that he was buried, and that he rose again the third day according to the scriptures.' Why does he bother to add this about 'according to the scriptures'? Why does he not merely say 'that Christ died for our sins, that he was buried, and that he rose again the third day' – why this dragging in and repetition of 'the scriptures'? To that there is only one answer. The Scriptures are the basis and the foundation of the whole teaching. This, as I reminded you at the beginning, was the thing that really gave birth to the IVF. Other student movements, following liberalism, modernism, and Higher Criticism, had departed from the faith. The primary trouble fifty years ago was this question of the Scriptures. It always has been and always will be. So you must always start with this; it is basic; it is the foundation of all our teaching.

What was Paul's preaching concerning the Scriptures? I can only give you the summary as he gives it here himself. The first thing we have to remember about the Scriptures is that they are revelation: 'I delivered unto you first of all that which I also *received*.' In other words, he reminds them of what he had told them when he first visited them, that he was not the propagator of some new philosophy, which he had thought out. There were many such people in the ancient world, and some at Athens thought that Paul was one of them. They said, 'What will this babbler say?' (Acts 17:18). But the apostle always made it perfectly plain and clear that he was only an instrument, the conveyer of a message which had been revealed and given to him: 'I also received.' Writing to these intellectuals, these philosophically minded people in Corinth, he said, You know, I have not arrived at this truth as the result of research, or enquiry, or endeavour. No – I have received it. He says elsewhere that he was not worthy even to receive it, for he had persecuted the church of Christ, and far from arriving at it as a result of reason and his own thinking and rumination, he was a man who had to be literally knocked to the ground on the way to Damascus. He received the truth in utter helplessness as a little child. Received! That is what he constantly says: 'A dispensation of the gospel is committed unto me' (1 Cor. 9:17).

The Christian truth is not something you arrive at as a result of a process of reason. Indeed, as he has made clear in the second chapter: 'But the natural man receiveth not the things of the Spirit of God: for they are foolishness unto him: neither can he know them' – he cannot, it is impossible – 'because they are spiritually discerned' (1 Cor. 2:14). Christian truth is not a matter of reason or of philosophy; it is something which is given. It is of God. It is God's truth. It is God speaking to man, not man trying to arrive at a knowledge of God, trying to understand his life and world, trying to concoct some proposals for dealing with the difficulties. No, it is the exact opposite. It is something that we *receive* entirely from God. It is revelation and it is all of grace.

At the same time the category of inspiration comes in. That is why Paul said in the second chapter, 'Which things also we speak, not in the words which man's wisdom teacheth, but which the Holy Ghost teacheth; comparing spiritual things with spiritual'. Not only have we the revelation from God; that revelation has been given to us as the result of this process of inspiration, *words* 'which the Holy Ghost teacheth'. This deserves separate attention and we cannot go into it now, but let us hold on to these things, let us remember that the writings of this man were divinely inspired. Peter, in referring to Paul and his writings, reminds his readers that the writings of Paul were in the same category as 'the other scriptures' (2 Pet. 3:15–16) – meaning the Old Testament – and, as Paul says, 'All scripture is given by inspiration of God' (2 Tim. 3:16). So he makes it abundantly plain and clear, and this is our position, that what we have here is the inspired Word of God. The message is entirely different from every other teaching confronting mankind.

Because it is a matter of revelation and inspiration, let us not forget that it is therefore ageless, and changeless. It is the faith once and for ever delivered to the saints (Jude 3). Someone may say, But surely you are not saying that we are in the same position as we were fifty years ago? Look what has happened since: we have split the atom, we have sent men up into outer space; we have made these astounding discoveries. Are you suggesting that the IVF should still hold on to its old position with regard to the Scriptures? The answer is quite simple. Because these are *entirely* from God – revelation and inspiration – the passing of fifty years, or of 5,000 years, makes not the slightest difference. This is in no sense the result of man's endeavour and discovery. It is all given, it is all from God. So that this question of change and of development, of modern knowledge and 'the assured results' of science and so forth, is completely irrelevant. We have the truth of God, not truths propounded by man.

Another deduction which we draw is this, that we must take the *whole* Scripture as the apostle is very careful to point out in this same chapter, the Old Testament as well as the New Testament. I have met many Christian people who seem to think that the Old Testament is irrelevant for them. They say they are only interested in salvation, they are not interested in the religion of the Jews and the Old Testament; they do not read it, they are only interested in the New. That is entirely wrong. The whole of the Scriptures are of God and we must accept them all. We must accept the history as well as the didactic teaching. We must take the whole of the revelation which God has been pleased to give us.

In other words, it is wrong to say that you go to the Bible only for 'religious' truth or truth concerning salvation. This has often been taught. It was taught very prominently in the last century by a German theologian called Ritschl; he drew this distinction. He argued that you must not go to your Bible for anything apart from 'religious' truth or truth concerning salvation. That is not true. The

Bible speaks concerning creation, the origin of the world, and the message of the Bible on salvation is not merely a personal one; it deals with a cosmic salvation. It is interested in the whole of life and the whole universe, because God the Saviour is first God the Creator. So we have to accept the history and the record of its beginning. In teaching this central doctrine of salvation in this very chapter, Paul refers to Adam, the historical Adam, the first man (1 Cor. 15:45). Salvation involves history; it involves the doctrine of creation; it involves the whole doctrine of man. Therefore it is vitally important that we take the whole of the Scripture, and do not pick and choose and say, because of our new knowledge, certain passages no longer apply. That is to deny the Scripture, the very basis and foundation of our faith, and we know from history that churches, movements, and individuals which have gone astray and become heretical have generally done so because they have started with that fatal distinction; they have ceased to believe, and to accept, the whole of the Scripture.

The Fall and Salvation

Secondly, Paul reminds them that he had taught them the doctrine of the fall and the need of salvation: 'Moreover, brethren, I declare unto you the gospel which I preached unto you, which also ye have received, and wherein ye stand; *by which also ye are saved*.' The need of salvation – here was one of the great strands in his preaching. The law comes before the gospel, conviction of sin before the offer of salvation.

Here again you notice that we are very much in the realm of history. Why does man need to be saved? Is it because he is not yet fully evolved or sufficiently evolved in the direction of perfection? Is that what we mean by salvation? Where does the need of salvation come in? The answer of the apostle is perfectly plain, and it is history again: 'as in Adam all die' (1 Cor. 15:22). There was once a perfect man, Adam, but he and the woman fell, and it is because of this fall that salvation became essential. God had made the world; He had made it perfect; He looked at it and saw that 'it was good'. He set man in paradise but man disobeyed God's special injunction. This is not myth, this is history, this is sheer fact. The apostle taught it, preached it, asserted it, and this has been a main plank in Christian preaching ever since and must always be. The whole case hangs

together, and if you remove any segment of it, it all collapses. The
need of salvation! Listen: 'If Christ be not raised, your faith is vain;
ye are yet in your sins. Then they also which are fallen asleep in
Christ are perished' (1 Cor. 15:17–18). This was a part of his
preaching. What does he mean by 'in your sins'? What does he mean
by 'perish'? He means that 'the wrath of God is revealed from heaven
against all ungodliness and unrighteousness of men, who hold
[down] the truth in unrighteousness' (Rom. 1:18). His teaching is
that Adam was the representative of the whole of the human race. He
was the first man, the head of humanity. When he fell, the whole race
fell with him and 'death passed upon all men, for that all have sinned'
(Rom. 5:12). To the Romans he says, they 'had not all sinned after
the similitude of Adam's transgression' (Rom. 5:14), but they all die;
'death has passed upon them all' because Adam was the first man and
the representative of the whole human race. Therefore it is true that
by nature we are 'in sin', and, in addition to that, we commit sins –
rebellion, disobedience, transgression. We are all guilty, and we are
all in our sins, and he says, If you die in your sins you will perish,
which means everlasting alienation from the life of God, and the love
of God; eternal misery and torment. Perishing!

This is why salvation is necessary. Man's first and greatest need is
not to be improved; it is not to be given better advantages; it is not to
be healed physically. Man's primary need is to be reconciled to God.
That is what Paul says in his Second Epistle to the Corinthians: 'We
are ambassadors for Christ', beseeching that men be 'reconciled to
God'. 'God was in Christ, reconciling the world unto himself'
(2 Cor. 5:19–20). It is all based on history, and so if you reject the
history of Genesis 1, 2, and 3 and the history of the fall, you are left
with no real explanation of the need of salvation; you have no
conception whatsoever of a cosmic and a total redemption, such as
that which was preached by this and the other apostles. This
therefore was one of the first and the central things which Paul taught
them.

Redemption by Christ Alone

Then the third great strand in the message was God's plan of
redemption. What of this? Well, the first thing he is anxious to say
about this is that it was revealed in the Scriptures. That is why he
keeps on repeating the phrase 'according to the scriptures'. He is

reminding them that the coming of the Lord Jesus Christ into the world was not a kind of afterthought; it was not something that God improvised. No! The doctrine of redemption was something that was planned before the foundation of the world; it antecedes creation and the fall. He has already made that clear in the second chapter, in the seventh verse: the gospel reveals the wisdom 'ordained before the foundation of the world unto our glory'. This is God's great plan of redemption. And what are the Scriptures, what is the Bible? It is, in a sense, the history of redemption. We are given an account of the creation of the world, including man, an account of how man and the creation fell from their original state. Then the great theme comes in. The gospel starts in Genesis 3:15. Having said, 'I will put enmity between thee' – the serpent – 'and the woman, and between thy seed and her seed', God declares this glorious promise that the seed of the woman shall bruise the serpent's head. It is the first promise of the coming of redemption. And as you go through the Old Testament there is the same great theme, not only adumbrated but worked out in detail. In that connection I must speak a word to those who see no point, as Christians, in reading the book of Leviticus. They say, What have I to do with all these regulations about meat offerings, and burnt offerings, and peace offerings, what has it all got to do with me? The answer is, that they all foreshadow the coming of the Lord Jesus Christ. These are types indicating the great antitype, God giving out in parts and portions what He was ultimately going to do; He has revealed it all in the Scriptures. That is why Paul keeps on saying 'according to the scriptures'.

Why did Christ die on the cross? What was He doing there? He was fulfilling the Scriptures – the promises, the burnt offerings, and sacrifices, the lambs that had been killed. This is God's lamb. This is fulfilment of the Scriptures.

Then you get these promises still more gloriously in the Psalms and in the great prophetic utterances of the prophets. 'Comfort ye, comfort ye my people, saith your God' (Isa. 40:1). Why? The deliverer is coming! 'Prepare ye the way of the Lord' (Isa. 40:3) – 'all the ends of the earth shall see the salvation of our God' (Isa. 52:10). It is going to come. This is prophecy and the fulfilment will be 'according to the scriptures'. Paul can say to these Corinthians in his Second Epistle: 'All the promises of God in him are yea, and in him Amen, unto the glory of God' (2 Cor. 1:20). Christ is the fulfilment of all the promises of the Old Testament Scriptures. You see the importance of Scripture and of history, and of the *whole* Scripture.

Then we come to the blessed person of the Lord Jesus Christ Himself, 'how that Christ died for our sins according to the Scriptures'. The person of the Lord Jesus Christ is crucial, vital, essential. There must be no question, no dispute, over the Son of God, the Lord of glory. He is God's lamb that takes away the sin of the world. The apostle is always asserting this. Christ, he says later on in this chapter, 'the second man is the Lord from heaven' (verse 47). He is 'the last Adam'. Here is a new head of a new race, and, as I have said, it is not only a question of individual salvation, He is the one through whom God is going to restore everything to its original perfection and glory. This is Paul's teaching here; it is his teaching everywhere.

What then are the important things about the Lord Jesus Christ? Well, many seem to think that the important thing is His teaching – the Sermon on the Mount, for example – His ethical, moral teaching. What we need, they say, is the application of this teaching to the problems confronting the world today. Others emphasize His example; they urge us to rise up and imitate Him. But have you ever noticed what it is to which Paul refers when he writes, 'I delivered unto you first of all that which I also received'? What was it? Christ is the great teacher, the great exemplar? Christ the great aesthete, the great 'pale Galilean'? Not at all! It was 'how that Christ *died*'. Of course it does not mean that the life and the teaching are not important; but it does mean that what saves you is that He *died*. Paul immediately comes to the death, the burial, and the literal, physical resurrection. These are the things, he says, that I preached to you. This was the essence of his message, this is the good news of salvation. This is the way of salvation and the only way. The wrath of God had already been revealed, in the Old Testament, but not in that fullness which we see at the cross where God put His own Son to grief for our salvation. It is by this crucial act and event that He saves us. We cannot save ourselves, *He* has done something that saves us: 'God was in Christ, reconciling the world unto himself' (2 Cor. 5:19). Paul presents us with the facts and he tells us their meaning: 'Christ died *for* our sins.' 'The Lord hath laid on him the iniquity of us all' (Isa. 53:6). 'He hath made him to be sin for us, who knew no sin; that we might be made the righteousness of God in him'

(2 Cor. 5:21). God does not impute trespasses to believers any longer, says Paul, for He has imputed them to Christ. This is the teaching that he gave them and it is *the* Christian message. Even when we are dealing with world conditions as they are today, our case is that man's primary need is to be reconciled to God, that there is no hope for him otherwise, and this is the way in which the reconciliation takes place.

But gospel history does not end with Christ's death and resurrection. There is the heavenly session where He is interceding for us. And still more important, in a way, there is His coming again; this new head of the new humanity is going to come again and He is going to finish this work of redemption. Paul puts it like this: 'Then cometh the end, when he shall have delivered up the kingdom to God, even the Father; when he shall have put down all rule and all authority and power. For he must reign, till he hath put all enemies under his feet' (1 Cor. 15:24–25). And we assert that Christ is reigning this afternoon. He permits things we do not understand, but He lives, He reigns, and at the appropriate, appointed time, He will come again, riding the clouds of heaven, conquering His enemies, judging the world, consummating His kingdom and handing it back to the Father in all its glorious original perfection. 'If in this life only we have hope in Christ, we are of all men most miserable' (1 Cor. 15:19).

I am not saying that you should not be concerned about the social, political implications of the gospel, that you should not be interested in art and life in this world while we are here, but with a world such as this today, and with these bombs being piled up, which may put everything to an end in a moment at any time, why do we not think more of what is before us, the glory that awaits us? Is this note as prominent as it once was? Are we as interested as we should be, as the New Testament is, in Christ's coming again, His conquering of all His enemies, His completion of the kingdom and his handing it back to the Father? This 'blessed hope', this cosmic redemption, this returning to God, the whole universe – yes, the physical universe – all is going to be changed. It is going to be purged of all the results of evil and sin and the fall, the briars and thorns, the diseases and the pestilences – all will be banished and the whole cosmos will be perfect, and returned to God. That is why we must see the doctrine of creation as the introduction to the doctrine of redemption and salvation.

Our Present Duty

All too hurriedly we have noted the things that the apostle himself tells us he preached to these people 'first of all'. But is there anything else? Well yes, we have to receive this; 'which also ye have *received*', he says. How did they receive it? The apostle has made it so plain that there can be no dispute about it. 'The natural man receiveth not the things of the Spirit of God ... neither can he know them' (1 Cor.2:14). There is only one way whereby anyone can receive this gospel, and that is that he be enlightened by the Holy Spirit. For by grace are ye saved through faith; and that not of yourselves: it is the gift of God' (Eph. 2:8). We need a spiritual understanding, and this gospel offers us a new birth. Then it becomes true what the apostle says, 'We have the mind of Christ'. 'But he that is spiritual judgeth all things, yet he himself is judged of no man' (1 Cor. 2:15–16). This blessed doctrine of the new birth and of regeneration! It is only as the result of this that we are able to see, believe, and receive the truth – and so the glory goes entirely to God.

Do we stop at receiving it? No. 'Moreover, brethren, I declare unto you the gospel which I preached unto you, which also ye have received, and wherein ye *stand*.' You have got to 'stand'. 'By which also ye are saved, if ye keep in memory what I preached unto you, unless ye have believed in vain.' It is not enough to receive it, you must stand in it, you must be firm and unshakeable in it. Paul was so concerned about this that when he comes to wind up his letter he repeats it again: 'Watch ye' – that is what I have been trying to exhort you to do – 'stand fast in the faith, quit you like men, be strong. Let all your things be done with charity' (1 Cor. 16:13–14). We have got to *stand* in this faith.

How do we do that? Again, fortunately, the apostle teaches us and here is his first injunction in that respect: 'Be not deceived: evil communications corrupt good manners' (1 Cor. 15:33). You will never stand in the faith unless you are careful about your relationships, your 'communications'. I agree with those commentators who say that this is a reference not only to one's behaviour but also to one's thinking and reading. 'Evil communications *corrupt* good manners.' Be careful with whom you associate, if you want to stand fast in the faith. It does not mean that you have to become a monk or an anchorite. No, but you have got to be careful, you have got to avoid false teaching, you have to avoid error and wrong practice.

The IVF deliberately separated itself from the SCM, believing that was the only way to safeguard this truth and to stand in it. It is still the same. Fraternizing with those who deny the gospel will never do us any good, indeed it will do us positive harm. 'Evil communications corrupt good manners.' Let us be careful that in our desire to be considered intellectually respectable, we do not expose ourselves to infections which can do us grievous harm in a spiritual sense. There were people who called this colossus of a man, this genius, a 'fool'. He was quite content to be a fool for Christ's sake. If you are out for intellectual respectability you will soon get into trouble in your faith. It does not mean you need to be obscurantist. I am not arguing for that, but I am saying that you will never make this gospel acceptable to the natural man. If you say that the new physics enables us to understand miracles in a way they could never be understood before, that does not help anybody to believe in miracles. There is nothing we know today that makes it easier for anybody to believe this gospel than it was for them to believe it in the first century. The natural man is opposed to it. Let us be careful lest in our desire to present the gospel in an attractive, a pleasing, and what we may imagine to be an acceptable manner, we do not philosophize it away or try to explain it away in terms of some modern knowledge. It cannot be done. The apostle has already said it all: 'If any man among you seemeth to be wise in this world, let him become a fool, that he may be wise' (1 Cor. 3:18). That is still the only rule. We must be ready to preach the scandal, 'the offence of the cross'. With the apostle we must determine 'not to know anything among you, save Jesus Christ, and him crucified' (1 Cor. 2:2). Take an interest in cultural things if you like, but be careful that you do not mix it with your presentation of the gospel. We have received it, let us stand in it, and let us tell others about it.

How? Not by pandering to modern ideas, not by using modern methods. There is only one way: 'it pleased God by the foolishness of preaching to save them that believe' (1 Cor. 1:21). 'Not with enticing words of man's wisdom, but in demonstration of the Spirit and of power' (1 Cor. 2:4). 'Not with wisdom of words, lest the cross of Christ should be made of none effect' (1 Cor. 1:17). If you try to make the cross something beautiful you are denying it. It is a 'scandal', an 'offence' to the natural man, for it condemns him utterly and completely. Let us preach it as it is, 'not in the words which man's wisdom teacheth, but which the Holy Ghost teacheth' (1 Cor. 2:13).

There is this old word that the apostle addressed to the church at Corinth in the first century, and it seems to me to come to us with a strange and alarming relevance in 1969 on this fiftieth anniversary of the founding of the IVF. In the name of God I appeal to you: stand in the truth that you have received; stand fast, stand firm! 'Let the world deride or pity', it does not matter, 'I will glory in thy name'. Believe the message, trust it utterly, absolutely, and look to the Holy Spirit of God to open the blind eyes and to give life and spiritual understanding to all those who are outside. It is the only way. Do not put the wrong things in the centre. There is only one thing that is in the centre: 'Jesus Christ, and him crucified', and all that that means and involves.

Sixteen

*

What Is an Evangelical?[1]

*

I

Jude, the servant of Jesus Christ, and brother of James, to them that are sanctified by God the Father, and preserved in Jesus Christ, and called: mercy unto you, and peace, and love, be multiplied. Beloved, when I gave all diligence to write unto you of the common salvation, it was needful for me to write unto you, and exhort you that ye should earnestly contend for the faith which was once delivered unto the saints (Jude 1–3).

This, as most of you realize, is a very interesting statement, for it is rather unusual in the New Testament. Here Jude is telling the people to whom he is writing that his original intention was to write a letter giving an exposition of the common salvation of the Christian faith, something similar or analogous, one imagines, to what the apostle Paul did in the Epistle to the Romans. That was what he intended to do, but he tells them here that he was not able to do so, that his great purpose had to be laid on one side. Why was this? It was because news had come to him of certain attacks upon the faith so that, in a sense, what he is saying is this: We have not the time, nor can we afford to enjoy the luxury of just expounding the truth and taking our time over it as we do so. A very urgent matter has arisen and all of us must now contend earnestly for the faith. And that is what Jude does and that is the reason why it is such a short letter.

Now I take this as my general text for these three lectures or talks which I propose to give. Nothing would give me personally greater pleasure than to take a verse or passage of Scripture and expound it. Nothing gives me greater joy at any time than to do that, but I believe

[1]A series of three addresses given at the IFES Conference at Schloss Mittersill, Austria, in 1971.

we are now in a position which is very similar to that in which this man Jude and others found themselves. A situation has arisen which compels us to consider the whole of the faith, and to defend the whole of the faith, urgently, and that is what I am going to try to do now with you.

I am proposing, in other words, to deal with the question, What is an evangelical? In the time of Jude this was the fundamental question which had arisen: What is the faith? What is a Christian? He says it is no use leisurely going over particular aspects of truth and of doctrine when the *whole* situation is being attacked and undermined. We have got to go back to the foundation, to the very basis. And I believe that we are now once more in such a situation. This is something that has arisen from time to time in the long history of the Christian church. Repeatedly, men and women in the church have had to go back to the origins, to define again and defend the very essence of the Christian faith.

The Constant Necessity for Definition

Now we are going to look at it in terms of 'What is an evangelical?' for we are meeting together under the auspices of the International Fellowship of *Evangelical* Students. There is the specific term. I want to try to show you that the situation today is such that we must not take this term 'evangelical' for granted. We must rediscover its meaning. We must define it again. And we must be ready to fight for it and to defend it.

There are those who might disagree with this and believe that there is no need to do this. They say, We all know what an evangelical is; it's a familiar term. In their view, as long as a man makes certain statements he is an evangelical, or if an organization makes certain positive statements, that organization is evangelical. I suggest that that is no longer true and that a situation has developed, and is continuing to develop, in which the whole question of the meaning of 'evangelical' has been thrown again into the melting pot. We must be sure and certain that we know exactly what we mean when we employ this term.

Why is this necessary? Well, my first answer would be that the history of the past, the history of the church throughout the centuries, shows very clearly that there is nothing static in the life of the church. There is always a process of change and of development, and unfortunately, as is true of nature, the process is generally one of degeneration. This, of course, is one of the main results of sin and of the fall. Sin has brought an element of degeneration into the life of man, and as a result of that, into the life of creation; so that even in the church herself there will be this tendency. In the New Testament you already see heresy, false teaching arising, subtle changes taking place with regard to what the Christian truth really is. The apostle Paul, in his great address to the elders of the church at Ephesus, as recorded in Acts 20, warns them of how, from among themselves, men will arise and teach false doctrines. Wolves, as it were, will come in and do harm to the flock of God. And this has continued ever since in the history of the church.

I shall never forget reading nearly forty years ago the opening sentence in a book on the subject of Protestantism. The first sentence reads thus: 'Every institution tends to produce its opposite.' That was the author's opening sentence in a book on Protestantism, and the thesis of the book, of course, was to point out – and he was able to do it very simply – that the position of most of the Protestant churches today is almost the exact opposite of their position when they originally came into being. I could easily take up the time in showing you this. Take Martin Luther and the beginnings of Protestantism as an example. You may remember how, in less than a hundred years from the rise of Lutheranism, there developed what we know as Lutheran scholasticism. A hardening process took place, subtle changes came in, so that by the middle of the seventeenth century Lutheranism presented a picture which was really very different from its origin under Luther. And the whole of the pietist movement with Spener and Arndt was a protest against this and an attempt to bring the church back to her origins.

The same thing happened among the reformed people: a hardening process took place; an intellectualism came in, so that you were soon confronted by something that had departed very seriously from the original position.

I could easily demonstrate this in the history of every denomination that is known to me personally, and of denominations and religious bodies in various other countries. This is a principle which we have got to recognize. It is no use assuming that because a thing has started correctly it is going to continue to be correct. There is a process at work, because of sin and evil, which tends to produce not only change but even degeneration.

Nor is this all. There is something further to point out as we look at the history of the church throughout the centuries. It is that this process of change is never a sudden one. It is always a subtle and slow process. You remember our Lord's own comparison about moth and rust. Rusting is a very slow process and if you do not watch out it will have developed in such an insidious manner that the first you know about it is that a girder on a bridge, or something like that, is broken. The change is almost imperceptible, and it is the same with the effect of a moth in a piece of clothing.

Perhaps the clearest demonstration of this that one can give is what happened in the last century, the nineteenth century, in connection with the so-called Higher Critical movement. At the beginning of that century there were a number of evangelical denominations and bodies. Then gradually a change came in, a change of emphasis, a change of teaching, but the striking thing about it was the slowness and the subtlety with which it came.

There were, of course, men who were very extreme, and who made bold statements, and almost everybody could see that they were wrong. They did not do the harm. They never do the harm. The obvious, open, arrogant heretic generally produces a reaction, and he is not the dangerous person.

The really dangerous man is the man who introduces some very slight or very subtle change. Now you will forgive me for giving an illustration out of the story of the church in the United Kingdom. It is, of course, the story with which I am most familiar, but the same thing could be demonstrated in the history of the church in America and other countries. There was a teacher in Scotland called A. B. Davidson. This is the kind of man who really did the harm. He was a professor in Old Testament and Hebrew, and he did the harm in this way. He was a very pious man, a very kindly man, and a very good man, with the result that most of his students did not realize that he was introducing a new element into his teaching as a result of accepting the Higher Criticism.

I remember a few years back noticing a thing which, if it had not been tragic, would have amused me very much. The centenary of the birth of this man, A. B. Davidson, was being celebrated, and I read two articles on him in the same week: one in a very liberal religious weekly, and the other in an evangelical religious weekly. They both praised him. The liberal paper praised him because he was the man who, above all others, had introduced the new 'scholarly view' of the

Old Testament, and had accepted the Wellhausen scheme and all the rest of it; so they praised him. But an evangelical writer was also praising him, and praising him for his devotional spirit and that he always started his theological lectures by praying. Now this is the sort of man who has generally done the greatest harm because, to all appearances, and if you looked simply on the surface, you could not see any change at all. It was the little things which he kept on introducing which were the real danger.

Now the great Charles Haddon Spurgeon saw all this, but when he began to denounce what he called the 'Downgrade' movement he was attacked ferociously by evangelical people. They said, What is the matter with Mr Spurgeon? He's become hypercritical; he's turning molehills into mountains; he's exaggerating! History has proved that he was not exaggerating. He saw these subtle changes. Others said of the men whose influence Spurgeon feared, They are still evangelical; they say this and they say that, but they are truly evangelical. They did not pay attention to some of the other things that these men were beginning to say, and therefore they missed the very subtle process which was insinuating itself into the life of the churches.

RECENT HISTORY AND CHANGES

I want to suggest that we are confronted today by this selfsame process and that even in the last ten years a very serious situation has arisen among evangelical people. My whole contention is that for us to assume that because we have once said that we are evangelical, therefore we must still be evangelical now and shall always be, is not only to misread the teaching of the New Testament, but to fail completely to grasp and to understand the great lessons which are taught us so clearly by history.

Let me further substantiate what I am saying. You have in America something which boasts the name of the 'new evangelicalism'; it is even announcing itself to you. A 'new evangelicalism' – it is no longer the old. There is a suggestion of some difference, whatever it may be. The people who belong to this school produce books, and it is my contention that these books show this very subtle change in the definition of what it means to be an evangelical. This change is not confined to America or to the term 'new evangelicalism'.

There are other particular instances I can give you. There was a great evangelical church in the United States called the Missouri Synod of the Lutheran Church. The Lutheran Church in the States is divided into a number of different bodies, but of all these divisions of Lutheranism, the *evangelical* body was the Missouri Synod. It was started in about 1860 by a German preacher and theologian by the name of Carl Walther. The Missouri Synod had stood throughout the years as a great bulwark of evangelicalism, but that is no longer true. Today, the Missouri Synod is in the midst of a serious conflict. It is divided more or less into two big groups. The subtle process has taken place, and they are in the throes of a great debate in an attempt to determine what is really evangelical and what is not.

Take another example from the United States. There is the denomination known as the Christian Reformed Church, with its headquarters in Grand Rapids in Michigan. Here again is a great denomination that has stood throughout the years as a defender of evangelicalism. They have a college and a seminary, Calvin College and Calvin Theological Seminary. They have Christian schools. They were once a body of evangelical people who stood united in the defence of the historic faith. But that is no longer true. The Christian Reformed Church is now divided right down the centre, and a debate is going on there, again in an attempt to determine what is evangelical. Can you introduce certain changes and still say that you are the same, that you are still evangelical? That is the question which lies behind the conflict there at this present time.

Then perhaps a still more striking illustration of the same thing is what is happening in Holland in connection with the Free University. You are familiar, I am sure, with something of the history of the Free University started by Abraham Kuyper in 1880. It was in order to defend the evangelical faith that he founded this university. Most of us here this morning who are over a certain age, and who are connected with the IFES, have throughout the years looked to the Free University for the defence of our evangelical position. But you can no longer do that. A change has come in the Free University of Amsterdam just as it has come in these bodies in the United States which I have mentioned. The Free University and its denomination are no longer where they were even ten years ago. Then they were outside the ecumenical movement and the World Council; now they are inside. And not only that. In the books and articles of Free University teachers there are plain and obvious demonstrations of a very subtle change, a change not only of emphasis but of belief with regard to certain vital and essential matters.

I am emphasizing the subtlety of the change. As it has always been in the past, so it is today. Some people are saying, But you're exaggerating; these men are still making great Christian affirmations; what right have you to say that they are changing? My answer is that these changes always happen in this subtle way; but let me add to that.

This kind of change has another characteristic and this again has been proved from New Testament times right down to this day. At the beginning the changes generally take place on the periphery and not at the centre. This, again, is a part of the subtlety of the process. You do not find men suddenly making different statements about certain central truths; the difference begins with something right on the outside. And because the change generally begins there, some people argue that there has been no change at all. They say, These men are all right on the great central matters. But no, although change may begin somewhere outside, on the circumference, *that* is the serious aspect of the matter, for this reason, that Christian truth is *one*. It is the glory of the Christian truth that it has many parts, but they are all interrelated. What the apostle Paul says about the church in 1 Corinthians 12, where he compares it to a body, is equally true with regard to the body or the corpus of the Christian faith. Every part belongs to every other part, and the result is that if you make what appears to be a minor change somewhere on the circumference it will soon have its effect even upon the centre. And again, as I have said, this is a principle that one could easily illustrate in the long history of the Christian church.

RE-EXAMINING OUR NAME

Here then are considerations which make it imperative for us to re-examine our whole position. So many of the men whom have undergone a great change in recent years, some of whom admit it openly, would still try to claim that they are truly evangelical. Therefore the problem is this: to define exactly what an evangelical is, and who exactly is evangelical.

I remember when we were beginning the IFES twenty-five, twenty-six years ago, that we were confronted by this same problem. We found that on the continent of Europe there was a tendency among some to regard anybody who was not a Roman Catholic as an evangelical. The use of the term evangelical was much broader, wider, and looser than it was in the case of Great Britain or America. There was a tendency to divide the religious situation into Roman Catholic and evangelical, and all who were not Catholic were automatically and inevitably evangelical. Now that is clearly much too broad a definition.

We must start by saying that the term evangelical is obviously a limiting term. I am not here this morning and on these subsequent mornings to discuss with you, What is a Christian? That is not what we are discussing. We are discussing, What is an evangelical? We, here in IFES, do not belong to a Christian body in that broad sense only. Of course we are Christian, but we claim to be evangelical Christians; that is what we are discussing together. There are individual Roman Catholics who are undoubtedly Christian. We are not discussing that.

Now if you use the term evangelical, obviously it has got some meaning. It is a limiting term. It is exclusive in certain respects. It puts certain things out, it emphasizes certain other things, and it is with this that I am concerned. I hope that this is quite clear. We are not simply defining the Christian in general, but we are defining the evangelical Christian, and we do that, of course, because we believe that ultimately the evangelical faith is the only true expression in doctrine of the Christian faith itself. You can be a Christian and yet defective in your doctrine, but our concern and our endeavour is to have the true doctrine presented in its fullness because we believe that it is only as this is believed and preached and propagated that men and women are going to be converted and added to the church. When the church has gone wrong in doctrine, she has ceased to be a converting influence. Here again is something that stands out very clearly in the long history of the church. That is why we should be so concerned about defining the meaning of this term evangelical and defending it even to our very 'latest breath'.

How, then, do we define the *evangelical* as distinct from the Christian in general? Here is the great question today, and I think you will find it to be the question you will have to face increasingly in these coming years. You are probably already having to do so in the various countries to which you belong. Where does one set the limits? Now as we come to this it seems to me there are two main dangers confronting us, and again I am saying this on the basis of the history of the past.

THE DANGER OF WRONG DIVISIONS

The first danger is to be too narrow, too rigid, and too detailed in definition. I call this a danger for the reason that it leads to what is called schism. What is schism? The best definition you will ever find of schism is in Paul's First Epistle to the Corinthians, especially in chapter 12 perhaps but it is also there in other places. Schism as it is defined by the great apostle is this: it is men and women who are agreed about the centralities of the faith disagreeing about things which are not essential; it is a tearing of the body. The only man who can be guilty of schism, therefore, is a man who believes the truth, the essential truth, but denies other things which are not essential.

Let me give you examples from the church at Corinth to illustrate what I mean. The church at Corinth was divided up into groups and factions. The church was guilty of schism. What were they dividing over? Let me remind you of some of the things which the apostle indicates. They were dividing up over their favourite preachers: some said, 'I am of Paul'; others said, 'I am of Apollos'; others said, 'I am of Cephas'. Here were people who were agreed about the centralities of the Christian faith, who were not only dividing but quarrelling over their favourite preachers and forming their groups, separating from one another over such matters as the excellences of the various leaders.

Another cause of division was the question of possession of intellect and of understanding. There were some more enlightened people there, and they could see that there was nothing wrong in eating meats which had been offered to idols. To them there was nothing wrong in it because the idol is imaginary; it has no being. Though meat has been offered to an idol in a temple, that obviously does nothing at all to the meat, because there is nothing there to taint it. That was their position, and they were eating this meat and justifying themselves in doing so. But then there were weaker brethren who could not see this. They were tied by tradition, by their background, and this practice was an offence to them, and they were dividing over it. They were agreed about the central verities and doctrines of the faith, but they were dividing up in terms of strong and weak brethren, more enlightenment and less enlightenment. This again is an example of schism.

The great illustration, of course, in the church at Corinth arises out of the question of the spiritual gifts. Now one and the same Spirit had given gifts to these various people. They were given to the body and Christians were all meant to be uplifted and edified as the result of the exercise of these gifts. But instead of the gifts being a cause of unity and of edification their abuse had become a cause of division and of schism. In this matter also the Corinthian Christians were acting independently and were jealous and envious of one another.

Now those are the ways in which the apostle shows us exactly what is meant by this term 'schism': people who were agreed about the centralities of the faith dividing and separating from one another over matters that were not essential to salvation, not absolutely vital. This is always one of the dangers afflicting us as evangelicals. We can be too rigid. There is this kind of fissile tendency which has manifested itself frequently in the long history of the Christian church. This has always been the great charge brought against Protestantism by Roman Catholicism, and there is an element of truth in it. Martin Luther, led by the Spirit of God, made this great move, and he caused a division. He separated; he went out; but the moment he did that, people began to separate from him. Soon there was the great division into Lutheran and Reformed, and then the Anabaptists in their various groups also came into being. The Roman Church said, That is it, the moment you leave us, this is what happens! And this has been a tendency among evangelicals.

I could give you some almost laughable illustrations of this. I hope I am not going to offend any national susceptibilities in what I am about to say, but the country that illustrates this particular point more clearly perhaps than any other is Scotland. There have been more divisions in the church in Scotland than in any other. They all tend to be Presbyterian, yet they are divided up into groups and denominations, and if you read their history, and particularly that of the eighteenth century, you will find differing groups which were known as the New Lights and the Old Lights, the Burghers and the Anti-burghers. Here were people who were agreed about the centralities of the faith, but they separated and formed separate churches over the question of whether or not you should take an oath to the borough to which you belonged.

Here I must tell you a rather amusing story vouched for as true. There was a minister in a certain church in Scotland, and he and his wife were very godly and very able people. But when the question of the burgher subscription came in, the husband and the wife took different sides and held different views. It is said that when this good man and his wife left the manse on the first Sunday morning after their difference they walked together as usual until they came to the building where the husband ministered; but this morning, as the minister turned to the right to go into the church, instead of his wife turning with him, she continued on the road. And as she continued walking, she called to him and said, 'You may still be my husband but you are no longer my minister.' So she proceeded to go and worship with the Anti-burghers! Such is one of the dangers by which we are confronted. We can be so rigid, so over-strict, and so narrow that we become guilty of schism.

Now, there have been divisions among the Baptists and among the people called Brethren. The Plymouth Brethren started out by saying that they did not believe in any denominations. They were all brethren, they were all loving, but look at the history of that body, look at the divisions among them – and these, not on central matters of the faith, but very frequently on matters which are far from being central. Similarly there have been endless divisions among Baptists, Methodists, and various other denominations. Think of the position in the United States. Look at the number of denominations. Look at the divisions that have taken place among men who have held to the same evangelical faith. They have divided on personalities; they have divided on subtle, particular emphases. I believe that this is something that is also very true today in South Africa and in other parts of Africa. There is a multiplicity of denominations, and men do not hesitate to set themselves up and to start denominations – not in terms of vital truth but in terms of matters which are not even secondary, but of third-rate, fourth-rate, even perhaps twentieth- or hundredth-rate importance!

This, then, is one great danger that we have to keep in our minds as we try to define what we mean by 'evangelical'.

SUCCUMBING TO THE ECUMENICAL SPIRIT

Then there is a second danger, and it is the exact opposite. It is the danger of being so broad, so wide, and so loose that in the end we have no definitions at all. As I see things today, this is perhaps the greater danger because we are living in what is called an ecumenical age. People have reacted, and rightly, against the divisions in the past, these wrong and sinful divisions. But the danger is that you react so violently that you swing right to the other extreme and say that nothing matters except that we have a Christian spirit.

I believe that this is the danger which is tending to threaten us as evangelical Christians at this present time. And I must give you what I see as some of the ways in which this ecumenical tendency, this wrong and false ecumenical tendency, is tending to show itself. Certainly we must all believe in unity. Our Lord has established that once and for ever in His great high priestly prayer (John 17). It is everywhere in the New Testament. Our great endeavour should be to be one, yet this must not lead to a looseness in our thinking. We must not become subject to a false, vague, nebulous, ecumenical type of thinking. There are certain factors which seem to me to be promoting this danger and threatening our whole position, and I must mention them.

I believe that one of the most potent factors in this respect has been the Billy Graham campaigns. Let me explain what I mean by that. He has believed in the widest possible sponsorship, and his motive has been a good one. He is anxious to evangelize, and that is right; but whether it is equally right to be sponsored by people who in reality deny your very message is another matter. This is what he has tended to do; he has brought together people who previously had practically nothing to do with one another. I have seen this in several countries, but I remember hearing it very strikingly after his visit to Scotland. I met people who said, You know, we've discovered from the campaign that these other people, the Church of Scotland people and others whom we did not know and with whom we had nothing to do in the past, we've discovered they're very nice people, and we've had a very happy time working with them. This was very subtle, because they found that they were nice people – whether they had thought before that these people had horns and long tails I do not know – but the point was that they had been impressed by their niceness, by their friendliness, and by their brotherliness. This has had the effect of making these people take the next step and say, Well, I wonder whether these doctrines we've been emphasizing are so important after all. Isn't the great thing about us that we are Christians, that we've got this loving spirit, and that we're prepared to work together? I believe that in a very subtle way the Graham and other campaigns have had this kind of influence and have been shaking people's convictions as to what exactly it means to be evangelical.

Another extraordinary way in which it is happening is one with which I am familiar in England. There is a very real danger at the present time that if a man denounces liberalism in any respect, he is regarded as an evangelical. There are some advantages, you know, in being old, and one of them is that you do know just a little bit about history. I am old enough to remember the beginning of the Barthian movement and events surrounding it. There was a great old professor in Scotland, Donald Maclean. He and another man started a journal known as *The Evangelical Quarterly*, which is still in circulation. This was a truly evangelical periodical which was started to defend the Christian faith against the modernism and liberalism which were rampant in the 1920s. I will never forget meeting Professor Donald Maclean. He was one of the first men who ever mentioned the name of Karl Barth to me, and he spoke of him in the most lyrical terms, giving me the impression that Karl Barth was one of the greatest evangelicals who had ever lived. Why did Maclean do this? Well, because of Barth's onslaughts on the old liberalism. You see the subtlety of the thing. Because Barth was so wonderful a critic of liberalism he was regarded as a true evangelical, something that he, of course, never was.

Let me give you another example. There is a man who is regarded as a very great Christian and one of the great defenders of evangelicalism in England today, a journalist by the name of Malcolm Muggeridge. He is being used by evangelicals in their conferences and in their campaigns. An evangelical evangelist was going to hold a campaign last September for a month in London and one of the key men of the whole of the campaign was to be this man Malcolm Muggeridge. Why? Well, because Malcolm Muggeridge is a very wonderful critic of the Church of England, makes fun of bishops and so on, and is a radical critic of the mere show and pretence of what is called the establishment. Not only that, he is a person who undoubtedly has changed his position from having been a man of the world and a cynic to being one who now says that what is needed is the spirit of Christ, and he claims to be a Christian. Having read his last book, which is called *Jesus Rediscovered*, I would not hesitate to say that Malcolm Muggeridge is not a Christian at all. He does not believe in the virgin birth, he does not believe in the miracles as facts, he does not believe in the atonement, he does not believe in the literal physical resurrection, he does not believe in the person of the Holy Spirit, he does not believe in prayer, yet he is being used in evangelical conferences and meetings. Why? Only because he has changed his general position and is now talking vaguely about Christ. The man has actually become a mystic and he imposes his mystical views upon the Christian faith. But evangelicals in this age of looseness are ready to lay hands suddenly upon any man who attacks the liberalism of the establishment and talks about Christ, without being careful to discover in detail what the man really believes.[2]

There have been many other examples of this. I find that C. S. Lewis has almost become the patron saint of evangelicals. He was never an evangelical and said so quite plainly himself. And I could give you many other illustrations and examples of the same thing.

Here then is a second factor which tends to produce this loose and vague idea, the ecumenical spirit that ultimately sells the pass and delivers us into a position in which we are no longer evangelical.

'THE HOLY SPIRIT, NOT DOCTRINE'

Then there is a third factor which to me is a very serious one at the present time, and that is what is known as the charismatic movement. I am sure that you are all familiar with this. This is a phenomenon that has been confronting us for the last fifteen years or so, and it is very remarkable. It began in America and it has spread to many countries, most countries probably by now. Why am I referring to the charismatic movement under this heading? Because this again is something that has tended to undermine an insistence upon careful definition of our terms, and it does it in this way.

The teaching of this movement is that nothing matters except 'the baptism of the Spirit'. Sometimes they may put it in terms of speaking in tongues, but at any rate they put it in general terms of 'the baptism of the Spirit'. Nothing matters but this! I could give you several examples of this thinking. I read a book by one of the leaders in the movement, David Du Plessis, in which he actually states that theology does not matter, that what matters is this experience. Now one can understand in a measure what he means by this. He may have set out to say that a dull, theoretical, intellectual orthodoxy is of no value, and that the Christian must have life. That is true, but when

[2]Muggeridge subsequently joined the Roman Catholic Church.

he goes so far as to say that nothing matters but this experience and that theology does not count at all, he is contradicting the statements and the teaching of the New Testament, and he is putting himself into a very dangerous position.

Have you read the little book called *Catholic Pentecostalism*? If you have, you will have discovered the same thing there. This is the thesis of the book. It is a very clever book, but a very subtle and dangerous one from our evangelical standpoint. This is the argument: they say, Here we are, people belonging to different religious and cultural backgrounds, but we are all one because we have all had the baptism of the Spirit, and we are all speaking in tongues. They say, *this* is the thing that really matters. The book does not go on to say that you may need to change your doctrine. Indeed the author actually argues to the contrary. He says that the danger in the past has been that when people have received this baptism of the Spirit and have started speaking in tongues, they have left their churches and have joined the Pentecostal Church. Now, he says, this is quite wrong. Let me quote the book: 'Most Pentecostalists historically have come from amongst the Methodists. The Methodists have generally been an emotional and an unintellectual people.' And the result is that when they get this 'baptism of the Spirit', they manifest it and show it by a lot of hyper-emotionalism and excitement, and so on. Now that, he says, is all right, that is their cultural background; the Spirit comes to them in that cultural medium. But we are Catholics, Roman Catholics; we have got a great body of dogma and of doctrine; we have got our great history, our sacramental teaching, and our sacramental life. When we receive 'the baptism of the Spirit' we must not give up and shed all we have got, join the Pentecostals and simply take over their cultural background. That is quite unnecessary. We receive 'the baptism of the Spirit' in our cultural milieu, and the effect that it should have upon us is not to make us shed our doctrines and become Pentecostals. It should give us a deeper understanding and appreciation of our great heritage. Thus you find that these Roman Catholics, who claim to have had 'the baptism of the Spirit', all go on to testify that the main effect of their 'baptism of the Spirit' has been to increase their intimate knowledge and communion with the virgin Mary. It has deepened their appreciation of the mass and all the other various Roman Catholic doctrines and dogma.

Now you can see the effect of all this. In the end it means that

doctrine does not matter at all. You can believe Roman Catholic
doctrine, or be Methodist, or be without any doctrine at all if you
like; it does not matter. The great thing is that you have this
experience. And so they have their conferences and their congresses
in which they all meet together, and they are virtually proclaiming
that doctrine does not matter at all. Now this, you see, undermines
the importance of arriving at definitions and descriptions of the faith.
As this is coming into evangelical circles, and has come, it threatens
our whole position as evangelical Christians and shows us the
desperate urgency of re-examining the position again and knowing
exactly what we mean.

Then, to speak of England in particular, there has been a great
change in the position of the evangelicals in connection with the
Anglican Church. Now this is not a value judgment of mine on them;
this is what they have said themselves. They had a conference in
Keele in 1967 and produced a report, which you can read for
yourselves. They condemned their own past; they condemned
themselves for not taking a more active part in the Church of
England. They condemned themselves for not being in the ecumenical movement and working actively in it, and they said this has been
wrong and they have changed their policy. So now you find
evangelical Anglicans taking an active part in the ecumenical
movement, and they are as concerned as anybody else about church
union with bodies that are not at all evangelical.

Here then is another factor which has tended to undermine the old
understanding of the meaning of the word evangelical and has
undermined our confidence in what has been said in the past.

Non-evangelical Opposition to Ecumenicism

The last factor that I must mention to you is this: there are various
denominations and church groupings that are opposed to the
ecumenical movement but not on evangelical grounds. For instance,
there are a number of men who are opposed to the ecumenical
movement because the ecumenical movement postulates bishops as
being essential to the united church. They know that in order to have
a world church there must be an acceptance of bishops and a
hierarchy; that is agreed by everybody. So there are now a number in
all the denominations who on political and general ecclesiastical
grounds say, We will never submit to bishops. They are therefore

outside the ecumenical movement. And here is the problem: we are also outside the ecumenical movement. So they have tended to come to us and say that we are all one: we are not in this world church; we are out together in the wilderness, so do we not all belong together? We have had approaches from these people. As a matter of fact I had a personal experience of this which was quite amusing. A little book of mine was published and, to my amazement, it was reviewed by a well-known professor belonging to one of the English denominations. He praised my book to the skies; I could scarcely believe it. I thought that either he or I had gone mad, or perhaps both of us. However, the explanation of the favourable review was this: this man is anti-ecumenical because he does not believe in bishops, and so being now predisposed in my favour he picked up everything he could to praise in my book and said nothing about the rest. Here, you see, is a very subtle danger, the danger of our coming together to fight the ecumenical movement, but we must not do so. Why? Because these men are not evangelical. They are liberal. It is another reminder that we must be careful that we define our position carefully.

I close then, for the moment, by saying this. What has been said of the church in the past is true today. The church, though she has been reformed, must be constantly re-formed, *semper reformanda*. Always reform! The church is always to be under the Word; she must be; we must keep her there. You must not assume that because the church started correctly, she will continue so. She did not do so in the New Testament times; she has not done so since. Without being constantly reformed by the Word the church becomes something very different. We must always keep the church under the Word, and we must keep a movement like the IFES under the Word. *Semper reformanda*! And we have got to do this with the term evangelical. Every generation has got to examine this for itself. You cannot receive these things by tradition alone. This has always been the danger. People have said, I've been brought up as an evangelical; I am an evangelical. Are you? We have got to ask ourselves the question, and we must not be satisfied merely with definitions drawn up in the past because every age has had its own particular problems, and all the great confessions and creeds were generally drawn up to face some particular problem or situation. So it behoves us in our day and generation to examine this term evangelical anew and afresh in the light of the Scripture and of history, and especially in the light of the dangerous tendencies that surround us at this present time.

With this general introduction I leave our subject this morning. I hope to continue tomorrow and to put before you certain guiding principles which will enable us to arrive at an answer to the question, What is an evangelical in our day and generation? Let us pray:

O Lord our God, we come to thee again and we thank thee that we are found among thy people. We know that it is all of thy grace, that left to ourselves we would not only be out in the world but in the depth of sin and of iniquity. We thank thee that we are what we are by thy grace, and we thank thee that thou hast given us an interest in these things and a concern about them. O God, we are amazed that thou hast ever looked on us, and in a measure made us guardians and custodians of the faith. We pray thee, O Lord, to give us great wisdom and understanding, to give us great circumspection to enable us to walk carefully, for the times and the days are evil. Wilt thou continue therefore to look upon this conference and to brood upon it with thy Spirit, guiding every aspect of this work, and leading us all together to submit ourselves to thy most holy Word and its divine instruction. Bless us, we pray thee, to that end and continue with us throughout the day. We ask it in the name of thy dear Son, our blessed Lord and Saviour, and the great Lord of the church, Jesus Christ. Amen.

II

In yesterday's lecture, I was suggesting that we are in the same position as that in which Jude found himself. He had intended to give an exposition of the Christian faith in a broad and general manner, but owing to certain circumstances which had arisen, he had to abandon that and, instead, had to exhort these people to contend earnestly for the faith, once and for ever delivered to the saints.

My theme is that we are in a similar position today, and that it behoves us to examine the situation in which we now find ourselves and to make sure that we are clear in our minds as to what is meant by being an evangelical. We are not discussing, What is a Christian? but we are discussing, What is an evangelical? It is a limiting term, and I argued that we are in such a subtle situation that it is no longer sufficient that we subscribe to some general basis of faith. That is no longer enough; we have got to be more particular, because these changes, when they come in, though they generally insinuate themselves on the periphery of the faith, gradually spread further and further towards the centre.

We are familiar with the fact, and it is not something new, that people are prepared to subscribe to bases of faith or to creeds and, at the same time, make what we call mental reservations. This, in the end, means that they deny some of the most essential articles of these bases. This, again, makes it necessary for us to be particular and careful.

At the same time let us remember that we are not merely to define what is bare orthodoxy. You can have a dead orthodoxy. I am concerned to define the evangelical in a way which goes beyond statements of belief. It is as important to define the evangelical as being against a kind of Protestantism or even reformed scholasticism, as it is that we should define the evangelical by contrast with those who are heterodox in their doctrine and their belief.

GUIDING PRINCIPLES: (1) THE PRESERVATION OF THE GOSPEL

Let it also be understood that our object in this discussion should not be merely the preservation of a tradition. Traditions may be good, but when they become traditionalism, they are bad. We should not be concerned primarily with merely maintaining some recognized position or continuing in some particular tradition. That is not our object. Still less should we be concerned simply to be polemical or to have argument for the sake of argument.

Neither are we to be concerned for separation as such; indeed I would go further and say that our object should be, not to exclude people, but to include as many as possible, and yet to be careful that we are maintaining our principles and our landmarks.

I said yesterday, and repeat it again today, that the evangelical Christian should be very concerned about unity. He, of all men, should be concerned about the unity of the Spirit of truth and of peace, for this is part of his whole attitude and his whole outlook.

So our real reason for definition, and contending for this faith, is that we believe it to be vital to the preservation of the true gospel. That is why I am so concerned about bearing the historical element in our minds. History shows very clearly that when this emphasis is lost, the true gospel becomes lost sooner or later, and preaching also is lost and in vain, so that the church ceases to evangelize and to gain converts and adherents.

That then is our object. We are not concerned merely to be polemical, as I said, but our intent is a very practical one. We are concerned about the souls of men and women. We are here to spread the good news of salvation and to win people out of darkness into light. That is why we should be so careful about the truth, and always contend for it.

What, then, is to be our method in defining what an evangelical is? The method, of course, is primarily biblical. The great slogan of the Reformation, *sola scriptura*, has always been the slogan of the true evangelical. The evangelical starts with the Bible. He is a man of the Bible. He is a man of the Book. This is his only authority and he submits himself in everything to this. We will open this out later but we must assert it at the outset. This, you see, is already a differentiating point. Others start with philosophy, and with a more general principle, but the evangelical starts always with the Bible.

GUIDING PRINCIPLES: (2) LEARNING FROM HISTORY

Secondly, with reference to method, I am again concerned to emphasize that, at the same time, we must be historical in our approach. I know that it is very difficult for many modern people to realize this, but we are not the first people to have lived in this world. That needs to be said very frequently at the present time. There have been great generations of people and of Christians before us. Though we have split the atom, we are not very different from those who have lived in previous ages, so it is important that we should be guided by history. A man who has no respect for history is a fool, and he will soon discover that, when he finds himself repeating the errors of those who have gone before him.

We are concerned about history. At the same time we must not be bound by it; we must not be slaves to it. These are always the dangers that afflict us. Some people dismiss the whole of history. They are going to have everything new and start everything afresh. We have a world of movements. There are people in the universities at the present time who are more or less suggesting that you scrap the whole of the past, that you start anew and afresh in politics, in social and economic affairs, and in everything else. This same attitude tends to come into the religious realm, but we must exclude it.

At the same time is is equally important that we must recognize that nothing in this world has ever been complete, that while we thank God for the great events of the past, the great Reformation and other minor reformations, we must not be slaves to them. That is the way to develop a kind of scholasticism and an arid intellectualism.

So we pay respect to history, and we are prepared to learn from it, but we are not totally subservient to it in a wrong sense. That is the second guiding principle.

GUIDING PRINCIPLES: (3) MAINTAINING NEGATIVES

The third is the importance of the place of negatives as well as positives. Now here, to me, is a tremendously important matter, and I am not sure that this is not going to be the most vital point in the dispute between evangelicals who are adhering to the old position and those who are tending to depart from it at the present time.

One of the first signs that a man is ceasing to be truly evangelical is that he ceases to be concerned about negatives, and keeps saying, We must always be positive. I will give you a striking example of this in a man whose name is familiar to most of you, and some of whose books you have read. This is what he has written recently: 'Whether a person is an evangelical is to be settled by reference to how he stands with respect to six points', which he then enumerates. His definition is by reference only to what a person is *for* rather than to what he is *against*. He goes on: 'What a man is, or is not, against may show him to be a muddled or negligent or inconsistent evangelical, but you may not deny his right to call himself an evangelical while he maintains these principles as the basis of his Christian position.'

Now that is the kind of statement which I would strongly contend against. I believe it is quite wrong. The argument which says that you must always be positive, that you must not define the man in terms of what he is against, as well as what he is for, misses the subtlety of the danger. If that argument is left uncontested the door is open to a repetition of such things as the Galatian heresy. You remember the Galatians and how the apostle has to deal with their heresy. It was the whole problem of Judaism, which emerges in several places in the New Testament. What was the Galatian heresy? Well, it stated that those people who had led the Galatians astray had not denied the gospel; they were not denying anything; what they were doing was to *add* something, namely circumcision, which, they said, was essential.

Oh yes, they said, you've got to believe the gospel, all these positives are quite right. But then they brought in their addition. So it is important, you see, that the evangelical should also have his negative criticisms and be ready to say that you must *not* believe this and you must *not* do that.

History is helpful at this point also, and I will take an example that is most obvious to me. You have heard of Puritanism. Puritanism was in England in the sixteenth century almost immediately after the Protestant Reformation. Puritanism was a section of Protestantism. The Reformation had come to England and the church had become Protestant. Who were these Puritans? They were men who said that the Reformation had not proceeded far enough, that it had done its good work in connection with doctrine, but it had ceased to do it in connection with practice. They argued that this was inconsistent, that some practices, still allowed, were denials of the changed doctrine, and they wanted the Reformation to be carried through in the matter of practice as well as of doctrine.

The Puritans and the others in the Church of England were all agreed about the doctrine; the difference came in with regard to the negatives, and that is why these negatives are always of such great importance. So we shall have to be careful to maintain this observation on the place of negatives in our definition of evangelical.

GUIDING PRINCIPLES: (4) NO SUBTRACTIONS OR ADDITIONS

A fourth general principle is this: that we must be very observant of people's *subtractions* from the truth on the one hand, and of their *additions* to the truth on the other.

I have discovered over the years that subtraction from the truth is something that members of churches are very, very slow to observe. I have almost come to the conclusion that the acid test to apply, to know whether a preacher is evangelical or not, is this: observe what he does not say! So often I have found that people have listened to a man and been carried away by him, and thought everything was wonderful, for the reason that he said nothing wrong, and they were quite right in their observation. The man had said nothing wrong, but the point was that he had not said certain things that an evangelical always must say; he had left them out.

I knew a minister who once went to listen to an American professor of theology called Nels Ferré. This minister was an evangelical but not a very well-instructed one. He listened to Nels Ferré and was completely carried away by him. He went back to his church and reported in lyrical terms on this marvellous address. What had happened? Well, what had happened was that Nels Ferré in that particular atmosphere had not said everything that he believed. All he had said then was perfectly right. He had not said anything specifically evangelical, neither had he, on that occasion, said anything of the heterodox thinking of which he was guilty.

There is no doubt that this question of subtracting from the truth, or leaving out part of the message is a very vital one at the present time. You hear people talking about the Bible, and they can talk about the cross, but it is important to notice what they do *not* say about them. The fact that they mention them is insufficient. You must be careful in your observation of what a man does not say, as well as what he does.

Then, on the other hand, you have got to be careful about additions. I have already referred to them in dealing with the importance of negatives. Only recently I came across a striking example of this point. There is a certain bishop in England who is well known as an extreme Anglo-Catholic. He has recently become one of the chaplains of a certain shrine, the Shrine of our Lady of Walsingham in England. Although this man is now an extreme Anglo-Catholic, in his student days he was a thorough evangelical. As he was talking to a friend of mine who is an evangelical, he said: 'You know, I haven't ceased to believe anything I believed as a student. What I have done is to add on.'

Now many of us have said throughout the years that in some respects we have found ourselves nearer to the Roman Catholics than to the liberals because the Roman Catholics, after all, believe in the being of God, the deity of Christ, the virgin birth, the two natures of Christ in one person, the miracles, the atonement, the literal, physical resurrection, and the person of the Holy Spirit. On these truths we have always found ourselves in closer agreement; and sometimes we have found that by reading books by certain Roman Catholic authors our faith was strengthened because they believe what we believe, whereas the liberals and the modernists deny all this. I say this to illustrate the same point, that the trouble with the Roman Catholic is what he adds on and what he adds to or subtracts from what is stated in his belief.

So we must be careful, and remember the warning in the book of Revelation, where we are told we must not add to, or take from, anything that is written in that particular book, and the command belongs equally to all the other books of the Bible. We have got to keep our eye on these two sides: what men do not say, and what they add on, over and above what we regard as the true faith.

These are the general principles to guide us in our definition of what constitutes an evangelical, and I trust that I have already made it plain that this approach is essential because of the subtlety of the situation in which we find ourselves. If you merely take here the short list of desiderata and then ask an individual if he can accept them, and sign his name to the basis of faith, he may mislead you and mislead himself, because you have not asked him certain further questions. You have not observed what he has not said, or you have not discovered what he adds on to what you have in your basis of faith.

Using these guiding principles, let us then try to approach a definition of an evangelical. All I want to do at this point is to deal with his *general characteristics*. This is something we have not been doing so far, but I believe that the general characteristics of the evangelical are almost as important as the particular doctrines to which he subscribes. There is a kind of ethos which to me is of very great importance. I am coming increasingly to the opinion that the way in which a man thinks tells you as much about him as what he actually says. His whole method of thinking is one which is of supreme importance. So I would call attention here to certain general characteristics of the evangelical person.

EVANGELICAL PRIORITIES

First of all, the evangelical is one who is entirely subservient to the Bible. John Wesley said that he had become 'a man of one book'. This is true of every evangelical. He is a man of one book; he starts with it; he submits himself to it; this is his authority. He does not start from any extra-biblical authority. He confines himself and submits himself completely to the teaching of the Bible. I shall, of course, deal more fully with this when we come to details; I am now simply giving you the general characteristics.

The next thing about the evangelical is that he uses this term as a *prefix* and not as a suffix. Here again, I think this is something that is going to be increasingly important in the years to come. What I mean by that is that the *first* thing about the man is that he is evangelical. The particular denomination to which he belongs is secondary; it is not primary. In other words, there is all the difference in the world between talking about an evangelical Baptist and a Baptist evangelical. I am contending that our man is evangelical first. He may be a Baptist, he may be a Presbyterian, he may be Episcopalian, but he is primarily, first and foremost, evangelical.

Let me give you one illustration. There was a great controversy in England a few years ago as a result of the conference at Keele to which I referred yesterday. One man, who had been an archbishop in Australia, wrote a letter to the press in which he said that he was very willing to admit that he was an Anglican before being evangelical. His first, his fundamental, his ultimate loyalty was to Anglicanism, not to evangelicalism. He said, 'I am an evangelical, but I am an Anglican first.' I contend that when a man says that, he has already said something that makes him suspect as an evangelical. Evangelical first! Any other difference is something that should follow.

WATCHFULNESS

Another characteristic of this evangelical is that he is a man who is *always watching*. Now all these things have to be said very carefully because there is a right and a wrong way to watch, but the evangelical is a man who is always watchful, and he is always watchful, of course, because the Scripture teaches him to be so.

'Watch and pray', says our Lord, and the apostle Paul, bidding farewell to the elders of the church at Ephesus, told them to do exactly the same thing. He warns them concerning the time following his departure: 'Take heed therefore unto yourselves, and to all the flock, over the which the Holy Ghost hath made you overseers, to feed the church of God. . . . For I know this, that after my departing shall grievous wolves enter in among you, not sparing the flock' (Acts 20:28–29). So he exhorts them to be watchful.

Or again, take 1 Corinthians 16 where there is a striking statement of this same lesson to be found. The apostle, having gone through the great series of controversial matters which was tearing asunder the life of the church at Corinth, winds it up by saying: 'Watch ye, stand fast in the faith, quit you like men, be strong. Let all your things be done with charity' (1 Cor. 16:13–14). It is an exhortation to watch, to be careful. As Christians we are always in the midst of foes, 'For we wrestle not against flesh and blood, but against principalities and powers, against the rulers of the darkness of this world, against spiritual wickedness in high [or, heavenly] places' (Eph. 6:12).

The New Testament gives many examples of this. Paul in his exhortations to Timothy is constantly making the same point. He says in 1 Timothy 6:3–4: 'If any man teach otherwise, and consent not to wholesome words, even the words of our Lord Jesus Christ, and to the doctrine which is according to godliness; he is proud, knowing nothing, but doting about questions and strifes of words', and so on. The New Testament indeed is full of these exhortations to us, to watch and to be careful.

John comforts the Christians, confronted as they were, even then, by antichrists and false teachers, that they 'have an unction from the Holy One' (1 John 2:20) and that they are to exercise this. They are to be discriminating; they are always to be examining; they are always to be watchful. And so when a man ceases to be watchful, he, to that extent, ceases to be an evangelical. The person who says, It is all right; you need not bother; we are all Christians and having a marvellous time together – and is not watchful, is already departing from the biblical position.

DISTRUST OF REASON

Then I come to another characteristic. This may very well be a highly controversial one, but in my estimate it is extremely important. It is, and I put it dogmatically and bluntly, that the evangelical *distrusts reason and particularly reason in the form of philosophy*. If you take a bird's-eye view of the history of the Christian church, this emerges very clearly indeed, and of course, the more you read of it in detail, the clearer it becomes. Every reformation has always expressed a distrust of reason and of philosophy. One of the earliest examples of this is to be found in Tertullian, one of the first great theologians of the Western church. He put it in a very striking form: 'What has Jerusalem to do with Athens? What has the temple to do with the porch and the academy?' He had, as you know, joined the Montanists, who were in rebellion against the tendencies to become subservient to Greek philosophy, that had come into the church.

I suggest to you that nothing is more important in our present situation than just this one particular point. Philosophy has always been the cause of the church going astray, for philosophy means, ultimately, a trusting to human reason and human understanding. The philosopher wants to encompass all truth; he wants to categorize and explain everything, and that is why there are no more important passages in the Scripture for us at the present time than the First Epistle to the Corinthians, starting in chapter 1, at verse 17, and going right the way through to the end of chapter 4, with especial reference to chapter 2. The apostle's whole contention in those chapters is that things were going wrong in Corinth because they were beginning to bring back faith in human wisdom, philosophy; and his point is to show that this is diametrically opposed to the preaching of the gospel. He says he has become a fool for Christ's sake: 'If any man among you seemeth to be wise in this world, let him become a fool, that he may be wise' (1 Cor. 3:18). Here 'a fool' means that you do not trust to philosophy and to human wisdom. This is really a most important matter.

Martin Luther used to refer to 'that old witch, Lady Reason', and those of you who are familiar with his writings know how he constantly emphasized this point, that reason is an old witch. He was concerned about this, of course, because it was of the essence of his argument against Rome. It is true still that the trouble with Roman Catholicism is that they *say* that they believe the Bible. Let us grant that they do, and that they are quite sincere in saying that, but what, then, is the trouble? The trouble is that they have *added* Aristotelian philosophy on to their belief in the Bible, and that ultimately they are interpreting the Bible in terms of Aristotelian philosophy. That is the great characteristic of the *Summa* of Thomas Aquinas, and it was as the result of this that the evangel, the true gospel, had become entirely hidden. So it is not surprising that Luther should have contended so strongly against this very matter, and this is not, by any means, confined to Luther either.

I mentioned just now the Puritans in England, and they are a very good illustration of this same point. The great controversy between the Puritans and the Church of England was very largely an argument over the place of reason. There was a man called Richard Hooker, who, in many ways, determined what is called Anglicanism. Hooker introduced the term 'natural reason', and natural reason can determine how you govern your church and do many other things. This was the very essence of the argument between the Puritans, who were the true evangelicals, and these others in the

Church of England, who, although they were Protestant, were not evangelical. It concerned this very matter of the place of reason.

We have got to be clear about what we mean by this because my statements can very easily be misunderstood. I base it all, as I said, on the teaching of 1 Corinthians 2 where Paul says: 'Now we have received, not the spirit of the world, but the spirit which is of God; that we might know the things that are freely given to us of God. . . . But the natural man receiveth not the things of the Spirit of God: for they are foolishness unto him: neither can he know them, because they are spiritually discerned' (verses 12, 14). These are things which are revealed to us and which the Spirit alone can enable us to receive. 'He that is spiritual judgeth all things, yet he himself is judged of no man' (verse 15). I am also thinking of the words of our Lord as quoted in Matthew 11:25–26: 'I thank thee, O Father, Lord of heaven and earth, because thou hast hid these things from the wise and prudent, and hast revealed them unto babes. Even so, Father: for so it seemed good in thy sight.'

Such is the basis for the evangelical's distrust of human reason, and, as I say, trace the history of the church and you will find that a failure to recognize danger in this area has been the problem all along. You see, when the apostles died, the whole question of authority arose in the church. Not only that, the church was being persecuted, and in the second century there arose a number of men in the church called apologists, some of whom had been trained as Greek philosophers. They were concerned to show that there was no contradiction between the gospel and Greek philosophy. Their motive no doubt was a very good one, but I suggest to you that in doing this they compromised the gospel, they turned it into a philosophy, and they lost something vital in the realm of the Spirit. The church eventually became institutionalized and this led to the Roman Catholicism of the Middle Ages, the period prior to the Protestant Reformation.

This tendency has kept on recurring, and that is why I think it is so important for us, because I believe it is happening again now. Let me state it still more bluntly by putting it to you like this, that the true evangelical is not only distrustful of reason, but he is also distrustful of scholarship. Here we are, belonging to IFES, students and members of universities, and I am saying that the evangelical is distrustful of scholarship, and I maintain that! What do I mean? Let me try to make it plain. The evangelical starts from the Scriptures.

He also reads the history of the church, and there he finds that the history proves what has been emphasized in the Scripture, that when men trust to reason and to understanding they go astray. He also finds that the men whom God has had to raise up and to use to call back people to the faith have often been very simple men. Not always, of course – I mentioned Luther and others, and I could have mentioned Calvin – but so often this has happened, that the revival in the church and the calling back of the people to the true faith has been done through the medium of someone quite unknown.

The sum of all I am saying is that the evangelical distrusts scholarship and is watchful of it. That does not mean that he is anti-intellectual; it does not mean that he becomes obscurantist; but it does mean that he keeps reason and scholarship in their place. They are *servants* and not masters.

THE PLACE OF REASON

What then is the place of reason in our faith and in our Christian life? I would define it like this. Reason must never determine *what* we believe. The business of reason is to teach us *how* to believe. It is an instrument, and the trouble arises always when people allow reason to determine what they believe. In other words, instead of submitting themselves to the Scripture, they turn to science, to philosophy, or to one of a number of other disciplines, and their position is determined by these things. They allow reason to determine what they believe instead of how they believe and how they think. Not *what* you think, but *how* you think, that is the place of reason, and I would say exactly the same thing about scholarship.

Now I am old enough to remember a generation of evangelicals who would have nothing at all to do with scholarship. Their attitude was, 'Scholarship is a menace and a danger; have nothing to do with it!' I knew men who were old when I was comparatively young who used to advise students for the ministry not to study theology. I recall one well-known evangelical leader who always used to tell such men, 'Whatever else you study at Oxford or Cambridge, don't study theology or you'll lose your faith.' That is something which I do not commend. I would condemn that attitude. That is the spirit of fear, and it leads to an obscurantism where you bury your head in the sand, and you are not aware of what is happening.

My contention is that the evangelical, while he realizes the danger of reason and scholarship, is not afraid of them. He does not run and hide, and just turn in on himself and the enjoyment of his own feelings. No, he is aware of scholarship, he meets it on its own level, but he does not submit himself to it. He does not go down on his knees because some man is a great scholar. He knows that the great scholar, even the great scholar in the Bible, may be an unbeliever, so he does not worship the scholar. It is when men begin to bow the knee to scholarship, submit themselves to it, almost worship it, and to regard it as the ultimate authority, that I suggest they have sold the pass and ceased to be truly evangelical.

The evangelical is not a bit afraid of scholarship. There is no need for us to be afraid of scholars if they are not Christians because they base their position on reason, and it is a simple matter to debate with them because they do not know the Scriptures. You can easily show them that what they have been saying they have spun out of their own minds. It is human reason, speculation, and philosophy, and not the true Christian teaching. The big principle that I would lay down is this, that in the attitude of the evangelical to reason and scholarship he is fully aware of the danger for he sees it so clearly in the Scripture. Paul becomes 'a fool', laughed at by the philosophers. They regarded his teaching as utter foolishness. This has always happened to the true Christian; it happens today. It is not surprising that the so-called great philosophers are sceptics and infidels. We should expect them to be, and we should not be frightened because they are. We should not apologize for the faith because they are not Christian. Rather we should see that this is a proof of the teaching of the Scripture; and we remember that when the church has gone down into the trough, in her deadest periods, it has invariably been when she has become subservient to philosophy.

Coming to more recent times, and to our own times, is it not a simple fact to say that the real damage to the life of the church in the last two centuries has been done mainly by theological seminaries? Is not that where the trouble has arisen? It has not arisen in the churches. It has arisen in the theological seminaries. Men who have felt called to the ministry and been recommended by churches for ministerial training have gone into the seminaries as evangelicals and true evangelists, and they have come out denying everything, sometimes even departing from the faith altogether. If that has not happened, they have come out dead, trying to be scholars and having lost the edge of their zeal and their enthusiasm. They are no longer truly presenting the truth. These are sheer facts.

Therefore, if an evangelical is not distrustful of reason and of scholarship, he is not only failing to understand the teaching of the Scripture; he is blind to this clear testimony of the history of the Christian church throughout the centuries. Why I am elaborating and emphasizing this is because the movements to which I referred yesterday, the 'new evangelicalism', and so on, are concerned with scholarship, in my opinion, in the wrong sense. This is a part of evangelicalism's inferiority complex. We want to be considered intellectual and respectable, and in doing that we are in grave danger of submitting ourselves to philosophy, to reason, and to scholarship, and it will lead to the same result with us as it has in the case of those who have gone before us.

OTHER MARKS OF AN EVANGELICAL

The next thing about the evangelical is that he *takes a particular view with regard to the sacraments*. I am not going to open this out this morning; I am hoping to do so tomorrow. The evangelical, speaking broadly, always takes a 'low' view of the sacraments. He recognizes only two, of course, like other Protestants, but his view of these often differentiates him, and generally does differentiate him, from those who are not evangelical.

The next point which I would make is that the evangelical *takes a critical view of history and tradition*. I have already emphasized that he pays attention to it, and great attention, and yet he is critical. The evangelical position, you see, is really always on a knife-edge. You have the two sides, two dangers, and the evangelical is here on this knife-edge between them. Let me put it in these terms: the evangelical emphasizes the principle of discontinuity rather than of continuity. Roman Catholicism obviously emphasizes the principle of continuity, tradition. So do most of the major denominations. I know it would be very interesting if I began examining you one by one this morning, and asked you why you belong to the denomination to which you belong. You would find almost invariably that it is an accident, that you did not decide it for yourself. Some of you have, perhaps, but not the majority. Most people are Baptists, Presbyterians, Methodists, whatever they are, simply because their parents were. They have been brought up in it. They are governed entirely by tradition. And you will find good people who, the moment you suggest that there is anything wrong with their denomination, can flare up, lose their tempers, and defend it to the last ditch, though they really know very little about it. Why? Because they are tied by this principle of tradition. And the idea of leaving their denomination is, to them, the greatest of all sins!

Now this is not evangelical. The evangelical believes in the principle of discontinuity. Looking at the history of the church, he sees how the church, which was a live, spiritual body, always tended to become hardened and fossilized into a dead institution. He realizes that this is the greatest danger, so, far from being afraid of the principle of discontinuity, he knows that he can only understand the true history of the living church in terms of discontinuity, the breaks that have taken place before the Reformation, and particularly at the Reformation, and since the Reformation.

In the same way, I could illustrate freely from the teaching of the Protestant fathers and others, that the evangelical is not tied by the decisions of early councils in the church. He does not slavishly fall down before them. He examines them, he examines everything in the light of the Scriptures, even the great pronouncements of the councils and everything else.

This leads me to the next thing, which is that an evangelical is a man who is *always ready to act on his beliefs*. I would say that this is a very striking characteristic of the evangelical. There are other people who are prepared to argue and discuss and even change their opinion, but they do not do anything about it. The evangelical, however, is a man who acts on his convictions. There would never have been Protestantism if this were not true.

Luther acted on what he came to see from the Scriptures, so did Calvin and Knox: all these men have done the same. And this, to me, is a very vital thing about the evangelical. He is not a theorist, he is not a theoretician; he is a living soul, he is a man who has got the Spirit in him, and he wants to act on what he believes. He is not afraid to change, and, of course, as I have already shown, it is because of this principle that *his* danger is to become guilty of schism. For, while I say that he distrusts reason, he does have a faculty of reason, and he uses it; he studies the Scriptures; he discovers the doctrine and he can judge that it is true and can see that the people with whom he is connected do not believe it. He says, I cannot go on like this, I am compromising my doctrine; I have got to act on the truth. That is the evangelical. But, as I say, his danger is to overdo this and to become guilty of schism. Nevertheless, he is a man who is ready to change and ready to act on his belief, and this is something that differentiates him from people who are not evangelical.

Let me come to the next principle which is this, *the evangelical is a man who always simplifies everything.* Everything becomes simple. This is a great characteristic of the evangelical. Contrast what the evangelical believes with all that a Roman Catholic is asked to believe, and you will see how the Reformation simplified belief. The reformers started with what they called the 'perspicuity', the clarity, of the Scriptures. Rome had made faith difficult and involved, as the Pharisees had made the Jewish law involved with their glosses upon it and their multitude of explanations. Religion became a great mass of instruction with authorities which had to be quoted to show your learning.

The effect of becoming evangelical is always to simplify and to make things clear. The evangelical is a clear thinker. The Catholic is never a clear thinker; he is involved, he is difficult, he is subtle. You find great trouble in following him because of his involved method of argumentation. Philosophy is difficult, but the gospel, by contrast, is essentially simple.

The gospel not only simplifies belief and the statement of beliefs; it always simplifies our view of church order and church government. This is an essential evangelical characteristic. The Roman Catholic line of thinking always has its hierarchies. Church government is always involved. The more evangelical a man is, the simpler will be his church order and his idea of church government.

The same applies to his idea of worship. Evangelical worship is always simple by contrast with other forms. The evangelical does not believe in vestments, putting on copes and mitres and changing vestments for different parts of the service. He does not believe in ceremonies and liturgies and processions. He dislikes formalism. He believes in freedom, the freedom of the Spirit. This is the essential characteristic. When the Spirit is lost, and the man ceases to be evangelical, you will find that he will always elaborate his service, he will bring in additions to his appearance, his clothing, and to what he does.

Formalism is the characteristic of the non-evangelical; freedom is the characteristic of the evangelical.

Indeed, this principle of simplicity is one that I could show you very clearly from the history of the church, even with respect to buildings. The church buildings of the evangelical are always simple, whereas those of the Catholics tend to be ornate and elaborate. This principle of simplification is one that emerges in the total life of the evangelical.

The next point which I hurry on to is that the evangelical is *always concerned about the doctrine of the church*. Now I am in some difficulty at this point because it has always been my criticism of the IVF in Britain and every similar movement in other parts of the world, that we have not paid sufficient attention to the doctrine of the church, and to that extent we have not been as evangelical as we should be. The evangelical throughout the centuries has been very concerned about the doctrine of the church. That is usually why he has left different sections of the church, or different bodies, or denominations. He is concerned about a pure church. His idea of the church is that it consists of the gathered saints. He does not believe in a state church. He is vitally concerned about his correct view of the nature of the Christian church. One can see very clearly in the history of the church that the great fight throughout the centuries has been the fight between institutionalism and a living body of believing people. The doctrine of the church, then, is a very vital one. I am sorry but I cannot digress further on this matter now. I merely bring it to your attention for the time being.

UPPERMOST CONCERNS

The next thing, clearly, about the evangelical is *the tremendous emphasis that he puts upon the rebirth*. This is absolutely basic to him; he is not interested in dead orthodoxy, he is not interested in Protestant scholasticism. This is to me a very important differentiating point at the present time. The evangelical is a man who emphasizes the rebirth: a new beginning, born of the Spirit, new life in Christ, and partakers of the divine nature. I need not emphasize this here, I am sure, but you will find that as men cease to be evangelical, they put less and less emphasis upon regeneration, and they tend to put more and more upon the activity of the human will and the decision of the individual person. But the evangelical sees everything in terms of regeneration, the action of God. He says, I am what I am by the grace of God; and he is amazed at himself. This is the characteristic evangelical, but let me add to this.

The evangelical, because of this, is not merely interested in the need for life and power, he emphasizes it with the whole of his being. Take the question of pietism. Pietism has almost become a pejorative term at the present time and a term of abuse. I am getting very tired of evangelicals attacking pietism. I maintain that the true evangelical is always pietistic and it is the thing that differentiates him from a dead orthodoxy. I referred earlier to the origins of pietism on the continent of Europe. Arndt, Spener, and Francke, and people who followed them – this pietistic movement – arose as a protest, because, unfortunately, within a hundred years of the Protestant Reformation, both the Lutherans and the Reformed people had settled down into a dead orthodoxy. The same recovery happened in England under a man called William Perkins. Calvin himself was known and described as a theologian of the Spirit, and that is right. In true evangelicals, as you find in the Puritans and in a man like Jonathan Edwards in America, the pietistic element is very prominent in their teaching, and it always must be. The evangelical is not *merely* an orthodox man. You can have men who are quite orthodox but who are dead, and you really do not feel you can have any fellowship with them; their religion is all intellectual. Now that is not evangelicalism.

The evangelical has a true and a correct evangelical belief, but he does not stop at that. He has this great emphasis upon life, so you will always find in evangelical circles that there is great emphasis on the study of the Bible, personal and corporate, that great attention is paid to expositions of the Scripture and to prayer. Prayer is vital in the life of the evangelical.

Even in connection with this movement, the IFES, I have known men from certain countries who have been utterly, entirely orthodox, but the churches to which they belonged not only did not have prayer meetings, but they did not believe in prayer meetings. You could not wish for anything better from the standpoint of orthodoxy, but they do not believe in prayer meetings. Prayer has very little place in their lives. Now while they may be orthodox, I take leave to suggest that they are not truly evangelical. This element of prayer is essential to the evangelical; it is his life; it is vital to him. You will find that evangelicals almost invariably have formed religious societies for reading the Bible, discussing it together, for prayer, and for sharing one another's experiences. You had these things in pietism on the Continent and among the Puritans in England; you had it in the class meetings of the Methodists and in the societies that came into being in the eighteenth century. This is the great characteristic of evangelicalism.

Not only that. Evangelicals pay great attention to the way in which people live. They are strict in their behaviour. This used to be one of the most prominent characteristics of evangelicalism. I remember in my first contacts with the student movement, the people of the SCM and others used to describe those who belonged to the evangelical unions, the evangelicals, in these terms, Ah, they're the people who don't go to cinemas, they don't drink, and they don't smoke. I do not think they say that about them now. There has been a great change, but I am one of those who believe that there was a great deal to be said for the old position. The evangelical is careful about his life, careful to maintain good works, to live a life above reproach, not to be a hindrance or an obstacle to a weaker brother. The great ethic, the emphasis on holiness of the New Testament, is something which true evangelicals have always set great store by. They were called Puritans for that reason; they were called Methodists because they were methodical and careful. They did not merely content themselves with an intellectual belief. No, their whole life had to be governed by their doctrine. 'Every man that hath this hope in him purifieth himself, even as he is pure' (1 John 3:3). The emphasis on holiness in personal life and in church life is a great characteristic of evangelicalism.

Yet another characteristic is *the evangelical's interest in revival*. The only people who are ever interested in revival are evangelicals, and a good way of testing the quality of a man's evangelicalism is his interest in revival. The institutional people do not often talk about revival. They try sometimes to pay lip-service to it but they do not believe in it. They are governed by their ecclesiology and so on. The true evangelical, on the other hand, is always longing for an outpouring of the Spirit, and the great evangelical reawakenings have always been a result of an effusion of the Holy Spirit. The evangelical by nature is tremendously interested in revival.

Then, of course, the evangelical *always gives primacy to preaching*. When people cease to be interested in preaching, they cease to be evangelical. If you put discussions before preaching you are beginning to deny your evangelicalism. The church starts with preaching. Revivals, reformations, have always been great restorations of preaching. To the evangelical, nothing compares with preaching. Even reading is very secondary to preaching – 'truth mediated through personality,' the impact of a man filled with the Spirit proclaiming the message of God!

My last point is that the evangelical is a man who is *always concerned about evangelism.* There are people who are orthodox, but who are not concerned about evangelism. To that extent they are not evangelical. The evangelical is a man who, because of what God has done for him, is anxious that others should have the same. Not only that, he sees something of the glory and the majesty and the sovereignty of God; he believes in hell, eternal punishment; and he is concerned about those men dying in spiritual darkness round and about him. They become a burden to him, and he is not satisfied until he has done his utmost to bring them to the knowledge of the truth as it is in Christ Jesus.

There, rather too hurriedly, I have tried to give you a general picture of the character of an evangelical person. In the next lecture I hope to consider what he believes in more detail. Let us pray:

O Lord our God, we again come unto thee, and we are increasingly amazed, O Lord, that thou hast ever looked upon us and entrusted these matters to us. God have mercy upon us. We humbly pray thee to look upon us and to speak to us through thy Word. Send thy Spirit upon it and upon us. Give us, O God, this living and live concern. Awaken us, O Lord, to the dangers of the hour in which we live, in the perils of this modern situation. Lord, keep us humble, keep us from a hypocritical spirit, but give us a single eye to thy glory and to thy praise, and then an interest in, and a concern for, the souls of men and women. Continue, O Lord, among us this day in thy benediction and in thy grace. We ask it in the name of Jesus Christ, our Lord. Amen.

III

I have been arguing that the great call that comes to us at this present time is that we should contend earnestly for the faith. Or, if you prefer it in the words of the apostle Paul, we must 'stand fast in one spirit, with one mind striving together for the faith of the gospel' (Phil. 1:27). We have considered reasons why, owing to certain tendencies which have arisen and certain statements which have been made, it has become essential for us once more to define exactly what we mean by an evangelical. What we could assume even ten years ago, we can no longer assume. Subtle changes are taking place as I described in the first lecture, and these compel us to ask again the question, What is an evangelical?

Yesterday we took a general view of the evangelical person, and I attach great importance and significance to the general view. A man's whole way of thinking, his outlook, sometimes tells us as much about him as what he tells us in detail. At times, indeed, it tells us even more.

We can now proceed to greater detail and ask what it is in particular that we desiderate in an evangelical, and what it is that an evangelical must believe? Obviously, as the centuries demonstrate so clearly, this is not an easy matter, but we must attempt it. Our primary concern, I would remind you once more, should not be to be exclusive. We must be as *inclusive* as we can and yet draw certain lines which we regard as being essential.

It can be taken for granted that we all agree that we must subscribe to a doctrinal basis such as that found in the constitution of the IFES. When this basis was drawn up, the object was to state things which we regarded, and still regard, as being essential and vital. You cannot read this doctrinal basis, however, without noticing that there are many doctrines in connection with the Christian faith that are not mentioned at all. These omissions raise the problem which we must consider.

FOUNDATIONAL AND SECONDARY TRUTHS

We clearly regard certain truths as being essential; there are others which, while we would say that they are important, and very important, we would not lay down as being *essential*. What we have to do, therefore, is to draw a basic distinction between truths and doctrines which we insist are essential or foundational, and others concerning which there can be a legitimate difference of opinion.

I am going to start with those truths which we regard as being essential; but my whole emphasis, and the case I am trying to present to you, is that it is not sufficient any longer merely to take these statements as they are. We have to elaborate them, we have to define them in greater detail, and we have to do this because of recent changes, and because we are confronted by the phenomenon of people subscribing to a basis of faith with what they call mental reservations. In view of that we are entitled to put certain questions to people, or if you like, we are entitled and compelled to define our statements in somewhat greater detail.

So what I am going to do is to assume these basic doctrines that are stated here in this basis, with which, I take it, you are all familiar, but I am going to draw out certain of these truths more particularly in the light of the present situation. In doing this, I am simply trying to do what has been done by our forefathers.

Take any confession of faith that has ever been drawn up in the past. You will always find that in addition to making statements of the truth as believed by truly Christian people, they have in addition gone beyond that, and they have defined these truths in the light of certain problems and circumstances that obtained at that time, in their day and generation.

For instance, it is obvious that in the Augsburg Confession, and in various other original Protestant confessions, the authors were deliberately expounding their positive belief in the light of erroneous Roman Catholic belief. This is always necessary. Take the earlier creeds, the Athanasian Creed and others. These were obviously written and elaborated, not merely to make positive statements of the faith, but to counteract certain heresies that had arisen at that time, such as the Arian heresy and others.

Now I suggest that we have got to do the same thing. That is why I have been asserting that we must not merely slavishly adopt, subscribe to, and continue to defend, the confessions and the creeds that have come down to us. We must go beyond that and show the relevance of these statements to our own day and generation.

JUSTIFYING A VITAL DISTINCTION

I am now going to do that, and I will also have to do a second thing, namely, to justify this distinction between doctrines that are essential (on which we must insist), and other doctrines which, while we regard them as true, we do not describe as being essential, and to differentiate between them. You can see why the need for this arises. The moment you state the basic and essential truths, you divide yourself off from people who are heterodox or who have virtually no belief at all, who merely say, perhaps, that they believe in God, while they do not even define what they mean by that. The moment you do this, you are confronted by a further problem. Having separated yourself from unbelievers, or from false professors of the Christian faith, you are now confronted by the problem of maintaining unity among yourselves. As I have tried to show, when people take doctrine seriously, a tendency develops in them, not perhaps to take it too seriously, but to become so particular and rigid that they demand too much, and put into the category of essential what should be regarded rather as non-essential. We have got to be careful that we do not fall into that error. While we must elaborate the meaning of essential truths even though it may cause division, it is also very right that we should establish this distinction between things which are essential and things which are not essential. If evangelicals do not do this, we shall be atomized and divided up in such a manner that we shall cease to count and cease to bear a corporate witness in this needy modern world.

This is a very old distinction which I am drawing between the essentials and the non-essentials. Let me give it to you in the words of Calvin in the *Institutes*, Book 4, Chapter 1, Section 12, where he puts it very clearly:

> For not all the articles of true doctrine are of the same sort. Some are so necessary to know that they should be certain and unquestioned by all men as the proper principles of religion. Such are: God is one; Christ is God and the Son of God; our salvation rests in God's mercy; and the like. Among the churches there are other articles of doctrine disputed which still do not break the unity of faith. Suppose that one church believes – short of unbridled contention and opinionated stubbornness – that souls upon leaving bodies fly to heaven; while another, not daring to define the place, is convinced nevertheless that they live to the Lord. What churches would disagree on this one point? Here are the apostle's words: 'Let us therefore, as many as are perfect, be of the same mind; and if you be differently minded in anything, God shall reveal this also to you' (Phil. 3:15). Does this not sufficiently indicate that a difference of opinion over these nonessential matters should in no wise be the basis of schism among Christians? First and foremost, we should agree on all points. But since all men are somewhat beclouded with ignorance, either we must leave no church remaining, or we must condone delusion in those matters which can go unknown without harm to the sum of religion and without loss of salvation.
>
> But here I would not support even the slightest errors with the thought of fostering them through flattery and connivance. But I say we must not thoughtlessly forsake the church because of any petty dissensions. For in it

alone is kept safe and uncorrupted that doctrine in which piety stands sound and the use of the sacraments ordained by the Lord is guarded.[3]

That, I think, is a very perfect statement of the position which I am trying to put before you. So, with that introduction, and bearing in mind the danger of going to the wrong extreme of laxity, looseness, and indifferentism on the one hand, and over-rigidity and too much particularity on the other, let us proceed to this task.

The first thing that I am anxious to do is to make some comments on these things which we agree are essential. I am saying that we have got to elaborate somewhat upon what we state here in this basis of faith. Indeed, I venture to suggest that we might even add something which will help to clarify the current situation.

THE NECESSITY OF OPPOSITION TO DOCTRINAL INDIFFERENTISM

In the light of the position in which we find ourselves I suggest that it would be a very good thing for us to state plainly and clearly that we are anti-ecumenical. Why do I start with a negative like this? For the reason that today we have to assert and defend the position that *doctrine is really vital and essential*. The ecumenical movement, while paying lip-service to a very minimum amount of credal statement, is merely based on doctrinal indifferentism. I think that this is generally agreed. You cannot have an ecumenical movement of the contemporary kind without such indifferentism. Even if ecumenists try to claim that they have a general subscription to a belief in Jesus Christ as God and Saviour, according to the witness of the Scriptures, we cannot regard this as sufficient, because they refuse to test subscription among themselves. In other words, they refuse any element of discipline, and this, it seems to me, is immediately something which proclaims indifferentism. There is no purpose in having a credal test unless you insist upon it, and unless you test people's subscription to it. We cannot admit this category of 'mental reservation'. Indeed, we are driven to say this by the notorious fact that there are men in the ecumenical movement who, in their own books and articles and statements, clearly show that they deny what we would regard as many of the essentials of the Christian faith.

[3]*Calvin: Institutes of the Christian Religion*, trans. F. L. Battles, ed. J. T. McNeill, vol. 2, SCM Press, 1961, pp. 1025–26.

There are men prominent in that movement, about whom it is doubtful whether they are even theists. It is not what I am saying about them; it is what they themselves say in their books, and we are all familiar with these facts.

Therefore we start by asserting the vital importance of doctrine, and of being clear with regard to our doctrine and belief, and so we have no fellowship with those who do not insist upon the centrality of doctrine. Though it sounds a negative point, it is ultimately a very positive one. Clearly we have nothing in common with people who do not insist in this way upon clear statements of doctrine and of truth.

Having said that, we now go on to deal with some of the particulars that are mentioned in our agreed basis of faith. I have to make specific comments on some of them.

SCRIPTURE: THE ONLY AND FULL AUTHORITY

The first is the doctrine of Scripture. The basis of faith says: 'We believe in the divine inspiration and entire trustworthiness of holy Scripture as originally given, and its supreme authority in all matters of faith and conduct.' I contend that it is not enough just to say that; we have got to go further. There are people who claim to subscribe to that doctrine, who, I would suggest, in some of their statements raise very serious doubts as to whether they really do accept it.

So we have to say some specific things such as that the Scripture is our *sole* authority, not only the 'supreme' authority, but our sole authority, our only authority. I say this to emphasize that we do not accept tradition as an authority in any sense of that term. We reject the Roman Catholic teaching with regard to tradition which is, as you know, that tradition is equal in authority with the Scriptures. Roman Catholics do not deny the authority of the Scriptures, but they give to tradition, the tradition elaborated in and by the church, an equal authority with the Scriptures. And in that tradition they would claim to have received revelation subsequent to the end of the New Testament canon.

We reject that, but we also reject another view of tradition which is much more subtle and much more dangerous, and which, one observes with great regret, has been creeping into the minds of some evangelical people in these last few years. What is this other idea of tradition? Well, it was a point of view first elaborated by John Henry

Newman in the last century. Newman wrote a book dealing with the development of doctrine in the church. And he put it like this, that we must not say that the church has received new revelation, rather that the church through her experience and understanding, as the centuries passed, has been able to discover what was before only implicit in the Scriptures, and has been able to draw it out. This is the new and more subtle form in which the idea of tradition is being re-introduced and given great prominence.

This is the way in which men can justify certain practices such as episcopacy and so on, and still claim to be guided by the Scripture. They say it is right and true to say that episcopacy is not actually taught as such in the Scripture, but it is there 'implicitly', and the mind and the experience of the church has been led by the Holy Spirit to draw it out, to discover it, and to spell out its meaning. In this way you have tradition coming in, not perhaps as an equal authority, but as a very important one, and one which justifies certain other beliefs and practices. I suggest that we must emphasize that the Scripture is our *sole* authority, and that with respect to authority we cannot give any place to tradition in any shape or form.

Certainly evangelicals say that we can learn from the expositions of Scripture by the fathers throughout the centuries, but we do not regard these sources as authoritative in any sense whatsoever.

Furthermore it seems to me that we have got to spell out much more clearly the whole notion of revelation. It is difficult to do that in a short statement. The basis speaks of 'the divine inspiration and entire trustworthiness', but we must go beyond that. We have got to assert today this category of revelation. We have got to exclude the notion that men have arrived at the truth as a result of searching and thinking, or by means of philosophy. We must affirm that it is entirely given, that 'holy men of God spake as they were moved by the Holy Ghost' (2 Pet. 1:21), or, as Paul is constantly reminding his readers, that his gospel is not his own, 'For I neither received it of man, neither was I taught it, but by the revelation of Jesus Christ' (Gal. 1:12). We have to underline in a new and very definite way the whole notion of revelation and also, in the same way, of inspiration, showing that by inspiration we do not mean that these men were inspired in the way that certain poets have been 'inspired' and given glimpses into truth, but that they were actually controlled by the Holy Spirit. 'Borne along', as Peter writes in 2 Peter 1:21, or as Paul puts it in 2 Timothy 3:16: 'All scripture is given by inspiration of

God'; it is 'God-breathed'. These things we must assert with particularity.

In the same way we have got to assert today that we believe that Scripture contains propositional truth. This has often been the dividing line between evangelicals and pseudo-evangelicals. I have noticed over the years that it is one of the first points that indicates a departure from an evangelical position when men begin to object to, and to reject, propositional truth, as Karl Barth did and as most of his followers still do. But we claim that in the Bible there are propositions, truths stated in propositional form, with regard to God and His being and His character, and many other matters. We have got to assert this element of propositional truth.

Likewise we have to assert particularly the supernatural element in the Scripture. What do I mean? Well, we have got to emphasize that we believe in prophecy in the sense of foretelling. The emphasis today is on 'forthtelling'. We admit that we agree that prophecy is forthtelling but, over and above that, it is foretelling. To me one of the profoundest arguments for the unique inspiration of the Scriptures is the truth of prophecy, the fulfilment of prophecy. We have got to emphasize this extraordinary manifestation of the supernatural.

We have also to insist upon a belief in the literal truth and historicity of the miracles of the Old and the New Testament, because there are people who say that they can still subscribe to our general statement about the inspiration and the authority of the Scriptures, who increasingly are denying the historicity of many of the Old Testament miracles, and indeed are trying to explain away some of the New Testament miracles in terms of science or psychology. We must assert the historicity of these manifestations of the supernatural.

Then the next thing to be said under this heading of Scripture is that we must believe the whole Bible. We must believe the history of the Bible as well as its didactic teaching. Failure here is always an indication of a departure from the true evangelical position. Today there are men who say, Oh yes, we believe in the Bible and its supreme authority in matters of religion, but, of course, we don't go to the Bible for science; we go to it for help for our souls, for salvation and help and instruction in the way to live the Christian life. They are saying that there are, as it were, two great authorities and two means of revelation: one of them is Scripture and the other is nature. These, they say, are complementary, they are collateral, and so you go to the Scriptures for matters concerning your soul, but you do not go to them to seek God's other revelation of Himself in nature. For that, you go to science.

You are familiar with this view which, it seems to me, is not only extremely dangerous, but tends to undermine our whole position. We have got to contest it, and contest it very strongly. There is one thing about this present tendency which is quite amazing to me, and it is that those who advocate it seem to think that they are saying something quite new; but it is not new. It is precisely what Ritschl and his followers were teaching a hundred years ago. 'Judgments of fact' and 'judgments of value', as they called them. It is just a return to that. That is how evangelicals in the last century went astray in the 1840s and subsequently. That is precisely how it came about. Their argument was that they were merely out to defend the truth of the gospel against this increasing attack from the realm of natural science. And that was the method they adopted. They held that the Bible is only concerned with 'religious' truth and so, whatever science may discover, it cannot affect this truth.

Our friends today with the same motive – and let us grant that their motive is good and true – are doing exactly the same thing. It seems to me that in so doing they are on the same path as the followers of Ritschl and others, and it always ends in the same result, namely that the gospel itself is compromised. We must assert that we believe in the historicity of the early chapters of Genesis and all other biblical history.

CREATION, NOT EVOLUTION

We accept the biblical teaching with regard to creation and do not base our position upon theories of evolution, whichever particular theory people may choose to advocate. We must assert that we believe in the being of one first man called Adam, and in one first woman called Eve. We reject any notion of a pre-Adamic man because it is contrary to the teaching of the Scripture.

Now someone may ask, Why do you care about this? Is this essential to your doctrine of salvation? Are you not falling into the very error of over-particularization against which you warned us at the beginning? I suggest that I am not, and for these reasons. If we say that we believe the Bible to be the Word of God, we must say that about the whole of the Bible, and when the Bible presents itself to us as history, we must accept it as history. I would contend that the early chapters of Genesis, the first three chapters of Genesis, are given to us as history. We know that there are pictures and symbols in the Bible, and when the Bible uses symbol and parable it indicates that it is doing so, but when it presents something to us in the form of history, it requires us to accept it as history.

We must therefore hold to the vital principle, to which I have referred earlier, of the wholeness and the close interrelationship of every part of the biblical message. The Bible does not merely make statements about salvation. It is a complete whole: it tells you about the origin of the world and of man; it tells you what has happened to him, how he fell and the need of salvation arose, and then it tells you how God provided this salvation and how He began to reveal it in parts and portions. Nothing is so amazing about the Bible as its wholeness, the perfect interrelationship of all the parts.

Therefore these early chapters of Genesis with their history play a vital part in the whole doctrine of salvation. Take for instance the argument of the apostle Paul in the Epistle to the Romans 5:12–21. Paul's whole case is based upon that one man Adam and his one sin, and the contrast with the other one man, the Lord Jesus Christ, and His one great act. You have exactly the same thing in 1 Corinthians 15; the apostle's whole argument rests upon the historicity. Indeed, it seems to me that one of the things we have got to assert, these days in particular – and it should always have been asserted – is that our gospel, our faith, is not a teaching; it is not a philosophy; it is primarily a history.

The apostles, you remember, on the day of Pentecost, filled with the Holy Spirit, were talking about the wonderful works of God. The works of salvation are God's acts! The Bible is a record of God's activity. Salvation is not an idea; it is something that results from actions which have taken place on the concrete plane of history. Historicity is a very vital matter. As I say, it is the very key to understanding the apostle Paul's elaboration of his doctrine of salvation.

In addition to that, of course, the whole question of the person of our Lord arises. He clearly accepted this history, he referred to Adam, and in speaking about marriage he clearly accepts the historicity of that portion of Scripture (Matt. 19:4–5). But quite apart from this, if you do not accept this history, and prefer to believe that man's body developed as the result of an evolutionary process, and that God then took one of these humanoid persons, or whatever you may call them, and did something to him and turned him into a man, you are still left with the question of how to explain Eve, for the Bible is very particular as to the origin of Eve. All who accept in any form the theory of evolution in the development of man completely fail to account for the being, origin, and existence of Eve. So there are scientific difficulties as well as these much more serious theological difficulties, but there is a general aspect to this particular matter which seems to me to be, in a sense, even more important.

These good friends who are thus, as they feel, safeguarding the Christian message of salvation by drawing this distinction are, I believe, doing precisely what the Roman Catholic Church did in connection with Copernicus and others. You remember how the Roman Catholic Church opposed the findings of these men. Why did she do so? Well, she did so because she was tied by Greek philosophical teaching with regard to the natural world. That teaching had come out of pure reason, not as the result of observation or of any scientific investigation. The philosophers had thought it through and they had laid down certain absolute propositions about the world and about the cosmos, so that when these scientific men came along and said that they had discovered this and that, it was rejected. Why? Because the church was not so much tied to the teaching of the Scripture as to the teaching of Aristotle and other Greek philosophers, and so she found herself in difficulties; she found herself denying what is truth and fact.

Now here, it seems to me, is the very thing that certain evangelical people are tending to do at the present time. They are tying themselves to modern, scientific teaching, and nothing is more dangerous than that. We must base ourselves exclusively on the Scriptures, and if this has always been true, it seems to me it is especially true today. We are living in an age of great change, great scientific change. The quantum theory and the work of Einstein have introduced a revolution into the whole realm of science. Take, for instance, the dogmatism with which the scientists spoke in the last century, how they talked about 'the absolute laws of nature', and so on, but they no longer do that, and they cannot do that. Everything today is indeterminate. Scientists now say that what we call the laws of nature are simply a very small section of the totality of truth. This is all we have discovered so far, but increasingly they are finding that their knowledge is very limited.

Modern science itself teaches us that we are not anti-scientific and we are not obscurantist if we do not accept statements as absolute truth and fact simply because they are made by certain prominent and great scientists. We know that great scientists have made very dogmatic statements in the past, which by now have proved to be wrong. They were teaching with great confidence, one hundred years ago, that the thyroid and the pituitary glands were vestigial organs, and people believed them. It was because they accepted such assertions that the faith of many evangelicals was shaken in the middle of the last century. Today we know that these assertions were wrong. All I am saying is that it is very dangerous for us to base our position, our exposition of the Scripture, upon the pronouncements of science. These are changeable, constantly moving. Indeterminacy is the rule today rather than determinacy, so we must be humble. And while we admit that we cannot explain everything and that there are certain things put before us for which we cannot account, what we must say is this: Because the Spirit has borne witness within us to the truth of the Scripture, we do believe that whatever is asserted in the Scripture about creation, about the whole cosmos, is true because God has said it, and though Scripture may appear to conflict with certain discoveries of science at the present time, we exhort people to be patient, assuring them that ultimately the scientists will discover that they have been in error at some point or other, and will eventually come to see that the statements of Scripture are true. Thus we base our position upon Scripture alone and this has always been the Protestant view of Scripture. There are two testimonies to the truth of the Scripture in all its parts: there is the external testimony of the Spirit in the Word itself; there is the *testimonium Spiritus internum*, the internal testimony of the Spirit in us, giving us assurance that this is the Word of God.[4]

You see the importance of the need to elaborate our doctrinal statements at the present time. There are some who say, Yes, I accept it; I haven't changed my view at all on your basis of faith and what it says about the Scriptures. But when you talk to them in detail, you find that they have departed in this very serious, and I suggest, radical manner from the true position of the evangelical.

[4]Further on this subject, see D. M. Lloyd-Jones, *Authority*, 1958 (Banner of Truth Trust, 1984).

THE FALL AND EVIL

We go on to assert that we must underline the fact of the historical fall of the first man, and that it happened in the way described in the third chapter of Genesis. Whether we can understand it or not is not the question. That is what we are told, and the apostle Paul in 2 Corinthians 11:3 reminds the Corinthians that 'the serpent beguiled Eve'. You cannot play fast and loose with these facts without involving the inspiration of the apostles, and, ultimately, the person of our Lord. You will soon be saying that He was a child of His own age, that He was ignorant in certain respects, and that He had simply the scientific knowledge of His own times, and so on. You begin to query and to question His statements, and ultimately you will have no authority at all.

Not only must we accept the historicity of Genesis 3 and its account of the fall. If you do not accept that as history, you are going to exclude from your belief one of the most amazing and comforting facts in connection with our faith, the proto-evangel of Genesis 3:15, the glorious promise that the seed of the woman shall bruise the serpent's head, the first prophecy concerning the virgin birth of Christ and how He was going to bring us this great deliverance. There is the first glimpse of the work, of the blessed work of the cross, all concretely stated in the historical account.

In the same way, we must assert the fact of the flood. I am not here making a complete statement, of course. Time prohibits that, but I am simply picking out certain things that we have to emphasize in a particular way at this present time. General statements are no longer enough. We must insist upon knowing what people believe in detail. We must test their statement that they accept the supreme authority of the Scriptures, and their trustworthiness in all these matters of faith and conduct.

Having dealt with our position on Scripture, we move on to certain other doctrines. Here also I want to make an addition to the basis of faith. I trust this will not surprise any of you. I am suggesting that we must make an assertion that we believe in the existence of the devil and his spirits. It is amazing to me that we do not say this. There are so many people who really do not believe in the existence of the devil and they do not believe in evil spirits. There are people known to us who are entirely orthodox, but if you start talking to them about devil-possession and exorcism, they show quite plainly that

they think you are talking nonsense. They do not believe in the
existence of evil spirits, or they tend to say that that was only true in
the time of our Lord, a position which I find amazing and
inexplicable.

There is here a twofold argument. They say that the gifts of the
Spirit were confined solely to the apostolic age, and that they
ceased with that age; and then by implication they seem to say
that the devil was kind and polite enough to stop his activities also
with the apostolic age. And so there is this utter confusion. No.
We must assert that it is a part of our whole position that we
believe in the supernatural realm, and in a spiritual conflict. Referring to this conflict, the apostle Paul writes, 'We wrestle not
against flesh and blood, but against principalities, against powers,
against the rulers of the darkness of this world, against spiritual
wickedness in high places' (Eph. 6:12). How often even in evangelical circles do we hear this asserted at the present time? Is there
not a tendency on our part to become intellectualists and to regard
these truths as almost abstract? We talk so little about 'leadings of
the Spirit' as the fathers used to, or 'prohibitions of the Spirit',
and the wonderful activities of the Spirit, and we seem to avoid all talk
of the activities of evil spirits, yet we are living in a world in which
demon-possession seems to be coming back very rapidly, and even
devil-worship and certain other terrible characteristics of the god-
less life.

So at this point we must assert our faith. We shall be regarded as
fools. Any man who believes in the devil today is regarded as almost
unintelligent, yet if you believe the Bible you must believe in this
tremendous person and his awful power. The Bible, in a sense, is a
record of the conflict between the forces of God and the forces of the
devil, and we are told that this is to go on until the final destruction of
the devil and all his forces.

Then we must go on to assert that man is spiritually dead, and that
he is totally incapable of any spiritual good, 'dead in trespasses and
sins' – not merely slightly defective – and that it is not true to say that
he has it in him, if he only applies himself, to believe in God and to
arrive at God. We must assert, as the Scriptures do, that man is
totally dead, that the advances of science make no difference
whatsoever to the fact that all men are 'by nature the children of
wrath, even as others' (Eph. 2:3), that 'all have sinned, and come
short of the glory of God' (Rom. 3:23).

ONE WAY OF SALVATION

When we come to the doctrine of the atonement, we must underline in a very special way the substitutionary aspect and element of the atonement, the penal, piacular aspect. These are things that I find are most indicative of a man's position. An evangelical may say, Well, of course, I'm not a great theologian; I simply accept, I simply repeat the Scriptures' statements. And he does not want to tie himself down to the fact that there is this penal element in the atonement. He may say, All I know is that Christ's work, his sacrifice, puts me right with God. I suggest this is not enough. He is really excluding the whole of the Old Testament teaching with regard to sacrifice if he speaks in that way, let alone the particular and explicit statements made in the teaching of the apostle Paul. So we have to underline and emphasize this substitutionary element.

We must also assert in a very special way justification by faith alone, faith only. We have got to assert that justification is not the result of regeneration, nor does it depend upon our regeneration. That is the Roman Catholic teaching, that we are justified because we have been regenerated as a result of our baptism. This error can come in, and is coming in today in very subtle forms, but we must assert that God 'justifieth the ungodly' (Rom. 4:5), that it is entirely a forensic action, a legal pronouncement by God, and that we play no part whatsoever in it. This is the traditional evangelical teaching which we must assert.

THE CHURCH: CONTEMPORARY ISSUES

When we come to the church we must again make certain specific statements. I personally would assert that no evangelical can possibly believe in a state or territorial church. We know that these institutions came into being solely as the result of certain events in history. There is no suspicion of a suggestion of it in the New Testament, and how could there be? What is there about being born in a certain country which makes anybody a Christian? Why should the church be merely the spiritual aspect of the life of the state? It is remote from the teaching of Scripture and we know that of all elements in the history of the church, perhaps nothing has been productive of greater confusion than this whole notion of the state or territorial church. We believe in the communion of saints, and a church consists of saints; it is a communion of saints.

And, of course, in our basis we must believe in purity of doctrine – and we must assert this – and of sacraments. Therefore we must believe in discipline. There is no purpose in having a basis or a confession of faith unless it is applied. So we must assert the element of discipline as being essential to the true life of the church. And what calls itself a church which does not believe in discipline, and does not use it and apply it, is therefore not a true church.

But there are certain negatives here which must come in, and we must not minimize the importance of negatives. We must reject completely every notion of apostolic succession. We must reject the distinction between clergy and laity because it is not found in the New Testament. We must also reject the notion that bishops are essential to the life of the church. Now you may ask, What has this got to do with evangelicalism? I reply that certain evangelicals have been committing themselves to statements such as this: that we believe that the authority of bishops is identical with the authority of apostles, being the personal authority of the Lord. Two evangelicals have subscribed to that statement within the last year or so. Another statement they have given is that the bishop gives expression to the headship of Christ over His church. Where is the biblical authority for this? The answer is that there is none. This is the so-called 'development of doctrine'. The church in her experience and wisdom, they teach us, has found a suspicion of a suggestion of this notion implicit in the New Testament, and she has drawn it out. I suggest that we as evangelicals must reject this completely.

Coming to the sacraments, we must reject every suggestion of sacerdotalism. We do not believe in priests or any priestly action. We do not believe that the sacraments act in and of themselves; the term is *ex opere operato*. We do not believe that. So we must reject statements to which the same two evangelical writers mentioned above have committed themselves, that there is an efficacy inherent in the sacramental act itself. As evangelicals we reject that. There is no efficacy inherent in the sacramental act itself. A sacrament is nothing unless there is in the recipient belief. There is no efficacy inherent in the act itself. We do not believe in the sheer unqualified efficacy of sacraments.

I would not be calling attention to these matters were it not that these are statements made by evangelicals. This is an illustration of the tragic shift that has been taking place in the last ten years, and this is again opening the door to sacramentalism, sacramentarianism, and sacerdotalism. So we must assert very strongly that we reject any suggestion of baptismal regeneration. It must be entirely excluded, not only in the Roman Catholic form, but in every form. We must likewise reject any notion of sacrifice in connection with the Lord's Supper. There is no repetition of sacrifice there, no element of sacrifice. We must assert that all we offer in that sacramental act is ourselves. We reject that we offer anything at that point, save ourselves.

There, as I see things, are the additions and the elaborations which we must make today in view of the situation in which we find ourselves. This present basis of faith, as it is, is not enough; neither is any other. We have got to ask these specific questions. We have got to make sure that we are clear about these particular matters.

Secondary Truths Not Essential to Unity

That brings me to my next heading. I have been dealing so far with the essentials. I am still left with what I have called the non-essentials.

What do we mean by non-essentials? We are clear about these matters with which we have been dealing. We have been defining our evangelical position. But I have left unmentioned many other things outside our basis. What about them? I put them in the category of non-essentials. When I say that they are not essential, I do not say that they are not important. They are very important, and they must be discussed by evangelical people, but we must discuss them as brethren. As Calvin said, on such matters we ought not to divide but to try to help one another. We recognize our limits, our defects, our ignorance. We believe that promise of Paul's in Philippians 3 that even in these other matters, light will be given to us if we are patient and if we seek it together.

But we call them non-essential because they are not essential to salvation. This seems to be the test. Another reason I give for calling them non-essential is that they cannot be proved one way or the other. I do not say the Scriptures are equivocal, but there are matters upon which the Scriptures are not so clear that you can say this *must* be believed.

Then there is another reason for calling some of these things non-essential. Sometimes it is a question of understanding or lack of understanding, and we must always remember that we are not saved by our understanding. This is a most important point. Our danger as evangelicals is to fall into the trap of thinking that we are saved by our understanding; but we are not. Thank God, we are saved in spite of ourselves, in spite of our ignorance and everything else that is true of us. And sometimes the difference between evangelical people is entirely due to a difference of understanding. I will give you an illustration of it in a moment.

There is also a difference between a defective understanding and a positive denial of truth by able people. What I mean is this. You may have certain simple Christian people, not over-gifted with intelligence, who find it very difficult to understand some matters, but there are other men, able men, gifted men, highly intelligent men, who deliberately reject the same truths which the first group finds difficult to accept and understand. Those two positions are very different. While we are patient, sympathetic, and lenient with the first, we must condemn and separate ourselves from the second.

These are some of the reasons for drawing a distinction between essentials and non-essentials. Let me mention a few things, therefore, which I put into the category of non-essentials.

One is the belief in election and predestination. Now I am a Calvinist; I believe in election and predestination; but I would not dream of putting it under the heading of essential. I put it under the heading of non-essential. Mark you, I would condemn Pelagianism; I would say that Pelagianism is a denial of the truth of the Scripture with regard to salvation – that goes out. But I am thinking of Arminianism in its various forms, and therefore I do not put this into the category of essential. I do not for the reason that this, for me, is a matter of understanding. You are not saved by your precise understanding of how this great salvation comes to you. What you must be clear about is that you are lost and damned, hopeless and helpless, and that nothing can save you but the grace of God in Jesus Christ and only Him crucified, bearing the punishment of your sins, dying, rising again, ascending, sending the Spirit, regeneration. Those are the essentials.

Now when you come to ask me, How exactly do I come to a belief in this? I say that that is a matter of the understanding of the *mechanism* of salvation, not of the *way* of salvation. And here, while I myself hold very definite and strong views on the subject, I will not separate from a man who cannot accept and believe the doctrines of election and predestination, and is Arminian, as long as he tells me that we are all saved by grace, and as long as the Calvinist agrees, as he must, that God calls all men everywhere to repentance. As long as both are prepared to agree about these things I say we must not break fellowship. So I put election into the category of non-essentials.

Another matter I would put into the same category is the age and the mode of baptism: the age of the candidate, and the mode of administering the rite of baptism. I would put that again in the non-essential category for the same reason, that you cannot prove one or the other from the Scriptures. I have been reading books on this subject for the last forty-four years and more, and I know less about it now than I did at the beginning. Therefore, while I assert, and we must all assert, that we believe in baptism, for that is plainly commanded, yet we must not divide and separate over the age of the candidate or over the mode of administration. In the same way, we must not divide on the question of assurance of salvation.

We must not divide even on the question of church polity. I find it very difficult to say that, and yet I must say it. I am so opposed to this tendency today to insist upon bishops. This is what is being done by the ecumenical movement. You will find everywhere and in every country that bishops are made essential to the new church. You have it in South India, you have it in North India. This I resent and reject; but for the sake of evangelical unity among evangelicals, I would even be prepared to consider at any rate the possibility of some form of modified episcopacy for the sake of unity. I put it into the category of non-essentials for that reason.

In the same way, clearly, we must not divide on the question of prophetic interpretation: pre-, post-, a-millennialist, and so on. Not one of them can be proved, so we must not put them into the category of essentials. You have your views; hold them. Let us discuss them together; let us reason together out of the Scriptures; but if we divide on these matters, I maintain that we are guilty of schism. We are putting into the category of essentials what is non-essential. Evangelicals have sometimes done this. I remember a man telling me that he was 'doubtful' about the late Dr Gresham Machen, and he was doubtful of him for this reason: this man was very prominent in the World Fundamentalist Association, in which you had to believe in pre-millennialism, and because Dr Gresham Machen did not believe in pre-millennialism this man was doubtful about his evangelical position.

In the same way, there are beliefs with respect to the way of sanctification which are non-essential. There are rival theories held by equally good evangelicals which we put into the category of non-essentials. We hold our own personal views and hold them strongly; we believe that certain teachings are wrong; but it is not essential to salvation to believe the contrary. We are saved, and these good friends and ourselves will arrive in heaven in spite of our views on the particular mode of sanctification.

I would put into the same category the whole question of the baptism of the Spirit and the *charismata*, the spiritual gifts. There are differences of opinion here. I regard these as very important, but I would not venture to put them into the category of the essential.

There, as I see things at any rate, are some of these matters which we have to underline and emphasize at the present time. We have got to be clear and specific in establishing the evangelical position, but having done that, we must be very careful to draw this distinction between essentials and non-essentials lest we become guilty of schism and begin to rend the body of Christ.

May I close on this note. Our object in all this, as I say, is to safeguard the gospel, to keep the evangel clear, to be concerned about the salvation of men and women and the spread of the Christian church. Let that be our only motive. Let us have a single eye to the glory of God and of the Lord Jesus Christ. Let us realize always that we are all of us saved in spite of ourselves, that none of us is perfect in understanding or in any other respect, that not to be in fellowship with those who are born again is to be guilty of schism, which is sinful, that we are therefore called upon, as the apostle exhorted the Philippians, to stand in rank together, whatever the cost, whatever suffering may be involved, but always with this one idea that God may be over all, that God may be glorified, and that the name of Jesus Christ our Lord may be magnified among the peoples of the earth. Let us pray:

O Lord our God, we come to thee again, and we see what children we are, beginners battling on the edge of this great ocean of truth. Lord, give us, and keep us to, that simplicity that is in Christ. Keep us from being puffed up with knowledge and self-conceit and understanding. O God, give us ever a childlike spirit. Deliver us from all false entanglements and intendments, and from every consideration save that thy name may be magnified and made glorious, and that through even our feeble instrumentality many may be convicted of sin, converted, led to Jesus' blood and become members together with us of the body of Christ. So hear us, we pray thee, give us wisdom and circumspection in these evil days. Guide and direct those here present who are leaders of this work in various countries – Lord, we know that our sufficiency is of thee – and grant them to know that though they may at times feel lonely and isolated, with no-one to help them and to stand with them, may they ever know that thou wilt never leave them nor forsake them. Grant that our confidence may ever be in thee and in the power of thy might. Bless thy servants as they commune together and meditate in the Executive and plan the future work. And in all the other meetings and activities of this day, we pray that all may experience thy benediction and thy grace. Pardon us, O Lord, for all the imperfection of our service and our every sin, as we ask these mercies, pleading nothing but the name and the merit of thy dear Son, our Lord and Saviour Jesus Christ. Amen.

Seventeen

*

A Protestant Evangelical College[1]

*

The Need for a New College

I address you tonight primarily as the chairman of the Sponsoring Committee, which has been responsible for calling this meeting to inaugurate the London Theological Seminary. I have a suspicion that many of you feel that the phenomenon with which you are confronted is that of a poacher turned gamekeeper! I agree that there is a good deal to be said for that feeling. My only defence is that I try always to be open to any conviction produced by facts; and whatever views I may have held in the past, and indeed still hold, I am here because I have been persuaded by the arguments that have been put before me.

I believe we are doing something here tonight which is of very great significance. We are inaugurating a new college, and we are concerned about the whole question of the training for the ministry. I want, therefore, to take advantage of this occasion to reconsider with you the whole question of the training for the ministry. That seems to me to be the most significant element in what we are doing here tonight.

Why should this question be reconsidered? There are many reasons, and it is these which have been moving us as members of the Sponsoring Committee. I believe it is true to say that by now virtually everybody is dissatisfied with the existing systems. During the last few months, and very largely as the result of that notorious book *The Myth of God Incarnate*, many have been expressing their amazement and surprise at the state of theological colleges. I have seen

[1] An address given at the opening of the London Theological Seminary on 6 October, 1977.

[356]

statements by bishops of the Church of England deploring the obvious gap between what is happening among so-called theologians in Oxford and Cambridge and the ordinary members of the Christian church. Many of them have said, and said rightly, that the colleges where men are supposed to be trained for the Christian ministry have lost all contact with the members of the Christian church. It is being recognized more and more that something has to be done.

Some, of course, have reacted strongly against the present state of such colleges and have tended to say that therefore we do not need any colleges at all. I believe that that is an error, as I am hoping to show. Another attitude, which is of concern to all of us at the present time, is the result of the new emphasis upon experience and the experimental aspect of the Christian faith. We thank God for this emphasis, but many such friends are tending to say that there is no need for ordained ministers as such, and therefore no need, obviously, for training ministers.

A further reason is that there are rumours, and more than rumours, of a move to have ecumenical colleges. So far the various denominations have had their own colleges; but there is a move afoot now to amalgamate all these and to have colleges in which men who are going to minister in the various denominations, even including the Roman Catholic Church, are going to be trained together and have a common course of instruction. This immediately stirs within us the feeling that we must have an evangelical college. I believe this ecumenical idea will come to pass, partly on economic grounds and because of various other difficulties. They cannot afford their separate colleges, so they are going to get together to establish ecumenical colleges. The Sponsoring Committee felt very strongly that over against that we must have an evangelical seminary, and not only an evangelical, but a distinctively Protestant, college. We are living in days, unfortunately, when it is no longer sufficient to talk about being evangelical. We must emphasize Protestant as well as evangelical, because we stand not only against ecumenicity but very definitely, and in particular, against Roman Catholicism. We are Protestants and this is to be a Protestant evangelical college. There are evangelicals today who are not only ready to fraternize, but are fraternizing, with Roman Catholics, and even considering with favour the possibility of eventually being one with the Roman Catholic Church. So we are Protestants as well as evangelicals over against a vague ecumenicity that ultimately includes Roman Catholicism.

Another element or factor which has influenced us is that we have
been hearing that certain free church evangelical students who are
hoping to enter, and some who have entered, free church ministries
have actually been going to Anglican colleges for their training. As a
Nonconformist and free churchman that is something which rouses
my ire, and if I had no other reason for supporting this venture, that
alone would be sufficient for me! And then, on top of this, it is
generally agreed that the existing colleges, for some reason or
another – and I hope to deal with some of them – have failed to
produce preachers. One of the most alarming and regrettable aspects
of our present church life is the paucity of preachers of the Word. We
have knowledgeable men; but what is needed above everything else
is preachers. Many hold the view, and I believe that there is
something to be said for it, that the existing colleges, far from
producing preachers, have on the whole tended to stifle and ruin
preachers. There are young men who have gone to college full of zeal
for preaching the Word of God but have come out tired intellectually, and weary, who have lost that first impulse which gave them the
desire to become preachers of the Word.

A final reason which I adduce is that we felt that it was essential
that the sponsorship of such a college should be as broad-based as
possible. There are among us certain 'empire builders' who are
always ready to start their own colleges, so we felt that we must have
a college which would be supported by, and which would minister
to, the various groupings of Protestant evangelicals in this country
today. The names of the members of this Sponsoring Committee
emphasize the wide and broad base on which this college is founded.
This is not some personal venture; it is the coming together of
Protestant evangelical groupings in this country to form a college
which will serve all the various free evangelical churches.

The Pitfalls and Purpose of Ministerial Training

How do we approach this whole matter of training preachers? I was
seriously tempted to deal with the subject solely from the historical
standpoint. The history of the theological colleges and seminaries is a
very fascinating one. Let me give a hurried bird's-eye view of the
history of this matter. The church as we know her started on the day
of Pentecost, and the first preacher under her auspices was a man
who, from the modern standpoint had had no training at all, a

fisherman, the apostle Peter. Of course he and the others had been with our Lord, and they had heard His preaching and His teaching; but there was no formal teaching, no formal training, to make them preachers. Peter stood up and 'filled with the Holy Ghost', he preached; and all those New Testament preachers, with the exception of the apostle Paul, were similar men. They could be described accurately as 'ignorant and unlearned men', yet they were mighty preachers.

At first that was the position, but gradually that was changed. As a result of the spread of the gospel in the Greek world, and its coming among the philosophers, it was felt that a greater intellectual content was necessary, that the gospel should be defended against the attacks that were made upon it, and that its superiority to every human philosophy should be made clear and manifest. So, slowly, the whole idea of training and preparing men came in, and developed very rapidly until, when you come to the Middle Ages and later, you have what is called a kind of scholasticism, and men entering the ministry were taught an admixture of philosophy and biblical teaching. They were taught philosophic systems and Roman Catholic dogma, with the result that the gospel, in a sense was entirely hidden out of sight.

Then came the Protestant Reformation in the sixteenth century. Now the Protestant Reformation, while it clearly saw the error of the teaching of Rome and introduced true gospel teaching and preaching, and while it corrected the doctrine, in my opinion did not deal in a fundamental manner with this further matter of training men for the ministry. It tended to take over the general idea of training, and though it gave men a different teaching, the method seems to me to have been very much the same. We can well understand that. They felt that they had to answer the case of Rome, and to point out its dangers to the people. The result was that, speaking very generally, Luther, Calvin, and all these great men perpetuated the kind of preparation which had already been employed. The teaching was changed but in a sense the method was not. The Puritans went further than the reformers in this matter; but I would argue that on the whole even they did not break free, as it were, from this older method, this older approach which had been in vogue for so many centuries.

It is when you come to the eighteenth century that you find a great change took place, which is of very great significance. With the advent of the Evangelical or Methodist Awakening a number of men came into being who were known as exhorters. These were men who were converted under the powerful preaching of the Methodists, both Calvinist and Arminian. Some of these converts were ordinary workmen, but in the class meetings and societies they began to display a gift of speaking, and increasingly they were called upon to speak and address meetings. In spite of the fact that they were not trained they became exhorters or lay preachers. The old idea still persisted, so they were not called preachers; they were called exhorters, because they had not had training. Some of these men were very powerful preachers, some of them exceptionally so; but as they had not received the customary training they were not ordained. This persisted to the end of that century.

When you come to the nineteenth century, something happened which we must examine very carefully. As that century proceeded it was felt that people had now become more educated and more learned, and so there grew a sense of increasing dissatisfaction with these simple, unlettered, sometimes uncouth preachers, and a corresponding demand arose for educated men in the pulpit. So the movement in the direction of theological colleges and seminaries was given a very great impetus; and it developed very rapidly until you arrive at the full-blown idea of theological colleges which flourished in the latter half of the nineteenth century and which has persisted more or less until today. Great emphasis was placed upon training, upon knowledge and learning – a knowledge of philosophy and of Greek and Hebrew. A knowledge of classical Greek was deemed to be essential in order to interpret the Greek of the New Testament truly, and so on. Now this became the pattern, and men were sent to such colleges to receive this education and learning and culture. That is what we have inherited.

My suggestion is that we have arrived at a point when all that has got to be reconsidered if we really want to have an efficient training of men for the ministry. I must not digress by pointing out that all that has been done during the last century has more or less come to nothing, and that we have come almost a complete circle. Having emphasized for so long, as the authorities did, that you must have a knowledge of classical Greek, it was then discovered that the Greek that was actually used was so-called Koine Greek, a much more common Greek; and that a knowledge of classical Greek might even be misleading in this respect. Not only that; they paid great attention to the dates of origin of the various books of the New Testament, and with great confidence they taught that most of the books of the New Testament were not written until the end of the first century and some even in the second century. By now, however, Dr John Robinson, of all men, has argued cogently that these books were written before AD 70; so all the fuss and bother, and all the weariness that endless generations of poor students have endured who had to grapple with this nonsense, has all proved to be completely valueless and useless!

That, then, is the position. What are we to do? The conclusion at which we as a Sponsoring Committee have arrived is that the whole question must be faced anew. We must make a fresh start; and we must not content ourselves with a mere modification of the present system and the present position. That, I believe, has been the main weakness and defect of the various Bible colleges that have come into being especially since the end of the last world war. They were established on the basis – and I was involved in the discussions – that what we needed to do was to safeguard the teaching; but the method of training was never considered at all. It was felt that all that was necessary was that we should guarantee that the teaching would be evangelical; but they made the fatal mistake of allowing the curriculum to be determined by the liberal outlook, sometimes even by secular universities such as the University of London. A secular university, which is what the London University is, was to determine the curriculum and the syllabus that evangelical ministerial students are to study! That was the fatal blunder; thus we have to reconsider this matter from the very foundation. We are not concerned, therefore, merely to start yet another college; we are starting an entirely different seminary, something which is based, not on the tradition we have inherited, but rather on our understanding of the New Testament teaching. We propose that an entirely new start should be made.

I therefore repeat my question: What is needed? I have already answered the question by asserting that the primary need is for preachers. God has done His greatest work in the world and in the church through preachers; and never was there a greater need of preachers than today. I am emphasizing preachers rather than teachers. What is the difference between a preacher and a teacher? The teacher is one who, essentially, imparts information, passes on knowledge. I am prepared to argue that there is less need of teachers today than there has been for a long time. This is so because the general level of culture and of knowledge is higher than it has ever been. Members of churches today, and others, have had a good education, generally speaking. They are able to read many translations of the Scriptures which were not available before. There are endless commentaries, and there is ample literature on religion in general, on theology and various other subjects, easily and cheaply available; so my argument is that there is less need today to give people information which they can find in books for themselves. The greatest need is not for teaching or lecturing; it is for preaching.

What is preaching? Preaching is proclamation; it is the powerful presentation of the great message of the Bible. It includes evangelism, of course. The preacher should be an evangelist, and should know how to bring people to conviction of sin and to faith in the Lord Jesus Christ, as the apostle Paul tells us he always did (Acts 20:21). He reminds the Ephesians that what he did among them was to tell them about the repentance that is toward God and the faith that is toward the Lord Jesus Christ. We need men who are able to do this with great power, but at the same time they must be able to build up the saints. I have often affirmed that the main function of the preacher is inspirational. It is not merely to dole out information, or lecture on the books of the Bible, or lecture on doctrine. He can tell people where they can read this. He does so up to a point of course, but his supreme task is to inspire the people. The people are reading the Bible, but they do not see much in it. The business of the preacher is to bring the Bible alive to them, to show them what is in it, to thrill them as they hear it from him, and then as they read it for themselves. He is to move people; he is to remember that they have hearts as well as heads, and that unless people are moved by the preaching, their head knowledge may even be a danger to them. To produce live, living witnesses, 'epistles of Christ', is the business of the preacher. He is not simply to give people knowledge and information. He is to produce saints, and these saints, as they mix with others, will be the means of convicting them and bringing them to the church. So the supreme need is that of preachers, not mere teachers, still less lecturers.

But the man of God is also to be a pastor. Because of the stresses of modern life, in a very special way, the pastoral side is an increasingly important one. There, then, is the need; and what we are aiming at in this new seminary is to supply the answer to it.

The Qualifications for Training

How can we do so? Let us start with our ideas with respect to the students. What are our desiderata with regard to the student? This is most important, because in many ways the wrong view has been held for many years. The churches and ministers – let us admit it – have been far too ready to 'lay hands suddenly' on any man. If any young man says vaguely that he would like to go into the ministry we immediately encourage him to do so. We may be quite wrong in doing so. This is a very serious and most crucial matter. I assume that we are all agreed that the minister is not a professional man. No man should go into the ministry as a profession. What then do we desiderate? Well, he must be a converted man; he must be a man who is aware of new life in hìmself; but he must also be a spiritually minded man. This is essential. He must have a sense of burden for the souls of men; he must be aware of a call which he finds irresistible. I have always maintained that if a man can stay out of the ministry he should do so. Every minister and preacher should be able to say, 'The love of Christ constraineth me.'

He must also be a humble man. This again is crucial. We read in the life story of George Whitefield that he felt that the task of the preacher, the minister, was so high and so sacred that he felt completely unworthy of it, and had to be persuaded by many others to go on with it. This sense of unworthiness seems to have gone, has it not? People rush into preaching and into pulpits lightly. The man who is to be a preacher must be a man who is aware of a sense of awe. He must be a humble man because of the greatness of the task. I need not surely say anything about his character. By character I mean in particular that the minister must not be a difficult man. I fear that I have known some ministers who have been very difficult, and their poor flock have had to accommodate themselves to him, to the preacher. This should never be the case. Over the years I have discouraged quite a number of men from entering the ministry because I felt that they were possessors of such a temperament, such a psychological make-up, that they were such awkward men, that anybody going to seek help from them would be ill at ease in their presence, and would more or less have to put the minister at ease! A minister, a man who preaches, who does pastoral work, must be of such a character, such a type, that people do not have difficulty in approaching him.

Those are general matters, but there are certain special matters upon which we must insist. A preacher should be a man of personality. That term unfortunately is much abused at the present time. People talk of television personalities – nothing but grinning ninnies! That is not what I mean by personality. I mean a man of strength, an arresting man, a man with an element of command about him. He has to stand in a prominent position, so a negative personality is surely a defect in any man who is going to be a preacher. He must also be a man of ability. Obviously if he is going to help others he must be a man of ability. He must know how to think, he must know how to study, but above all he must know how to speak. A man may be a very good man, he may be a very godly man, but if he cannot speak except in a halting, stumbling manner, he has no business to be in the pulpit. By definition the preacher is a speaker, a proclaimer. So he must have a gift of speech. I have referred to the eighteenth century and the class meetings, and how they detected this gift in some of the converts. In their class meetings they would find that there were certain men who could pray more freely than others, who could speak more freely not only in giving their experience, but in giving their opinion upon a verse. It was thus discovered that they were natural preachers, and so the people would then urge them to speak regularly. They had a speaking ability. This seems to have been largely forgotten during the present century, and it has led to very woeful and sad results. Furthermore, the prospective preacher must have the confidence of the church to which he belongs. This is, again, most important, and we are very concerned to emphasize this in connection with this college. Our desire is that everything that is done here should be closely in touch with the churches from which the students and the candidates come. They are to remain in contact with the churches constantly, with their minister, their deacons, elders if they have any. We are very insistent upon the fact that men should have the confidence of their churches and should remain in contact with them.

When we come to the tutors I need not say much. What I have to say is inevitable in the light of what I have been saying about the students. The tutors must not be academics primarily. Theological teachers and tutors have often been academics who know nothing about church life, who know nothing about handling people, and, often, who cannot preach. Such have been the men who have been teaching others how to be preachers and pastors!

It is idiotic. We must have men who are themselves pastors and preachers and not mere academics; and the men we have appointed as tutors of the London Theological Seminary are men who conform to this pattern. They are men, incidentally, who have been to colleges either in Oxford or Cambridge or to London University, and some of them have even been to two of them. So they are men of learning, men of academic knowledge and standing; but we have not appointed them for that reason. We have appointed them because they are also men who are preachers, and who have warm pastoral hearts, because they are men who are spiritually minded and concerned about revival in the church. Such are the members of the faculty of this new seminary. Not one of these men is leaving his church. They are all continuing as ministers and pastors in their local churches, but they are giving this extra time, taking on this extra task and labour, in order to train preachers and pastors for the future.

A Biblical Approach to Seminary Studies

We come now to the question of how they are to train these students. I start by saying that it is unlike every other kind of training. It is entirely unique. It is entirely different from the study of science or philosophy or literature or art or any other subject. This is so because every Christian in a sense has the same knowledge as the preacher and the pastor. It is a question of degree. When you take up any other subject you start knowing virtually nothing. If you want to study medicine or science your personality as such is not involved; but here it is involved. In addition, every Christian has a certain minimum knowledge. Our entire approach therefore has to be very different. We start by realizing that here we are in a new realm, an entirely different realm, and the matter must not be considered in an academic or scientific manner. It must be considered always in a spiritual manner. I recently came across a statement by Anselm, who was many centuries ago Archbishop of Canterbury. He wrote a book *Cur Deus Homo*, and in it he said something which we must bear in mind, and which is the justification for any training at all:

As, on the one hand, right order requires that we believe the deep things of the Christian religion before presuming to subject them to the analysis and test of reason; so, on the other hand, it looks to me like indolent neglect if,

[365]

already established in the faith, we do not take the trouble to gain an intellectual intimacy with what we believe.

Note that Anselm says, that you *believe* first. Reason is not the controlling factor; this is supra-reason, it is above and beyond reason. He says we must start with belief and not with reason and philosophy; but he goes on to say that it is very unreasonable, on the other hand, it is 'indolent neglect', if we say that because we have faith we do not need to go any further. We should now try to reason out and to understand, as far as we can with our enlightened spiritual reason, the things we have already believed in the realm above reason. That seems to me to be the basis from which we start.

Let me emphasize that we are not interested in mere scholarship or any kind of scholasticism. That has been, as I have said, the tragedy of the last hundred years in particular. The men who have been concerned with theological education during the past century remind me forcibly of the Pharisees and scribes of whom our Lord said that they 'pay tithe of mint and anise and cummin, and have omitted the weightier matters of the law' (Matt. 23:23). They have wasted time and energy and wearied the poor students and, in turn, members of congregations, with details of so-called historical and literary criticism, and in quoting authorities; and in the meantime the great principles of the Christian faith have been forgotten. It is not surprising that some of these colleges have been closed and that their premises are being sold. We are concerned here with spiritual knowledge.

That brings me to my next point which is that there are to be no examinations in this college. You see, we are departing entirely from what has been customary. Colleges founded on the wrong idea have had examinations, and have gone in for degrees and diplomas. We are turning our backs upon that entire outlook. The men who come here to be trained are not going to be regarded as children, or placed under a law. We are not going to tell them when they must get up in the morning and when they are to go to bed, and how they must spend their time. We are assuming that they are men who are called of God and who feel a burden for the age in which we live. If they waste their time they will be proclaiming that they will be disasters in the ministry if they are ever called by a church. We are not interested in diplomas and degrees which do not belong to this realm. There is a sense in which it is almost blasphemous that there should be examinations in connection with this knowledge with which we are concerned.

At this point I venture to offer a criticism of a great evangelical scholar who at the opening of a famous seminary nearly fifty years ago uttered these words: 'We believe that a theological seminary is an institution of higher learning whose standards should not be inferior to the highest academic standards that anywhere prevail.' I dissent from that completely and entirely, and regard it as an entirely wrong approach. This college is not an academic institution and it should not be compared in any way with any institution of higher learning. We are in an entirely different realm here. So we are not going to have any degrees or diplomas or even any examinations. The students will proclaim what they are by their response to this; and when they appear before churches it will be obvious to the church members.

We start, in other words, on the assumption that preachers are born. No college, or any other institution, can ever produce a preacher. That they can do so has been another of the fallacies of the past hundred years. A preacher is born, as such, and I am not sure but that the same applies to pastors. However, they need to be helped in the development of the gifts they have, in order that they may become effective preachers and pastors. This being a theological seminary, no women will be admitted, and the students will not be trained here for posts as religious teachers or instructors in schools. We are out to produce preachers and pastors, not experts in religious education, not even foreign missionaries as such. Preachers and pastors! Such men may, of course, go to preach in other countries, but we are not concerned here, as most Bible colleges are, in that wider programme.

We agree that these men, whom we have defined and described, need some further help. What are we going to give them? Our idea is that we should provide here primarily a basic teaching. This is not to be a college to produce experts or specialists. It is to produce men who will be preaching Sunday by Sunday to congregations of ordinary people. Should a student appear who has a greater aptitude for study than the average, and who feels that he would like to go on to obtain further knowledge or learning or instruction, and to become a specialist in some branch or other, he will, of course, be at full liberty to do so; but the object of this seminary is not to produce such men.

May I use, to illustrate this point, an analogy from the realm of medicine. The great fallacy in medical training for a long time has been that instead of training men to be general practitioners, they have been training them to be specialists. Here in the great London hospitals, where training is given, all sorts of rare diseases are met, and unusual and difficult cases are seen; and so the poor student, the qualified student, generally goes out into practice knowing a great deal about rare, exceptional diseases but often feeling that he knows very little about the common cold or some of the childish ailments with which he will have to deal in his surgery day by day. At long last this has been recognized, and medical students are now given training by general practitioners. But in the past it was not so, and medical doctors had all this abstruse and rare knowledge which was of little value in general practice. Using that analogy, we are concerned here primarily about 'general practitioners', preachers of the Word regularly Sunday by Sunday in their churches and chapels. If they want to go on to specialize they are at full liberty to do so, but this college, in particular, does not cater for that.

The Essentials in a True Curriculum

What, then, will be taught here? The first thing, of course, is knowledge of the Bible, because a preacher is one who is going to expound the message of the Bible. What does this involve? We start with the vexed question of languages, Hebrew and Greek. As the article written by Mr Graham Harrison, one of the tutors, has indicated, we propose to give students sufficient instruction on this matter to enable them to use the commentaries in an intelligent manner. Much of the trouble in the past has been due to the fact that students have had to struggle and labour with Greek and Hebrew. This has not proved to be of much help to them when they have become ministers because they do not know enough to pit their opinion against the authorities who write the commentaries. They have had to waste much time over this.

There are those at the present time, as there have been before, who dispute and deny what I am asserting. I heard of a youngish minister recently who said in a conference that unless a man had a thorough knowledge of Hebrew and Greek he could not possibly be a preacher. The great authority, whom I have already quoted, who gave that address nearly fifty years ago, said the same. He said that if you are to tell what the Bible says you must be able to read the Bible for yourself, and you cannot read the Bible for yourself unless you know the language in which it was written. That, to me, is an extraordinary statement to make. Such men hold the view that unless a man has a knowledge of Hebrew and Greek he cannot be a preacher of the Bible. What is the answer to them? I have already given one answer. The apostles could not come up to this standard; and not only the apostles, but also the men in the eighteenth century to whom I have referred. Some of the greatest preachers in the eighteenth century were not only men who did not know any Greek or Hebrew; some of them had virtually had no school education whatsoever. Some of those who preached in Wales had had some three or six months in a school where they were taught a little English. This is surely a very serious matter. Charles Haddon Spurgeon was never in a theological seminary, neither was Joseph Parker, and they were the two greatest English preachers of the last century. The same applies to others who are well known for their great preaching ability and their books of sermons.

So to say that a man cannot preach, and cannot even read his Bible if he does not know Greek and Hebrew, I am afraid, must be categorized as sheer nonsense. This is most serious, for it seems to me to show an ignorance of the spiritual character of the biblical message. How anyone who has ever read the First Epistle to the Corinthians, chapter 2 can make such statements I cannot understand. We are not in the realm of things natural; these things are 'spiritually discerned', are understood in a spiritual manner. A man does not understand the Bible simply by knowing Greek or Hebrew. He understands the Bible because he has the Spirit of God in him. 'The princes of this world', says Paul, did not know and receive this message, and they rejected Christ; 'But God hath revealed them unto us by his Spirit: for the Spirit searcheth all things, yea, the deep things of God'. He goes on to say, 'We have received, not the spirit of the world, but the spirit which is of God; that we might know the things that are freely given to us of God. Which things also we speak, not in the words which man's wisdom teacheth, but which the Holy Ghost teacheth' (1 Cor. 2:8, 10, 12–13).

The key to an understanding of the Bible is not a knowledge of the original languages. You can have such knowledge and still be ignorant of the message, as so many are and have been, unfortunately. It is the man who has a spiritual understanding who

[369]

understands the Word of God. Of course, as the Protestant reformers, William Tyndale and others said, the Word of God must be in a language that a man can understand. Today, we have it in a language we can understand. We have it in English in many versions and translations; so what preachers need today above everything else is the power of the Spirit illuminating their minds. John in his First Epistle, chapter 2, verses 20 and 27 teaches, You have no need that anyone teach you. Why? Because they had an 'unction', an 'anointing'. So to say that a man cannot read his Bible, and that he cannot preach if he lacks a knowledge of Greek and Hebrew seems to me a serious misunderstanding of the biblical message, and of the true character of preaching. True preaching is the conveying of this message. The early church did this even when she had not got our New Testament documents. They preached a message which they had heard, and had believed, though they were 'unlearned and ignorant men' who knew nothing of the nuances of Hebrew and Greek deemed so essential today.

What is needed by preachers today is a sufficient knowledge of Greek and Hebrew to enable them to use their commentaries, to read the many translations available, in an intelligent manner, and to be able to follow the argumentation of the authorities for one view rather than another. No student who comes here – indeed, I go further, ninety-nine per cent of students who go to any place of learning – will ever know enough Greek and Hebrew to argue with the great professors. So what is needed is a basic knowledge of these languages. They have the Bible in a language they understand; and what they need now is to be taught the Bible message – the whole message, and the particular messages of the particular books – more thoroughly.

So they will be trained in what is called exegesis, a true understanding of what the text is saying; but, still more important, hermeneutics, the grasping of the message, and how to use this, how to convey it, how to apply it, how to present it to the people. A man may be an expert at exegesis but if he is poor at hermeneutics he will be a very poor preacher.

Moreover the students will be taught theology, but they will not be taught philosophy here. We have not catered for any teaching of philosophy except in apologetics, which will come at the end. Theology is knowledge of God derived from the biblical revelation. Theology is most important; some of us have been trying to teach and to emphasize this for many years, and have held it to be the queen of the sciences; but we must realize that there are certain dangers connected with teaching theology. Increasingly I have come to the view that the teaching of theology should never be separated from the Bible. If I were pressed hard I would be prepared to say that theology should never be taught except through sermons! The great danger is to turn theology into an abstract, theoretical, academic subject. It can never be such because it is knowledge of God. So the students here are to be taught biblical theology, the doctrines that emerge as you study through the Bible carefully. Then, having got their biblical theology, they must learn how to systematize that, how to put it all together in a more logical form in order that it may control their thinking and preaching. It is most important that it should be presented in the right way, never abstractly, but always as something which comes out of the Scriptures.

What is the purpose of theology? Here, again, there have been many mistakes in the past. Theology has to be handled very carefully. What is the function of theology and doctrine? First and foremost it is never meant to be a prison house. It is never meant to be a strait-jacket. There have been many men for whom theology has been just that. They are in a strait-jacket, hemmed in by their theology, and always afraid that they may say something wrong. That is not the business of theology. Theology is not a prison, or something which fetters a man; it is to be thought of, rather, in terms of what the skeleton, the bony structure of a man's body is to his body. Or, if you like, theology can be compared to the scaffolding that you put up when you are going to erect a great building. It must be there if you are to have good preaching, but you must not preach it in a skeletal or structural manner. It is there to give body to the sermon, and to safeguard you from saying anything wrong or from going astray. Theology, again, may be compared to railway lines which guarantee that you are going in the right direction and make sure that you are going to arrive at the right destination. But it implies movement! It is not something restricting, prohibiting, that shuts you down, something that inhibits freedom and liberty and power. The moment a man is hemmed in and tied down by his theology he is showing that incidentally he is a very poor theologian, and certainly he has a wrong view of the purpose of theology.

Theology means a knowledge of God, and the greater the theologian the more he should bow down in the presence of His majesty. The end and object of theology is to make a man say, 'great is the mystery of godliness' (1 Tim. 3:16); and if it does not bring him to that he had better examine himself carefully. The business of the tutors is so to present theology that it leads to that wonderful result. Theology is that which tells me, indeed commands me, 'Put off thy shoes from off thy feet, for the place whereon thou standest is holy ground' (Exod. 3:5). You cannot discuss theology while smoking pipes or cigarettes or drinking beer. It cannot be done in a jocular, light-hearted manner. It means knowledge of God, so it must be done 'with reverence and godly fear' (Heb. 12:28). That is the end and object of theology. So the students will be taught that while all true preaching is theological, they are not to preach theology.

What else will be taught? Church history. I regard this as extremely important. It includes the history of the great doctrines, how they came into being, how they developed, and the disputes concerning them. We live in an age of transition, an age which is doubting everything; and we can learn a great deal from the past. We are back again in a situation similar to that in the early centuries of the Christian era; so this history of doctrine is going to be of extreme importance. Not only the history of doctrine but also the history of the denominations. The denominations are talking about amalgamating, of becoming one great church; and some people are fighting a kind of last-ditch stand for their particular denomination. Most of them do not know why they belong to that particular body, and have no idea as to how their denomination ever came into existence. Their attitude is, It is my denomination, and I am going to fight for it to the last drop of my blood. So it is good that people be taught how the denominations first came into being. That is a part of church history. So too are the biographies of the saints of God that have adorned the church. How wonderful it all is! These young men are to be exhorted to read such histories, not merely to obtain information, but also to keep them humble, so that when they begin to be puffed up and think that they are great preachers, reading about a man like Whitefield will soon bring them to the conclusion that they have never preached at all, and are never likely to do so! Church history also includes the stories of revivals and spiritual awakenings. We are living in a barren age spiritually; things are difficult and the churches are having to struggle. Our greatest need is a mighty spiritual awakening, a great revival of religion. The young men who study here will be told about such great events in the past and directed to books which will give them yet greater knowledge about them.

What of apologetics? It should only come in at this point because its value and function is mainly negative. Its business is to refute the arguments brought against the Christian faith, and to expose the futility of the teaching of the various cults and ideas that are round and about us at the present time. Ministers and pastors of churches are constantly having to deal with either members of their churches or hearers in their congregations, who have suddenly heard of a cult which seems to offer much more than they have, and they are attracted to such movements. They must be able to tell them why they should not do so. There have been institutions and colleges which have been virtually controlled by apologetics; but that surely is entirely wrong. That is to be negative; and we are to be positive. We must certainly know something about the arguments against false teaching, and we must be able to 'contend for the faith'. That is the place of apologetics; but it only comes in at that point.

There is no time to say anything about the pastoral side. As I have said there is a sense in which pastors are born, but they can be helped and encouraged by men who have long experience at such work, and also warned of certain pitfalls. Men need help about such matters, and that will be provided for them here; but we have made no provision for the teaching of psychology. That has been the vogue for years: pastoralia, psychology, etc. Pastors are men called to deal with problems of a spiritual nature, and that can be done primarily out of our knowledge of the Word of God.

Conclusion

To sum up, what is the business of this college? What do we hope it is going to do? Let me quote some words written by Peter Brown in his excellent biography of the great St Augustine: 'The problem is no longer one of training a man for a task he will later accomplish. [That is not the business of a theological seminary.] 'It is one of making him wider – of increasing his capacity, at least, to take in something of what he will never hope to grasp completely in this life.' That is the most you can do for any man called to the ministry. Here is a man: he has been converted, born again, and he has been reading his Bible; he has a certain amount of knowledge. The business of this college is to make him 'wider', not in the sense of going in for a study of philosophy, but to widen the knowledge he already has, to give him a deeper understanding, to make him a more profound thinker.

Indeed, if I were asked to sum up in one word the main function of such a seminary I would say that it is to teach men to think, so that when they have left the college they can, and will, go on thinking, and when they are asked certain questions, not simply turn to the notes which they took down when they were in college and read out the answers. The tragedy of so many men who have been to theological colleges and seminaries is that they have never really thought after they have left college. They have lived on what they were told and the notes they took down in a mechanical dictation system in their seminary, to which they simply refer.

What happens in college should be only a beginning. Its purpose is to widen a man, to increase his capacity to take in something of that which he will never hope to grasp completely in this life. This is so because it is a knowledge of God. The business of the college is to give men a greater love of the Word than they have ever had, a greater desire to dig into its profundities and its mysteries, to read everything they can which will help them to that end, and then to go on doing this, to go on learning and increasing and developing in every respect until they are called home to their eternal reward. And above that, it is, as I said, to inspire these men, to send them out with a burning desire to preach the 'unsearchable riches of Christ'. If men's hearts are not warmer when they go out from this college than when they came in, these tutors will have failed.

I was reading the other day a statement in a letter written by a man called Robert Roberts of Clynnog. He was a Welshman who lived at the end of the eighteenth century, a seraphic preacher. He came up to London to preach to his fellow countrymen for eight weeks in 1797. He was not very good at English, but he was a wonderful Welsh preacher. While he was here in London he visited some of the English churches. He found them packed out with great congregations; and among the places he visited was Whitefield's Tabernacle in Tottenham Court Road. Concerning that particular visit he wrote to a friend: 'I felt while I was there a groaning in my heart and spirit which said, "Behold the fire and the wood: but where is the lamb for a burnt offering?"' He went on, 'Here is an altar, here is an offering, but where is the fire? Here I am looking at Whitefield's pulpit, but where is his God?'

The business of a college is to help these future preachers to provide the wood, and to provide the offering, which in a sense is the knowledge of salvation in our Lord Jesus Christ. This is what we can do, but if the fire does not descend upon it, it will be lifeless, more or less useless and valueless. You may be in the pulpit of Whitefield, you may have Whitefield's knowledge, and even more than he had, for he was not a very learned man, but the secret of Whitefield was his God, and without Him we avail nothing. Our great concern is that this seminary should not be a dry-as-dust academic institution, trying to produce men with first-class honours and high degrees and diplomas awarded by secular universities such as the University of London. No! We are hoping to encourage men who will be able to put everything in order on the altar so that the fire of God the Holy Spirit may descend upon it. And we have every confidence that the members of this faculty whom we have appointed, and who are so ready to give their services, will never lose sight of that objective. We have every confidence that their greatest desire is that the fire may descend upon the offering that is on the altar. Let us pray for them, and pray for the prosperity and the future of this seminary. Pray also for the students who shall come here. Do everything you can to help them and to encourage them. Pray for the members of the faculty and the students, that they may be given strength and understanding and, above all, spiritual insight, so that everything that shall be done here shall redound to the praise and the honour and the glory of the great God whom it is our privilege to try to serve.

Index

Index